Further praise for the Dictionary and Introduction to Global Environmental Governance

'Words matter – they transform ideas into action. This power of communication is amplified with a common vocabulary. Saunier and Meganck's ambitious glossary makes a valuable contribution to enhancing the potential of global environmental agreement.'
Elizabeth Dowdeswell, Former Executive Director, UNEP

'Saunier and Meganck have zeroed-in on one of the most confounding issues related to Global Environmental Governance: language and most importantly its context. This book will become the "yellow pages" for students and practitioners alike, assisting them in becoming "fluent" in the ways of GEG and envirospeak.'
James Gustave Speth, Dean, Yale School of Forestry, Former Administrator of UNDP

'This book helps clarify the steps needed to overcome a major obstacle towards measurable progress on the goals set by governments: clarity of purpose.'
Ambassador Jack Vaughn, Founding Chairman, Conservation International

'Unlike the world of GEG, which borders on chaos, this book contains a profoundly unambiguous message, with prose that borders on the poetic.'
Dr Robin Rosenberg, Dante B. Fascell North-South Center, University of Miami

'Finally a volume that dares to take on the complex challenge of Global Environmental Governance and, in the process, succeeds in mobilizing the scholarship necessary to introduce the subject in a way that is both comprehensible and engaging. Bravo gentlemen!'
Dr Noel Brown, Former Head of UNEP USA Office

'The book is full of extremely useful information that stimulates thinking, and opens new avenues for research, policy formation and actions in Global Environmental Governance.'
Ambassador Vicente Sánchez

Dictionary and Introduction to Global Environmental Governance

To Kenton R. Miller: critic, colleague, mentor, friend.

Dictionary and Introduction to Global Environmental Governance

Richard E. Saunier and Richard A. Meganck

London • Sterling, VA

First published by Earthscan in the UK and USA in 2007
Copyright © Richard E. Saunier and Richard A. Meganck, 2007

This book was originally published in 2004 by A.A. Balkema Publishers, a member of Taylor & Francis Group plc, London, UK under the title: *C.H.A.O.S.S.: An Essay and Glossary for Students and Practitioners of Global Environmental Governance.* ISBN 90 5809 704 8 (hardback), ISBN 90 5809 705 6 (paperback).

The views expressed in this book are those of the authors and do not necessarily reflect the policies of UNESCO or UNESCO-IHE, their Executive or Governing Boards or the Member States.

ISBN-13: 978-1-84407-425-9 (hardback)
Typeset by Safehouse Creative
Printed and bound in the UK by Bath Press, Bath
Cover design by Yvonne Booth

For a full list of publications please contact:

Earthscan
8–12 Camden High Street
London, NW1 0JH, UK
Tel: +44 (0)20 7387 8558
Fax: +44 (0)20 7387 8998
Email: earthinfo@earthscan.co.uk
Web: **www.earthscan.co.uk**

22883 Quicksilver Drive, Sterling, VA 20166-2012, USA

Earthscan is an imprint of James and James (Science Publishers) Ltd and publishes in association with the International Institute for Environment and Development

A catalogue record for this book is available from the British Library

Library of Congress Cataloging-in-Publication Data
Saunier, Richard E.
  [C.H.A.O.S.S.]
  Dictionary and introduction to global environmental governance / Richard E. Saunier and Richard A. Meganck.
        p. cm.
  "Originally published: Leiden ; London : A.A. Balkema, 2004, under the title C.H.A.O.S.S. : an essay and glossary for students and practitioners of global environmental governance.
  ISBN–13: 978–1–84407–425–9 (hardback)
  ISBN–10: 1–84407–425–0 (hardback)
 1. Environmental responsibility–International cooperation–Dictionaries.
2. Environmental policy–International cooperation–Dictionaries. 3. Globalization–Environmental aspects–Dictionaries. 4. Environmental management–International cooperation–Dictionaries. I. Meganck, Richard Albert. II. Title.
  HC79. E5S2675 2007
  333.703–dc22

                                                                    2006100473

Mixed Sources
Product group from well-managed forests and other controlled sources
www.fsc.org Cert no. SGS-COC-2121
© 1996 Forest Stewardship Council
FSC

Contents

List of Tables

Acknowledgments

What is written here is not new and the ideas have been debated, acknowledged, criticized, supported, damned and praised by a long list of colleagues and mentors, most of whom we still count as friends. Over the years, in a great variety of meetings, bus commutes, long flights, cheap bars and, increasingly, in expensive hotels, as well as on hillsides and mountain tops, the faces and names have pretty much stayed the same. In the beginning the conversations were of conservation and the push for wilderness legislation, then came the intense interest in 'the environment' and debates on sustainable development – and now, on environmental governance. Throughout it all there was plenty of helpful critique and support and we would be remiss if we did not at least acknowledge the value of the comments and criticisms of the most important. Thus, in no particular order, subject matter, level of importance or agreement, we owe a debt of thanks to the following individuals: Arthur Heyman, Kenton Miller, Joshua Dickinson, Axel Dourojeanni, Boris Utria, Chris McKay, Dianne Wood, Gilberto Gallopin, Ariel Lugo, James Nations, Joanne Martin-Brown, Juan Jose Castro-Chamberlain, Kirk Rodgers, Brian Thomson, Margaret Catley-Carlson, Larry Hamilton, Aaron Wolf, John P. Beno, Elizabeth Dowdeswell, Lidia Brito, Peter Jacobs, Luis Bojorquez, Manuel Ramirez, Martin Goebel, Michael Freed, David Munro, Noel Brown, Pablo Gonzalez, Neal Bandlow, the late Peter Thatcher, Richard Sandbrook, Yadira Soto, Robert Goodland, Ilona Van der Wendon, Stephen Bender, Ted Trzyna, Walter Vergara, William Possiel, Ralph Daley, Yolanda Kakabadse and Silvio Olivieri.

Comments from several reviewers triggered significant changes in the text while others provided us with necessary encouragement. These include Ambassador Jack Vaughn (US), Ambassador Luigi R. Einaudi (US), Ambassador Michael King (Barbados), Ambassador Vicente Sanchez (Chile), Andras Szöllosi-Nagy, Andrea Merla, Gus Speth, Alfred Duda, Bart Schultz, Antonio Rengifo, Cristina Gonzalez, Ewoud Kok, Laura Kwak and Peter Stroo, Joyeeta Gupta, Len Berry, Mantha Mehalis, Mohamed T. El-Ashry, Rick Schulberg, Robin Rosenberg, Todd Baldwin and Tom Lovejoy.

We used a great many individual and institutional sources to build the glossary and list of acronyms. We appreciate their work and they are named on pages 41–46. Finally, we once again want to thank our spouses Gayle Saunier and Janet O. Meganck for their support and love through 30 years of friendship between our families.

Biographies

RICHARD E. SAUNIER, PhD was the Senior Environmental Management Advisor in the Department of Regional Development and Environment of the Organization of American States from March 1975 until his retirement in December 1996. From 1970 to 1975, he held staff positions with the US Peace Corps in Paraguay, Peru and Washington, DC and, during 1967–1969, he was visiting professor of forestry at the Universidad Austral de Chile in Valdivia, Chile. He holds degrees from Colorado State University (BSc) in forestry and range management, and from the University of Arizona (MSc, PhD) in range ecology and watershed management. His interests and recent experience are in environmental management policy and program evaluation and in the identification and mediation of resource use conflicts. Together with Richard A. Meganck, he is the co-editor of *The Bottoms Up of International Development*, published by Infinity Publishing in 2002, *Conservation of Biodiversity and the New Regional Planning* published by the OAS and the IUCN in 1995, and *C.H.A.O.S.S.: An Essay and Glossary for Students and Practitioners of Global Environmental Governance* published by A.A. Balkema Publishers in 2004.
rsaunier@comcast.net

RICHARD A. MEGANCK, PhD is the Rector of UNESCO-IHE Institute for Water Education in Delft, The Netherlands. Prior to his appointment in The Netherlands in 2003, Dr Meganck was the Director of Sustainable Development and Environment at the Organization of American States. His career spans 30 years in international development and the management of natural resources in both the United Nations and Inter-American systems, during which time he has undertaken more than 400 technical and administrative missions to 105 countries throughout the world. He holds BS and MS degrees from Michigan State University in natural resource development policy and watershed management and a PhD from Oregon State University in natural resource management. He has published more than 90 articles and three books. Dr Meganck began his professional career as a faculty member in the College of Forestry at Oregon State University and served as a US Peace Corps Volunteer in Colombia, South America in 1971–1972.
r.meganck@unesco-ihe.org

KENTON R. MILLER, PhD has held the highest positions in international conservation. Beginning in 1976, he served seven years as Chairman of IUCN's World Commission on Protected Areas. From there he was elected to be Director General of IUCN where he served five years. In 1982 Dr Miller was Secretary General of the 3rd World National Parks Congress in Bali, Indonesia. As WRI's Director of the Biological Resources Program, he lead the cooperative project between UNEP, IUCN and WRI, which developed the *Global Biodiversity Strategy*, launched at the 4th World Parks Congress in Caracas, Venezuela, in 1992. Following his PhD studies at the State University of New York, College of Forestry and Environmental Sciences, he began his career as a field researcher and post-graduate educator in Central and South America under the auspices of FAO, which provided him with the opportunity to practice wildland management and national park planning throughout the region. Subsequently, his conservation activities carried him to all continents including Antarctica. Later, as Associate Professor at the School of Natural Resources, University of Michigan, he established the Center for Strategic Wildland Studies. Until his retirement Dr Miller was Vice President for International Conservation and Development, at the WRI. In 2001, he was again elected to chair IUCN's WCPA for a four-year term. He is recipient of the Golden Ark award, and an Honorary Doctorate from the International University in Costa Rica.

JOYEETA GUPTA, PhD has Bachelors' degrees in economics (Delhi University) and law (Gujarat University), India, a Master's degree in law from Harvard Law School, US and a PhD in law from the Vrije Universiteit in Amsterdam, The Netherlands. Since 1993, she has been working at the Institute for Environmental Studies at the Faculty of Earth and Life Sciences Vrije Universiteit. She holds a part-time position as Professor in Policy and Law of Water Resources and the Environment at UNESCO-IHE Institute for Water Education in Delft. Dr Gupta's areas of expertise are in the multidisciplinary (legal, political and policy) analysis of international environmental and water agreements and multi-level environmental governance. In particular, her focus has been on the climate change regime, which she has examined from the North–South perspective and the perspective of Europe. She has also looked at domestic implementation issues especially in relation to energy in Brazil, China, India, Indonesia and Kenya. Although her area of research thus far has been climate change, she has been teaching water law and politics for the last 12 years. Joyeeta Gupta has published extensively in the area of environmental governance, climate change and North–South relations. She is Editor-in-Chief of *International Environmental Agreements: Politics, Law and Economics*, is on the editorial board of several important journals, and serves on a number of international scientific panels and boards.
j.gupta@unesco-ihe.org

Preface to the Second Edition

For those of you familiar with the first edition of this book, two things are noticeable when you pick up this one: first, this volume is a good bit thicker and second, it has been graced with a new name. Given the creativity of Global Environmental Governance (GEG) wordsmiths, we knew that a second edition would eventually be required – we just did not know it would be so soon. However, the large number of GEG meetings held during the period since the original publication resulted in a few hundred additional terms and acronyms now incorporated in this edition. Included among these, for example, are the many groupings of countries – what Alan Beattie describes as the 'Gang of Gs' (G3, G4, G5, etc.) –13 more than we had in the first edition. That so many groupings appear necessary, if nothing else, is an indication that complexity is still a large part of GEG.

Our basic thesis, that communication in general and the special language of GEG in particular have a great deal to do with the success or failure of governance activities still holds true. For example, many of the experts involved in GEG deliberations knew that the careless ease with which the term 'precautionary principle' was used would eventually come back to haunt. It did, with the result that the European Commission felt it necessary to give it a 29-page definition, which, you will be happy to hear, we did not include. As further evidence that we are not alone in our concern about the GEG process, France recently published both the *Petit Décodeur*, a dictionary of the 3000 most commonly used administrative terms and *Lara*, a computer anti-jargon spellchecker.[1]

Which brings us to the name change. In short, GEG remains on the edge of chaos but not under the umbrella of C.H.A.O.S.S. (our acronym – Can Humans and Other Species Survive?). As evidence of the former, we see problems in furthering regional alliances, the global threat of terrorism and increased isolationism in the name of national security, the never-ending crises confronting Africa and the stubborn numbers of people who still survive with few benefits from technology or those elaborated in the Millennium Development Goals. All of this has led the President of the UN General Assembly, Dr Jan Eliasson of Sweden,[2] to reflect on the 'diminished system of global government,' feeling that 'multilateral cooperation is at a cross roads,' which, for our purposes, is a fair definition of the 'edge of chaos.'

As evidence of the latter, we find a bit of confusion (not unannounced during the peer review process) concerning the acronym C.H.A.O.S.S. that some felt made the book's distribution more difficult. The message came in two parts: first, a few seemed to wonder how we could put together a dictionary with the title misspelled. Most understand that an acronym is not a word but we are aware of the problem – especially when miscommunication makes the book show up on the science and mathematics shelves rather than on those dedicated to environment or governance. Since the purpose of the book is to attempt to reduce the level of miscommunication, we felt it best to make the switch.

R.E.S.
R.A.M.
5 August 2006

Notes

1   John Henley (2005) 'Parlez-vous bureaucratique?' *The Guardian*, 18 February.

2   Michael Vatikiotis (2005) 'A troubled world seen from a Swedish idyll,' *The International Herald Tribune*, 10 August.

Foreword

With globalization, a nation's developmental/environmental problems are increasingly inter-linked with the economies and policies of other countries as well as of local communities. As such, governance in today's world is organized at different administrative levels, and policies at all these levels need to be closely coordinated and linked; a process that is referred to as multi-level governance. Three tendencies are increasingly visible, a tendency to regulate everything at a global level to create harmonized conditions and political viability, a tendency to address policy problems at the community level through stakeholder participation in order to achieve legitimacy and effective implementation, and a tendency to create the conditions in which private and other nongovernmental actors can more actively participate in the governance process. Although these tendencies can pull in opposite directions, the centrality of governance through bilateral, multilateral and global interstate negotiations remains obvious, and such negotiations are becoming increasingly frequent as time passes. The recent challenges to the United Nations (UN) system by the US should not be construed as a weakening of the power of the UN, but recognition that if the US accepts and ratifies a UN agreement, it can be held accountable within its own borders for non-implementation of the agreement by non-state actors.

Given this reality, it is vital that students of international relations and international law, diplomats and other negotiators and observers understand the conditions and realities within which global policy making is undertaken. Many of the conferences that are a part of this process are attended by more than 1000 delegates, with multiple plenary sessions and often dozens of non-plenary sessions and informal side-meetings. The terminology in these sessions is increasingly more complicated and acronyms are frequently used. How decisions are actually taken often remains a mystery for those present in the negotiating room, since many of the decisions are prepared and pre-negotiated with a few key parties long before the plenary debate actually starts. This is also because, although countries are officially represented by negotiators and diplomats, in many of the more technical negotiations, scientists are sent who may be extremely well qualified in their own field, but are very 'green' when it comes to figuring out the intricacies of international negotiation. Many negotiators are often faced with a fait accompli. Only those more intimate with the global process know how influential the UN rules of procedure are in the process of global diplomacy, and those who know how to use and abuse these rules effectively have control over the process and its outcomes.

The realities of negotiations are often not considered in international relations theories, international law discussions, nor in negotiation theories. It is here that the present book fills a vital gap in the available knowledge and in making the whole process more accessible to the future negotiator and researcher of the international processes. It combines an abstract essay discussing the nature of the chaos in global governance with a very practical glossary that immediately makes many of the terms accessible and comprehensible to the outsider.

From an international relations perspective, most global developmental and environmental problems are closely inter-linked and are essentially 'wicked' or 'unstructured' problems that reflect issues where there is poor alignment between the costs of taking action and the benefits from the action, where the science is limited in its ability to actually address the issue because of the high level of complexity and uncertainty, and where there is little or no agreement on the underlying values that should determine how problems are to be addressed. Under such circumstances, all global processes can be viewed as social learning processes and there is an expectation that such processes will eventually lead to problem solving. For many of us in the social sciences, there is a 'method in the madness.' This is described in the present book as the emergence of procedures that flow out of the 'edge of chaos' where we now find ourselves.

Against this background, the essay in this book has a fresh approach, as it examines the international process from the perspective of those who participate in the international governance process. The context, process, architecture and implementation of diplomatic encounters are described in brief but colorful detail. The book uses the metaphor of chaos to describe the international arena where few consensus definitions exist, even for key terms such as sustainable development and environment, where the concept of ecosystem is seldom understood, where the term ecology is used as an ideology rather than as a science that has useful insights and where a lack of political will is used as an excuse for not getting our homework done. The book then refers to additional tools to help deal with the critical challenges in global environmental governance. The book argues that the lack of political will reflects an absence of finished homework and that the consensus is probably at best only symbolic. It then develops a strategy to deal with this challenge.

The book makes pleasant and informative reading, which in itself is a very useful and rewarding effort. If at all one needs to find fault in the book, it is in its confidence that opposing views will be able to understand the terms and problems of one another. This may sound strange to the social scientist for whom problems are socially constructed, perceptions are reality, and 'normal' (as opposed to post-normal or public interest) science does not have solutions for so-called 'wicked' problems. On the other hand, too much relativism may also cloud one's perspective and a confident, eloquently argued portrayal of the global problems can help to clear ones own doubts as to how these problems are to be addressed and may help us prepare to participate more effectively in the international negotiating arena.

Joyeeta Gupta
Delft, The Netherlands
4 December 2006

Introduction

There is no human failure greater than to launch a profoundly
important endeavour and then leave it half done.

Barbara Ward

The idea for the essay that follows and its accompanying dictionary and list
of acronyms occurred to us as the global community prepared for the 2002
World Summit on Sustainable Development (WSSD) – an arduous, two-year
process fraught with misunderstanding and acrimony.[1] Reaction to the Summit outputs only strengthened our wish to offer something that would help
reinvigorate a productive conversation on the problems suffered by Earth
and its inhabitants. After all, at one time they were of sufficient moment
for governments to pay many millions of dollars for their resolution. To our
knowledge, few, if any, of them have gone away.[2]

Opinions concerning the relevance and efficacy of the WSSD vary, of
course. As with the previous world meetings of this nature, some participants
have said that not only did nothing of value occur, the dialogue required for
that to happen did not exist.[3] Referring to the meetings of the WSSD, for example, President Hugo Chavez of Venezuela summarized it as a 'dialogue of
the deaf', a statement often repeated by governments and nongovernmental
organizations (NGOs) from the South.[4] In addition to a perceived lack of
dialogue, others cite the assumed obstinacy and far from satisfactory efforts
by governments to meet the goals set at earlier summits of this kind, as well as
a failure to set urgent goals for the future and provide for those already established.[5] On the other side, officials of UN agencies, and some governments
from the North, publicize the decisions to implement *Agenda 21* as signs of
success and are now busily working on a number of partnerships established
to further sustainable development.[6] Still, in an acknowledgment that serious
problems do exist, the UN has announced a moratorium on such large environmental meetings.[7] That pronouncement, of course, applied only to the
UN, and not other groupings such as the World Water Council, which, four
years later, sponsored the Fourth World Water Forum in Mexico City, which
was attended by 20,000 people from 140 countries. There, the conclusion
was that water mattered and that its protection was urgent.[8] According to
the final news release from that conference, President Jacques Chirac, '…ex-
pressed the feeling of urgency relating to the challenge of water that everyone faces, and called for a collective and lasting commitment from everyone.'[9] We can hope, but the 'urgency' surrounding many other issues such
as climate change, HIV/AIDS, nuclear proliferation, energy, the threat of
pandemic diseases, the increasing occurrence of catastrophic natural events,
genocide, war and enduring poverty make for a long list of upcoming governance meetings both large and small.

Little doubt exists that stubbornness and biased attention to data are scattered among the diplomats, scientists and concerned citizens who work on the issues central to these meetings. More often than not, though, bickering and bias help expose the real reasons for the gamut that a Global Environmental Governance (GEG) idea must run. These include, but are not confined to, the complex differences in economic and social policies and cultural values among the nearly 200 sovereign nations that can become involved in the issues, the application of 'soft' and 'hard' power preferences by major states[10] and the thousands of NGOs that now help to frame the GEG agenda.

Proving themselves helpful in many ways, NGOs also bring with them a long list of added concerns and demands for attention.[11] Likewise, corporations, newly converted either by conscience or by economics, add an array of ideas rivaling the products and services they market. A large and growing number of disenchanted, not to say disenfranchised, individuals and groups outside the gates also now claim a voice. Caused as much by differences in what all sides are hearing as it is a difference in their ultimate goals, some of these groups prefer disruption to dialogue to get their points across.

The make-up of state delegations can also create its share of disorder. Rarely are the economists and attorneys who frequently form part of a delegation fully prepared to discuss biology and chemistry. Their colleagues, the chemists and biologists, by and large know little of diplomacy; and, despite near heroic efforts, none of these groups can fully understand and recommend completely effective remedies for the variety and potency of the problems we face.

Further, though present early on in the debates on international environmental management, the themes of human rights and poverty have taken on new weight, and cracks in the wall of those who want to stay fixed on 'the environment' writ as natural resource conservation and pollution control are beginning to show. For some, 'sustainable development' in its many forms seems to have usurped the concerns of much of the environmental movement. Even for those who may feel that inequity and poverty are not a part of the environmental agenda, these two realities alter what we can and cannot do.

Correctly, the search for pathways to accommodate these many differences is high on the agenda of the diplomats and scholars active in the themes of GEG.[12] However, the problems of environmental governance at a very practical level can also lie with words that are misunderstood and misinterpreted as well as with those that are known but not heeded. Thus, in addition to the scholarly work meant to elucidate and treat the complexities of GEG, tools are required that can help orient and facilitate the productivity of those directly involved in negotiating international instruments and of those who prepare and report on the many congresses, conferences and other meetings along the way. More specifically, it seems necessary to crack open the closed and often confusing language that leads to unnecessary complications, and that can make for decisions and negotiations based on partial or mistaken information.

Jargon and acronyms are the standard (and necessary) language of global environmental governance. We offer you PIC-INC. If you had to say the phrase, 'Intergovernmental Negotiating Committee for the Preparation of the Conference of Parties of the Rotterdam Convention for the Application of the Prior Informed Consent Procedure for Certain Hazardous Chemicals and Pesticides in International Trade' at any interval short of every few years, you would most certainly opt for PIC-INC, its acronym.

Likewise, Alan Beattie notes the proliferation of 'Gs': 'so attractive is the allure of G-membership that generally the only way of shrinking a group is to shut it down and start again. But new gangs are created faster than the old ones are dissolved.'[13] For now, the list includes G3, G4, G5 old, G5 new, G6 old, G6 new, G7 old, G7 new, G8, G8+, G8+ new, G10, G13, G15, G20, G21, G33, G90 and G77 + China which now has well over a 100 members.

Because of PIC-INC, the 'G syndrome' and countless other bits of GEG jargon, acronyms and abbreviations, it appeared to us that GEG students and even long-term practitioners could use an easily accessible and sizeable dictionary of these things. Such a dictionary and a listing of acronyms make up the bulk of this introduction to GEG.

GEG is a continuing process that occupies the time and energy of thousands of dedicated people during hundreds of meetings. Available minutes of these meetings, however, record discussions that seem repetitive, disjointed and, many times, misdirected.[14] The turmoil that arises between the official and the unofficial, the governmental and nongovernmental, and the boardroom and the street, too often reflects a curious blend of obscure, but important, scientific fact and popular, but meaningless, science fiction. Because of weaknesses in how many interested parties handle the most basic of GEG terms, we have included a short essay on some of the more important of these that should help enrich the debate if not clarify the issues.

We do not mean by any of this to suggest a failure of the GEG process or of the range of instruments successfully concluded because of it. We have watched that process closely over a fair number of years, and respect the dedication and energy brought to it by a great many individuals and institutions. Yet, how this unique and valuable culture communicates within itself often seems a significant contributing factor in the problems – real and imagined – so often cited by others.

Consequently, rather than 'failed,' we choose to describe the current state of the global governance process as 'chaotic,' a portrayal that few who are active in it today would deny. However, though it is possible to depict the present system with the dictionary definition of chaos as 'turmoil and turbulence,' we do not want to emphasize those aspects of it here. We prefer, instead, to see it in terms of the complexity sciences where slight initial differences, imprecision, positive feedback for something less than optimal and increasing complexity take a system to a 'place' at the edge of chaos where it will either stagnate in the channel it has created, die altogether, skid into ceaseless chaos or escape to something better.[15] It is this last alternative that makes the 'edge of chaos' a potentially constructive place to be – and, to a large degree, that is our message.[16]

Complexity concepts, of course, are often misinterpreted and misused from the point of view of mathematics and the physical sciences and we are aware of the damage we may do in the eyes of these disciplines. Our intent, however, is only to make a 'metaphorical application' of their ideas.[17] We do not mean, in any way, to explore what mathematical modeling may say about global environmental governance. Nevertheless, it does seem to us that the richness of the ideas coming out of the complexity sciences can usefully describe GEG and, as a result, lead to a fruitful rethinking of the governance process.

We also understand that some of what we have written here will be of little value to the many diplomats and scholars who dedicate themselves to global environmental governance. If they happen to find this book in their hands, we suggest that they skip over the next half dozen pages. However, we do want them to look at the remainder of the essay since it represents at least one view from the field that they may or may not be missing. And, for better or for worse, we offer it as an effort to help ensure that the 'profoundly important endeavor' of global environmental governance not be left half done.

Notes

1   The WSSD took place from 26 August to 4 September 2002 in Johannesburg, South Africa.
2   For a recent analysis and the problems and future of GEG see James Gustave Speth and Peter M. Haas (2006) *Global Environmental Governance*, Washington DC, Island Press.
3   For a critique of the 1992 UNCED see Adil Najan (1995) 'An environmental negotiation strategy for the south,' *International Environmental Affairs*, vol 7, no 3, pp249–287; and for the 2002 WSSD see Tom Bigg (2003) 'The World Summit on Sustainable Development: Was it worthwhile?' in T. Bigg (ed) *Survival for a Small Planet*, Earthscan, London.
4   The quote by President Chavez is from Robin Pomeroy (2002) 'Earth summiteers cast doubt on future world meets,' *Reuters News Publication Service*, 4 September. A view from NGOs in the South can be found in Anju Sharma, Richard Mahapatra and Clifford Polycarp (2002) 'Dialogue of the deaf,' *Down to Earth*, Delhi, Centre for Science and Environment, pp25–33.
5   As given in a press release from the World Resources Institute (2003) 'WRI Expresses disappointment over many WSSD Outcomes,' http://newsroom.wri.org, accessed on 6 October 2003.
6   UN Department of Economic and Social Affairs, Division of Sustainable Development (UNDESA/DSD), 'Partnerships for Sustainable Development,' www.un.org/esa/sustdev/partnerships/partnerships.htm, accessed on 13 November 2003.
7   Geoffrey Lean (2002) 'U.N. creates watchdog group in lieu of future summits,' *London Independent*, 8 September.
8   See Robert Varady and Matthew Iles-Shih in a 2005 paper: 'Global water initiatives: What do the experts think?' presented at the Workshop on Impacts of Mega-Conferences on Global Water Development and Management in Bangkok, Thailand. They document the growth in professional societies and intergovernment and nongovernmental organizations of prioritizing water as a subject of critical importance. Of course, they also note the complexity of developing a coordinated international agenda on this topic given the plethora and increasing size of national, regional and international conferences.
9   Jacques Chirac, 'Message from the President of the French Republic to the Closing Session of the 4th World Water Forum', accessed 30 November 2006 at www.elysee.fr/elysee/elysee.fr/anglais/speeches_and_documents/2006/message_from_the_president_of_the_french_republic_to_the_closing_session_of_the_4th_world_water_forum.44782.html.
10   Robert Kagan (2002) 'Power and weakness,' *Policy Review on Line*, accessed 15 August 2003 at www.policyreview.org/JUN02/kagan.html; also Andrew F. Cooper, John English and Ramesh Thakur

(2002) *Enhancing Global Government: Towards a New Diplomacy*, Tokyo: UNU Press.

11   Elizabeth Corell and Michele M. Betsell (2001) 'A comparative look at NGO influence in intergovernmental environmental negotiations: Desertification and climate change,' *Global Environmental Politics*, vol 1, no 4, pp86–107.

12   Ronald B. Mitchell (2002b) 'Of course international institutions matter: But when and how?" in Frank Bierman, Rainier Brohm and Klaus Dingwerth (eds) *Proceedings of the 2001 Berlin Conference on the Human Dimensions of Global Environmental Change: Global Environmental Change and the Nation State*, PIK Report No. 80, Potsdam: Potsdam Institute for Climate Impact Research, pp16–25; and Ronald B. Mitchell (2003) 'International environmental agreements defined,' accessed 15 October 2003 at www.uoregon.edu/~rmitchel/IEA/overview/definitions/htm.

13   Alan Beattie (2005) 'Welcome to the Group of 78,' *The Financial Times*, 16 April.

14   Hillary French (2002) 'Reshaping global governance,' in Christopher Flavin et al. (eds) *State of the World 2002 – Progress Towards a Sustainable Society*, London Worldwatch Institute and W.W. Norton and Company, pp174–198.

15   Edward N. Lorenz (1993) *The Essence of Chaos*, Seattle: University of Washington Press, pp161–179; and M. Mitchell Waldrop (1993) *Complexity: The Emerging Science at the Edge of Order and Chaos*, New York: Touchstone.

16   A fascinating paper on the rise of water as a topic on the international agenda is provided by Robert Varady and Matthew Iles-Shih in a 2005 paper: 'Global water initiatives: What do the experts think?' presented at the Workshop on Impacts of Mega-Conferences on Global Water Development and Management in Bangkok, Thailand. They document the growth in professional societies and intergovernment and NGOs of prioritizing water as a subject of critical importance. Of course, they also note the complexity of developing a coordinated international agenda on this topic given the plethora and increasing size of national, regional and international conferences.

17   Stephen Kellert (1995) 'When is the economy not like the weather? The problem of extending chaos theory to the social sciences,' in A. Albert (ed) *Chaos and Society*, Amsterdam: IOS Press; and Robert Axelrod (1997) *The Complexity of Cooperation*, Princeton: Princeton University Press, pp3–9.

part one

Global Environmental
Governance:
An Essay

Global Environmental Governance: An Essay

Governance and government

> The art of international diplomacy is to convert the obnoxious into the incomprehensible.
>
> Widely held principle of GEG

First a few words concerning a phrase you have already read many times in this document: 'global environmental governance' (also known as GEG). Each of the three words is important. The concept of 'governance' requires discussion because of the subtle but significant differences between it and the concept of 'government.'[1] Though they cover much of the same ground, governance is more than government. For example, according to the United Nations Centre for Human Settlements (UNCHS), the differences are between 'a single authority and shared purposes and responsibilities.'[2] Further, governance includes all of the ways that individuals and institutions plan and manage their common affairs and consists of 'formal institutions, informal arrangements,' and what citizens know and do.[3] However, governance does not, as often believed, reduce the importance of a government since, as noted by the UNCHS, government still 'holds the regulatory powers and the majority of fiscal responsibility;' and, its 'normative and political legitimacy' helps to create and sustain the structures that encourage us to act together.

'Global,' in the context of governance, likewise is different from 'intergovernmental' and 'international.' While 'intergovernmental' treats the official affairs between and among governments, 'international,' in addition to considering the relationships among governments, also includes the common contacts and dealings of their citizens. 'Global' has a far broader meaning than either of the two previous ideas and embraces the official and unofficial governance activities of a long list of institutions including governments, businesses, nongovernmental organizations (NGOs), universities, research centers, and foundations. Use of 'global' acknowledges that a large number of institutions inside and outside of government and across national and institutional boundaries are responsible for much of the administration and management of our planet.[4] 'Environmental' is a term of such importance that it has a section of its own and we encourage you to read the rest of the essay to see why.

As in all other issues of global governance, global environmental governance is founded on a few basic rules.[5] First, the fundamental premises outlined in the 1648 Westphalia Settlement concerning the absolute sovereignty and legal equality of nation states are at its center. Without these concepts, relationships between states in international forums would appear as little more than political parlor games and weight-lifting contests. Second, GEG follows international law – the compendium of binding agreements reached over years of interaction at various levels by which governments adjudicate differences and work toward positions of common interest and which subsequently become national law (Appendix 1). In addition, GEG is guided by a growing number of principles (Appendix 2) and other non-binding instruments with the important caveat that, although agreed upon by consensus, these principles are not always accepted by all cultures in the same way.

A significant additional feature of global environmental governance is the role of civil society in decision making accepted by governments at the United Nations Conference on Environment and Development (UNCED) in Rio de Janeiro in 1992.[6] Principle 10 of the Rio Declaration states, in part, 'Environmental issues are best handled with the participation of all concerned citizens, at the relevant level.' More importantly, governments enabled this process with the additional statement that, 'States shall facilitate and encourage public awareness and participation by making information widely available. Effective access to judicial and administrative proceedings, including redress and remedy, shall be provided.'[7]

Global environmental governance, which, in the run-up to the World Summit on Sustainable Development seems to have undergone a metamorphosis to become 'global sustainable development governance,' has at least three core components: process, architecture and implementation. Ideally, GEG will reflect the interdependence of these components in that they should occur in a closely coordinated sequence. However, in the world of GEG, things may not work as they should and order may appear only after time, frequent false starts and many frustrations.

The *process* of GEG can begin almost anywhere and often leads nowhere, as shown in the increasingly long list of unratified, totally abandoned or archaic instruments.[8] GEG *architecture* consists of the formal and informal, and public and private institutions that guide *implementation* – which often moves forward before it has a clearly defined destination or formal support.[9]

Process

The visible portion of the GEG process is made up of a large variety of assemblies, conferences, congresses and summits – so many in fact, that someone once defined sustainable development as the 'mantra that launched a thousand meetings.' Important examples of these meetings, of course, are the 1972 UN Conference on the Human Environment, the 1992 UN Conference on Environment and Development, and the 2002 World Summit on Sustainable Development. However, other meetings are now also considered as part of the GEG process; for example, the 1995 World Summit for Social Development, the 1996 Summit of the Americas on Sustainable Development, the 2001 Doha Ministerial Conference of WTO and the 2006 World Water Forum.

For every major meeting there are literally hundreds of other preparatory meetings sponsored by a galaxy of interests including those that offer the science that informs the negotiations.[10] These interests repeatedly break into sub-groups to deal with specific issues or aggregate into coalitions according to geography, economics, culture, ideology and the question of the day. In formal meetings, a secretariat faithfully records the discussions and decisions for later review, debate, amendment and action. A major part of the process is the effort to get it all down on paper in the proper language as an instrument that will enter into force when signed (by the executive branch of governments) and ratified (by the legislative branch of governments) by a sufficient number of states or other institutions.[11]

Meetings called on behalf of GEG can be large or small, formal or informal, inclusive or exclusive and may represent sectoral, geographical or cultural concerns. A speech, an article, or a background paper for any number of unofficial gatherings can initiate a new, or rekindle an old, GEG effort. The formal process established to negotiate an intergovernmental treaty or convention is a series of meetings of an International Negotiation Committee (INC). However, rather than in official open meetings, negotiators often come to agreement first in hallways or during coffee breaks, cocktails and impromptu late night working sessions where, despite the rhetoric, transparency can be an early casualty.[12] Similar meetings of NGOs (see Appendix 3) and, more recently, of the business community, mirror all of this in terms of complexity, cost, variety of interests, the amount and accuracy of information and secrecy.[13]

Architecture

GEG architecture – the agreements and the institutions required to interpret and administer the instruments of governance is likewise complex.[14] The organizations surrounding an agreement consist of a variety of formal and informal advisory committees (panels, subsidiary bodies, bureaus, etc.) as well as the conferences or meetings of the parties that negotiated and/or signed on to the treaty or protocol.[15] Secretariats, programs and commissions are part of this architecture. For example, the United Nations Environment Programme (UNEP) encourages and facilitates implementation of the mandates of the 1972 UN Conference on the Human Environment and the UN Commission on Sustainable Development (CSD) reviews progress on the approved agendas of the 1992 Earth Summit.[16] Most of the treaties and conventions that have entered into force now will also have a secretariat to track ratification, help insure implementation, and provide support to their administrative bodies.[17]

Agreements can be statements or declarations (sometimes defined as 'soft law') and conventions, treaties or protocols (sometimes defined as 'hard law'). These different kinds of instruments bind the parties with different levels of authority.[18] A record of agreement for any of these instruments generally consists of an opening statement (*chapeau*), references to prior agreements, a set of principles and statements regarding what the parties have agreed to do. Prescribed actions may follow as a part of the instrument itself, as an addendum, or as a separate text. Each institution and meeting has an identifying code for the documents that are produced (see Appendix 4 for help in deciphering these codes).

There are at least four varieties of conventions in GEG. Framework conventions, such as the UN Framework Convention on Climate Change and the Convention on Biological Diversity, require additional, separately negotiated protocols to reach the objectives laid out in the convention and a government may sign and even ratify a convention without signing or ratifying any of its protocols. Self-contained agreements such as UN Convention to Combat Desertification and the Convention on International Trade of Endangered Species do not necessarily need further protocols for implementation. Umbrella agreements, such as the Convention on Migratory Species of Wild Animals, allow other allied accords within the wider mandates of the convention. The fourth is an agreement open for signature to both governments and NGOs, as, for example, the Ramsar Convention on Wetlands.

Signing an instrument does not legally bind a nation to abide by its directives – only ratification can do that and only then if enough of its signatories ratify to allow entry into force.[19] However, signing does indicate that a state, or other institution, will do nothing to impede the work of the treaty secretariat or another state party toward meeting the objectives of the instrument that it signed.[20]

Implementation

As difficult and complex as the process and architecture of governance may be, they can appear easy compared to the implementation of what has been decided. Implementation of GEG frequently causes seemingly endless anxiety, frustration, debate, accusations and delays. All of this happens because implementation means financing the work of the agreement's plan of action; the staffing of a secretariat or other institution(s) designed to insure that the agreement meets its objectives; and intense negotiations to decide just where the secretariat will be located and what the limits to its authority should be. National, and regional, prestige and additional income to a nation's economy are involved.

Debate on implementation also revolves around the issues of (a) funding

·for the programs mandated by a treaty and (b) sovereignty – with the developing world generally insisting that funding be 'new and additional' and the bi- and multilateral development agencies insisting that certain conditions be met before the funding matters can be resolved.[21]

Monies for program and project implementation traditionally come from bilateral grants and low interest loans or multilateral loans that may be concessional in that they generally include lower interest rates and longer payback periods than those from commercial banks. More recently, funding and other assistance comes from NGOs and foundations, as foreign direct investments from corporations and other businesses or as some combination of public and private funds.

Whatever the case, funding is nowhere near what is required to fulfill current commitments to agreed upon targets for GEG. For example, the total annual official development assistance (ODA)[22] was between 50 and 60 billion dollars when the 180 governments attending the 1992 Earth Summit approved *Agenda 21*, a program that itself calls for 200–500 billion dollars annually. However, instead of increasing from 50 billion dollars to 500 billion dollars, or even 200 billion dollars, total ODA has dropped each year since. It now sits close to an average of 0.5 percent of GNP for the wealthier nations despite calls that it should rise to 1.0 percent and agreement by these nations that it should be at 0.7 percent of GNP.[23]

Though much of GEG has little or no funding, some parts of it do.[24] The Global Environment Facility, for example, supports implementation of the Convention on Biodiversity, the Framework Convention on Climate Change, the Convention on Persistent Organic Pollutants and the work of the Montreal Protocol Secretariat as well as work on international water and land degradation. Various trust funds support implementation of other individual agreements and ensure participation of delegates from Third World countries in many international meetings.

Fraying edges

GEG, its process, architecture and implementation are not static and in some thematic areas, both the substance and the rules that guide debate are rapidly evolving. Although governments generally adhere to the fundamental rules of how they are to interact, several recent actions seem to question the established codes of behavior.

- There is a trend toward greater polarization and hardening of positions between regions on certain issues – the rancorous debate over the Kyoto Protocol on global warming at COP-8 (October 2002) that has jeopardized the entire process is an example.[25]
- Increased belief among Member States that anything emerging from the United Nations is either biased or controlled by perverse interests regardless of the issue or decision.[26]
- Although science, rather than real or perceived power, was

to drive the agenda of international negotiations, large and powerful countries and donor nations appear more aggressive in their attempts to influence the outcome of the GEG process for unilateral purposes.

- Movements like these force smaller countries to either align themselves with a larger country or vote as a geographic or interest-driven coalition to get a piece of the action. The Small Island Developing States (SIDS), for example, often votes as a group to garner the attention of the larger countries and to have a discernable influence on the outcome.

- In other instances, nations actually 'sell' (or 'buy') votes in exchange for support, trade concessions or even direct aid.[27]

- Unilateral, and at times contravening, actions with regard to the Law of the Sea, CITES principles, the Kyoto Protocol, International Criminal Court, Convention on Biological Diversity, Persistent Organic Pollutants, the Convention on Cultural Diversity and the Basal Convention on the Movement of Hazardous Materials jeopardize core values of the United Nations as well as 'unanimity' as the accepted protocol for reaching consensus at intergovernmental meetings.

- Criticism of long accepted tenants for policy application such as the precautionary principle.

- Disenfranchisement, perceived or real, of many of the world's citizens has caused opposition to global governance as the backbone of globalization. It is a significant uprising that will get stronger as it matures.

- Accusations that UN officials themselves are corrupt and working against the very decisions taken in the General Assembly or the Security Council, and the impact this may have on public perception and respect for the UN.

- The different preferences (and capacities) by states to use 'hard power' (military, economics) or 'soft power' (negotiation) in the conduct of international affairs.

- The disturbing trend to consider United Nations and other aid and humanitarian workers (PVOs, NGOs, bilateral or multilateral organizations) as legitimate targets of violence in war-torn countries and regions when they are perceived to be supporting the aims of an invading or occupying force.

As a result, what may be emerging are the doctrines of 'preemption' and 'retroactivity' – even the use of threat and unilateral force that could significantly alter the GEG process. Some see a direct link between these and a so-called predominance doctrine or the willingness to go it alone on issues as disparate as war and intellectual property rights vis-à-vis the Convention on Biological Diversity.[28] In this scenario, power leads to unilateralist actions whether for vested interests (political, economic, etc.) or humanitarian or altruistic goals. A former Finnish Ambassador to the UN noted that while the use of preemption as a strategy is historic, the context of employing it today has changed substantially.[29] Time will tell if these trends are merely opinions reflecting current events or if they will survive at the expense of what were once global values.

Success and failure

Successes do occur despite, but not necessarily because of, the way institutions formulate and administer GEG. Almost paradoxically, success within the complexities of GEG seems to depend on several relatively simple attributes: personalities, relationships, trust, mutual respect and a sympathetic understanding of others' interests. Rather than blocking coalitions, casting blame and participating in ideological battles, joint problem solving is necessary. The process calls for high levels of expertise – technical as well as diplomatic – throughout the system. All participants must know and adhere to the decision-making procedures and a fixed and accepted set of rules. Conference officers should be stern, dedicated, unbiased and knowledgeable of the history and substance of the issues. Also required are documents in the appropriate languages and a fully prepared secretariat, including translation and interpretation services as well as a cadre of dedicated note-takers. Besides these, the process should include the support, criticisms, ideas and energy of civil society.[30]

Equally important is that communication between the negotiators be efficient and with a minimum of error. Although, as is often the case, the negotiators may not agree on the definitions, as much as possible, all participants should seek to understand what the others are saying – even those populations who choose (or who are forced) to stay outside the gates. After all, what good is an instrument that contains all the right words if the parties that agreed to them understand them in mutually exclusive ways?

Chaos

> Squalid poverty lives side by side with over-abundance on our Earth. We have reached the Moon but we have not yet reached each other. Many species of our co-inhabitants on the globe ... have forever disappeared. Many beautiful rivers have become sewers endangering the oceans. We must heed the omens. We must pass from words to deeds. We must pass from rights to obligations. We must pass from self-interest to mutual interest. We must pass from partial peace to total peace.
>
> U. Thant

Though not the first expression of concern for the condition of our Earth and its inhabitants, these words of UN Secretary General U. Thant over 35 years ago (1970) lay the foundation for a question that must have an affirmative response from any effort to build an effective architecture of global environmental governance: 'Can Humans and Other Species Survive?'

Despite successes, the responses of the international community to the complexities that surround us have been messy and confused and the answers to the question have divided as often as they have united the peoples of our planet.

Arguments can be made that chaos is to be both expected and welcomed in something as complex as GEG, if for no other reason than that it creates the tension required for questioning and creativity to take place. Nevertheless, this chaos, unattended, slows the process because of needless repetition, sidetracks the debate to unproductive bickering and further misunderstanding, raises the already excessive financial and human costs, and dampens the enthusiasm required to overcome the frequently tedious and thankless job of organizing a united attack on the problems we face today.

If GEG is looked at through the lens of the complexity sciences, it is the former rather than the latter point of view that is of interest. Global environmental governance, like other social systems, is an open, non-linear, complex and, therefore, unpredictable system that follows the trajectory:

> Order → Complexity → Edge of Chaos → Chaos, disintegration, death, or emergence to a new order depending on the rules the system follows.[31]

Accordingly, a system begins its evolution from initial orderliness. However, as new information, projects, interests, misunderstandings, adjustments, constraints and disturbances of any kind are added, the system becomes progressively more complex. It also becomes increasingly disorganized since, following the complexity sciences, small initial differences can later become major forces that push a system towards chaos or a variety of undesirable kinds of stability. Likewise, positive feedback, especially if for something less than optimal, will lead the system to increasing disorder and eventually to the 'edge of chaos.' It is here, at the edge of chaos, where an array of 'choices' becomes available. 'Attractors' – the points around which order is generated, influence these choices and there are three of them: 'point,' 'cyclic' and 'strange.' If the system 'falls' toward either of the first two, stagnation – even death – is the result. If it is the third, the consequence is chaos.[32]

Fortunately, though, there is a fourth 'emergence' alternative, where creativity and innovation can take the system to something still complex but also newly ordered and, hopefully, in social systems, one having more value. Institutional examples of the first two attractors include all-important and immoveable organizational goals despite the change taking place around them. Cultures, core values and ideologies can be examples of strange attractors. With complex, open, non-linear systems, however, change or evolution of the system will always occur. Given the alternatives of death, eternal repetition, or endless chaos, it seems to many that the ideal policy would be one that influences, rather than attempts to stifle, this change.

Environment and sustainable development in GEG

GEG stands at the edge of chaos. Hints of this can be seen in the moves by individual states toward unilateral actions, in the professionally belligerent, and, for our purposes, in the significant variation of estimates for the number of international environmental agreements (anywhere from 16 to nearly 1000) given by GEG scholars and negotiators. These seemingly innocuous numbers indicate far more than innocent discrepancies because they depend on the informant's understanding of what the term *environment* may mean,[33] how it fits with his or her view of development,[34] and the relationship these concepts have with one's appreciation of what *sustainable development* may be.[35] Much of this confusion rests on the relationships between the terms of 'conservation,' 'environmental protection,' 'environment and development' and 'sustainable development' that have evolved over the last 50 years. This evolution, though normally positive, has also created many of the troubles that plague our search for successful models of global environmental cum sustainable development governance.

Various GEG negotiators, and others, have long acknowledged the lack of consensus definitions for both 'environment' and 'sustainable development.'[36] Lack of common, workable definitions of these terms is one piece of the problem. Another is the growing distrust of sustainable development by some environmentalists and the accusations by non-environmentalist promoters of sustainable development that 'representatives from the environmental ministries and departments dominate sustainable development.' The following excerpt from the minutes of a recent meeting of a group of experts requested by the Open-ended Intergovernmental Group of Ministers illustrates the confusion:[37]

> The Chair recalled that the Open-ended Intergovernmental Group of Ministers had asked for a clearer definition of international environmental governance and asked the experts to contribute to the debate on whether governance should refer to environmental issues or to sustainable development.
>
> The experts explored empowering the concept of sustainable development, to ensure the full integration of environmental policies with development. There was agreement that the problem is essentially political insofar as the key economic actors have not been engaged. This was taken as an indication that the sustainable development agenda lacks maturity. As a result, environmental actors are left to work only with the 'converted' in trying to deal with the wider issues of sustainable development.
>
> This led to a critical discussion on the Commission on Sustainable Development (CSD), with one participant observing that it had been impossible to get down to real work because the only people in the conference room were ones with an environmental portfolio.
>
> There were differences of opinion over the question of the existence of a governance process that addresses sustainable development and that the only meaningful systems of governance address

the environment. Some pointed out that the major environmental agreements also address sustainable development such as those designed to modify production and consumption patterns.

Participants discussed the role UNEP could play in international environmental governance cum sustainable development governance. There was a consensus that, on the whole, the CSD adds little to the debate on sustainable development.

These comments reflect the diversity of understandings of environment and sustainable development extant in GEG – again, in large part, the result of 50 years of evolution. For example, a biologist at the time of the World Conservation Strategy[38] would have a different understanding of sustainable development from that of the forest manager in the 1950s or from an attorney at an environmental NGO who picked it up in the 1970s. All three of these interpretations are different from that of a diplomat who learned about it from the Brundtland Commission Report in 1987,[39] or a businessperson who discovered the term in 1992 at the United Nations Conference on Environment and Development. These would be different from the view of almost anyone else who first learned about sustainable development during the Millennium Summit in 2000. All of these interpretations are possible, of course, but all of them are also incomplete. Taken together though, they are resources useful in our search for sustainability rather than something illegitimate or lacking in context.

GEG at the edge of chaos

Typically, the course followed in taking an idea through to a formal instrument of GEG begins with great enthusiasm and focus. Based on mutual concerns, states and/or other like-minded groups have common objectives that look down the line to the institutionalization of jointly made solutions. Negotiations commence but, almost immediately, positions begin to move away from one another. Multiple parties automatically mean multiple issues and unpredictable allies. The uncertainties of biased science and technology, whether real or imagined, begin to appear and, eventually, the realities of power differences become clear. Time frames evaporate and the cadres of early negotiators disappear – replaced by new people who perceive the potential outcomes as negative or competitive instead of common and convergent.[40] Negotiations continue and then, because of an immovable cut-off date, something less than originally hoped for is produced and signed.

Work towards improving global environmental governance requires a long institutional memory since the time counted from the recognition of a need for an agreement to its entry into force can easily exceed half of a career. By default, memory is held more by the community of observers (secretariat staffs and interested NGOs) than by the corps of official government negotiators for whom each new meeting seems a repetitive exercise for those who have been there, or a bizarre new learning experience for those who have just arrived. It seems that the numbing collection of concepts, jargon and acronyms that the newcomer encounters is never quite mastered before reassignment to different tasks in a different branch of the diplomatic corps.

Critics who say that official delegations to GEG events, including the meetings of the UN Commission on Sustainable Development, too often represent a country's environmental ministry or department have a point. However, the name 'environment' hides important details – like the fact that the representatives can be located in, and reflect the views of, a variety of sectoral institutions that includes natural resources, agriculture, forestry, fisheries, health, education, culture, social development, housing, youth, labor, tourism, recreation, foreign affairs, finance, planning, science, cooperatives, energy, industry and, even, public works. Now and then, they may even find themselves in the office of the chief of state where they can exercise genuine power. More often, they fill a more or less powerless office of their own. The handful of ministers with a 'sustainable development' title fair no better, and spend their time defending their role vis-à-vis their colleagues with 'substantive' portfolios. Recognizing this diversity of content, delegations from the richer and larger nations have representatives from several different offices, including foreign affairs, who often disagree with their colleagues from the substantive units on the positions their government should take. Disagreements, however, rarely take place on technical grounds. Rather they are between the technical and political elements or official positions that a delegation must publicly uphold.

Even if initially unified, the position of a delegation will vary over time. Governments, and a nation's policies, change with each election and, with each new government, a different set of negotiators arrives on the scene. During their initial meetings, at least, new delegates are unprepared for what they find despite what they may understand of their government's policies and positions on any given topic.

Generally, delegations contain both specialists and generalists. The predicament of the specialist is that the problem areas covered by GEG are often so broad that the specialist understands only a very small portion of the technical issues and almost nothing of diplomacy. The trouble with the generalist is that his or her understanding of a specific problem area is often nowhere close to what is necessary. Anything other than a solution based on an increasing number of vagaries required to reach consensus is impossible. Indeed, part and parcel of many of these agreements is the adjustment of once valid concepts and the invention of a language intentionally made unintelligible to everyone.[41] Agreement to use a term or concept that means different things to different people, however, can be a costly bit of trickery.[42]

The 1972 UN Conference on the Human Environment was the first international conference of its size to include a side gathering of a substantial number of civil society representatives. With each conference since then, civil society has moved closer to the official deliberations as well as to become better funded, larger in number, more varied in interests, better prepared and increasingly more aggressive and effective in the promotion of its points of view.[43] As the influence of these groups grows, it adds both good and bad consequences in terms of complexity and results. Little doubt exists that the process achieves a better technical and, in many ways, political outcome because of the input and influence of civil society. However, the result often attempts to meet too many demands, appears disjointed, and almost certainly has a budget designed to meet negotiated objectives unacceptable to many governments that will claim they look more like a wish list than a realistic effort to find solutions that fit within national priorities and resources.

Not only are the nongovernmental camp followers of GEG growing in number, they are also growing in variety and in strength sufficient enough to force new socio-economic topics like trade, debt relief, economic theory, the selection and assignment of subsidies, lifestyles, marketing, gender, war, democracy and human rights onto the environmental agenda.[44] It is the flip side of the successes of the environmental movement that previously forced systems thinking, impact studies, health and civil participation onto the agendas of development and governmental policy. Environmentalists may complain, but this is the logical extension of their early successes and, even, of the concept of environment itself.

Add to all of this the number of languages (including several different varieties of English) and the fuzziness created by the simultaneous interpretation of invented jargon.[45] Add as well the heat created by cultural differences, ancient animosities, current competitions and unfortunate histories. Add also the open and inadvertent skewing of information because of late night meetings, institutional loyalties, ephemeral alliances and financial inequities. Include, then, the intricacies of working through national, institutional and delegate egos, as well as the delicacies of managing several simultaneous, cross-cultural flirtations, dalliances and true loves (both institutional and personal), and there is little doubt that GEG stands at the edge of chaos.

We, the authors, of course, can do nothing about any of this. We have neither the authority nor the ability to do so. We do have, however, the opportunity to look at the language of GEG and we will do so now.

Chaos is born

If language is not correct, then what is said is not what is meant. If what is said is not what is meant, then what ought to be done remains undone. If this remains undone, then morals and acts deteriorate and justice goes astray. Hence, there must be no arbitrariness in what is said. This matters above everything.

Confucius

Mathematical models used in the development of the science of complexity show that chaos occurs in complex systems because of their sensitivity to initial conditions and, the models suggest, very small differences at the beginning of an operation will grow at an enormous rate. Likewise, as stated earlier, imprecision along the way, and positive feedback for something less than optimal will take an increasingly complex system to a 'decision point' where it will either stabilize itself in death or monotony, stay in the furrow it has created to spend an eternity in chaos, or emerge to something still complex but once again ordered.

That such theories can describe social as well as physical systems is now widely accepted.[46] In the physical sciences, complexity and chaos can be explained because of the power of modern computers. For the social sciences, however, Confucius (see above) had it figured out long before the experts in non-linear programming.

Does Chaos Theory hold for global environmental governance? Our guess is, 'yes.' The differences and imprecision in how individuals and institutions in the environmental/sustainable development movement understand the words – not to mention the concepts – of 'environment,' 'ecology' and 'ecosystem' and the positive feedback surrounding the *politics* of 'sustainable development' as well as the confusion elicited by such notions as the 'precautionary principle' do seem to influence the course of GEG.[47]

For many years, it has been a hobby of ours to ask students, teachers and technical and administrative staff of environmental management courses, government offices and NGOs to define these four terms: environment, ecology, ecosystem and sustainable development. No grades were involved but it is clear that few of the responses were coherent enough to serve as a guide to global environmental governance (see Appendix 5 for a collection of their responses). However, since even a professional could have a problem giving cold definitions to such requests, we need to look at what they give us in print, where they have sufficient time to reflect on what they say.

Environment

Table 1 presents the ways environmentalists often use the term 'environment' when they talk or write to one another. In an attempt to classify the various uses, we have come up with four categories and several sub-categories of meanings. There could be many more. How the word is used is instructive, but the wide variation in how it is used (the 'small initial differences' of Chaos Theory) is even more interesting. More importantly though, is that almost none of the uses really reflect the essential qualities of the scientific concept of environment: that is that the characteristics of an environment change in time and space and that these characteristics largely dictate the health, welfare and behavior of the object or system at its 'center.'[48]

Does this variety of uses cause problems for environmental governance? Again, our answer is 'yes' and, this time, it is more than just a guess. For example, the confusion sown by being unacquainted with the concept of environment surfaces in the following discussion found in a UNDP report of a survey of environmental projects:[49]

> (p.6) As a first step, it was decided that UNDP would prepare a compendium of environmental projects, building on its own Official Development Assistance information base with contributions from forum members. The idea was to better understand the impact of aid to the environment sector.
>
> In 1996, UNDP published the *Compendium of Environmental Projects in Vietnam – 1985–1995* summarizing a decade of international assistance to the environmental sector ...
>
> The team collating the compendium had to define an 'environmental'

Table 1 Contexts in which the word 'environment' is defined

I. Building blocks	II. Economic uses	III. Spatial uses	IV. Ethical/ spiritual uses
1) Architectural	1) Inputs	1) Ecosystems	1) Home
Built environment	Natural resources	Forest	Nature
Natural environment	System services	Rangeland	Place
2) Geographical	2) Outputs	Planet	Planet
Terrestrial environment	Contamination	2) Comprehensive	Earth
Aquatic environment	Products	Watershed	2) Spiritual
3) Institutional	3) Other	Landscape	GAIA
Home environment	Occupational health		Wilderness
Work environment	Environmental engineering		Culture
Social environment			Deep ecology

project. This caused problems, as it is always difficult to define what activities constitute environment projects and programs.

In the years immediately following [UNCED], aid agencies reported on their performance in this field using different criteria and by 'repackaging' existing projects. The result was that it became impossible to gain an accurate picture of the true extent of environment investment ...

To get around this problem ... UNDP adopted the definition that 'an environmental project is one where the main objective of the project is either the preservation of the natural environment or supporting the sustainable management of natural resources.'

UNDP also noted that 'even given this broad definition the problem of concisely classifying projects remains.' It found that the best way to identify what is or is not an environment project was to illustrate the type of donor projects that did or did not fall into this category. Thus, donor projects identified as 'environment' included:

• all forestry projects;
• all soil degradation and salinization projects, minus irrigation activities;

- watershed and water pollution projects;
- environmental research and training, but not general agricultural research;
- integrated community and rural development projects, excluding commercially oriented agricultural and credit fund projects;
- disaster planning and mitigation;
- rehabilitation of sea dykes projects;
- urban and regional development plans;
- integrated pest management projects;
- energy efficiency projects (e.g. wood stoves, solar or wind power).

The internal inconsistencies included in this list should be apparent to most readers. For example: do 'all forestry projects' include high grading, clear-cutting, and the use of exotic species in plantations? Most urban and regional plans are terribly conflictive; integrated pest management is included in the list but agricultural research is not; salinization projects [desalinization projects?] are in, but irrigation – the activity perhaps most responsible for salinization – is out; and the debates surrounding the location of wind powered generators, waste treatment plants and sanitary landfills (pollution control) are classic in NIMBY wars as well as in the battles for environmental justice.

By no means is such confusion isolated; nor is it new. In the early 1980s, the Committee of International Development Institutions on the Environment (CIDIE), which is made up of the environmental offices of UNEP, UNDP, the World Bank, IDB, ADB, AfDB, EIB, EBRD, OAS, ECE and a few other part-time associates, was likewise concerned with isolating 'environmental projects' from the rest of their agencies' portfolios. The group also needed a common basis for understanding the environmental management issues then confronting their agencies. Of the 35 issues suggested as being 'environmental' by the eight CIDIE representatives (Table 2), two of them were mentioned seven times, four were mentioned three times, seven twice, and 22 of them were mentioned only once. No consensus was ever developed and the problem of what is and is not an environmental project remains unresolved. It is apparent that, in terms of its common usage, an 'environmental project' is anything anyone wants to say it is.[50]

Other contradictions are evident in how nonprofessionals and professionals alike understand the term 'environment.' Most will say, for example, that environment has to do with 'natural resources,' as in the extract of the UNDP report given above, but many others are fond of using the phrase 'environment and natural resources,' which seems to say that environment and natural resources are separate entities. There also is the widely accepted idea that 'environment is everything' (see Appendix 5), which, if true, complicates things for those who prefer to talk about an 'environmental sector,' again as in the 1996 UNDP report.

Perhaps there are practical and operational reasons for many of the ways the term 'environment' is used. Our conclusion, however, is that this word is the most used, yet least understood, term employed in environmental

Table 2 CIDIE member institutions' interpretations of the issues requiring treatment as an 'environmental project'

Member institutions	Interpretation
ADB	Reforestation, water supply, sanitation, solid waste disposal, urban renewal, land-use and capability assessment, watershed management, soil conservation, agro-forestry, industrial and urban pollution, regional planning.
EIB	Water supply, sewerage, wastewater treatment, oil tanker cleaning, industrial pollution, afforestation, pasture improvement and erosion control, soil saturation.
WB	Reforestation, soil conservation, rangelands and watershed management, water resources and slum upgrading, pollution control, natural resource development.
UNDP	Afforestation, energy conservation, pollution control, wildlife conservation, water supply and sanitation, flood warning, occupational safety and health, environmental legislation, environmental management surveys and studies.
IDB	Conservation or enhancement of the environment, flood control, land erosion, air, land and water pollution, transfer and utilization of science and technology.
AfDB	Sanitation, health, water, forestry, irrigation, agro-industry, mining, rural development, industry and energy.
ECE	Desertification and afforestation, wildlife conservation, renewable sources of energy, water management, village water supplies, soil conservation, fish stocks conservation.
OAS	Any development project is an environmental project.

management as well as in the search for sustainable development and global governance. It has been misused for decades, of course, and too few writers use it in a way that sufficiently expresses what it has always meant: *Anything outside an object (or system) of interest that influences the health, welfare and behavior of that object (or system) of interest at a given moment in time.*[51]

Human environments, of course, are no different from other environments in terms of definition; they also are predominately local, always personal, continuously changing, and are a primary influence on the health, welfare and behavior of the individual or population at their 'center.' Therefore, any use of the term 'human environment' that faithfully reflects the concept of environment will convey the idea that outside of naming a specific time, a specific place and a specific owner, something called 'the environment' does not exist.

Ecology

When asked to give a definition of 'ecology' most people will get it more or less right and call it a 'science.' They will then immediately use the term to mean something entirely different.[52] An interesting example of the correct definition and incorrect use of the term appears in a publication of the Asian Development Bank in which 'concepts of ecology' and 'protection of ecology' show up in the same sentence after earlier defining the term only as the '... study of the interrelationships of organisms to their environment.'[53]

Ecology is, indeed, a science – at least it is a science according to the *Ecological Society of America* (ESA), which, despite its name, is an association of professional ecologists from around the world. The full definition given by the ESA is '*Ecology is the scientific discipline that is concerned with the relationships between organisms and their past, present, and future environments.*'[54] Note the plural 'environments.' Note also that ecology is not a synonym for environment and that there is only one definition given. Used in any other way – as if 'ecology' were a worldview, a synonym for environment or as an adjective to describe a problem, is 'language that is not correct.' To use it in any other way, without giving a definition of what one means by it, is confusing and impedes our capacity to 'do what needs to be done.'

Nevertheless, many of its users, though continuing to define it as a science, will say that the public long ago co-opted the word 'ecology' and that one can now correctly use it to mean other things.[55] There is no doubt that definitions change because a word is misinterpreted and used erroneously so often that it eventually comes to mean something else. Alternatively, the definition can be modified because new information shows it to be in error as a descriptor for some phenomenon or object. Unfortunately, where ecology is concerned, co-optation is closer to the first than it is to the second – which brings up a question: Why should global environmental governance accept the careless use of words or, even more importantly, why should it accept the *ideological* use of words that, by definition, were designed to be free of ideology? If the word 'ecology' is co-opted by an ideology, does the science itself also become ideological in the eyes of many? Observation tells us that the answer to that question is also a regrettable 'yes.'

Ecosystem

Even ecologists have trouble saying what an ecosystem is, yet the word is used by almost everyone else both as if they know for sure what it means and as if everybody who is listening has a perfect understanding of what is being said.[56] However, as with 'environment' and 'ecology,' the popular view of 'ecosystem' omits some very important parts.

For instance, according to the generally accepted *concept*, the borders of an ecosystem are not a given, are never precise, and, more importantly, are always defined by the person who locates the boundary around the ecosystem in question:[57] '[The] boundary is based on the observer's needs, the actors, and the context, rather than on any intrinsic property of the system itself.'[58] Other people, for other purposes or using other measurement instruments and scales, will put the line elsewhere.[59] Likewise, ecosystems, being non-linear and open, are neither static nor in equilibrium. They are always changing and this change can be rapid or slow, catastrophic or evolutionary, human controlled and influenced, or without any human intervention whatsoever.[60] These characteristics of ecosystems, of course, cause problems for such concepts as 'ecosystem balance,' 'ecosystem health' and 'ecosystem fragility' as well as for some interpretations of 'ecosystem restoration.'

Balance

For example, one of the myths surrounding the issue of sustainable development closely ties sustainability to an assumed 'balance of nature' where disturbances initiated by humans lead to disharmony and development failure. However, science has discovered such balance, when it occurs, to be highly dependent on the scales of time and space.[61] Indeed, for all practical purposes, this kind of balance does not last and development, like environmental management, if it is to be sustainable, must either adapt to such change or fail – the reverse of what is often stated.

Further, though science *has* looked into the stability of ecosystems and, therefore, their instability under conditions of stress, few studies have truly investigated their 'fragility.'[62] Yet, there is a long list of ecosystems that have been labeled as fragile in the public press: from the Arctic to the tropics, from reefs and estuaries to alpine ponds, rainforests, grasslands, deserts and, incidentally, urban neighborhoods. Given its ubiquity in popular writing and its absence in scientific literature, however, one could suspect that the term *'fragile ecosystem'* is used more often to promote a particular view of how to treat a specific place than it is to inform the public of scientific fact.[63]

Ecosystem health

Ecosystem health is similarly an invented attribute of ecosystems and not something included in the concept. It becomes a valid piece of the model only if a management objective is assigned to the manipulation of the ecosystem in question.[64] That is, if one is to talk of ecosystem health, one also must state the objective desired for that ecosystem be it a cornfield, windbreak, pristine mountain lake or tropical estuary and be it (the objective) food, fiber or spiritual tranquility. It is possible to design any number of objectives and activities to make use of the attributes of any system. Manipulation of the system to meet an objective, of course, includes the tools required for conservation or preservation as well as for other forms of development. Characteristically, if there is more than one objective for that system at a given time, the result will always be conflict over how 'best' to use its structure and function on the one hand and just who is going to make that decision on the other.[65]

Ecosystem restoration

Likewise, given the dynamics of ecosystem change, *ecosystem restoration* is a difficult term to understand and an even more difficult task to pull off.[66] Succession, a notion put forth by ecologists to describe ecosystem formation, is really a continuum of evolving structure and function altered by forcing functions known and unknown to the restorer. The decision as to where along this continuum one can say an ecosystem is now 'restored' is a decision made according to the desires (objectives) of the restorer, which may or may not be what the system looked like when it was 'in equilibrium' or what it may have been like before humans got there.[67] Indeed, according to the Society for Ecosystem Restoration, ecosystem restoration can be based on conservation goals, economic need, ethical or cultural values, aesthetic principles or, even, political considerations.[68]

Positive feedback

Because of the unquestioning use of concepts such as the 'precautionary principle' and the acceptance of the term 'sustainable development' across a broad span of sectors and the numerous problems they create in terms of definition and practical application, their handling within GEG falls into the category of positive feedback for something less than optimal.

The Precautionary Principle (PP)

The emergence of increasingly unpredictable and unquantifiable risks such as those associated with genetically modified organisms (GMOs), and global climate change have led the scientific community to develop an anticipatory model to protect against such risks.

Over the last 20 years or so, PP has become one of the most frequently cited rationales for international treaties and declarations. It is also one of the most criticized and hotly debated issues in the GEG process.[69] Simply stated, PP is a strategy to cope with scientific uncertainties in the assessment and management of risks – a 'better safe than sorry' approach to policy making – that covers a multitude of interpretations that vary from a guarantee against serious and irreversible harm and the promotion of inter-generational equity to a means to delay and block needed development. Despite these differences, PP, in the last 40 years, has gained currency as a guiding principle in a wide variety of GEG-related issues, including the 1992 UNCED conference and the United Nations Framework Convention on Climate Change (UNFCCC) negotiations.

In spite of this, though definitions are similar, there is no universally agreed-to definition of the PP nor uniformity as to the degree of its authority.[70] For example, the World Commission on the Ethics of Scientific Knowledge and Technology (COMEST) complains that 'the triple negative notion in the Rio Declaration that the "*absence* of rigorous proof of danger does *not* justify *inaction*," forces but does not require consideration of PP';[71]

the German Government (1984) suggests that 'damages done to the natural world should be avoided in advance and in accordance with opportunity and possibility'; the London Declaration on the Protection of the North Sea (1987) states that an 'approach is necessary which may require action to control inputs of such substances even before a causal link has been established by absolutely clear scientific evidence'; and the EU Directive on the Precautionary Principle (2000) states that it applies 'where scientific evidence is insufficient, inconclusive or uncertain and preliminary scientific evaluation indicates that there are reasonable grounds for concern that the potentially dangerous effects on the environment, human, animal or plant health may be inconsistent with the high level of protection chosen by the EU.' What is remarkable in these and other documents is the change in interpretation over time, how it has been applied to an ever widening range of sectors, and moved from general guidance to mandatory actions and measurable targets and that even the most strict interpretations also provide language along the lines of 'according to their capabilities' or that the PP 'shall not be used as a reason for postponing *cost-effective* measures to prevent environmental damage.' It is as if PP is such an on-target principle that we cannot afford to use it. Alternatively, it is something that sounds so good that we all want it but if fully implemented, progress will come to a halt.[72]

Sustainable development[73]

Treatises on the history, definition and principles of sustainable development and sustainability have become unmanageable. Discussions regarding the origins of these terms appear to depend as much on an author's interests as it does on research. What appears obvious, however, is that there are at least two levels of conceptual intensity that fall out of the hundred or so definitions of sustainable development – the abstract and the practical. Each of us is captivated by, and intuitively understands, the abstract idea of sustainable development. What we grasp of it at a practical level, is something else altogether. Being understood differently by each, sustainable development is a term that most politicians, entrepreneurs and environmentalists enthusiastically embrace; development *and* conservation together are a heady mix. Add to that the positive feedback every time anyone uses the term, no matter the context and content, and we have the stuff of conflict and chaos.

At a practical level, the concept is fraught with the same contradictions as the concept of development, which are serious. For example, according to Denis Goulet, development decision making suffers from a 'failure to confront the inherent conflicts between the technical, political and ethical rationalities' of the process where a decision that favors any one of the three very often conflicts with one or both of the other two.'[74] Likewise, the three principles of sustainable development most often cited (protection of nature for its own sake, efficiency in the use of resources, and intergenerational equity) are mutually exclusive ideas according to David J. Pannell and Steven Schilizzi.[75]

This does not mean that we must rid ourselves of the term by any means. The idea is certainly a giant step forward from unsustainable development and every initiative that takes us forward is an improvement on what we have. However, GEG could make more progress if the supporters of sustainable development would accept that the concept has both abstract and practical levels. Then, believing the abstract to be possible, they could dedicate themselves to work through the difficulties and contradictions of development rather than denying that such contradictions exist just because someone adds the word 'sustainable' to the project or policy. The alternatives, the ones based on what we would like to know rather than on what we do know; or the ones that respond to pressures – be they from the despoilers, or from the conservationists – lead us only to unproductive chaos. Indeed, the best understanding of the concept and, therefore, the best way forward, is to appreciate sustainability as does Terri Meyer Boake: 'It's not a topic, it's an attitude.'

Complexity

According to W. Brian Arthur, who helped formalize Chaos Theory:[76]

> [complexity] tends to increase as functions and modifications are added to a system to break through limitations, handle exceptional circumstances or adapt to a world itself more complex... Where forces exist to weed out useless functions, increased complexity delivers a smooth, efficient machine. Where they do not, it merely encumbers.[77]

This statement by Dr Arthur is one that the practitioners of GEG need to heed as they try to 'break through limitations, handle exceptional circumstances and adapt to a more complex world.' For example, based on the conflict seen during both the run-up and the WSSD event itself, the process of GEG is neither 'smooth' nor 'efficient.'

Some of the reasons for this lack of smoothness and efficiency, already mentioned, consist of the divergent policies, ideologies, social and economic conditions and cultures of nearly 200 independent states and their governments as well as the policies, ideologies and cultures of thousands of NGOs. Likewise, the broad and changing makeup of each of the governments and nongovernmental organizations tend to promote disappointment rather than firm progress in their search for the means to govern well. Finding a route through and around these permanent fixtures on the GEG landscape requires a concerted effort on the part of scholars and diplomats. One part of that effort, we believe, is to improve the language and the manner in which it is continuously assembled around the process, architecture and implementation of GEG because it is here that many of the 'useless functions' may be most easily weeded out. One of these encumbrances, in our view, is the term 'political will.'

Political will

As previously stated, Chaos Theory includes the idea of 'attractors.' An attractor is the mathematical conceptualization of some stable point in a complex system. These are the 'organizers' of chaos, that is when a complex system is on the 'edge of chaos' the influence of an attractor may push (or drag) the system to a new order that can include death – the ultimate in stability, or endless repetition – only slightly more desirable than death. Certain systems also exhibit behaviors that settle on 'strange,' or chaotic, attractors. Hooked to a strange attractor, the behavior of the system varies unpredictably and spends its life in chaos. In GEG, our guess is that the term 'political will' – something that GEG has yet to define or even explain – is a strange attractor.

How obsessed is GEG with the idea of political will? An internet search for a combined 'political will' and 'environment' produces over 3 million references while a search for 'political will,' 'sustainable development' and 'sustainability' yields nearly 2 million references. That is a lot of cyberspace dedicated to something that few have ever tried to explain. Even more unsettling, however, is that the majority of these references relate to discussions held during meetings dedicated to GEG and nearly all of them include what can only be described as an excuse that pushes the blame for failure or inaction onto someone else: 'The effort we spent so much time planning, failed because of a lack of political will.'

However, to say that a project, program or policy failed because of a 'lack of political will,' is little more than a pretext to escape the guilt for something we did not do: we did not finish the assignment and our homework was handed in half done. Is it not somewhat embarrassing that we would spend millions upon millions of dollars to develop action proposals whose objectives are nothing less than the salvation of the world as we know it and then not do our homework?

To make some sense of the issue, we at least need a definition of what 'political will' is. To start, we will make a leap of faith and say that 'political will' involves a political decision. The question then becomes, 'How are political decisions made?' Since a political decision is probably not much different from any of the other decisions we make – only the names and intensities change, we have decided that we make decisions based on the route of least conflict for ourselves, the decision maker.

'Ha!' some of you will say, 'I knew it all the time. Politicians are such cowards!' Take it a step further, though, and ask 'conflict with what or with whom' and 'how strong' and 'how much' and the whole thing gets a good deal more complicated; so complicated in fact that we find ourselves admiring the politicians who have to make political decisions.

Making a decision requires deliberation. Deliberation is required because one has to balance the amount and kinds of conflict the decision will cause with a number of different entities or ideas, pretty much all of them important. Here are a few: constituents, support base, mentors, peers, opposition, leaders, law, constitution, other priorities, scientific information, aspirations and conscience. Multiply all of that by the many individuals who will

24

become involved in a decision on GEG and 'political will' becomes a strange attractor. Thus, relying on political will without doing our homework is costly, dangerous and naïve. However, since progress in GEG does indeed depend on the decisions of politicians, we need to know just what the homework is that went missing.

The answer to that homework question is easy; doing it is quite a bit more difficult. That is, our homework is to discover and manage the conflict that is at the center of emerging change; something few of us are very good at doing. We have difficulty in managing the many conflicting demands made by humans on the systems we share because the competing demands are not discovered early enough, they are known but not included in the analysis and treatment, or, more likely, there is no *real* consensus gathered around the process, the product, or both, before a governance proposal is put forward.[78] The reactions of unsatisfied or disenfranchised affected parties (including a significant portion of the political establishment) are major reasons for failed GEG proposals and actions. They fail because of unresolved conflict.

Emergence

There are at least two ways to manage emerging change in complex social systems such as GEG; they include the participation of civil society and the creative management of conflict.[79] These are important enough that there ought to be whole divisions of GEG practitioners schooled in these two methods for minimizing conflict, the reason being that if we can offer a program or policy to a decision maker that meets a desired objective and minimizes the conflict that the decision will bring, we will have done our homework.

Participation of civil society

Based on Principle 10 of WCED, two regions have established formal mechanisms to involve civil society in government decision-making processes: the Aårhus Convention, in Europe,[80] and the *Inter-American Strategy for the Promotion of Public Participation in Decision-Making for Sustainable Development* (ISP) in the Americas.[81] Both instruments include a set of principles that help guarantee civil society input into decision making. These mechanisms, combined with the growing activism of transnational elements of civil society, are radically transforming international negotiation, diplomacy and governance.

Europe's 'Aårhus Convention' (The United Nations Economic Commission for Europe Convention on Access to Information, Public Participation in Decision-making and Access to Justice in Environmental Matters) was adopted in June 1998 and entered into force in October 2002. Not only was it the first formal agreement of its type in the world, it represents a departure from the standard convention in that it links environmental rights and human rights and acknowledges the obligation owed to both present and future generations.[82] It establishes that sustainable development can be achieved only through the involvement of all stakeholders and it links government accountability and environmental management. The Convention focuses on interactions between the public and public authorities in a democratic context and it is forging a new process for public participation in the negotiation and implementation of international agreements.

The subject matter of the Aårhus Convention also goes to the heart of the relationship between people and their governments. It is not just a convention concerned with environmental management; it is also an agreement that demands government accountability, transparency and responsiveness. The Aårhus Convention grants the public rights and imposes obligations on parties and public authorities regarding access to information, to justice and to the process itself.

The *Inter-American Strategy for the Promotion of Public Participation* also has its origins in UNCED. UNCED led to the first hemispheric 'Specialized Summit of the Americas on Sustainable Development.' This summit, convened in Santa Cruz, Bolivia in late 1996, instructed the Organization of American States to formulate an inter-American strategy to promote public participation in decision making for sustainable development. In a show of consistency, subsequent summits and meetings of ministers (Chile 1996; Quebec City 2001) endorsed the concept of public participation in government decision making.

Consequently, early in 1997, the OAS General Secretariat began formulation of the ISP as an open, transparent and participatory initiative itself. A Project Advisory Committee (PAC) that included members from governments, private business and labor, as well as women and indigenous people, provided strategic guidance and advice. The core of the Strategy is the Policy Framework that contains the following six basic principles:

- a proactive role of governments and civil society to assure opportunities for public participation;
- inclusion of a diversity of interests and sectors;
- responsibility to share the commitments and burdens of development;
- comprehensiveness to ensure participation in all phases of the decision-making process, with sufficient flexibility to make midstream adaptations;
- access to relevant information, to the political process and to the justice system;
- transparency of information within, among and between government and civil society organizations to ensure the efficient use of resources.

These principles, in turn, gave rise to the following recommendations:

- Create or strengthen existing formal and informal communication mechanisms to encourage information sharing, collaboration and cooperation among civil society groups, within and between levels of government, and between government and civil society.
- Create, expand and put into practice legal and regulatory

       frameworks that allow for the participation of civil society in development decisions.

- Support institutional structures, policies and procedures that actively promote and facilitate government and civil society interaction in development decisions.
- Build and strengthen the capacity of individuals, within government and civil society organizations, to participate in development decision making with an increased base of knowledge on sustainable development issues and public participation practices.
- Procure and expand financial resources to initiate, fortify, and/ or continue participatory practices in development decision making.
- Create, strengthen and support formal and informal fora in which development activities are discussed and related decisions taken.

All this, of course, may (will) create any number of temporary problems and will often slow progress considerably. However, the advantages do seem to outweigh the disadvantages and the participation of civil society does represent an emerging solution to which GEG must pay close attention.

Conflict management

In terms of GEG decision making, we have come a long way in the years since the 1972 Stockholm Conference but there is still a long way to go. Along the route, we will need to work harder at conflict management – something that is a great deal different from the frequently acrimonious negotiations that currently take place in GEG.

Obviously, conflict management has been around forever and it is something we still need.[83] Unfortunately, however, where GEG is concerned, conflict management is too often seen as compromise and a loss or restriction of power when what it should be seen as is the opportunity to create.[84] Does that sound naïve? Of course it does; at least it does to us. But it also sounds necessary. We do live in a world of inequities in information, finances, organization, abilities and opportunity as well as hidden agendas and unarticulated, though strongly felt, needs. Human values are as diverse as personality, and all of them are important. Memories are long and history carries more weight than it should. Conflict is everywhere.

However, although conflict is often insane, it also tells us that inequities do exist, that noise makes problems easier to identify and that there is value in debate. Because of all of this, conflict management is not just a means to resolve disputes. It also is an opportunity to use the relationship revealed by a conflict to engage in productive debate, and to look for new and different solutions to the problems uncovered because of that conflict.

According to Dudley Weeks, who teaches conflict resolution at the American University in Washington, DC, at least four of our perceptions of conflict need to be changed:[85]

- that 'conflict is always a disruption of order,' a negative experience when in fact it is an outgrowth of diversity that can be used to clarify a relationship and additional ways of thinking;
- that conflict is always a battle between competing and incompatible self-interests while forgetting the presence of needs or goals that the two [or more] parties might actually share;
- that a conflict defines the entire relationship when the reality is that it is only one part of a complex relationship;
- that the conflict involves two absolutes, between right and wrong or between good and evil when, many 'values' are, in fact, subjective preferences.

Accordingly, conflict management may well be the single most important ingredient for successful global environmental governance that we know of – if we view conflict in positive ways rather than as something that requires the choosing of sides and destructive engagement to the bitter end.[86]

Justice and the problem of environment vs. environments

Perhaps some of you have noticed that we, the authors, have had a difficult time in keeping our eyes fixed on what we set out to do in writing this essay: to discuss only the language problem in GEG and leave the problems of power imbalance, cultural differences and all those 'non-environmentalists' trying to get into GEG to someone else. We had an idea all along, however, that in the end these two problems would turn out to be essentially the same thing. Since it is something that GEG is going to have to face squarely, we should do it also. It has to do with how one understands the concept of 'environment.'

The many differences in how the term is used do not appear bothersome within defined communities. For example, all architects recognize that a sleeping environment is different from an eating environment and those differ from a work environment. Biologists understand that a fluvial environment is different from a terrestrial environment and any sociologist can tell you the differences between the environments of a *barrio bajo* and a *barrio alto* in Latin America or between Upper and Lower Manhattan in New York City. Few can tell you what 'the environment' is, however, and therein lies the problem.

A strong disconnection exists between what many people vaguely believe the term to mean and the reality that those who formulated the concept meant it to describe: a system outside of another system that influences the interior system's health, welfare and behavior. Given that concept, our work is much more than the 'preservation of nature,' our challenges greater than the 'sustainable management of natural resources,' the labor of environmental governance is more than biodiversity conservation, and work on the problems of ozone depletion and climate change – though all of these are extremely important and correctly form a part of what GEG is about.

The concept of environment, however, demands that GEG go beyond pollution control and resource preservation. It obligates us to understand and use the term as a plural rather than as a singular. 'Whose environment is to be conserved, whose environment is to be developed, and whose environment will be impacted' by either of those actions are questions asked by the developing countries in every environmental meeting since Stockholm. Indeed, Principle 1 of the Stockholm Declaration affirms that 'Man has the fundamental right to freedom, equality and adequate conditions of life, in *an* environment of a quality that permits a life of dignity and well-being' (emphasis added).[87]

Environmental quality is the link between environment and poverty, between environment and health, and between environment and development. It has to do with how well a specific environment satisfies the needs of those who are at its center. Each of us, individually or in small groups, lives in different and ever-changing environments. Some of these environments are rich and rewarding. Others are totally lacking in the means required to satisfy human needs. A singular entity labeled 'the environment' does not exist, and calls to protect 'the environment' as described by the powerful and the favored disenfranchise the powerless and less fortunate.

Regrettably, the question, 'Whose environment are we talking about?' has always received the wrong answer. To respond directly or indirectly that there is only 'the environment,' that it belongs to everyone and that it must be protected, can misrepresent development choices, misdirects human energy and other resources, and hides conflict instead of managing it. Thinking of environment as a singular confounds the issues. Thinking of environment as a plural permits isolation and treatment of problems and allows us to understand the sources of conflict. Use of the plural allows a proper response to the complexity of our universe; use of the singular oversimplifies to an extreme. Use of the singular buries conflict until it explodes and becomes unmanageable. Use of the plural allows civilized discussion, trust and a coordinated search for solutions in the forums of global environmental governance, use of the singular is a major reason why GEG finds itself where it is.

What about 'the environment' of planet Earth – the 'global environment'? Does it exist? Obviously it does. However, that environment is only one of a countless number and has little to do with the way most individuals or groups perceive the problems found in their own private and local environments.[88] What about the ozone hole and climate change? Are they not environmental problems? Certainly they are. However, rightly or wrongly, the citizens of extreme latitudes are much more concerned about ozone depletion than are those individuals living in regions that are nearer the equator – which just happens to coincide with many of the areas of our world that suffer the most from poverty and disease. Obviously also, climate change will affect different parts of the globe in different ways, some of which, at least in the short term, may even be positive for a portion of the world's population.[89]

Environment and development are not opposites and the problems of environment and development are not a question of having one or the other in varying degrees. A short comparison will explain: for forest dwellers, deforestation may or may not be an environmental problem that forest protection may or may not solve. Poverty and inequity, on the other hand, entangled as they are with hate and corruption, as well as with international trade, national debt, local incompetence, gender issues, power imbalance and far from adequate education and health care, are most certainly environmental problems that only development, and good governance, can unravel.[90] That, in part, is now the future challenge to GEG – a quantum leap in complexity, a long way from the still valid concerns of national parks, wilderness and wildlife – but environment, nonetheless.

Notes

1   Oran R. Young (1997b) 'Global governance: Drawing insights from the environmental experience,' in O. R. Young (ed) *Global Environmental Accord: Strategies for Sustainability and Institutional Innovations*, Cambridge: MIT Press; chapter 2 of UNCHS (2002) *Cities in a Globalizing World Global Report on Human Settlements 2001*, London: Earthscan, 344pp; and Ronnie D. Lipschutz (1999) 'From local knowledge and practice to global environmental governance,' in Martin Hewson and Timothy J. Sinclair (eds) *Approaches to Global Governance Theory*, Albany, NY: State University of New York Press, pp259–283.

2   UNCHS pp90–92, and the CGG (1995) 'The concept of global governance' in CGG (ed) *Our Global Neighborhood: The Report of the Commission on Global Governance*, Oxford: Oxford University Press.

3   UNCHS, pp90–92.

4   A number of works are available that seek to explain the ways and means of how this is done. Four among many are that of Patricia Birnie and Alan E. Boyle (1992) *International Law and the Environment*, Oxford: Clarendon Press, 563pp; the even larger and more wide-ranging David Hunter, James Salzman and Durwood Zaelke (1998) *International Environmental Law and Policy* New York: Foundation Press, 1567pp; that of Lamont Hempel (1996) *Environmental Governance: The Global Challenge*, Washington DC: Island Press, 291pp. and the recent publication of James Gustave Speth and Peter M. Haas (2006) *Global Environmental Governance*, Washington, DC: Island Press. Other frequently updated sources such as the *Earth Negotiations Bulletin* published by the International Institute for Sustainable Development and the Fridtjof Nansen Institute's *Yearbook of International Cooperation on Environment and Development* (London: Earthscan) for example, are excellent archival sources of facts and analysis. Of course, the treaties, and the records provided by their secretariats, fill in the necessary background and can be easily accessed through the United Nations Treaty Data Base at http://untreaty.un.org or the Columbia University CIESIN Data Base at http://sedac.ciesin.columbia.edu.

5   For a comprehensive discussion of these 'rules,' see chapters 1 and 2 of Birnie and Boyle (1992).

6   The documentation of UNCED in convenient form can be found in Michael Keating (1993) *The Earth Summit's Agenda for Change: A Plain Language Version of Agenda 21 and the other Rio Agreements*, Geneva: Centre for Our Common Future, 70pp.

7   The full text of the Rio Declaration can be found at www.unep. org/documents/default.asp?documentID=78&articleID=1163.

8   For example, the European Multilateral Agreement on Investments appears abandoned and the proposed Vienna Convention on the Law of Treaties between States and International Organizations or between International Organizations has seen little activity since 1986. Although accepted by UNGA RES 37/7 (1982), the largely NGO sponsored *World Charter for Nature* is looked upon as 'pre-sustainable development' and insufficient to provide a complete ethical base for today.

9   This was particularly evident with early treaties but, even with these problems, there were successes. The 1940 Western Hemisphere Convention on the Conservation of Natural Resources, for example, proved widely useful for the formation of numerous national parks and reserves in Latin America despite a lack of funding for a secretariat or any concerted official effort for its promotion. A discussion of the 1940 convention can be found in Kenton R. Miller (1980) 'Cooperación y asistencia internacional en la dirección de parques nacionales' in *Planificación de Parques Nacionales para el Ecodesarrollo en Latinoamerica*, Madrid, Fundación para la Ecologia y la Protección del Medio Ambiente.

10   Victor Kremenyuk and Winfried Lang (1993) 'The political, diplomatic, and legal background,' in Gunnar Sjostedt (ed) *International Environmental Negotiation*, London: Sage Publications, pp3–16.

11   The peculiarities of all of this can be confounding to newcomer and veteran alike. Neither should venture into a meeting without first reading Joyeeta Gupta's *"On behalf of My Delegation..." A Survival Guide for Developing Country Climate Negotiators*, Climate Change Knowledge Network/Center for Sustainable Development in the Americas (no date) Accessed 22 July, 2002 at www.unitar.org/cctrain/Survival%20Negotiations%(nAIP)w ww/index.htm or Felix Dodds and Michael Strauss (2004) *How to Lobby at Intergovernmental Meetings*, London: Earthscan. A more general discussion of the whole procedure is given in Richard Elliot Benedict (1993) 'Perspectives of a negotiation practitioner,' in Sjostedt, pp219–243 and Birnie and Boyle (1992) pp32–81.

12   This is not to denigrate the value of the debate that goes on in 'unofficial' meetings where discussions can be much more straightforward than those that take place in plenary sessions.

13   CCX, the Chicago Climate Exchange, a private consortium of 14 founding members recently signed a legally binding document (2003) agreeing to reduce greenhouse gases by 4 percent each in four years. See www.chicagoclimatex.com.

14   See especially chapters 1 and 2 of Birnie and Boyle (1992) for an excellent in-depth discussion of GEG architecture.

15   Commonly, Conferences of the Parties (COP) are administrative assemblies of parties to a convention or treaty while Meetings of the Parties (MOP) are administrative assemblies of parties to a protocol.

16   UNEP (1997) *Compendium of Legislative Authority 1992–1997*, Oxford: United Nations Environment Programme/Express Litho Service, 287pp. and Keating (1993).

17   Intergovernmental treaties and conventions are generally deposited with international organizations that will then dedicate an office to act as the secretariat.

18   Kenneth W. Abbott and Duncan Snidal (2000) 'Hard and soft law in international governance,' *International Organization*, vol 54, no 3, pp421–456.

19   Ratification is seldom automatic. Indeed, if the treaty severely affects domestic interests, a legislative body may opt to not ratify even though the executive branch of the government signed the instrument (see Abram Chayes and Antonia H. Chayes, (1991) 'Adjustment and compliance processes in international regulatory regimes,' in Jessica Tuchman Mathews (ed) *Preserving the Global Environment: The Challenge of Shared Leadership*, New York and London: W.W. Norton and Company, pp280–308.

20   Fortunately, the Vienna Convention on the Law of Treaties, signed at Vienna 23 May 1969 and entered into force 27 January 1980, governs all of this. Every negotiator should have a copy. It can be found at www.fletcher.tufts.edu/multi/texts/BH538.txt.

21   An important related issue is that of how agreements are to be enforced (See Ronald B. Mitchell (2002a) 'International environment,' in Thomas Risse, Beth Simmons and Walter Carlsnaes (eds) *Handbook of International Relations*, London: Sage Publications; and Daniel W. Drezner (2002) 'Bargaining, enforcement, and multilateral sanctions: When is cooperation counterproductive?' *International Organization*, vol 54, no 1, pp73–102.

22   ODA is the official development assistance coming from the 22 members of the Organisation for Economic Co-operation and Development (OECD).

23   In 2004, the US Government doubled it percentage of GDP dedicated to ODA to 0.2 percent (Japan raised its giving rate to 0.23 percent of GDP in 2005), while several European countries began increasing ODA levels to meet the 0.7 percent commitment, raising the global average figure to near 0.5 percent in 2005. Another method of ranking giving has recently been published by the Centre for Global Development and the Carnegie Endowment for International Peace (2003) 'Ranking the rich,' *Foreign Policy*, May/June, pp56–66, which use other criteria to indicate support to the poor (trade, immigration and

peacekeeping policies) in addition to aid and investment.

24   Hillary French (2001) *Vanishing Borders*, London: Worldwatch Institute and W.W. Norton and Company.

25   One of the more significant of these was when the US Ambassador to the UN claimed in 2005, to the amazement of many, that his government had signed the Millennium Declaration as a broad statement of intent, but not the *goals* and targets themselves – a distinction that could and should have been made clear at the signing rather than five years into the program.

26   Victor Davis Hanson (2004) 'The U.N.? Who Cares...' *The Wall Street Journal – Europe*. 23 September.

27   Third Millennium Foundation (2002) *Briefing on Japan's 'Vote-buying' Strategy in the International Whaling Commission*, Paciano: Third Millennium Foundation.

28   Max Boot (2002) 'The big enchilada: American hegemony will be expensive,' *The International Herald Tribune*, 15 October.

29   Max Jakobson (2002) 'Preemption: Shades of Roosevelt and Stalin,' *The International Herald Tribune*, 17 October.

30   James K. Sebenius (1993) 'The Law of the Sea Conference: Lessons for negotiations to control global warming,' in Sjostedt, pp189–215.

31   Lorenz 1993, p228.

32   Lorenz 1993, pp222–235.

33   For example, Ronald B. Mitchell for the specific purpose of preparing a list of international environmental agreements, discusses this problem and defines agreements as being 'environmental' if they '... seek, as a primary purpose, to manage or prevent human impacts on natural resources; plant and animal species (including in agriculture); the atmosphere; oceans; rivers; lakes; terrestrial habitats; and other elements of the natural world that provide ecosystem services,' *International Environmental Agreements Defined* accessed at www.uoregon.edu/~rmitchel/IEA/overview/definitions/htm on 5 July, 2003. Ronnie D. Lipschutz, on the other hand, in his book *Global Environmental Politics from the Ground Up* (accessed at http://ic.ucsc.edu/~rlipsch/pol174/syllabus.html on 15 July, 2003) prefers 'habitat' as a more suitable approach to defining the global environment.

34   Herman E. Daly (1996) *Beyond Growth: The Economics of Sustainable Development*, Boston: Beacon Press.

35   Richard E. Saunier (1999) *Perceptions of Sustainability: A Framework for the 21st Century*, Washington DC: Trends for a Common Future 6. CIDI/Organization of American States. See also, Simon Dresner (2004) *Principles of Sustainability*, London: Earthscan.

36   Becky J. Brown et al. (1987) 'Global sustainability: Toward definition,' *Environmental Management*, vol 11, no 6, pp713–719; J. Pezzey (1992) *Sustainable Development Concepts: An Economic Analysis*, World Bank Environment Paper No. 2, Washington, DC: The World Bank; and Birnie and Boyle (1992), p2.

37   IISD (2001) 'Summary Report from the UNEP Expert Consultations on International Environmental Governance, 2nd Round Table, 29 May 2001,' *IISD Linkages*, vol 53, no 1.

38   IUCN, UNEP and WWF (1980) *World Conservation Strategy: Living Resource Conservation for Sustainable Development*, Gland: IUCN.

39   World Commission on Environment and Development (1987) *Our Common Future*, Oxford: Oxford University Press.

40   Christophe Dupont (1993) 'The Rhine: A study of inland water negotiations,' in Sjostedt, pp135–148.

41   Which caused Rosemary Righter to repeat an observation in a recent article in *The Times of London* (2003) that 'The art of international diplomacy is to convert the obnoxious into the incomprehensible.'

42   In diplomacy, 'constructive ambiguity' in language is often used to get through a hard place so that negotiations can continue – maybe to a place where there is so much agreement that the point of ambiguity can be discarded altogether. Ideally, it has two characteristics: first, it is deliberate and all sides know and agree to what is going on and second, it reduces the differences to the lowest common denominator rather than to paper them over. It can be a dangerous tactic if the problem is not eventually resolved because the realities of the differences will always come back to cause even more difficulties.

43   Recent developments include the decisions to permit 'official non-government observers' at many sessions of intergovernmental organizations and meetings, and the development of formal mechanisms for civil society involvement in government decision-making and international meetings.

44   UNEP (2002) *Global Environment Outlook 3*, London: Earthscan.

45   In this regard, the EU is certainly the record holder with 21 official languages among its 25 members, 3 working languages and even 3 official alphabets. All this 'linguistic diversity' comes with a hefty price tag. In 2005, written and spoken translation services cost €1.1 billion and the language directorate is the EU's largest department with 1650 full-time translators plus 550 support staff. In 2005 they translated 1,324,231 pages! For more on this topic see: Matthew Brunwasser (2006) 'For Europe, a lesson in ABCs (of Cyrillic),' *The International Herald Tribune*, 9 August.

46   A. B. Cambel (1993) *Applied Chaos Theory: A Paradigm for Complexity*, San Diego: Academic Press, Inc.

47   See Tim O'Riordan and James Cameron (eds) (1994) *Interpreting the Precautionary Principle*, London: Earthscan; T. O'Riordan et al. (2001) *Reinterpreting the Precautionary Principle*, London: Cameron May; and Carnegie Council (2004) 'Human rights dialogue: Environmental rights,' *Human Rights Dialogue*, Series 2, no 11, Spring.

48   Gilberto C. Gallopin (1981b) 'The abstract concept of environment,' *International Journal of General Systems*, vol 7, pp139–149.

49   UNDP (1996) *Compendium of Environmental Projects in Vietnam – 1985–1995,* Ha Noi, Viet Nam.

50   Birnie and Boyle have an interesting discussion on the topic of the many ways the word 'environment' is used. Summarizing their discussion, they repeat the unfortunate words of Caldwell (1980): '...it [environment] is a term that everyone understands and no one is able to define.' The words are unfortunate because the concept of environment is well understood in science and definitions that faithfully reflect that concept are available in any dictionary or encyclopedia.

51   Gilberto C. Gallopin (1981a) 'Human systems: Needs, requirements, environments and quality of life,' in G. E. Lasker (ed) *Applied Systems and Cybernetics. Vol. 1. The Quality of Life: Systems Approaches,* Oxford: Pergamon Press; and Amos H. Hawley (1986) *Human Ecology: A Theoretical Essay,* Chicago: The University of Chicago Press.

52   Mojan Wali in the June 1995 *Bulletin of the Ecological Society of America* vol 76, pp106–111) lists 337 different uses of the terms 'ecology' and 'ecological' found in the published literature he reviewed.

53   Asian Development Bank (1986) *Environmental Guidelines for the Development of Ports and Harbours,* Manila: ADB, p3.

54   www.esa.org/aboutesa/.

55   Lynton Caldwell (1980) *International Environmental Policy and Law,* Durham: Duke University Press.

56   John E. Fauth (1997) 'Working toward operational definitions in ecology: Putting the system back into ecosystem,' *Bulletin of the Ecological Society of America,* vol 78, no 4, p295; Alice E. Ingerson (2002) 'A critical user's guide to "ecosystem" and related concepts in ecology,' Institute for Cultural Landscape Studies, the Arnold Arboretum of Harvard University, accessed 10 June 2003 at www.icls.harvard.edu/ecology/ecology.html.

57   John C. Maerz (1994) 'Ecosystem management: A summary of the Ecosystem Management Roundtable of 19 July 1993,' *Bulletin of the Ecological Society of America,* vol 75, no 2, pp93–95.

58   There is some debate on this issue but the broad outcome seems to be that of general system theory, which suggests that we isolate systems mentally for the purpose of study. See Victor Marín (1997) 'General system theory and the ecosystem concept,' *Bulletin of the Ecological Society of America,* vol 78, no 1, pp102–103 and Bernard Pavard and Julie Dugale, 'An introduction to complexity in social science,' p17, accessed 15 July 2003 at www.irit.fr/cosi/training/Complexity-tutorial/htm.

59   Take, for example, the many differing definitions of 'wetland' being debated for regulating land-use. Closer to the subject of GEG are the discussions of Article 3.3 of the Kyoto Protocol and how one distinguishes between 'forested,' 'reforested' and 'afforested' areas.

60   James J. Kay (1991) 'A non-equilibrium thermodynamic framework for discussing ecosystem integrity,' *Environmental Management*, vol 15, no 4, pp483–495.

61   Daniel B. Botkin (1990) *Discordant Harmony: A New Ecology for the Twenty-first Century*, Oxford: Oxford University Press, 256pp.

62   C. S. Hollings (1973) 'Resilience and stability of ecological systems,' *Annual Review of Ecology and Systematics*, vol 4, pp1–24; Ariel E. Lugo (1978) 'Stress and ecosystems,' in J. H. Thorp and J. W. Gibbons (eds) *Energy and Environmental Stress in Aquatic Systems*, DOE Symposium Series; and Kay 1991.

63   Try an interesting experiment with reference to science vs. advocacy: Type 'ecosystem fragile' and 'ecosystem stress' into a search engine and see how many of the references under each can be classified as 'advocacy' or 'science.'

64   Robert T. Lackey (2001) 'Values, policy, and ecosystem health,' *BioScience*, vol 51, no 6, pp437–443.

65   OAS (1987) *Minimum Conflict: Guidelines for Planning the Use of American Humid Tropic Environments*, Washington DC: Organization of American States, 198pp.

66   James G. Wyant, Richard A. Meganck and Sam H. Ham (1995) 'The need for an environmental restoration decision framework,' *Ecological Engineering*, vol 5, pp417–420.

67   Kay 1991.

68   SER (2003) 'Global rationale for ecological restoration,' IUCN-CEM 2nd Ecosystem Restoration Working Group Meeting, 2–5 March, Taman Negara, Malaysia.

69   See Tim O'Riordan et al. (1994) *Interpreting the Precautionary Principle*, London: Earthscan; T. O' Riordan et al. (2001) *Reinterpreting the Precautionary Principle*, London: Cameron May.

70   European Commission (2000) *Communication from the Commission on the Precautionary Principle*, EU COM(2000)1, http://europa.eu.int/comm/environmental/docum/20001_en.htm. February, Brussels.

71   COMEST (Commission on the Ethics of Scientific Knowledge and Technology) (2005) *The Precautionary Principle*, Paris: UNESCO.

72   COMEST 12.

73   Much of this discussion follows Richard E. Saunier (1999) *Perceptions of Sustainability: A Framework for the 21st Century*, Washington DC: CIDI Organization of American States.

74   Denis Goulet (1986) 'Three rationalities in developmen decision-making,' *World Development*, vol 14, no 2, pp301–317.

75   David J. Pannell and Steven Schilizzi (1997) 'Sustainable agriculture: A question of ecology, equity, economic efficiency or expedience?' *Sustainability and Economics in Agriculture*, SEA Working Paper 97/1' GRDC Project, University of Western Australia.

76   See chapter 1 of M. Mitchell Waldrop (1993) *Complexity: The Emerging Science at the Edge of Order and Chaos*, New York: Touchstone.

77   W. Brian Arthur (1993) 'Why do things become more complex?' *Scientific American*, May, p144.

78   Consensus, of course, is an important goal of negotiations meant to lead to a binding treaty based on an agreement to use the words that are used. Unfortunately, this does not necessarily include agreement on their definitions.

79   There are others, all of which tend to fit into these two responses. Gender issues, for example, are important, as are issues surrounding youth, indigenous peoples, etc. Including these interests in the analysis reduces future conflict – and produces a better product. Likewise, if one asks of any environmental impact, 'Who created it?' and 'Who felt it?' one immediately realizes that the 'impact' is really a conflict between two or more interests that can be treated. That is something far different from identifying an impact of a development activity on something called *the environment* – a problem that cannot be treated.

80   UNECE (2002) *Introducing the Aårhus Convention*. Accessed 15 August 2001 at www.buwal.ch/inter/e/ea_zugan.htm.

81   OAS (2001) *Inter-American Strategy for Public Participation in Decision-Making for Sustainable Development*, Washington, DC: General Secretariat, Organization of American States.

82   The XXXII General Assembly of the OAS (Barbados, 2002) also followed this path in passing Resolution 1896, which clearly joins the right to environmental goods and services, such as clean air and water, to human rights via the Inter-American Human Rights Commission.

83   William I. Zartman (1993) 'Lessons for analysis and practice' and Jeffery Z. Rubin (1993) 'Third party roles: Mediation in international environmental disputes,' both in Sjostedt.

84   Dudley Weeks (1992) *Eight Essential Steps to Conflict Resolution*, New York: G.P. Putnam's Sons, 290pp.

85   Weeks 1992.

86   This issue is also being given serious institutional consideration in selected quarters. UNESCO, together with the members of the UN Water Family and other private sector, NGO and academic institutional partners, is spearheading the establishment of the Water Cooperation Facility (WCF) – a mediation center for parties with conflicts over the access and use of transboundary water or shared river basins, lakes or reservoirs. This facility will hopefully help resolve disagreements long before they involve rooms filled with lawyers or formal proceedings at the PCA, ICJ or other such arbitration or juridical bodies. It is also interesting to note that the acronym WCF was originally denoted the Water 'Conflict' Facility, but wiser heads prevailed with the word 'Cooperation.'

87   The text of the Stockholm Declaration can be found at www. unep.org/document/default.atp?documentID=978&articleID=1501.

88   Thomas F. Saarinen (1974) 'Environmental perception,' in Ian R.

Manners and Marvin W. Mikesell (eds) *Perspectives on Environment*, Washington DC: Association of American Geographers, pp252–289.

89   IPCC (2001) 'Climate change 2001: Impacts, adaptation and vulnerability,' *IPCC Third Assessment Report*, WMO/UNEP. See especially para. 1.21 of that report: 'Climate change represents opportunities and risks for human development,' at www.ipcc.ch.

90   Akiko Domoto (2001) 'International environmental governance: Its impact on social and human development,' *Inter-linkages*, World Summit for Sustainable Development, United Nations University Centre, 3–4 September.

part two

A Dictionary of Selected Terms, Concepts, Jargon, Acronyms and Abbreviations Used in Global Environmental Governance

Sources Used to Develop the Dictionary and List of Acronyms

Much of this book is about words and how they are used in global environmental governance; that is why we have included more than 2500 definitions and about 3000 acronyms that represent the institutions, devices, dreams and jargon invented by our colleagues. We are well aware that this does not do justice to the creativity of GEG wordsmiths. However, having now collected a dictionary of some magnitude, we are also aware of the amount of time and work that goes into such an exercise. Because of this, we want to acknowledge the work of all the others who have attempted such a thing and to say 'thank you' for knowingly or unknowingly allowing us to use their work. You will notice that many of the entries end with some hieroglyphics of our own – an attempt to identify our sources and the following is a translation of these hieroglyphics. Where a term is from an article or paper with a known author, their contribution is acknowledged as in a text and the source is then given in the bibliography.

We are also quite aware that many readers will disagree with some of the definitions we have chosen to include; we disagree with many of them as well (mostly those that run counter to what we have said in the essay), but for better or worse, they have come into common usage in international fora. Let the debate continue; clarification is needed and, for our part, welcome.[1]

ACCU	Asia/Pacific Cultural Centre for UNESCO. www.accu.or.jp/litdbase/glossary/
AD	Deardorff's Glossary of International Economics. www.personal.umich.edu/~alandear
AFESD	Arab Fund for Economic and Social Development. www.arabfund.org
AIT	Asian Institute of Technology. www.nano.ait.ac.th

AM	*Dictionary of Environmental Economics*, www.earthscan.co.uk
AMNH	American Museum of Natural History. www.Cbc.amnh.org/symposia/archives/seascapes/glossary/html
APO	Productivity Organization. www.apo-tokyo.org
ASEAN	Association of Southeast Nations. www.aseansec.org
AU	African Union. www.africa-union.org/root/au/AboutAU/au/au_in_a_nutshell_en.htm
BCHM	Belgium Clearing House Mechanism. webbie.kbinirsnb.be/beh_chd/belgium/glossary/glos-_a.htm
BLD	*Beck's Law Dictionary: A Compendium of International Law Terms and Phrases.* http://people.Virginia.edu/~rjb3v/latin.html
BWP	Bretton Woods Project. www.brettonwoodsproject.org/about/glossary.html
CAF	Andean Development Corporation. www.caf.org
CAN	Climate Action Network. www.climateactionnetwork.org
CBD	Convention on Biological Diversity, Secretariat. www.biodiv.org/secretariat
CCP	Copenhagen Consensus Project. www.copenhagenconsensus.com
CD	Convention to Combat Desertification. www.unccd.int
CEDAW	Convention on the Elimination of all forms of Discrimination Against Women. www.un.org/womenwatch/daw/cedaw
CF	Canter Fitzgerald. www.co2e.com/corporateoveriew.asp
CFR	Council on Foreign Relations. www.cfr.org/publication
CGC	Center for Green Chemistry. www.greenchemistry.uml.edu/
CGD	Center for Global Development. www.cdgev/rankingtherich/home.html
CI	Conservation International. www.conservation.org
CIPA	*World Directory of Environmental Organizations 1996.* www/cipahq/prg/landmarks.htm
CITES	Convention on International Trade in Endangered Species of Wild Fauna and Flora. www.cites.org
CIVICUS	CIVICUS. www.civicus.org
CMS	Convention on the Conservation of Migratory Species of Wild Animals. www.unep-wcmc.org/cms
CNS	Center for Nonproliferation Studies. cns.miis.edu/pubs/week/020805.htm
Co	Chaordic Commons. www.Chaordic.com
COICA	Coordinating Group of Amazon Basin Indigenous Organizations. www.coica.org
CONGO	Conference of Non-Governmental Organizations in Consultative Relationship with the United Nations. www.ngo.org/congo.html
CSD	Commission on Sustainable Development. www.un.org/esa/sustdev
CSG	Complex Systems Glossary. The Complexity and Artificial Life Research Concept for Self-Organizing Systems. www.calresco.org

CW	Country Watch. www.countrywatch.com
DESIP	Demographic, Environmental, and Security Issues Project. www.igc.apc.org/desip/toc.html
DFID	Department for International Development (UK). www.dfid.gov.uk
EC	Earth Council. www.earthcouncil.ac.cr
ECA	Environment Canada. www.ec.gc.ca/
ECLAC	United Nations Economic Commission for Latin America and the Caribbean. www.eclac.org
ECO	The Ombudsman Centre for Environment and Development. www.omced.org
eD	eDiplomat. www.eDiplomat.com
EEA	European Environmental Agency. www.eea.eu.int/; glossary.eea.eu.int/EEAGlossary/
EES	Encyclopedia of Environmental Science. www.wkap.nl/prod/b/0-412-74050-8
EM	Evomarkets. www.evomarkets.com/ghg_glossary.html
ENB	Earth Negotiations Bulletin. www.iisd.ca/linkages
ENN	Environmental News Network. www.enn.com
ES	Euroscience. www.euroscience.org
ESA	Society of America. www.esa.org
ESS	Earth System Sciences. www.ess.uci.edu
EU	Council of European Ministers www.europeanunion.org
FAO	Food and Agriculture Organization of the United Nations. www.fao.orgWAICENT/faoinfo/economics/ESN/codex/default.htm
FOEI	Friends of the Earth International. www.foei.org
FSC	Forest Stewardship Council. www.fscoax.org
GBA	*Global Biodiversity Assessment.* www.unep_wcmc.org/assessments
GBS	*Global Biodiversity Strategy.* www.wri.org/biodiv/pubs_description.cfm?pid=2550
GCC	Global Climate Coalition. www.globalclimate.org
GEF	Global Environment Facility. www.gefweb.org/gefgloss.doc
GP	Greenpeace International. www.greenpeace.org
GPF	Global Policy Forum. www.globalpolicy.org/security/issues/diamond/kimberlindex.htm
HH	*Wycoff & Shaw's Harper Handbook* 3rd ed
IDB	Inter-American Development Bank. www.iadb.org
IEA	International Energy Agency. www.iea.org
IFAD	International Fund for Agricultural Development. www.ifad.org
IISD	International Institute for Sustainable Development. www.iisd1.iisd.ca/glossary.asp
ILO	International Labor Organization. www.ilo.org
IMF	International Monetary Fund. www.imf.org
IPCC	Intergovernmental Panel on Climate Change. www.ipcc.ch
IPS	Institute for Policy Studies. www.ips-dc.org/projects/legalscholars/

IPU	Parliamentary Union www.parlinkom.gv.at/portal/page?_pageid+1033, 658150&_dad+portal&_schema=PORTAL
ISO	International Organization for Standardization. www.iso.org
ITTO	International Tropical Timber Organization. www.itto.or.jp
IUCN	World Conservation Union. www.iucn.org
IUFRO	International Union of Forest Research Organizations. www.iufro.org/
LEAD	Leadership for Environment and Development. www.fa.lead.org
LLL	'Lectric Law Library. www.lectlaw.com
MBDC	McDonough Braungart Design Chemistry. www.mbdc.com/c2c_gkc.htm
MW	Merriam Webster
NAFTA	North American Free Trade Agreement. www/nafta-sec-alena.org
NASA	Air and Space Administration. www.nasa.gov
NGS	National Greenhouse Strategy of Australia. www.ngs.greenhouse.gov.au/glossary
NRDC	Natural Resources Defense Council. www.nrdc.org/reference/
NS	The Natural Step. www/naturalstep.org
OAS	Organization of American States. www.oas.org/
OECD	Organisation for Economic Co-operation and Development. www.oecd.org
Ox	Oxfam. www/oxfam.org
PAHO	Pan American Health Organization. www.paho.org
PEW	PEW Center on Global Climate Change. www.pewclimate.org/
PIC	Rotterdam Convention. www.chem.unep.ch/pic
PL	*Pequeño Larousse.* www.larousse.es/larousse/product.asp?sku=1
PPRC	Practical Solutions for Environmental and Economic Vitality. www.pprc.org
R	Real Alternatives Information Network. www.web.net/rain/main.htm
RC	Ramsar Convention. www.ramsar.org
RFF	Resources for the Future. www.rff..org
RMI	Rocky Mountain Institute. www.rmi.org/
SACN	South American Community of Nations. www.comunidadandina.org/ingles/sudamerican.htm
SETAC	Society of Environmental Toxicology and Chemistry. www.setac.org
SFI	Sustainable Forestry Initiative. www.afandpa.org/forestry/sfi_frame.html
SFWMD	South Florida Water Management District. www/sfwmd.org
SNW	Sustainable Northwest. www.sustainablenorthwest.org
SWF	State of the World Forum. www.worldforum.org

TFDD	Transboundary Freshwater Dispute Database. www. transboundarywaters.orst.edu
TI	Transparency International. www.transparency.org/
TWAS	Third World Academy of Sciences. www.twas.org
TWN	Third World Network. www.twnside.org.sg/title/brie6-cn.htm
TWNSO	Third World Network of Scientific Organizations. www. twnso.org
TWOWS	Third World Organization for Women in Science. www. twows.org
UN	United Nations (Main web page) www.unitednations.org
UNCED	United Nations Conference on Environment and Development. www.unep.org/unep/partners/un/unced/home.htm
UNCHS	UN Habitat. www.unchs.org
UNCLOS	United Nations Convention on the Law of the Sea. www. un.org/depts/los
UNDP	United Nations Development Programme. Governance for Sustainable Human Development. http://magnet.undp.org/policy/glossary.htm
UNECE	United Nations Economic Commission for Europe. www. sustainabledevelopment.gov.uk/publication/pdf/strategy/new%20glossary.pdf
UNED	United Nations Environment and Development Forum. www. earthsummit2002.org/
UNEP	United Nations Environment Programme. www.unep.org
UNEP-CAR-RCU	United Nations Environment Programme – Cartagena Convention – Regional Coordinating Unit. www.gpa.unep.org
UNESCO	United Nations Educational, Scientific and Cultural Organization. www.unesco.org
UNESCO-IHE	Institute for Water Education. www.unesco-ihe.org
UNFAO	United Nations Food and Agriculture Organization. www. fao.org
UNFCCC	United Nations Framework Convention on Climate Change Secretariat. www.unfccc.de/siteinfo/glossary.html
UNFPA	United Nations Population Fund. www.unfpa.org
UNIAEA	United Nations International Atomic Energy Agency. www. uniaea.org
UNICEF	United Nations Childrens Fund. www.unicef.org.uk/c8
UNMD	United Nations Millennium Declaration. www.un.org. millennium
UNMP	United Nations Millennium Development Project. www. unmillenniumproject.org/htm/about/htm; unmp.forumone.com/index.html
UNOCHA	United Nations Office for Coordination of Humanitarian Affairs. www.reliefweb.int/w/rwb.nsf

UNT	United Nations Treaty Collection, Treaty Reference Guide. untreaty.un.org/english/guide/asp
UNW	United Nations Wire. un.wire@smartbrief.com
USAID	United States Agency for International Development. www. USAID.org
USDA	Forest Service. www.fs.fed.us/
USDOS	US Department of State. www.state.gov
USEPA	US Environmental Protection Agency. www.epa.gov
USGS	United States Geological Survey. http://Interactive2.usgs. gov/glossary/index.asp
VTPI	Transport Policy Institute. www.vtpi.org
VC	Vienna Convention on the Law of Treaties. www.un.org/ law/ilc/texts/cvkengl.html
WB	World Bank. www.worldbank.org
WBCSD	World Business Council for Sustainable Development. www. wbcsd.org
WC	WIDECAST Wider Caribbean Sea Turtle Conservation Network. www.widecast.org
WCMC	World Conservation Monitoring Centre. www.unep-wcmc. org
WDp	Washington Diplomat. www.washdiplomat.com/glossary. html
WEF	World Economic Forum. www.weforum.org
WFp	Water footprint. www.waterfootprint.org/
WHO	World Health Organization. www.who.int
WIPO	World Intellectual Property Organization. www.wipo.int
WP	Wikipedia. http://en.wikipedia.org/wiki/Main_Page
WR	World Reference.com. www.worldreference.com
WRI	World Resources Institute. www.wri.org
WSF	World Social Forum. www.forumsocialmundial.org.br
WSSD	World Summit on Sustainable Development. www. johannesburgsummit.org/html/documents
WTO	World Trade Organization. www.wto.org/english/thewto_ e/minist_e/min99_e/english/about_e/23glos_e.htm
Wu	Wuppertal Institute. www.wupperinst.org/sites/links.html
WWF	Worldwide Fund for Nature. www.wwf.org

Note

1. We have included a good number of definitions that some readers may disagree with, which we may even question. Many definitions were undoubtedly written by lawyers, politicians, accountants and others who filled a void left by not having enough scientists.

Dictionary

Aa

A21 major groups – A term used in the text of *Agenda 21* indicating nine sectors of society fundamental to achieving sustainable development: children and youth, indigenous people, women, NGOs, local authorities, workers and trade unions, scientific and technological community, farmers, and business and industry. (UN)

A posteriori – Relating to or involving inductive reasoning from particular facts or effects to a general principle; derived from or requiring evidence for its validation or support; empirical; open to revision. (WR)

A précis – An abstract, abridgement, condensation, digest, synopsis or a summary of the essential thought of a longer piece. (HH)

A priori – Relating to or involving deductive reasoning from a general principle to the expected facts or effects; known to be true independently of or in advance of experience of the subject matter, requiring no evidence for its validation or support. (WR)

Aårhus Convention – The Convention on Access to Information, Public Participation in Decision-making and Access to Justice in Environmental Matters of the UNECE entered into force on 30 October 2001. Its purpose is to link environmental rights to human rights through stakeholder involvement, and it establishes that the achievement of sustainable development is through government accountability linked to environmental protection. (UNECE)

Aårhus Protocol on Persistent Organic Pollutants (POPs) – A protocol to the Convention on Long-Range Transboundary Air Pollution designed to reduce air pollution from 16 persistent organic chemicals including DDT, aldrin, dieldrin, PCB and the industrial byproducts, dioxins and furans. Thirty-three governments signed the protocol in 1998 but it has not yet entered into force. (UNECE)

Abatement – The reduction of the degree or intensity of pollutants or emissions. (EM)

Absorptive capacity – The capacity of an environment to assimilate waste products from an economic activity.

Acceptance – A decision having the same legal effect as ratification and consequently expressing the consent of a state to be bound by a treaty once the minimum number of states has signed and ratified. (VC)

Accession (1) – A sample of a crop variety collected at a specific location and time. (GBS)

Accession (2) – The act whereby a state accepts the offer or the opportunity to become a party to a treaty already negotiated and signed by other states. It has the same legal effect as ratification. (VC)

Accession countries (1) – Countries that become party, through signing and ratification, to an agreement or treaty already in force. (VC)

Accession countries (2) – Countries in the process of joining the European Union. (EEA)

Acclimation – A change that occurs in an organism that allows it to tolerate a new environment. (CBD)

Accord – An international agreement originally meant to describe something less than a convention or treaty but now all three terms are generally considered as synonymous. (UNT)

Accountability – The requirement that officials answer to stakeholders on the disposal of their powers, duties and decisions; act on criticisms or requirements made of them; and accept the responsibility for their failure, incompetence or deceit. (UNDP)

Accreditation – A formal registration process that enables representatives of an NGO to attend meetings of an intergovernmental organization after providing information regarding its organization, objectives and work program, and after its acceptance by the international organization.

Accuracy – The closeness of a measured value to the true value. (SFWMD) See '**Precision**.'

Acid rain – The precipitation of dilute solutions of strong mineral acids, formed by the mixing in the atmosphere of various industrial pollutants, primarily sulfur dioxide and nitrogen oxides, with naturally occurring oxygen and water vapor. (NRDC)

Acquis communautaire – Used in EU law to refer to the total body of EU law accumulated to date. (EEA)

Acre-feet/foot (ac-ft) – The volume of liquid required to cover one acre to a depth of one foot. (SFWMD)

Act – In the legislative sense, a bill or measure passed by a legislative or governing body. (MW)

Activated sludge – A secondary sewage treatment process that involves mixing of primary effluent with bacteria-laden sludge, followed by agitation or aeration to promote biological treatment. (USEPA)

Activities Implemented Jointly (AIJ) – Initiatives taken by countries to jointly implement activities to reduce GHG emissions that, unlike joint implementation (JI), cannot be credited against current commitments of parties to the UNFCCC. (UNFCCC)

Ad hoc group – A group formed for a specific purpose and no other, which is generally disbanded when the task is completed. (PL)

Ad interim (a.i.) – Designates that a particular official is in charge on a temporary basis until either a person is designated to a particular post or returns to his post; for example: Ambassador, a.i.; or *Chargé d'Affaires, a.i.* (eD)

Ad referendum – An agreement reached by negotiators subject to concurrence by their governments. (BLD)

Adaptation (1) – Special traits that help a plant or an animal survive in its environment. (CSG)

Adaptation (2) – Policies and actions that minimize adverse impacts of climate change. (UNFCCC)

Adaptation Fund – A fund established to support concrete adaptation projects and programs in developing countries that are Party to the Kyoto Protocol and financed through a share of proceeds from project activities of the clean development mechanism and other sources. (UNFCCC)

Adaptation measures – Actions in response to, or in anticipation of, climate change made to reduce or avoid adverse consequences or to take advantage of beneficial changes. (NGS)

Adaptive management – A type of natural resource management where adjustments are made in response to project monitoring, new scientific information, and changing social conditions that may indicate the need to change a course of action.

Additionality – An intervention that adds to, rather than replaces, other financial inputs. (DFID)

Adoption – The formal act that establishes the structure and content of a proposed treaty text that takes place through the expression of the consent of the states participating in the treaty-making process. However, adoption does not yet mean that a State consents to be bound by a treaty. (VC)

Adsorption – An advanced method of treating wastewater in which activated carbon removes organic matter. (USEPA)

Advanced informed agreement – The principle that international exchange of transgenic plants and microorganisms that could adversely affect plants should not proceed (a) without the informed agreement of, or (b) contrary to the decision of, the competent authority in the recipient country. (BCHM)

Advanced treatment technologies (ATTs) – Biological and chemical treatments designed to reduce chemical levels in storm water or other runoff to very low concentrations. (SFWMD)

Advanced wastewater treatment – The process that removes pollutants not adequately removed by secondary treatment, particularly nitrogen and phosphorus; accomplished by means of sand filters, micro-straining or other methods. It is similar to tertiary treatment. (EEA)

Adverse effects of climate change – Changes in the physical environment or biota resulting from climate change that have significant deleterious effects on the composition, resilience or productivity of natural and managed ecosystems or on the operation of socio-economic systems or human health and welfare. (UNFCCC)

Adverse impact – A detrimental effect on an environmental change relative to the legally mandated, desired or baseline conditions. (SFWMD)

Aerosols – Non-gaseous microscopic particles and droplets (.01 – .00001 cm), other than water or ice, suspended in the atmosphere – the most abundant being particles of mineral dust, sulphuric acid, ammonium sulphate, pollens and carbon or soot. (UNFCCC)

Affected public – Individuals and communities that experience the impacts of a project, action or policy.

Affordable safe minimum standard approach – A management approach in which the fewest activities required to avoid damages due to climate change require a balance between the acceptance of risk and the affordability of abatement costs. (UNFCCC)

Afforestation – The establishment of forest cover on land not previously forested. (UNFCCC)

African Development Bank (AfDB or ADB) – The regional development bank for Africa established in 1964 and which formally began operations in 1967. AfDB headquarters was moved in 2003 from its formal location in Abidjan, Côte d'Ivore, given the level of political instability in that country, to a temporary location in Tunis, Tunisia. The Bank has a membership of 53 African and 24 non-African member states from the Americas, Asia and Europe. (CIPA)

African Union (AU) – A pan-African organization formed in July of 2002 in Durban, South Africa to replace the Organization of African Unity (OAU). The AU has a security council, and a legislature and an economic development plan, called the New Partnership for Africa's Development (NEPAD).

Agence Française Développement **(AFD)** – The principal agency through which France provides technical assistance and delivers foreign aid.

Agenda – A formally adopted program of work. (MW)

Agenda 21 – A blueprint of 40 chapters, the fulfillment of which would help lead to the sustainability of development. Nearly 180 governments at the Earth Summit in Rio de Janeiro in 1992 agreed to *Agenda 21*. (UNCED)

Agreements – Legal instruments that are generally less formal and more narrowly focused in subject matter than are treaties. (MW)

Agrément – Diplomatic courtesy requires that before a State appoints a new chief of diplomatic mission to represent it in another State, it must first be ascertained whether the proposed appointee is acceptable to the receiving State. Granting its *agrément* to the appointment signifies the acquiescence of the receiving State. (eD)

Agro-ecosystem – A dynamic association of crops, pastures, livestock, other flora and fauna, atmosphere, soils and water. Agro-ecosystems are contained within larger landscapes that include uncultivated land, drainage networks, rural communities and wildlife. (FAO)

Agro-forestry – As defined by ICRAF, agro-forestry is a collective name for all land-use systems and practices in which woody perennials are deliberately grown on the same land management unit as crops or animals. This can be either in some form of spatial arrangement or in a time sequence. This definition provides a classification of agro-silvicultural (trees and crops) and silvopastoral (trees with pastures) practices, sequential and simultaneous systems as well as mixed arrangements of trees and crops. (EES)

Aid – The transfer of goods and services between nations, commercial banks, international agencies or nongovernmental agencies generally in the form of grants and loans. Internationally, aid refers to net flows of official development assistance (ODA for countries on Part I of the DAC list) and official assistance (OA for countries on Part II of the DAC list). (DFID)

Aid insurance – A concept that provides an immediate payout by the insurer as an alternative to soliciting and disbursing funds on an emergency basis after a disaster has occurred. The concept has its origins in the fact that late aid is ineffective aid, particularly in life-threatening situations. (UNW) See **'United Nations Central Emergency Response Fund.'**

Aide mémoire – A signed and dated summary of the points made in an official conversation left with the parties to the conversation, either at the time of the conversation or subsequently, as an aid to memory. (eD)

Airbase – The European air quality database including air quality information and information on monitoring networks and stations, as collected by the European Topic Centre on Air Quality. (EEA)

Air pollution – Toxic, radioactive gases or particulate matter introduced into the atmosphere usually as a result of human activity. (NRDC)

Air pollution criteria – The levels of pollution and length of exposure above which adverse health and welfare effects may occur. (USEPA)

Air pollution episode – A period of abnormally high concentration of air pollutants often due to low winds and temperature inversion that may cause illness or death. (USEPA)

Air pollution standards – The level of pollutants prescribed by regulations that may not be exceeded during a given time period in a defined area. (USEPA)

Air Quality Visualization Instrument for Europe on the Web (Airview) – A computer based program that allows the user to consult a database and visualize air quality data (raw data or statistics) in the form of maps, graphs or tables. (EEA)

Albedo – The ratio of reflected solar radiation to incoming solar radiation, where both the incoming (down welling) and reflected (upwelling) radiation streams are measured on a plane horizontal to the surface and integrated over the complete spectral (wavelength) range of solar radiation. For a single wavelength, or for a narrow spectral band, the ratio is usually termed spectral albedo or spectral reflectance. (EES) See '**Urban heat island**.'

Alicante Declaration – An ISGWAS-sponsored agreement launched in Alicante, Spain and opened for endorsement in January 2006 aimed at improving understanding and management of groundwater. (ES)

Alien species – A species occurring in an area outside of its historically known range as a result of intentional or accidental dispersal by human activities. (GBS)

Alliance of Small Island States (AOSIS) – The coalition of over 40 Pacific and Caribbean nations that lobby for action by developed nations to reduce greenhouse gas emissions because of the threat of rising sea levels and increased storm activity that may accompany global warming.

Alphabet, official – An alphabet officially recognized for use in communications in an international organization. The EU has three official alphabets: Latin, Greek and Cyrillic. (EU)

Alternat – The principle that provides that a state's own name be listed ahead of the other signatory, or signatories, in its own official copy of the signed instrument. It is a practice devised centuries ago to handle sensitivities over precedence and where ordering all states alphabetically does not suit the signatories, for example when certain states are always listed near the bottom of the list of signatories. In most cases, the states listed after the *Alternat* are listed either alphabetically or in order of signing or ratification. (eD)

Alternative energy – Energy derived from non-fossil fuel sources. (IPPC)

Alternative fuels – Alternative fuel is any method of powering an engine that does not involve petroleum (oil). Some alternative fuels are electricity, methane, hydrogen, natural gas and wood. (WP)

Ambassador – A diplomatic envoy of the highest rank accredited to a government, generally for a specific period or assignment. (MW)

Ambassador at Large – A Minister of the highest rank not accredited to any particular government, but rather to an organization for a specific task or theme. (MW)

Ambassador, Extraordinary and Plenipotentiary – The chief of a diplomatic mission; the ranking official/diplomatic representative of his country to the country to which he is accredited, and the personal representative of his own head of state to the head of state of the host country. (eD)

Ambassador, Goodwill – See '**Goodwill Ambassador**.'

Ambassador Without Portfolio – An Ambassador without a substantive or technical portfolio in government, but who undertakes special missions at the request of the Head of State and/or Foreign Minister and for whom the title 'Ambassador' provides the necessary rank to undertake such missions, such as access to high-level authorities and/or signing authority. (MW)

Ambassadress – A (misused) term to indicate a female ambassador. The correct term regardless of gender is Ambassador, although Madame Ambassador is also acceptable. (MW; eD)

Ambient-based standards – Air and water quality standards based on an ambient quality goal, normally set at a level needed to prevent negative human health and environmental impacts. (AM)

Ambient permit system (APS) – An ambient permit entitles the environmental regulator to vary permitted emissions according to the impacts they have on a receptor, such as a wildlife sanctuary or a drinking water extraction site. (AM)

Amendment – A proposed or effected alteration to a document made by parliamentary procedure. (MW)

Andean Community of Nations (CAN) – A trading bloc (formerly the Andean Pact) dating from 1969 that includes Bolivia, Colombia, Ecuador, Peru and Venezuela. In mid-2006, Venezuela announced its intentions to leave the Community because two of its members had signed trade agreements with the US, compromising the original intent of the CAN. See '**South American Community of Nations**.'

Andean Development Corporation (CAF) – Formed in 1968, the CAF is a multilateral financial institution that promotes sustainable development and regional integration by attracting capital resources for a wide range of financial, value added services to the public and private sectors of shareholder countries. CAF has a current membership of 16 countries in Latin America and the Caribbean. Its principal shareholders are the five countries of the Andean Community: Bolivia, Colombia, Ecuador, Peru and Venezuela. The Corporation also has 11 extra-regional partners: Argentina, Brazil, Chile, Costa Rica, Jamaica, Mexico, Panama, Paraguay, Spain, Trinidad & Tobago and Uruguay, and 18 private bank members from the Andean region. (CAF)

Andean Free Trade Association (AFTA) – See '**South American Community of Nations**.'

Annex B Countries – Developed country Parties to the Kyoto Protocol that have agreed to a target for their GHG emissions (generally includes the OECD member states, Central and Eastern Europe, and the Russian Federation. (UNFCCC)

Annex I Parties – Parties to the United Nations Framework Convention on Climate Change who pledged to reduce their greenhouse gas emissions by the year 2000 to 1990 levels. Annex I Parties consist of the Organisation for Economic Co-operation and Development (OECD) member states and industrialized countries with economies in transition (Central and Eastern Europe excluding the former Yugoslavia and Albania). (UNFCCC)

Annex II Parties – The developed country parties and other parties included in Annex I of the UNFCCC that are also Parties to the Kyoto Protocol. (UNFCCC)

Annex III Parties – Developing country parties with economies that are highly dependent on the exploitation, production, processing and exportation of fossil fuels. (UNFCCC)

Annotated agenda – A draft agenda that includes explanatory text.

Anthropocene – A new geological epoch so named because humans have come to rival nature in their impact on the physics, chemistry and biology of the global environment showing 'hotspots' in the Earth's defenses against catastrophic change. Examples of 'hotspots' include sea level rise, changes in ocean circulation patterns, breaking and moving of the west Antarctic ice sheet, the increasing pace of glacier retreat, change in the Asian monsoon system patterns and force, acidification of soil and large water bodies, and carbon exchanges between the oceans and the atmosphere. (ES)

Anthropocentric environmental ethic – A view of the environment that is human-centered. (AM)

Anthropocentrism – A belief that our larger brains, which are the source of our particular mobility and dexterity, advanced reasoning powers, and the source of our perceptiveness, indicate that the human race has been chosen to dominate the rest of nature. (EES)

Anthropogenic – A thing or phenomenon made by people or that result from human activities. (MW)

Anticorruption strategy – See 'World Bank Anticorruption Strategy.'

AOSIS – See the 'Alliance of Small Island States.'

Appellate Body – An independent body that considers appeals when one or more parties to a dispute requests clarification or a review of a decision. (MW)

Approach – A way of thinking or of doing things based on values used to attack a problem. (MW)

Appropriate technology – Technology that provides solutions to the problems of local communities that are sustainable, in the sense that the technology can be maintained by the community without introducing dependence on outsiders. A term that refers to using the simplest and most benign level of technology that can effectively achieve the intended purpose (AM; WP)

Approval – See 'Acceptance.'

Aquifer – Underground formations that are sufficiently permeable or porous to yield groundwater in usable quantities. Aquifers, which can be thought of as underground lakes or reservoirs, form a vital water resource that contain about 95 percent of the world's readily available freshwater and are found throughout the world, in both wet and arid zones. (EES; SFWMD)

Arab Fund for Economic and Social Development – A financially autonomous Pan-Arab regional organization comprising all Arab countries that are members of the League of Arab States. Its functions are to assist the economic and social development of Arab countries through (1) financing development projects, with preference given to overall Arab development and to joint Arab projects; (2) encouraging investment of private and public funds in Arab projects; and, (3) providing technical assistance services for Arab economic and social development. (AFESD)

Arab League – See 'League of Arab States.'

Archipelagic State – A State constituted wholly by one or more archipelagos (islands) including parts of islands, interconnecting waters and other natural features that are so closely interrelated that such islands, waters and other natural features form an intrinsic geographical, economic and political entity, or which historically have been regarded as such. (UN)

Artesian (aquifer or well) – Water held under pressure in porous rock or soil confined by impermeable geologic formations. (USEPA)

Artesanal fisheries – Small-scale fisheries carried out by people who rely on fishing to support their families and other local people. This type of fishing is not fully commercial in nature. The fishing technology may be very sophisticated, but it is not highly dependent on outside sources of capital and materials. (AMNH)

Article 8(j), Working Group on – A working group mandated by COP/CBD to provide advice on the application and development of legal and other appropriate forms of protection for the knowledge of indigenous and local communities embodying traditional lifestyles relevant to the conservation and sustainable use of biodiversity. (ENB)

Aruba Protocol – The protocol from Oranjestad, Aruba (1999) concerning Pollution from Land-based Sources and Activities in the Wider Caribbean Region that is one of three protocols to the 1983 Cartagena Convention for the Protection and Development of the Marine Environment of the Wider Caribbean Region. (CBD)

Ash – Incombustible residue left over after incineration or other thermal processes. (NRDC)

Asia-Pacific Economic Cooperation (APEC) – APEC was established in 1989 to further enhance economic growth and prosperity for the region and to strengthen the Asia-Pacific community. This forum is dedicated to facilitating economic growth, cooperation, trade and investment and is the only intergovernmental grouping in the world operating on the basis of non-binding commitments. APEC has 21 members – referred to as 'Member Economies' including: Australia; Brunei Darussalam; Canada; Chile; People's Republic of China; Hong Kong, China; Indonesia; Japan; Republic of Korea; Malaysia; Mexico; New Zealand; Papua New Guinea; Peru; The Republic of the Philippines; The Russian Federation; Singapore; Chinese Taipei; Thailand; the US; and Vietnam.

Asia-Pacific Partnership on Clean Development and Climate (AP-PCDC) – Inaugurated in January 2006 in Sydney, Australia this grouping includes the six largest polluters (US, Australia, Japan, China, South Korea and India), accounting for nearly half of the world's greenhouse gases, who claim that their national efforts to reduce greenhouse gas emissions will complement those of the Kyoto Protocol. They also feel that the private sector must take the lead in addressing climate change by developing new technologies that help curb greenhouse gas emissions. (UNFCCC)

Asian brown cloud – The haze of pollutants trapped by a temperature inversion over the northern Indian Ocean, much of South Asia, India, Pakistan, Southeast Asia and China that occurs for three to four months each winter and which could have serious effects on the human health and climate of the region. (EES)

Asian Development Bank (ADB) – An international development finance institution established in 1966 for the Asia-Pacific region. It has an Office of the Environment established in 1987 to facilitate the integration of environmental planning at all levels of Bank operations. ADB headquarters are located in Manila, Philippines. (CIPA)

Assembly – A gathering of individuals or delegations for the purpose of deliberating and approving legislation, declarations and policy. (MW)

Assessed contribution – Funds that a member state is required to contribute based on a formula applied to all states that are normally dedicated to support the core (regular fund) functions of the organization. The 2007 assessed contributions to the UN by the largest donors expressed as a percentage of the total regular fund include: US 22 percent, Japan 19.5 percent, Germany 8.6 percent, UK 6.1 percent, France 6.0 percent, Italy 4.8 percent. The 25-member EU jointly contributes 37 percent of the UN regular fund budget. (UN) See '**Capacity to pay, principle of**,' '**Assessed contribution investment, concept of**.'

Assessed contribution investment, concept of – The return on the 'investment' realized by donors to the UN regular fund (paying assessed contributions) through contracts received for services or materials back to the UN system acquired through a competitive and transparent process. The amount of the contribution is not related to the awarding of consultancy or other contracts. (UN)

Assimilative capacity – In relation to water quality, the capacity of a natural body of water to receive wastewaters or toxic materials without deleterious effects and without damage to aquatic life or humans who consume the water. (USEPA)

Assistance – Support for projects that can include technical advice and assistance as well as funds. (DFID)

Associated project – A GEF project that is either physically dependent on another agency's project or whose success could depend upon the implementation of another project. Opposite of a freestanding project. (GEF)

Association of Caribbean States (ACS) – The Convention establishing the ACS was signed in July 1994 in Cartagena, Colombia, with the aim of strengthening the regional integration process, in order to create an enhanced economic space in the region; preserving the environmental integrity of the Caribbean Sea, which is the common patrimony of the peoples of the region; and promoting the sustainable development of the Greater Caribbean Region. The Association comprises 25 Member States and three Associate Members.

Association of Southeast Asian Nations (ASEAN) – ASEAN was established in August 1967 to: (i) accelerate the economic growth, social progress and cultural development in the region through joint endeavors in the spirit of equality and partnership in order to strengthen the foundation for a prosperous and peaceful community of Southeast Asian nations, and (ii) promote regional peace and stability through abiding respect for justice and the rule of law in the relationship among countries in the region and adherence to the principles of the United Nations Charter. There are currently ten Member Nations participating in this forum: Brunei Darussalam, Cambodia, Indonesia, Laos, Malaysia, Myanmar, Philippines, Singapore, Thailand and Vietnam.

Association of Southeast Asian Nations Eminent Persons Group –
An idea to create an EU-like region (one currency, borderless society, legally
binding with powers to impose sanctions on members who do not follow
its rules, etc.) was first given serious consideration in 2006. At their January
2007 meeting, the heads of state created the Eminent Persons Group to
draft an ASEAN charter. The ASEAN charter will address trade, human
rights, environmental regulations, transnational crime, maritime security,
disaster reduction and relief, and mitigation of communicable diseases
among other issues. (ASEAN)

Asylum fatigue – The reactions or policies of governments that negatively
affect asylum seekers, which cloud the concepts of who asylum seekers are
and what needs to be done to help them. The term came into use in 2006
when the UN High Commissioner for Refugees observed the confusion
between legitimate asylum seekers and illegal immigrants. (UNW)

Asylum shopping – A EU trend by asylum seekers where people apply for
refugee status in several countries simultaneously or in a specific country
based on the policies and therefore the country most likely to accept them.
The EU is considering the adoption of a common asylum policy to combat
this tendency. (EU)

Atmosphere – The 500km thick envelope of air surrounding the Earth
and bound to it by the Earth's gravitational attraction, which supports the
existence of all flora and fauna. Four gases dominate the atmosphere: nitrogen (78.08 percent), oxygen (20.94 percent), argon (0.93 percent), and
carbon dioxide (0.034 percent). (EES; NRDC)

Atmospheric inversion – An upper layer of warm air preventing the rise
of cooler air and the pollutants trapped beneath it. (USEPA)

Atomic energy – Energy released in nuclear reactions. When a neutron
splits an atom's nucleus into smaller pieces, it is called fission. When two
nuclei are joined together under millions of degrees of heat, it is called fusion. (NRDC)

Attaché – Government attachés are either junior officers in an embassy or,
if more senior, officers who have a professional specialization such as 'labor
attaché,' 'commercial attaché,' 'scientific attaché,' 'cultural attaché,' 'military attaché,' etc. and who are responsible for or advise the Ambassador on
those aspects of the embassy portfolio. (eD)

Attractor – A point to which a system tends to move, a goal, either deliberate or constrained by system parameters (laws). The three permanent
attractor types are fixed point, cyclic and strange (or chaotic). (CSG)

Audit – A systematic retrospective examination of the whole, or part, of a
project or program to measure conformance with the plan and/or policies.
(MW)

Australian Agency for International Development (AusAid) – The principal agency through which Australia provides technical assistance and delivers foreign aid.

Authentic text – The text of a treaty that is established as definitive and where states cannot unilaterally change its provisions. Usual forms of authentications are by signature, signature *ad referendum* or the initialing by the representatives of the states that negotiated the treaty. (VC)

Authentication – The procedure whereby the text of a treaty is established as authentic and definitive usually by signature or initialing by representatives of the negotiating states. (UNT)

Bb

Background level (1) – The concentration of a substance in an environmental media (air, water or soil) that occurs naturally and not because of human activities. (EEA)

Background level (2) – In exposure assessment, the concentration of a substance in a defined control area, during a fixed period before, during or after a data-gathering operation. (EEA)

Balance of payments – A set of accounts for a given period, usually a year, which summarizes the financial transactions of the institutions and residents of one country with the institutions and residents of the rest of the world. The set of accounts consists of a current account, which shows expenditures the country made during the period on the purchase of goods and services from abroad, and the revenue derived from the sale of goods and services to the rest of the world; and a capital account, which shows the flows of private and public investment and of other transfers. (DFID)

Balkanization – A term that emerged in response to small-scale independence movements and the increasing trend of mini- or micronationalisms that occur along ethnic, cultural and religious fault lines. The term finds its roots from the divisive and conflict-ridden Balkan region of Europe and generally describes the process of geopolitical fragmentation, and political dissolution across the world. (CW) See '**Micronationalism**.'

Bamako Convention on the Ban of the Imports into Africa and the Control of Transboundary Movement and Management of Hazardous Wastes within Africa – This agreement provides guidelines for the management of hazardous wastes by member states of the Organization of African Unity (now African Union). It was adopted in Bamako, Mali in January 1991 as an alternative to the Basel Convention as OAU member states felt that the ban on movement of hazardous wastes included in the Basel Convention were not strict enough. To date 22 countries have signed and 18 countries have ratified the Convention. (UNT)

Bank – A bank is an institution that provides financial services, particularly taking deposits and extending credit. See '**Development bank**.'

Bankable – A term used primarily by the international technical assistance agencies and development banks to describe a cost-effective project proposal. (WB)

Barbados Declaration and Plan of Action – The formal statement produced by the Global Conference on the Sustainable Development of Small Island Developing States (SIDS) held in Bridgetown, Barbados, 25 April–6 May 1994. The Barbados Declaration made a commitment to specific policies, actions and measures to be taken at the national, regional and international levels to enable SIDS to achieve sustainable development. It recognized the special constraints to sustainable development that SIDS face by virtue of their small size and called for the assistance of regional and international entities, both governmental and non-governmental, to engage in a program of action aimed at the sustainable development of the SIDS. (UNDP)

Barcelona Convention – See '**Mediterranean Action Plan**.'

Barefoot College – Established in 1972 in the village of Tilonia, India, the college, built by the poor, serves only those earning less than an average of US$1.00 per day. The idea is to recognize and apply traditional knowledge, village wisdom and local skills for the development of poor communities thus reducing dependency on outside expertise. Using this approach, there are presently 20 such 'colleges' in 13 Indian States specializing in the development of drinking water resources, income generation, electricity and power, as well as social awareness, decision skills and the conservation of ecological systems supporting rural communities. (UN) See '**Gross village product**.'

Barometer of sustainability – See '**Sustainability assessment measures**.'

Base floor salary scale – A universally applied scale for UN staff at the Professional (P-level) and higher categories (D-level and unclassified) and reflecting the minimum net salary received by United Nations staff around the world but excluding other benefits awarded based on the level and posting of the staff member (post adjustment, education allowance, rental subsidy, vacation, health insurance, home leave, separation bonus, hazardous duty allowance, pension, travel conditions, daily subsistence allowance, etc.) (UN)

Base water flow – The sustained or dry weather flow of streams resulting from the outflow of permanent or perched groundwater, and from the drainage of lakes or wetlands, during dry weather. Also included is the flow from glaciers, snow and other possible sources not directly attributable to runoff. (FAO)

Basel Convention – The Basel Convention on the Control of Transboundary Movements of Hazardous Wastes and Their Disposal entered into force in 1989 with the goal to protect human and environmental health by minimizing hazardous waste production. The convention requires that the production of hazardous wastes is managed using an 'integrated life-cycle approach,' which involves strict controls from production to storage, transport, treatment, reuse, recycling, recovery and final disposal. (UNT)

Baseline (1) – Information collected before or at the start of a project to provide a basis for planning and/or monitoring subsequent progress and impact. (WB; SFWMD)

Baseline (2) – The reference point for calculating incremental costs. The GEF funds the difference between the cost of a project undertaken with global environmental objectives in mind and the costs of the same project without global environmental concerns. The baseline is the latter project that yields only national benefits. (GEF)

Basic human rights – The rights outlined in the 'United Nations Universal Declaration of Human Rights' (See Appendix 1).

Basle Agreement – A 1988 agreement that established the G10 methods for qualifying credit worthiness and credit risk for countries.

Beijing Declaration – The Beijing Declaration and its Platform of Action are the products of the Fourth World Conference on Women, which was held in Beijing, China in September of 1995. The Platform for Action is an agenda for women's empowerment. It aims to remove all the obstacles to women's active participation in all spheres of public and private life through a full and equal share in economic, social, cultural and political decision making. (UNT)

Bellagio Principles – In 1996, the International Institute for Sustainable Development convened assessment specialists at the Rockefeller Foundation Conference Center in Bellagio, Italy to develop principles to guide the assessment of progress towards sustainable development. The Bellagio principles state that assessments should meet the following criteria:

- **Guiding vision and goals** – Be guided by a clear vision of sustainable development and goals that define that vision.
- **Holistic perspective** – Include a review of the whole system as well as its parts and consider the well being of sub-systems and both positive and negative consequences of human activity in monetary and non-monetary terms.
- **Essential elements** – Consider equity and disparity within the current population and between present and future generations.
- **Adequate scope** – Adopt a time horizon long enough to capture both human and ecosystem time scales.
- **Practical focus** – Be based on an explicit set of categories that link visions and goals to indicators.
- **Openness** – Include transparent methods and accessible data; they should make explicit all judgments, assumptions and uncertainties in data and interpretation.
- **Effective communication** – Be designed to meet the needs of the users and aim for simplicity in structure and language.
- **Broad participation** – Obtain broad representation of key

professional, technical, and social groups, while also ensuring the participation of decision makers.

- **Ongoing assessment** – Develop a capacity to repeat measurement to determine trends and be responsive to change and uncertainty and adjust goals and frameworks as new insights are gained.
- **Institutional capacity** – Continuity of assessing progress should be assured by clearly assigning responsibility and support in the decision-making process, providing institutional capacity for data collection, and supporting development of local assessment capacity. (IISD)

Bench – In a land-use sense, a steep cut into a hillside to create a horizontal strip of cultivable land. (FAO)

Bench-scale tests – Laboratory scale testing of technologies prior to field-testing. (USEPA)

Beneficiary – The people, communities, organizations or nations expected to benefit from the project or program. (WB)

Beneficiary pays principle – A concept that implies that the beneficiaries of a high quality or improved environment should compensate resource users for the ongoing costs of maintaining ecological functions and services that do not bring direct market benefits and are not required of all people. (AM) See '**Polluter pays principle**.'

Benefit–cost ratio – A decision criterion that uses the net present value of the benefit related to the net present value of the costs. (WB)

Benefit sharing – One of the three objectives of the Convention on Biological Diversity, it is the 'fair and equitable sharing of the benefits arising out of the utilization of genetic resources, including by appropriate access to genetic resources and by appropriate transfer of relevant technologies, taking into account all rights over those resources and to technologies, and by appropriate funding.' The Convention also encourages 'equitable sharing of the benefits arising from the utilization of knowledge, innovations and practices of indigenous and local communities embodying traditional lifestyles relevant for conservation and sustainable use of biological diversity.' (CBD)

Berlin Declaration – A global initiative for the promotion of sustainable tourism, signed in Berlin, 8 March, 1997. (UNFCCC)

Berlin Mandate – A negotiated process from COP 1 (1995) of the UN-FCCC that dealt with the inadequacy of the measures committed to under the UNFCCC where developed countries were to return their greenhouse gas emissions to 1990 levels by the year 2000. The Berlin Mandate enables parties to take action for the period beyond 2000, including a strengthening of developed country commitments, through the adoption of a protocol or other legal instruments. (UNFCCC)

Bern Convention – The Convention on the Conservation of European Wildlife and Natural Habitats was adopted in Bern, Switzerland on 19 September 1979 and came into force on 1 June, 1982. Forty-five European and African States as well as the EC are parties to the convention. It has a three-fold objective: to conserve wild flora and fauna and their natural habitats; to promote cooperation between states; and to give particular emphasis to endangered and vulnerable species, including endangered and vulnerable migratory species. (EEA)

Best alternative to a negotiated settlement (BATNA) – A resistance level in negotiations corresponding to the best option outside the current relationship.

Best management practice(s) (BMPs) – A practice or combination of practices determined by a state or a designated planning agency to be the most effective and practicable means (including technological, economic and institutional considerations) of controlling point and non-point source caused by nutrients, animal wastes, toxics and sediment pollutants to levels compatible with environmental quality goals. (SFWMD)

Bifurcation – A point at which a system splits into two alternative behaviors, either being possible, the one actually followed often being indeterminate or unpredictable. (CSG)

Big Table – An informal consultation between finance ministers from eleven African countries and their counterparts from the development co-operation ministries of the Organisation for Economic Co-operation and Development (OECD).

Bilateral – Describes instruments or processes that reciprocally affect two nations or civil society parties. (MW)

Bilateral(s) – Those national government agencies or organizations implementing the terms of an agreement or carrying out policies between two nations. (USDOS)

Bilateral debt swap – A form of debt exchange, negotiated between a creditor nation and a debtor nation that results in a particular public external debt (or a portion thereof) being cancelled in exchange for counterpart funding for a specific purpose. (AM) See **'Debt for nature swap**.'

Bilateral treaty – An agreement between two states. (MW)

Bill – A proposed law, to be debated and voted on. (NRDC)

Billanthropy – Philanthropy by billionaires. A large donation ('Bill'ions) in line with the objectives of the Millennium Development Goals or to specific UN programs or other altruistic or humanitarian goals, such as those made by the Bill and Melinda Gates Foundation and Warren Buffet to address the HIV/AIDS crises and other health and education issues, or that made by Ted Turner in support of the health, humanitarian, socio-economic and environmental challenges of the 21st century, Li Ka-Shing in support of medical, education, cultural and community welfare projects in China, and that of Richard Branson in support of efforts to address climate change. (UNW)

Bioaccumulation – The intake of a chemical and its concentration in the organism by all possible means, including contact, respiration and ingestion, relative to its concentration in the background environment over time. (EES; SFWMD)

Bioaccumulation factor (BAF) – The ratio of a contaminant concentration in living tissue to its concentration in the organism's diet. (SFWMD)

Bioassay – The determination of the activity of concentration of a chemical by its effect on the growth of an organism under experimental conditions. (EEA)

Biochemical oxygen demand (BOD) – The amount of oxygen used for biochemical oxidation by a unit volume of water at a given temperature and for a given time. BOD is an index of the degree of organic pollution in water. (EEA)

Biocentrism – The concept that all living creatures are of equal importance in the grand scheme of nature. (EES)

Bioconcentration – The intake and retention of a substance in an organism entirely by respiration from water in aquatic ecosystems or from air in terrestrial ecosystems. (EES)

Bioconversion – The conversion of organic materials into energy sources such as methane by processes such as fermentation involving living organisms. (EES)

Biodegradable – Any material or product capable of being broken down into innocuous products by the action of living organisms. (EES)

Biodiversity – The variability among living organisms from all sources including, *inter alia*, terrestrial, marine and other aquatic ecosystems and the ecological complexes of which they are part: this includes diversity within species, between species and of ecosystems. (CBD) The totality of genes, species and ecosystems in a region or the world (GBS).

Biodiversity Clearing-house Mechanism – A network of parties and partners working together to facilitate implementation of the UNCBD. It also facilitates access to and exchange of information on biodiversity around the world. Created in accordance with Article 18 of the UNCBD. (UN)

Biodiversity, economic value of – The economic value of biodiversity consists of several components: direct-use value, indirect-use value, option value, bequest value and existence value. Direct value derives from the direct use of the biological resource such as in attracting tourism based on a reef system, a particular plant or natural phenomenon. Indirect value refers to the role of biodiversity in supporting human activities, for example the water produced by a managed forest. Option value is the value placed on preserving a resource presently for possible future use. Bequest value is the value that people place on preserving natural assets for future generations. Existence value is the value that people place on the knowledge that a particular resource exists. (AM)

Biodiversity hotspots – Biodiversity hotspots hold especially high numbers of endemic species, yet their combined area of remaining habitat covers only 2.3 percent of the Earth's land surface. Over 50 percent of the world's plant species and 42 percent of all terrestrial vertebrate species are endemic to the 34-biodiversity hotspots. To qualify as a biodiversity hotspot, a region must meet two strict criteria: it must contain at least 1500 species of endemic vascular plants (> 0.5 percent of the world's total), and it has to have lost at least 70 percent of its original habitat. (CI)

Bioenergetics – The study of the flow, exchange and transformation of energy along trophic pathways in ecosystems, populations and organisms. (EES)

Biogeochemical cycle – The chemical interactions among the atmosphere, biosphere, hydrosphere and the lithosphere. (EES)

Biological corridor – A management area in which methods are used to maintain the migrations and movement of species between areas of natural distribution. (WWF)

Biological diversity – See '**Biodiversity**.'

Biological resources – (Biotic resources) includes genetic resources, organisms or parts thereof, populations or any other biotic component of ecosystems with actual or potential use or value for humanity. (CBD)

Biomagnification – A process that occurs when a chemical is passed up the food chain to higher trophic levels, such that in predators it exceeds the concentration to be expected where equilibrium prevails between an organism and its environment. (EES; SFWMD)

Biomass – All the living matter in a given area. Also the amount of plant and crop material that could be produced in an ecosystem for making biofuels and other raw materials used in industry, for example. (ESS; SFW-MD)

Biome – The complex of living communities maintained by the climate of a region and characterized by a distinctive type of vegetation, such as tundra, tropical forest, steppe and desert. As a subdivision of the biota, the biome includes humans, characterized by a particular assemblage of animals, plants and other living things. (EES)

Bio-piracy – The exploitation of a community's genetic resources for drug, fertilizer or product development without a fair return or a negotiated agreement benefiting the owners of the resource base. (UNW)

Bioprospecting – Activities that entail the search for economically valuable genetic and biochemical resources from nature. (BCHM)

Bioregions – A territory defined at a given scale by a distinct combination of biological, social and geographic criteria, rather than by geopolitical considerations. (EES)

Bioremediation – The metabolism and consequent chemical transformation of hazardous chemicals to less hazardous chemicals by microorganisms. The microorganisms facilitating this process are typically bacteria, but occasionally may be fungi. The matrix to be treated can include contaminated soil, ground or surface waters, wastewater, sludge, sediment or air. (EES)

Biosecurity – Policies and programs designed to prevent the harmful introduction of plant and animal pathogens into agriculture and food production systems. (UN)

Biosphere – The terrestrial and atmospheric areas occupied by life, including the hydrosphere (the very thin fluid outer region of the Earth's surface), the lithosphere (solid portion – rocks, soils, sediments – of the earth), and the atmosphere (gaseous layer surrounding the planet). (EES; MW)

Biosphere reserve – A classification of land-use established under UNESCO's Man and Biosphere Programme that includes allied areas of increasing protection intended to demonstrate the relationship between conservation and development. (UNESCO; EES)

Biota – A term for all of the organisms, including animals, plants, fungi and microorganisms, found in a given area. (GBS)

Biotechnology – Any technological application that uses biological systems, living organisms, or derivatives thereof, to make or modify products or processes for a specific use. Examples include pharmaceuticals, vaccines, improved breeds of plants and animals, biomass fuels and foodstuffs. (CBD; EES) See '**Genetically modified organism**.'

Biotic – Of or relating to life. (NRDC)

Biotic resources – Those components of biodiversity of direct, indirect or potential use to humanity. (GBS)

Bird flu – The H5N1 avian virus is a type of influenza virulent in birds. It was first identified in Italy in the early 1900s and is now known to exist worldwide. (WHO)

Birth rate – The number of babies born annually per 1000 women of reproductive age in any given set of people. (NRDC)

Blast fishing – A method of fishing (usually on reefs) that involves the use of dynamite or homemade explosives to harvest large numbers of fish.

Bloc – A group of people with the same interest or goal, usually used to describe a voting bloc, a group of representatives intending to vote the same way. (NRDC)

Blocking coalition – A group of opposing interests that could prevent a winning coalition from coming into existence or being sustained. (BLD)

Blood diamond – A diamond mined in a war zone and sold, usually clandestinely, in order to finance an insurgent or invading army's war efforts. Nongovernmental organizations have also alleged the use of these diamonds in financing other illegal or terrorist activities. (WP)

Blood lead levels – The amount of lead in the blood as compared to WHO standards. Human exposure to lead in blood can cause brain damage, especially in children. (WHO; NRDC)

Blue Helmets – Members of the UN peacekeeping forces/missions, distinguished by their blue protective helmets. UN peacekeeping is a way to help countries, torn by conflict, create conditions for peaceful elections and/or catalyze negotiations between warring factions. UN peacekeepers – soldiers and military officers, civilian police officers and civilian personnel from many countries – monitor and observe peace processes that emerge in post-conflict situations and assist ex-combatants implement the peace agreements they have signed. Such assistance comes in many forms, including providing security, confidence-building measures, power-sharing arrangements and electoral monitoring/support. (WP)

Blue Plan – See '**European Blue Plan**,' '**United Nations Environment Programme Blue Plan**.'

Blue sector – A catchall label for 'environmental' projects that cover issues related to oceans.

Black water/issues – See '**Water**.'

Blue water/issues – See '**Water**.'

Body (1) – The main part of a text or of an agreement. (MW)

Body (2) – The attendees at a conference or meeting. (eD)

Boiled-frog syndrome – An oft-used fable relating to the tendency, in addressing complex issues in intergovernmental settings, to postpone taking definite decisions or to the slow process in attaining measurable results in reducing greenhouse gases, and the resulting tendency to continue to discuss the issue rather than come to conclusions. Meanwhile in spite of the slow process of climate change, the frog eventually 'boils and dies,' preempting or compromising a decision that would have had a positive and measurable impact.

Bolivia Summit – The 1996 Specialized Summit of the Americas on Sustainable Development held in Santa Cruz, Bolivia in an attempt to prioritize actions called for in *Agenda 21*. (OAS, 2001)

Bona Fides – In law and international parlance, 'good faith' is the mental and moral state of honest, even if objectively unfounded, conviction as to the truth or falsehood of a proposition or body of opinion. (WP)

Bonn Convention – Convention on the Conservation of Migratory Species of Wild Animals (1979), which prohibits the commercial capture of some 50 species of migratory animals and which urges Parties to the Convention to conserve and restore the habitats of these species. (UNT)

Bonn Guidelines – Voluntary guidelines that are the result of Decision VI/24 of COP-VI of the Convention on Biological Diversity that deal with access to genetic resources and the fair and equitable sharing of the benefits arising from their utilization. They are meant to assist parties, governments, and other stakeholders when establishing legislative, administrative or policy measures on access and benefit sharing and/or when negotiating contractual arrangements for access and benefit sharing. (CBD)

Bore hole – A well or hole in the earth to the point where water can be extracted. (MW)

Boreal forest – The northern hemisphere, circumpolar, tundra forest type consisting primarily of black spruce and white spruce, mixed with balsam fir, birch and aspen. (EEA)

Bout de Papier – A very informal means of conveying written information; more informal than an aide mémoire or a memorandum. (eD) See '**Verbal Note.**'

Brackets – Square brackets [ ] are used to surround words or phrases that are in dispute or that are alternative wording proposed by a delegation when drafting legal instruments and indicate that no agreement has been reached. (UN; eD)

Bretton Woods Conference – An international conference held 1–22 July,

1944 at Bretton Woods, New Hampshire. Attended by representatives of 44 countries, the conference established the International Monetary Fund and the International Bank for Reconstruction and Development (World Bank). (BWP)

Brown cloud – See '**Asian brown cloud.**'

Brownfields – Abandoned, idled or under-used industrial and commercial facilities where expansion or redevelopment is complicated by real or perceived environmental contamination. (NRDC)

Brown sector/issues – A catchall label for 'environmental' projects that cover issues related to urban and industrial areas. (EES)

Brown water/issues – See '**Water.**'

Brundtland Commission Report – The report of the World Commission on Environment and Development (WCED): *Our Common Future* (1987). Dr Gro Harlem Brundtland, then Norwegian Prime Minister, chaired the WCED (WCED, 1987).

Bubble – The idea that emissions reductions anywhere within a specific area count towards a common reduction goal – as if a giant bubble were placed over the various sources to contain them in a common area. (EM)

Bubbles – A term used in the negotiation of multilateral instruments to indicate informal consultations on specific topics that take place in formal negotiations. (UN)

Bucharest Convention on the Protection of the Black Sea Against Pollution – Adopted in 1992 (entered into force in 1994), its objectives are to undertake all necessary measures consistent with international law and in accordance with the provisions of this Convention to prevent, reduce and control pollution thereof in order to protect and preserve the marine environment of the Black Sea. (EEA)

Bucharest Population Conference – The first World Conference on Population held in Bucharest, Romania in 1974, attended by more than 1200 representatives of 135 nations.

Budget – A formal projection of income and spending for a predetermined period, traditionally submitted by the chief executive of an organization for consideration and approval by its governing body. (NRDC)

Buenos Aires Plan of Action (BAPA) – A schedule adopted by COP-4 (1998) of the UNFCCC for reaching agreement on the details of how to implement the Kyoto Protocol.

Buffer zone – The region near the border of a protected area designated as a transition zone between the protected area and other areas managed for more intensive objectives. (EES)

Bully pulpit – A term describing an office of sufficient prestige, whether public or private in nature, that it provides the incumbent the opportunity to speak out on almost any issue of public interest. The UN Secretary General, the Pope and the US President and others of their stature are oftentimes described as having a bully pulpit at their disposal. (MW)

Burden sharing – An EU concept of emissions sharing allowances among the 15 Member States of the EU (expanded to 25 members in 2005). An agreement on burden sharing was reached in June 1998 and made legally binding as part of the EU's instrument of ratification of the Kyoto Protocol. (EEA)

Bureau – Group of national representatives that acts between sessions according to the mandates given it by the Parties to a convention or the governing council of an institution. The Bureau presides over the work of a general assembly and facilitates agreement among the parties or members. (BLD)

Bureau of Oceans and International Environmental and Scientific Affairs (OES) – The US Department of State's focal point for foreign policy formulation and implementation in global environment, science and technology issues. (CIPA)

Bushmeat – Edible meat obtained from wild animals. (CBD)

Business as usual scenario – Baseline scenario that examines the consequences of continuing current trends in population, economy, technology, human behavior or any specific activity. (EEA)

Business Council for Sustainable Development – See '**World Business Council for Sustainable Development**.'

Business for Diplomatic Action® – Born in the aftermath of the September 2001 terrorist attacks on New York City and Washington, DC, this group comprises US businessmen and academics committed to improving the image of the US abroad by mobilizing the private sector in support (human and financial resources, best practices, exchange programs, etc.) of public diplomacy efforts. (USAID)

By-catch – The portion of a fishing catch discarded as unwanted or commercially unusable. (NRDC)

Byproduct – A useful and marketable product or service deriving from a manufacturing process that is not the primary product or service being produced. (EEA)

Cc

C8 for Kids – A UNICEF-hosted children's version of the G8 meeting, first held in conjunction with the G8 meeting convened in Dunblane, Scotland 3–5 July, 2005. During the parallel summit, 'under-eighteen' advocates from eight of the world's poorest countries – Bhutan, Cambodia, Moldova, Yemen, Guinea, Sierra Leone, Lesotho and Bolivia – met with their counterparts from selected G8 countries – Russia, France, Italy, Germany and the UK – to debate and firmly place their issues on the agenda of the G8 meeting. This forum is held in coordination with G8 meetings. See '**Model United Nations**.' (UNICEF)

Cairo Plan – Recommendations for stabilizing world population agreed upon at the UN International Conference on Population and Development, held in Cairo in September 1994. The plan calls for improved health care and family planning services for women, children and families throughout the world, and emphasizes the importance of education for girls as a factor in the shift to smaller families. (UNT)

Cairus Group – Group of agricultural exporting nations lobbying for agricultural trade liberalization formed in 1986. Membership consists of Argentina, Australia, Bolivia, Brazil, Canada, Chile, Colombia, Costa Rica, Guatemala, Indonesia, Malaysia, New Zealand, Paraguay, Philippines, South Africa, Thailand and Uruguay. (WTO)

Canadian International Development Agency (CIDA) – The principal agency through which the federal government of Canada provides technical assistance and distributes foreign aid.

Canalization – The restriction of possible state space exploration by constraints imposed upon the system either from outside or self-generated. This helps to preserve stability or the 'status-quo' but may also prevent better optima from being reached. (CSG)

Cancer – Unregulated growth of changed cells; a group of changed, growing cells (tumor). (NRDC)

Capacity building – A collection of activities including human resources development through education and training, institutional and infrastructure development, and formulation of enabling policies (WCED). A coordinated process of deliberate interventions by insiders and/or outsiders of a given society leading to (i) skill upgrading, both general and specific, (ii) procedural improvements, and (iii) organizational strengthening. (WB)

Capacity development – The process by which individuals, organizations, institutions and societies develop their abilities individually and collectively to perform functions, solve problems and set and achieve objectives. (UNDP)

Capacity to pay, principle of – The basis for calculating the UN assessment (dues) of any Member State to the regular fund to the UN Secretariat in New York City or any of the Specialized Organizations of the UN system. (UN) See '**United Nations Economic and Social Council**.'

Capital costs – The total expenditure incurred on a project (labor, equipment and infrastructure) from the beginning of its planning and construction to its delivery, excluding the costs of operation and maintenance. (WB)

Captive breeding programs – The founding and management of captive populations of species at risk based upon sound scientific principles for the purpose of securing their survival through stable, self-sustaining populations. (IUCN)

Carbon-14 dating – A process whereby carbon atoms are measured (by converting C^{14} into CO_2 gas; or by using accelerator mass spectrometry) resulting in numerical dating of fossils, artifacts and deposits whose age previously had to be estimated. (EES; WP)

Carbon cycle – The reservoirs of carbon (atmosphere, terrestrial and marine biomass, soil organic matter, fossil fuels and other sediments, the ocean, atmosphere, etc.) and the chemical processes governing the exchanges of carbon between them.

Carbon dioxide (CO_2) – A naturally occurring greenhouse gas in the atmosphere, concentrations of which increase (from 280 parts per million in pre-industrial times to over 350 parts per million since the 1970s) as a result of burning of coal, oil, natural gas and organic matter. (NRDC)

Carbon dioxide equivalents – A metric measure used to compare the emissions from various greenhouse gases based upon their global warming potential (GWP) commonly expressed as 'million metric tons of carbon dioxide equivalents (MMTCDE)' or 'million short tons of carbon dioxide equivalents (MSTCDE).' Multiplying the tons of the gas by the associated GWP derives the carbon dioxide equivalent for a gas. (EEA)

Carbon dioxide fertilization – A process leading to the enrichment of the atmosphere with CO_2. (EEA)

Carbon Emissions Trading – The trading of permits to emit carbon dioxide (and other greenhouse gases, calculated in tons of carbon dioxide equivalent, tCO2e) as a means of assisting emitting countries to meet

C

their obligations under the Kyoto Protocol to reduce carbon emissions and thereby mitigate global warming. The world's only mandatory carbon trading program is the European Union Emissions Trading Scheme (EUETS). Created in conjunction with the Kyoto Protocol, it caps the amount of carbon dioxide that can be emitted from large installations, such as power plants and factories, in EU Member States. (UNW; EU)

Carbon footprint – A concept representing the effect human activities have on the climate in terms of the total amount of greenhouse gases produced measured in units of carbon. (WP)

Carbon neutral audit – A combination of reduction of energy consumption and offsetting of remaining emissions in order to achieve net zero CO_2 emissions as measured through a carbon audit for greenhouse gases. It establishes if the claimed reductions in emissions, or carbon sequestration, has actually occurred and is stable. (WP)

Carbon neutral shipping – See '**Carbon offsetting**.'

Carbon offsetting – The practice whereby people calculate how much carbon dioxide emissions their actions produce and counter it by donating money toward clean energy and other environmentally friendly programs. Examples include contributions to have enough trees planted to offset your carbon footprint, and 'carbon neutral shipping' whereby a cataloge retailer and purchaser jointly or individually contribute an amount of money equal to shipping costs to a conservation fund. (UNW) See '**Green upgrades.**'

Carbon sequestration – The uptake and storage of carbon, including anthropogenic carbon dioxide that would otherwise affect global climate change, in large-scale carbon sinks or reservoirs that absorb more carbon than they release (i.e. oceans and immature forests). (UNEP)

Carbon sink – Forests and other ecosystems that absorb carbon, thereby removing it from the atmosphere and offsetting CO_2 emissions. The Kyoto Protocol allows certain human-induced sinks activities undertaken since 1990 to be counted towards Annex I Parties' emission targets. (EEA)

Carbon tax – A charge on fossil fuels (coal, oil, gasoline, natural gas, etc.) based on their carbon content and resultant environmental impact. When burned, the carbon in these fuels becomes carbon dioxide in the atmosphere, the chief greenhouse gas. (NRDC)

Carcinogen – Any substance that causes cancer. (MW)

Caribbean Community and Common Market (CARICOM) – Established by the Treaty of Chaguaramas, Trinidad and Tobago, and signed by Barbados, Jamaica, Guyana and Trinidad & Tobago, it came into effect in August 1973. There are currently 15 member states.

Caring for the Earth – The 1991 sequel to the *World Conservation Strategy* (published in 1980). Like the earlier WCS, *Caring for the Earth* was sponsored by the IUCN, UNEP and WWF. It sets forth 132 actions required to 'increase human well-being and halt the destruction of the Earth's capacity to support life.' (CIPA)

Carrying capacity – A term used to describe the maximum number of individuals of a particular species that a given environment can support over time and within set management objectives and methods. (EES)

Cartagena Convention – The Convention for the Protection and Development of the Marine Environment of the Wider Caribbean Region, adopted in Cartagena, Colombia on 24 March 1983 and entered into force on 11 October 1986 as the legal instrument for implementation of the Caribbean Action Plan. (UNEP-CAR-RCU)

Cartagena Protocol – A protocol of the CBD on biosafety developed at an extraordinary Conference of the Parties in Cartagena, Colombia in 1999 and adopted by more than 130 countries on January 29, 2000, in Montreal, Canada. It provides a framework for addressing environmental impacts of bio-engineered products (referred to as living modified organisms or 'LMOs') that cross international borders. (CBD)

Catchment area – A river or lake drainage basin. (UNDP)

Caucus – A closed meeting of a group of people with a similar agenda, usually to debate and/or decide on a policy or position. (MW)

Center of crop diversity – Geographic area containing a high level of genetic diversity for crop species in *in-situ* conditions. (CBD)

Center of origin – Geographical area where a domesticated or wild plant species developed its distinctive properties. (CBD)

Central Group-11 (CG-11) – A coalition of governments that brings together the countries with economies in transition listed in Annex I of the UNFCCC minus the Russian Federation and the Ukraine. (UNFCCC)

Certification – A written testimony to certain facts used to satisfy regulatory bodies or customers that a person's or thing's capability, qualities, performance, etc. meet specified standards. See '**Sustainability assessment measures**,' '**Cradle to cradle certification**,' '**Certified emission reductions**,' '**Fair-trade**,' '**Certified wood (1) (2)**.'

Certified emission reductions (CERs) – Verified and authenticated reductions of greenhouse gas from the abatement or sequestration projects that are certified by the Clean Development Mechanism. (UNFCCC)

Certified wood (1) – Timber, or processed wood certified to have been grown on a sustainable plantation or in a sustainable fashion. (FSC)

Certified wood (2) – The principle that materials going into wood-based products must come from a sustainable forest or contain certified recycled and/or recovered content. Most forest products are currently certified by two international NGOs: the Forest Stewardship Council or the Sustainable Forestry Initiative. (FSC; SFI)

CFCs – See '**Chlorofluorocarbons**.'

Chain of custody – A term used in certification (QA/QC, ISO, FSC or SFI processes) that tracks all stages of the production, handling, distribution and sale of the product to be certified to insure that the product meets the standards set by the certifying institution. See '**MDIAR agreement**.'

Chair – The title of the person charged with facilitating the work of a meeting, and for ensuring that the rules of procedure for that meeting are upheld.

Chancery – The office where the chief of mission and his staff work. This office is often called the embassy but this is a misnomer. Technically, the embassy is where the ambassador lives, not where he works, although in earlier times when diplomatic missions were smaller, this was usually the same building. Today, for clarity's sake, many diplomats now distinguish between the two by using the terms 'embassy residence' and 'embassy office.' (eD)

Chaord – Any auto-catalytic, self-regulating, adaptive, non-linear, complex organism, organizati or system, whether physical, biological or social, the behavior of which harmoniously exhibits characteristics of both order and chaos. (Co)

Chaos – A system whose long-term behavior is unpredictable, tiny changes in the accuracy of the starting value rapidly diverge to anywhere in its possible state space. However, there can be a finite number of available states, so statistical prediction can still be useful. (CSG)

Chaos Theory – An attempt to uncover the statistical regularity hidden in processes that otherwise appear random. Systems described as 'chaotic' are extremely susceptible to changes in initial conditions. As a result, small uncertainties are magnified over time, making chaotic systems predictable in principle but unpredictable in practice.

Chapeau – An opening paragraph to a statement or declaration used to outline or introduce the topic at hand rather than to directly enter into the discussion.

Chargé d'Affaires, a.i. – Formerly, a *Chargé d'Affaires* was the title of a chief of mission, inferior in rank to an ambassador or a minister. Today with the *a.i.* (*ad interim*) added, it designates the senior officer taking charge for the interval when a chief of mission is absent from his post.

Charrette – A short period of intense, cross-disciplinary, collaborative planning that empowers community participants and thereby encourages their support for, and ownership of, the final product.

Charter – A term used for particularly formal and solemn instruments, such as the constituent treaty of an international organization. (UNT)

Chemical oxygen demand (COD) – The amount of oxygen consumed by a chemical oxidizing agent in a quantity of water, determined by the total amount of organic material that can be oxidized in the water column. (USEPA)

Chemtrail Shield – A belief held by certain segments of the environmental movement that a secret chemical spraying program in the upper atmosphere has been in effect since the early 1990s. They point to changes in the appearance of the sky from one of crisscrossing contrails that normally dissipate in a matter of minutes, to a spreading mass of milky clouds lasting for hours. While still unconfirmed by any government, the belief of the proponents of this effort is that this program is justified as a protective shield to increasing concentrations of harmful UV rays reaching the surface of the Earth, due to a decrease in the stratospheric ozone layer. The opponents argue that the composition of the chemical spray, which includes barium and aluminum, is having a number of negative health-related effects on large numbers of unsuspecting people. See '**Contrails**.'

Chief of Mission – The ranking officer in an embassy. (MW)

Chilling effect – A situation where compliance with trade rules proves to be a barrier to the use of trade provisions to stop environmentally damaging activities (i.e. POPs: Biosafety Protocol intellectual property debate).

China-Europe Dialogue and Exchange for Sustainable Development (CE-DESD) – A nongovernmental organization aimed at facilitating international partnerships for sustainable economic activities, development and peace between China and Europe; fostering awareness and harmony of man and his natural environment; and connecting values and culture with economic, social, technological, environmental and leadership issues. The Foundation will achieve these goals through the implementation of inter-cultural, people-to-people and business-to-business dialogues; organization of seminars, conferences, training, twinning and exchange programs; and project management, communication and logistic services to partnerships.

China-US Center for Sustainable Development (CUCSD) – The mission of the CUCSD is to accelerate sustainable development in China and the US through a new form of cooperation among governments, the business community, universities, research institutions and nongovernmental organizations. The Center focuses on three priority actions: (a) creating sustainable enterprises that enable commerce, community and nature to thrive and grow in harmony, (b) cooperating on strategic initiatives of importance for both China and the US, and (c) building capacity for sustainable development through training and education. CUCSD's headquarters are located in Portland, Oregon.

Chlorofluorocarbons (CFCs) – Chemicals used for refrigeration, air conditioning, packaging, insulation, solvents or aerosol propellants and that, under certain conditions, break down ozone. (EES)

Choke points – A UN term first used by Secretary General Kofi Annan in 2006 to describe the most volatile hotspots where the slightest spark of violence could trigger massive economic and political shockwaves, potentially affecting the entire world. The first such listing included the Strait of Hormuz connecting the Gulf of Oman and the Persian Gulf, the Abqaiq oil processing facility in Saudi Arabia, the Strait of Malacca connecting the Indian and Pacific oceans between Malaysia and Indonesia, the Suez Canal connecting the Red Sea with the Mediterranean, and the Druzhba pipeline, which is the world's longest oil pipeline from Russia to multiple points in Europe. (UNW)

CIVICUS – An international alliance dedicated to strengthening citizen action and civil society throughout the world. Its members include nearly 500 nongovernmental organizations, associations, private foundations and individuals from 91 countries. It works to promote an enabling architecture for civil society; promote citizen participation in civil society; and build a global civil-society movement. (CIVICUS)

Civil society – Extra-governmental individuals and groups, organized or unorganized, who interact in the social, political and economic domains and who are regulated by formal and informal rules and laws. Civil society offers a dynamic, multilayered wealth of perspectives and values, seeking expression in the public sphere. (UNDP). A classification that includes those political, cultural and social organizations of modern societies that are autonomous of the state but part of the mutually constitutive relationship between state and society. (Lipschutz, 1999). The web of associations, social norms and practices that comprise activities of a society as separate from its state and market institutions. Civil society includes religious organizations, foundations, guilds, professional associations, labor unions, academic institutions, media, pressure groups and political parties. (WB)

Classical statist approach to international law – A view of international law wherein states are the only recognized and legitimate 'subjects,' everything else is an 'object,' and only states can create and employ international law. It is premised on ideas regarding the 'sovereign equality of states,' a duty of non-intervention on the part of states in the internal affairs of other states, and state consent to international obligations. (ECO)

Clean Development Mechanism (CDM) – CDM is a means by which non-Annex I Parties to the Kyoto Protocol (developing countries) can be assisted in development efforts and contribute to the stabilization of GHG concentration in the atmosphere at a level that would prevent dangerous anthropogenic interference with the climate system and to help developed countries and countries with economies in transition to meet their quantified emission limitation commitment. (UNFCCC; EEA)

Clean fuels – Fuels that produce lower emissions than conventional gasoline and diesel. Refers to alternative fuels as well as to reformulated gasoline and diesel. (NRDC) See '**Alternative fuels**.'

Cleaner production – The continuous application of an integrated preventive environmental strategy to processes, products and services to increase overall efficiency, and to reduce risks to humans and the environment. Cleaner production can be applied to the processes used in any industry, to products themselves and to various services provided in society. (UNEP)

Cleanup – Treatment, remediation, destruction/disposal of contaminated material. (NRDC)

Clearances – A message or other document conveying a policy or an instruction is 'cleared' in a foreign office, or large embassy, when all officials who have responsibility for any of its specific aspects have signified their approval by initialing it. See '**Visa**' when referring to UN and other international organizations. (eD)

Clear cutting – A commercial timber management technique in which all trees, with the possible exception of 'seed' or 'specimen' trees and buffers bordering water courses (depending on the policies of a given country), are harvested from a delimited forested area. (USEPA)

Clearing House Mechanism (CHM) – A mechanism generally operated by a convention's secretariat to promote and facilitate technical and scientific cooperation or to facilitate the exchange of scientific, technical and legal information and assist developing country parties in the implementation of the MEA concerned. (UNFCCC)

Climate Action Network (CAN) – Formed in 1989, CAN is a global network of over 287 nongovernmental organizations (NGOs) working to promote government and individual action to limit human-induced climate change to ecologically sustainable levels. CAN members work to achieve this goal through the coordination of information exchange and NGO strategies on international, regional and national climate issues. (CAN)

Climate change – A change of climate that is attributed directly or indirectly

C

to human activity that alters the composition of the global atmosphere and which is in addition to natural climate variability observed over comparable time periods. (UNFCCC; EES)

Climate Change Protocol – See '**Kyoto Protocol**.'

Climate models – Large and complex computer programs used to simulate global climate based on mathematical equations derived from the physics that govern the earth atmosphere system. (IPPC)

Climate system – The totality of the atmosphere, hydrosphere, biosphere and geosphere and their interactions. (UNFCCC)

Climate variability – Refers to change in patterns, such as precipitation patterns, in weather and climate. (PEW)

Clinton Global Initiative – A nonpartisan project of the William J. Clinton Nonprofit Foundation started in 2005 and bringing together some of the world's best minds and most distinguished problem solvers to identify immediate, practical solutions to some of the world's most challenging issues including, but not limited to, reducing poverty, addressing climate change and strengthening governance. However, unlike other world conferences, it requires each participant to make a personal commitment to take specific action on one of the topics discussed. The 2005 conference resulted in formal pledges of US$1.25 billion, and the 2006 conference in pledges of US$2billion.

Closure/Cloture – The formal close of debate in a legislative or governing process, many times ending with a vote or consensus decision. (MW)

Clubbable – A term that refers to the potential of a non-EU state to be invited to join the EU that came into common usage in 2005 in relation to the possibility of Turkey gaining the support it needed to be asked to join the EU.

Club of Madrid – A group comprising 66 former heads of state and government created for the purposes of promoting democracy and addressing priority issues for world peace and stability. (WP)

Clustering – A suggested method to reduce conflict and overlap between international legal instruments, which includes placing treaties or conventions having similar subject matter or that cover the same geographic area in the same administrative unit.

CNN effect – The effect that continuous and instantaneous television coverage may have on making and conducting foreign policy and/or the conduct of international organizations, NGOs and private sector entities.

Coalition – A temporary alliance of distinct parties, persons or states that is generally established to further joint action on a specific matter. (MW)

Coastal zone – The part of the land affected by its proximity to the sea, and that part of the sea affected by its proximity to the land. (EEA)

Cocoyoc Declaration – The published report of the 1974 UNEP/UNCTAD symposium held in Cocoyoc, Mexico that identified the maldistribution of resources as a factor in environmental degradation. The symposium, chaired by Barbara Ward, called for development action focused on filling basic human needs. (UNT)

Codex Alimentarius – The international 'food code' or set of standards implemented through a commission responsible to the Directors-General of the Food and Agriculture Organization (FAO) and the World Health Organization (WHO). The standards are established to protect the health of consumers and ensure fair practices in the food trade; promote coordination of all work on food standards undertaken by international, governmental and nongovernmental organizations; and to determine priorities and guide the preparation of draft standards. (FAO)

Co-financing – An arrangement whereby an international bank attracts a second lender to finance part of a loan. Such an arrangement spreads the risks to the banks and obtains a second opinion as to whether the project is bankable and interesting. (DFID)

Co-generation – The use of waste heat from electric generation, such as exhaust from gas turbines, for either industrial purposes or district heating. (IPCC) Also, the use of a public power grid by private energy producers.

Co-incineration – Joint incineration of hazardous waste of any kind with refuge and/or sludge. (EEA)

Cold War – The post-1945 struggle between the US and the Soviet Union that ended with the collapse of the Berlin Wall in 1989 and the dissolution of the Soviet Union in 1991. (UN)

Coliform Index – A rating of the purity of water based on a count of coliform bacteria. (USEPA)

Collaboration – Cooperation with an agency or instrumentality with which one is not immediately connected. (MW)

Collective decision-making process – The negotiation of international agreements where the established procedures include decision criteria of fair representation and treatment of all parties, transparency, equity and efficiency.

Comity – The agreement between countries to recognize and respect the laws and institutions of each. Somewhat similar to international law except that international law is binding while comity is not. (MW)

Command and control – In relation to policy and management, command-and-control instruments (e.g. mechanisms, laws, measures) rely on prescribing rules and standards and using sanctions to enforce compliance with them. (EEA)

Commercial extinction – A term most commonly used in reference to fish populations and its depletion to the point where fisherman cannot catch enough to be economically worthwhile, or to commercial wildlife populations to the point where hunters or trappers can no longer realize gainful employment from their killing or capture. (EEA; NRDC)

Commission for Environmental Cooperation (CEC) – An international organization created by Canada, Mexico and the US under the North American Agreement on Environmental Cooperation (NAAEC). The CEC was established to address regional environmental concerns, help prevent potential trade and environmental conflicts, and to promote the effective enforcement of environmental law. The Agreement complements the environmental provisions of the North American Free Trade Agreement (NAFTA) See '**North American Agreement on Environmental Cooperation**'; **North American Free Trade Agreement**.'

Commission on Global Governance (CGG) – An independent group of 28 public figures who, based on the belief that the end of the Cold War offered opportunities to build a more cooperative, safer and fairer world, published *Our Global Neighborhood* (1995) and *Millennium Year and the Reform Process* (2000).

Commission on Sustainable Development (CSD) – A commission of the UN Economic and Social Council created in December 1992 to ensure effective follow-up of UNCED; and to monitor and report on implementation of the Earth Summit and the WSSD agreements at the local, national, regional and international levels. (CSD)

CSD – Development Water Action and Networking database (CSD-WAND) – Developed by UNDESA, the CSD-WAND is a tool for the implementation of the CSD's decisions and provides increased information to those working on water and sanitation issues. (UN)

Commitment authority – The power that GEF has to make commitments based on the amount of resources it has received or that donors have committed. The authority covers contributions received in the form of notes and cash deposits, and investment income generated on cash deposits, less actual project disbursements and anticipated administrative costs of the GEF. (GEF)

Commitment to Development Index – The Washington, DC-based Center for Global Development/*Foreign Policy* magazine Commitment to Development Index ranks 21 of the world's richest countries based on their dedication to policies that benefit the 5 billion people living in poorer nations worldwide. Moving beyond standard comparisons of foreign aid volumes, the index also rates countries: quality of foreign aid, openness to developing country exports, policies that influence investment, migration policies, support to the creation of new technologies, security policies, and environmental policies. (CGD) See '**Sustainability assessment measures**.'

Committee – A group of people selected from a larger group to discuss, investigate or report on a particular subject.

Committee of the Whole (COW) – A committee created by a COP to facilitate the process of text negotiation. The COW then turns over the draft text to the COP for further work and formal adoption during a plenary session. (BCHM)

Common but differentiated responsibilities – Principle 7 of the Rio Declaration, which reads, 'States shall cooperate in a spirit of global partnership to conserve, protect and restore the health and integrity of the Earth's ecosystem. In view of the different contributions to global environmental degradation, States have common but differentiated responsibilities.'

Common concern of humankind – A principle supported by numerous international meetings that represents an effort to provide a basis for international action to protect the global climate. However, since climate change is not imposed by one state upon another state, the traditional legal principles governing transboundary pollution do not apply. But if the atmosphere is a 'common concern of humankind,' all states have an interest and duty to protect it from serious harm. A state on one side of the globe is thus 'affected' by a state on the other side of the globe that is emitting greenhouse gases into the atmosphere. (UNFCCC)

Common good – Freely accessible good for which there is strong competition between users. This is the case with fishery resources, certain forest areas and certain grazing rights without an agreement; unrestricted exploitation of the resource may lead to it becoming exhausted. (UNCLOS)

Common heritage of mankind – A concept initially used by Arvid Prado in 1967, which stated that the seabed and the ocean floor (and presumably other of the global commons) are beyond national jurisdiction, are the common heritage of mankind, not subject to national appropriation in any manner whatsoever and should be used and exploited for peaceful purposes and for the exclusive benefit of mankind as a whole. (UNCLOS)

Common property resource – A resource where the rights of use are communally shared and owned and where formal or informal use regulations are employed. (BLD)

Commonwealth of Nations – The Commonwealth of Nations, usually known as The Commonwealth, is an association of 53 independent sovereign states, almost all of which are former territories of the British Empire. It was once known as the British Commonwealth of Nations or British Commonwealth, and some still call it by that name, for historical reasons or to distinguish it from the other commonwealths around the world, such as the Commonwealth of Australia and the Commonwealth of The Bahamas. (WP)

Communiqué – A brief public summary statement issued following import bilateral or multilateral discussions. (eD)

Community – An integrated group of species inhabiting a given area. (GBS)

Community-based organizations (CBO) – Organizations that are voluntary, not-for-profit, nongovernmental and run by citizens with aims and activities limited to a locality that has a unique identity, as a city or neighborhood.

Community of Democracies (CD) – A term coined by then US Secretary of State Madeline Albright in the year 2000, the CD was a response to the fact that for the first time in history, most countries had some form of representative government. Meetings of invited governments are generally held every two years and meant to advance principles strengthening democratic governments. (USDOS)

Community of practice (CoP) – A group of people informally bound together by shared expertise and passion for a joint enterprise in a common context. (Wenger, 1998)

Competent authority (1) – A governmental entity empowered by the Member States as responsible for performing the duties arising from enforcing a given law or policy. (EEA; WP)

Competent authority (2) – A governmental authority designated by a party to be responsible for receiving the notification of a transboundary movement of hazardous wastes or other wastes, and any information related to it, and for responding to the notification. (UN; EEA)

Competition – The idea that to survive, agents must fight each other and that only one of them can be successful. This assumes that resources are limited (insufficient for both) and is often a negative-sum strategy, i.e. 'win–lose' or 'lose–lose.' (CSG)

Complex – Intricate association of individual parts forming a whole. (MW)

Complex adaptive system – A form of system containing many autonomous agents who self-organize in a co-evolutionary way to optimize their separate values. (CSG)

Complex systems – Systems that interact non-linearly with their environment. Their components have properties of self-organization that make them non-predictable beyond a certain temporal window. (Pavard and Dugale, 2003)

Complexity theory – A field of research that explores systems in which a great many independent agents interact with each other in a great many ways. (Waldrop, 1993)

Compliance monitoring – In a water quality management program, compliance is associated with meeting permit conditions as well as ambient standards. Ongoing monitoring provides periodic water quality data used to assess compliance. (SFWMD)

Complimentarity, principle of – The cornerstone of the International Criminal Court (ICC), which holds that the ICC will only conduct a small number of prosecutions and only when national courts are unwilling or unable to prosecute war or other international crimes. The ICC believes that national court systems should be the first line of investigation of these crimes. The ICC does not seek to supplant these courts, but to reinforce the national courts (i.e. complimentarity). The principle of complimentarity was also the result of an astute political judgment in that Member States were more likely to ratify this concept if it provided respect for national court systems. (UN)

Composting – A process whereby organic wastes, including food wastes, paper and yard (garden) wastes, decompose naturally, resulting in a product rich in minerals and ideal for gardening and farming as soil conditioners, mulch, resurfacing material, or landfill cover. (NRDC)

Comprehensive Environmental Restoration Plan (CERP) – The framework and guide for the restoration, protection and long-term management of a given ecosystem. (EES)

Concessional financing – Usually, money loaned by development banks at below market interest rates and often below the cost of borrowing for the lending agency to promote a specific goal. (WB)

Concessional/Concessionary loan – Loan provided to poorest countries with lower interest rates and longer repayment periods than are typical of standard market or multilateral loans, that is less than market interest rates and extended grace period. (WB)

Conciliation – A term meaning to unite or to make compatible different viewpoints in a document.

Concordat – A treaty to which the Pope or the Holy See is a party. Such notations have been attached to environmental agreements/principles such as the access to potable water, when the Holy See determines that basic human rights are involved. (eD; UN)

Conditionality (1) – The practice of attaching conditions to international economic concessions or development assistance funds, or to the opening of international markets. The obligations accepted by a developing country in relation to its policies or institutions as part of an aid transaction. (DFID)

Conditionality (2) – A rule of the International Monetary Fund that a member's right to the use of credit tranches and credit facilities will be conditioned on its progress in regularizing its balance-of-payments obligations and in developing sustained economic growth. (WB)

Conditions – The existence of, or setting of, certain requirements before agreement can be reached or work can begin. (MW)

Conference (or Congress) – International meeting. In the diplomatic sense, a congress has the same meaning as a conference. (eD)

Conference of the Parties (COP) – The supreme body of any Multilateral Environmental Agreement (MEA). The role of the COP is to promote the MEA and its objectives and to review its commitments, effectiveness and implementation. COPs generally meet once a year to review implementation and take decisions on how to improve the implementation process. (eD)

Conference-room papers (CRP) – A category of in-session documents containing new proposals or outcomes of in-session work for use only during the session. (BCHM)

Confined aquifer – An aquifer delimited by a layer of impermeable rock or soil above and/or below the body of water. (USEPA)

Conflict – A condition where two or more parties have differing interests or perspectives that require resolution to achieve a positive outcome. (MW)

Conflict diamond. See '**Blood diamond**.'

Congress (1) – A meeting of elected or appointed representatives. (MW)

Congress (2) – A national legislative assembly. (MW)

Congress (3) – The highest legislative body in a given country charged with making law. (MW)

Congressional Record – A document published by the US government printing office recording all debates, votes and discussions taking place in the US Congress (legislature); available for free inspection at all government document repositories, as well as in some major libraries. (NRDC) See '**Gazette**.'

Consensus – A decision of an assembly that has agreement from all voting parties or members. An agreement adopted without a vote when there are no stated objections by any of the delegations. Abstentions may be voiced and noted in the conference record and not affect a consensus decision. (BLD)

Consequential equity – A principle of equity that refers to the outcomes of a decision in terms of burden sharing among and within countries as well as between present and future generations. (CSG)

Conservation – The management of human use of the biosphere so that it may yield the greatest sustainable benefit to current generations while maintaining its potential to meet the needs and aspirations of future generations. (GBS)

Conservation categories of IUCN – Species conservation groupings that indicate the degree of threat to survival for taxa. The six IUCN categories are given a capital letter to distinguish them from general usage of the terms as follows:

- *Threatened Categories*
  - *Extinct (Ex)* **Taxa that are no longer known to exist in the wild after repeated searches of their type localities and other known or likely places.**
  - *Endangered (E)* **Taxa in danger of extinction and whose survival is unlikely if the causal factors continue operating. Included are taxa whose numbers have been reduced to a critical level or whose habitats have been so drastically reduced that they are deemed to be in immediate danger of extinction.**
  - *Vulnerable (V)* **Taxa believed likely to move into the Endangered category in the near future if the causal factors continue operating. Included are taxa of which most or all the populations are decreasing because of over-exploitation, extensive habitat or other environmental disturbance; taxa with populations that have been seriously depleted and whose ultimate security is not yet assured; and taxa with populations that are still abundant but are under threat from serious adverse factors throughout their range.**
  - *Rare (R)* **Taxa with small world populations that are not at present Endangered or Vulnerable, but are at risk. These taxa are usually localized within restricted geographical areas or habitats or are thinly scattered over a more extensive range.**

C

  - *Indeterminate (I)* **Taxa known to be Extinct, Endangered, Vulnerable, or Rare but there is not enough information to say which of the four categories is appropriate.**
- *Unknown Categories*
  - *Status Unknown (?)* **No information is available with which to assign a conservation category.**
  - *Insufficiently Known (K)* **Taxa that are suspected but not definitely known to belong to any of the above categories, following assessment, because of lack of information.**
- *Not Threatened Category*
  - *Safe (nt)* **Neither rare nor threatened.**

Conservation easements – Regulations that limit activities permitted in the process of using a natural resource. For example, allowing indigenous peoples to use a protected forest for certain subsistence and/or economically productive activities, allowing a public access path to cross a private parcel of land separating two public parcels. (AM)

Conservation International (CI) – A US-based, international organization, that applies innovations in science, economics, policy and community participation to protect the Earth's richest regions of plant and animal diversity in biodiversity hotspots, high-biodiversity wilderness areas as well as important marine regions around the globe. With headquarters in Washington, DC, CI works in more than 40 countries on four continents.

Constructive ambiguity – A method used in diplomacy that inserts temporary language into a document that is the lowest common denominator acceptable by the parties in disagreement, but which allows negotiation to proceed – hopefully to full agreement on other more important issues. The wording must be revisited or implementation of the agreement will be made more difficult later. (eD)

Consul General – See '**Consulate**.'

Consulate – An office established by one state in an important city of another state for the purpose of supporting and protecting its citizens traveling or residing there. In addition, these offices are charged with performing administrative duties such as issuing visas to host country nationals wishing to travel to the country the consulate represents. All consulates, whether located in the capital city or in other communities, are administratively under the ambassador and the embassy. In addition to carrying out their consular duties, they often serve as branch offices for the embassy. Consulates are expected to play a particularly significant role in connection with the promotion of their own country's exports and other commercial activities. Officers performing consular duties are known as consuls or, if more junior, vice consuls. The chief of the consulate is known as the consul, or consul general. (eD)

Consultative group – Groups established to treat specific themes or geographic regions where the members are usually both public and private and where their support may or may not include financing.

Consultative Group on International Agricultural Research (CGIAR) – CGIAR was created in 1971 as an association of public and private members to support a system of 16 Future Harvest Centers that work in more than 100 countries, with a mandate to mobilize cutting-edge science that will reduce hunger and poverty, and improve human nutrition and health, while emphasizing environmental protection. (FAO)

Contact group – A group called into being to resolve a specific issue on which there is disagreement. Membership is ostensibly open to all parties, but is usually limited to those parties individually invited by the chair to participate because of their differing viewpoints. (ENB)

Contaminant – A substance that is not naturally present in the environment or is present in unnatural concentrations that can, in sufficient concentration, adversely alter an environment. (MW)

Continental shelf – The seabed and subsoil of the submarine areas that extend beyond a coastal state's territorial sea throughout the natural prolongation of its land territory to the outer edge of the continental margin. A coastal state may claim a continental shelf of up to 200 miles from the baselines from which the territorial sea is measured even if the continental margin is not that far seaward; but its maximum claim can be no more than 350 miles. (EES)

Contingency plan – An alternative for action if things do not go as planned or if an expected result fails to materialize. (MW)

Contingent valuation – Valuation technique that asks people directly how much they are willing to pay for improving environmental quality. See '**Defensive expenditure**.' (EEA)

Contra legem – 'Against the law' (term used to describe an equitable decision of a court or tribunal that is contrary to the law governing the controversy). (BLD)

Contracting state – A State that has consented to be bound by the treaty, whether or not the treaty has entered into force. (VC)

Contrails – Condensation trails sometimes called vapor trails or artificial cirrus clouds made by the exhaust of aircraft engines or wingtip vortices that precipitate a stream of tiny ice crystals in the moist, frigid upper air layer of the troposphere between 9 and 12km in height with temperatures between -37°C to -57°C. (WP) See '**Global dimming**,' '**Global cooling**,' '**Haze**.'

Convention – When signed and ratified, a binding agreement between two or more states that deals with specific matters of mutual interest and which defines the duties of the Parties to the Convention that sets out the political and legal framework for actions that may be listed or that may need to be developed. (VC)

Convention Concerning the Protection of the World Cultural and Natural Heritage – A convention adopted in November 1972 at the 17th General Conference of UNESCO. The Convention is responsible for the establishment and recording of the World Heritage List of cultural and natural properties, submitted by the States Parties. These sites are considered to be of outstanding universal value. The Convention provides technical cooperation under the World Heritage Fund to States Parties whose resources are insufficient to safeguard World Heritage properties.

Convention for the Prevention of Marine Pollution by Dumping from Ships and Aircraft – The Oslo Convention came into force in April 1974. It grades pollutants into three levels of toxicity – black list (most detrimental, organo-halogens, organosilicons, carcinogenic compounds, mercury and mercury compounds, and persistent plastics and other synthetic materials); the grey list (harmful, arsenic, lead, copper, zinc and their compounds, containers, scrap metal, tar-like substances and bulky wastes, and substances that although not necessarily toxic may become harmful in large quantities); and the white list (least toxic, but requiring approval before dumping from local authorities). The Convention also provides regulations for the disposal of these pollutants. (AM)

Convention for the Protection of the Ozone Layer – A multilateral treaty adopted at Vienna on 22 March, 1985, and in force from 22 September, 1988. It requires States Parties to cooperate in undertaking scientific research to protect the Earth's ozone layer.

Convention on Biological Diversity (CBD) – The Convention on Biological Diversity was negotiated under the auspices of UNEP and opened for signature at UNCED in June 1992. It entered into force on 29 December, 1993 and has three goals: to promote the conservation of biodiversity, the sustainable use of its components, and the fair and equitable sharing of benefits arising out of the utilization of genetic resources. (ENB)

Convention on Early Notification of a Nuclear Accident – A 1986 Convention that aims to provide relevant information concerning nuclear accidents as early as possible to minimize transboundary radiological consequences. (VC; UNIAEA)

Convention on Environmental Impact Assessment in a Transboundary Context (Espoo Convention) – The Espoo (EIA) Convention sets out the obligations of parties to assess the environmental impact of certain activities at an early stage of planning. It also lays down the general obligation of States to notify and consult each other on all major projects under consideration that are likely to have a significant adverse environmental impact across borders. The Espoo Convention was signed in Espoo, Finland and entered into force in 1997. (UNT)

Convention on International Trade in Endangered Species of Wild Fauna and Flora (CITES) – CITES bans or regulates international trade in endangered species to combat their over-exploitation. The text was opened for signature in Washington DC on 3 March, 1973 and entered into force on 1 July, 1975. (CITES)

Convention on Nuclear Safety – The Convention establishes a legal obligation on the part of the Parties to apply certain general safety principles to the construction, operation and regulation of land-based civilian nuclear power plants under their jurisdiction and submit periodic reports on the steps they are taking to implement the obligations of the Convention. The Convention was opened for signatures in September, 1994 and entered into force in 1996. (VC; UNIAEA)

Convention on Supplementary Compensation for Nuclear Damage – The Convention on Supplementary Compensation for Nuclear Damage was adopted on 12 September, 1997 and was opened for signature on 29 September, 1997 at the 41st General Conference of the International Atomic Energy Agency in Vienna. The Convention allows for compensation for damage within a country's exclusive economic zone, which includes loss of tourism or fisheries related income. (VC; UNIAEA)

Convention on the Conservation of Migratory Species of Wild Animals – A 1979 UNEP sponsored Convention and its amendments to protect the habitat of migrating species whether within a single country or of a transboundary nature. (UNEP)

Convention on the Elimination of All Forms of Discrimination Against Women (CEDAW) – CEDAW was adopted in 1979 by the UN General Assembly and is often described as an international bill of rights for women. Consisting of a preamble and 30 articles, it defines what constitutes discrimination against women and sets up an agenda for national action to end such discrimination. (CEDAW)

Convention on the Law of the Non-Navigational Use of International Watercourses – The so-called International Water Convention was first proposed in 1954. Work was initiated on a draft text in 1971 and finally adopted by the UNGA in 1997. The Convention attempts to promote cooperation between riparian states by setting principles, norms and rules that give guidance for regulating conflicting uses. It is among the most contentious of texts ever negotiated in the UN and the date of its eventual entry into force is still listed as 'unpredictable.' (UNT)

Convention on the Physical Protection of Nuclear Material – This 1980 Convention provides for certain levels of physical protection during international transport of nuclear material and establishes a general framework for cooperation among states in the protection, recovery and return of stolen nuclear material. (UNIAEA)

**Convention on the Protection and Use of Transboundary Water-
courses and International Lakes (Helsinki I)** – The Helsinki I Convention, which entered into force in 1996, is intended to strengthen national
measures for the protection and ecologically sound management of transboundary, surface and groundwater. The Convention obliges parties to prevent, control and reduce water pollution from point and non-point sources
and also includes provisions for monitoring, research and development,
consultations, warning and alarm systems, mutual assistance, institutional
arrangements, and the exchange and protection of information, as well as
public access to information. (UNT; EU)

Convention on the Rights of the Child (CRC) – The treaty that fully
articulates the human rights of children and the standards to which all governments must aspire. The Convention, entered into force in 1989, is administered by UNICEF. Ratified by nearly all countries, it is the most universally
accepted human rights instrument in history. (UN)

Convertible currency – A currency that can be exchanged freely for other
currencies at market rates, or for gold. (WB)

Cooperation – The idea that agents can increase their fitness by mutual help
rather than by competition. This assumes that resources adequate for both
exist, or are created by the interaction. (CSG)

**Coordinating Group of Amazon Basin Indigenous Organizations
(COICA)** – COICA is a coordinating body for more than 400 indigenous
groups. Now headquartered in Quito, Ecuador, it was founded in Lima, Peru
in 1982 to help native people defend their rights, fight for the survival of
their culture, exchange experiences and find solutions to their various common problems. (COICA)

Copenhagen Consensus Project (CCP) – A concept conceived by the
Danish economist Björn Lomborg, which brings together a panel of eminent
development specialists who attempt to prioritize a range of ideas for meas-
urably improving the quality of lives of people living in developing countries.
The argument is made that there is only so much ODA, loan or investment
money available and that it should be spent on the highest priority projects.
(CCP)

CORINE – A program for the Coordination of Information on the Environment proposed in 1985 by the European Commission that is to gather information on priority environmentally related topics for the European Union.
(EEA)

Corporate social responsibility – A concept whereby companies voluntarily integrate social and environmental concerns into their business and the
way they interact with stakeholders. This generally implies going over and
above legal requirements, integrating economic, social and environmental

concerns into their business plans, and adopting new approaches to business management. (EEA; WP)

Corridor – A band of vegetation, usually older forest, which serves to connect distinct patches on the landscape. (EES)

Corruption – Inducement to wrong by improper or unlawful means such as bribery. (MW)

Cost–benefit analysis – A decision tool that assesses projects through a comparison between their costs and benefits, including social costs and benefits. (DFID)

Cost–benefit approach – A method of analysis used in circumstances where components of the real costs or benefits of a project would not be adequately represented by market prices and may not be traded at all. It assumes that benefits and costs are ultimately defined in terms of human preferences. (WB)

Cost-effectiveness – The relation between the costs (inputs) and outputs of a project. The most cost-effective is the most economical in terms of tangible benefits produced by money spent. (DFID)

Cost-efficiency – The relation between the costs (inputs) and outputs of a project. A project is most cost-efficient when it achieves its outputs at the lowest possible cost compared either to alternative methods of delivery or alternative outputs achieving the same objective. (DFID)

Cotonou Agreement – A partnership agreement between the EU and the countries of Africa, the Caribbean and the Pacific signed in June 2000 in Cotonou, Benin. The agreement replaced the Lomé Convention and has poverty reduction as its main objective, 'to be achieved through political dialogue, development aid and closer economic and trade cooperation.' (AD)

Council (1) – An executive or governing body whose members are equal in power and authority. (CONGO)

Council (2) – The GEF governing body that consists of 32 members representing constituency groupings and meets semi-annually. It develops, adopts and evaluates the operational policies and programs for GEF-financed activities. (GEF)

Council for International and Economic Cooperation (CIFIC) – Creating a new agenda-setting body for the international financial system is the primary objective for CIFIC, as the G7 does not include some of the critical actors (China, India, Brazil), and the G20, with 40 ministers and central bank governors around its table, is considered too large

C

to be effective. A new body, provisionally named CIFEC, is being debated as the agenda-setting body, providing strategic direction for the functioning and development of the international financial system and exercising informal oversight to the various multilateral institutions and forums involved in international economic cooperation. As proposed, CIFEC would have no more than 15 member country members, represented by their finance ministers. The Secretary General of the UN, the Managing Director of the IMF, the President of the World Bank, and the Director General of the WTO would be invited to its meetings. (CFR)

Council of Europe – The Council of Europe is an intergovernmental organization established to protect human rights, pluralist democracy and the rule of law; promote awareness and encourage the development of Europe's cultural identity and diversity; seek solutions to problems facing European society; and help consolidate democratic stability in Europe by backing political, legislative and constitutional reform. (EU)

Council of European Ministers – The political leadership of the EU comprising sectoral ministers from all 25 States, according to what is on the agenda, and the president who is appointed by the European Council. For example, if a decision must be taken on agricultural matters, the national governments send their Ministers of agriculture. (EU)

Council on Environmental Quality (CEQ) – US Government agencies established by the National Environmental Policy Act of 1969 to formulate and recommend national policies and provide analysis concerning US participation in international agreements and treaties relating to environmental quality issues. (EES) See '**Bureau of Oceans and International Environmental and Scientific Affairs**.'

Countries with economies in transition (EIT) – The countries of Central and Eastern Europe and former republics of the Soviet Union that are in transition to a market economy. (WB)

Country – The largest local administrative subdivision of most States. (MW) See '**Nation**,' '**State**' and '**Territory**.'

Country desk – A US State Department term indicating the office dealing with a given country or countries. (USDOS)

Country of origin of genetic resources – The country that possesses those genetic resources in *in-situ* conditions. (CBD)

Country profile – A socio-economic, political, environmental and demographic overview of a nation that emphasizes the interests of the institution making the overview.

Court (I) – A judge or judges in session with the aim of conducting judicial business. (MW)

Court (2) – A formal faculty comprising a judge or judges convened for interpreting a law or its application. (MW)

Cradle to cradle certification (C2CCertified) – This certification provides a company with a means to differentiate its product within the marketplace, defining tangible achievement and providing credibility. Within the certification process, MBDC evaluates a material or product's ingredients and the complete formulation for human and environmental health impacts throughout its life-cycle and its potential for being truly recycled, upcycled or safely composted. Certification of a finished product also requires the evaluation of energy-use quantity and quality (i.e. relative proportion of renewable energy), water-use quantity, water-effluent quality and workplace ethics associated with manufacturing. Criteria fall into the following five categories: materials, material reutilization/design for environment, energy, water and social responsibility. (MBDC) See '**Sustainability assessment measures.**'

Cradle to cradle, concept of – A design paradigm originated by architect William McDonough, and chemist Michael Braungart, based on principles and an understanding of the pursuit of value, processes for product and material research and development, and for educating and training. (MBDC)

Cradle to grave, concept of – Cradle to grave assessment considers impacts at each stage of a product's life-cycle, from the time natural resources are extracted and processed through each subsequent stage of manufacturing, transportation, product use and, ultimately, disposal. (EEA)

Credentials – A document issued by a State authorizing a delegate or delegation of that state to attend a conference, including, where necessary, for the purpose of negotiating and adopting the text of a treaty. (UNT)

Creditor Reporting System (CRS) – A database jointly established by the OECD and the World Bank in 1967 that reports official development assistance (ODA) and official aid (OA) and other lending to developing countries and countries in transition by OECD member countries and Bretton Woods institutions. (DFID; WB)

Creeping normalcy, concept of – A political term used to refer to slow trends concealed within noisy fluctuations. If the economy or the environment deteriorates slowly it is difficult to realize that each successive year is on average slightly worse than the preceding year. Therefore, one's baseline standard is what is considered normalcy (Jared, 2005). See '**landscape amnesia**;' '**Boiled-frog syndrome.**'

Crises management – Management that responds to unforeseen circumstances with no time to plan. (DFID)

Critical load – The notion of critical load presumes an ecological threshold or intolerance to the accumulation of a pollutant in an ecosystem. (EES)

C

Critical mass (1) – The minimum mass of fissionable material that will support a sustaining chain reaction. (NRDC; MW)

Critical mass (2) – The minimum amount or number required for something to happen. (MW)

Cross compliance – Most frequently used to indicate the attachment of environmental conditions to agricultural support policies. In the EU debate, the terms cross-compliance and environmental conditionality are often used interchangeably to describe the linking of a farmer's eligibility for agricultural subsidies to environmental conditions. (EEA)

Crosscutting issues (also cross-sectoral issues) – Topics of concern to several different sectors or interests that include subjects such as education, finance and budgeting, personnel management and security, trade, technology transfer, consumption and production patterns, science, capacity building and information.

Cultivar – A cultivated variety (genetic strain) of a domesticated crop plant. (GBS)

Cultural diversity – The variety of human social structures, belief systems, and strategies for adapting to situations in different parts of the world. (GBS)

Cumulative impacts – The impacts (positive and negative, direct and indirect, long-term and short-term) arising from a range of activities throughout an area or region, where each individual effect may not be significant if taken in isolation. Such impacts can arise from the growing volume of traffic, the combined effect of a number of agriculture measures leading to more intensive production and use of chemicals, etc. Cumulative impacts include a time dimension, since they are calculated based upon the impact on environmental resources resulting from changes brought about by past, present and reasonably foreseeable future actions. (EEA)

Customary international law – Usual and expected, although unwritten, rules of behavior regarding relations between states. (BLD)

Cuzco Declaration – See '**South American Community of Nations**.'

Cyclical macro-economic policies – Spending more when the economy is doing well and cutting drastically when the economy is doing poorly. These policies tend to lead to a widening of the income–spending gap, leading to higher debt levels. (WB) See '**Tailor-made economies**.'

Dd

D8 – A group of the largest Muslim developing countries (based on a combination of the population of the Muslim community and the size of the economy) established to improve the lives of the citizens of these countries and to push for the integration of their economies (Bangladesh, Egypt, Iran, Indonesia Malaysia, Nigeria, Pakistan, Turkey).

DAC – See '**Development Assistance Committee**.'

Daily subsistence allowance (DSA) – An amount of money given to a traveler on official mission to cover housing and food expenses. (UN)

Danish International Development Agency (DANIDA) – The principal agency through which Denmark provides technical assistance and distributes foreign aid.

Darwin Declaration – A declaration by the Darwin Workshop on Removing the Taxonomic Impediment (February 1998) that recognizes the lack of sufficient infrastructure, training, research and access to taxonomic information required for the conservation, sustainable use and equitable sharing of benefits from biodiversity.

DATA – NGO established to track the pledges of the 2005 (Gleneagles, Scotland) G8 meeting on debt relief, trade policies, and AIDS-HIV treatment to the world's poorest countries. (UNW)

Davos moment – A reference to the World Economic Forum held in Davos, Switzerland, those 'only-at-Davos experiences' when one has the unexpected opportunity to mix with the rich and powerful and be witness to the rather extraordinary synergy that occurs when powerful people share a public moment.

Davos (Switzerland) Symposium – See the '**World Economic Forum (WEF)**.'

DCM – A US Government abbreviation used to indicate Deputy Chief of Mission. (USDOS)

DDT – Dichlorodiphenyltrichloroethane, an insecticide that is highly toxic to biota, including humans. This is a persistent biochemical that accumulates in the food chain. (EEA)

De facto – In fact (as opposed to in law, *de jure*). (BLD)

De jure – In law (as opposed to in fact, *de facto*). (BLD)

De lege ferenda – What the law ought to be (as opposed to what the law is). (BLD)

Debate Europe – A mechanism established in 2001 and strengthened in 2006 to facilitate public input on issues of importance to the continent that will be debated in one of the EU governing bodies. By involving citizens and civil society closely in these debates, fresh impetus can be given to the whole process of European expansion and integration. This debate will make it possible to better define objectives, establish a delimitation of powers, develop more in-depth policies and improve the Union's methods and instruments. (EU)

Debt buy-back – Purchase by a debtor of all or a part of its debt, usually at a discount from the original face value. (WB; AM)

Debt for nature swap – Debt-for-nature-swaps convert unpaid or uncollectible loans to indebted countries into funds for conservation activities in those countries. A swap occurs when a country allows a foreign investor to acquire a portion of its debt held by a creditor bank. The debt is subsequently donated or purchased at a discount, usually by a non-profit NGO, and is then converted into national currency bonds and expended as per the terms of a contract between the creditor bank(s), the purchasing NGO and the Government. (EES)

Debt relief – Debt relief may take the form of refinancing, reorganization, rescheduling or cancellation of repayments and/or interest due on a loan. A loan is refinanced when the creditor country makes a new loan to enable the debtor country to meet the debt service payments on an earlier loan. A loan is rescheduled when the amortization or interest payments or both on the outstanding portion are rearranged to make payment easier. (DFID)

Decentralization – The general term for a transfer of authority and/or responsibility for performing a function from the top management of an organization or the central governance level of an institution to lower level units or the private sector. (UNDP)

Decentralized energy path (DE) – The generation of electricity at the point of its use regardless of plant size, fuel or technology.

Decision – A formal agreement that leads to binding actions. It becomes part of the agreed body of decisions that direct the work of a COP or other governing body.

Decision 21/21 – A decision of the UNEP Governing Council that established an Open-ended Intergovernmental Group of Ministers to undertake a comprehensive policy-oriented assessment of weaknesses in existing international environmental institutions and examine options for strengthened international environmental governance. (UNEP)

Declaration – A joint statement by two or more states that is binding on those states making the declaration (mandatory declaration). Non-mandatory declarations may be non-binding. The term may also refer to an 'interpretive' declaration from a state as to its understanding of some matter covered by a treaty but these are not the same as reservations. (UNT)

Declaration and Plan of Action of Barbados – The formal statement produced by participating states in the Global Conference on the Sustainable Development of Small Island Developing States (SIDS) held in Bridgetown, Barbados, 25 April–6 May, 1994. The Barbados Declaration made a commitment to specific policies, actions and measures to be taken at the national, regional and international level to enable SIDS to achieve sustainable development. It recognized the special constraints to sustainable development that SIDS face economically, environmentally and socially by virtue of their small size. It called for the assistance of regional and international entities, both governmental and nongovernmental, to engage in a program of action aimed at the sustainable development of the SIDS. (UNEP; UN)

Decomposition (biological) – The action of microorganisms breaking down organic compounds into simpler ones and resulting in the release of energy. (SFWMD)

Deep ecology – A philosophy that argues that humans are part of a larger ecological system, and that the realization of this interconnectedness is fundamental for maintaining the health and integrity of ecosystems. (AM)

Defensive expenditure – A factor calculated from what people or communities are observed to spend to protect themselves against a potential or an actual decline in their environmental quality. People buy goods and services, which help them to preserve the environment and reduce personal or community risk levels. (EEA) See '**Contingent valuation**.'

Definitive signature – A way of establishing the consent of the state to be bound by a treaty that is not subject to ratification, acceptance or approval. (UNT)

Deforestation – The change of forested lands to non-forest lands, with a depletion of tree cover to less than 10 percent. The removal of forest stands by cutting and burning to provide land for agricultural purposes, residential or industrial building sites, roads, etc., or by harvesting the trees for building materials or fuel. (IPCC; EES) See '**Clear cutting**.'

Delegation – A group representing others, which may include high-level representatives of relevant ministries including foreign affairs, technical experts and, increasingly, NGO representatives; the grant of authority to a person to act on behalf of one or more others, for agreed purposes. (UN; eD)

Demarsch/Demarché – A diplomatic or political initiative or maneuver. A petition or protest presented through diplomatic channels. (MW)

Democracy deficit – A democracy deficit is considered to be occurring when ostensibly democratic organizations or institutions (particularly governments) are seen to be falling short of fulfilling the principles of democracy in their practices or operation. (WP)

Demographic, Environmental and Security Issues Project (DESIP) – A project that is intended to help illuminate connections between environmental scarcity and political conflict. The project was to compile information on the world's wars and trouble spots but now includes information on the demographic, political and environmental factors that impact human and other life on the planet. (DESIP)

Department for International Development (DFID) – The principal organization through which the UK provides technical assistance and distributes foreign aid.

Dependency – A land or territory geographically distinct from the country governing it, and held in trust or as a possession. (MW)

Depletion quotas – Quotas that set limits on the amount of a resource that can be used or extracted. (AM)

Deposit-refund system – Surcharge on the price of potentially polluting products. When pollution is avoided by returning the products or their residuals, a full or partial refund of the surcharge is granted. (EEA)

Deposition – The transfer of substances in the air to surfaces, including soil, vegetation, surface water or indoor surfaces, by dry or wet processes. (EEA)

Depository – The institution acting as the custodian of a treaty and that is entrusted with several specific functions regarding the commitments of the parties: accepts notifications and documents related to treaties, examines whether all formal requirements are met, registers and deposits all related documents, and notifies the parties of all relevant actions regarding the treaty. (UNT)

Desalination/Desalinization – The removal of salt from brackish or seawater in order to make it drinkable. The removal of salt from the upper horizons of the soil to make it more productive. (EES; USEPA)

Desert – A dry place classified by UNESCO as arid, semi-arid or hyper-arid. (UNESCO)

Desertification – The progressive destruction or degradation of vegetative cover especially in arid or semi-arid regions bordering existing deserts. (FAO; EES)

Desertification Convention – See '**United Nations Convention to Combat Desertification in Countries Experiencing Serious Drought and/or Desertification, Particularly in Africa (UNCCD).**'

Détente – An easing of tension between states. (eD)

Detritus – Plant or animal debris that occurs as small particles after having been attacked by organisms of decay. (MW)

Developed country – Generally, a highly industrialized country usually from the so-called 'North' or 'West.' Economies used to be classified as developed if they were members of OECD. But today there is some confusion as different organizations use different definitions. The OECD membership, for example, includes poorer countries such as Mexico and Poland, yet excludes wealthier countries such as Hong Kong, Singapore and the United Arab Emirates, which have GDP rankings equivalent to several European nations. *The Economist* gave the following examples in discussing the complexity of country classifications: 'JP Morgan Chase and the United Nations count Hong Kong, Singapore, South Korea and Taiwan as emerging economies. Morgan Stanley Capital International includes South Korea and Taiwan in its emerging-market index, but keeps Hong Kong and Singapore in its developed-markets index. The IMF schizophrenically counts all four as "developing" in its International Financial Statistics but as "advanced economies" in its World Economic Outlook.' (*The Economist* 2006)

Developing country – Low- and middle-income countries in which most people have a lower standard of living with access to fewer goods and services than do most people in high-income countries. There are currently about 125 developing countries with populations over 1 million; in 1998, their total population was more than 5.0 billion. The term is used to categorize countries eligible for official development assistance. (WB)

Development – Process of increasing capacities in the context of a defined goal or set of goals, commonly of a particular sphere at the level of either a community, state or an organization (social development, economic development, institutional development, etc.) (UNDP) A process made up of activities leading to the use, improvement, or conservation of natural and economic goods and services in order to maintain and improve the life quality of a targeted human population. (OAS, 1987) The growth of a person or society toward its full potential. It is often used to mean 'industrialization' or 'modernization' of countries of the South, with the underlying assumption that the industrial model is worth emulating. (R)

Development Assistance Committee (DAC) – A forum for consultation among most of the donor countries, together with the EC, on how to increase the level and effectiveness of aid flows to all aid recipient countries. DAC sets the definitions and criteria for aid statistics internationally. (DFID) The following includes member states and supporting agencies within those countries. See '**ODA(1); ODA(2).**'

D

- Australia
  - AusAid, Australian Agency for International Development
- Austria
  - BKA, Federal Chancellery
  - BMA, Federal Ministry of Foreign Affairs
  - OeKB, *Oesterreichische Kontrollbank* AG
- Belgium
  - DGIC, Directorate General for International Cooperation
  - MF, Ministry of Finance
- Canada
  - CG, Canadian Government
  - CIDA, Canadian International Development Agency
  - IRDC, International Development Research Centre
- Denmark
  - DANCED, Danish Cooperation for Environment and Development
  - DANIDA, Danish International Development Agency
  - MFA, Ministry of Foreign Affairs
- EC
  - EDF, European Development Fund
  - EIB, European Investment Bank
- Finland
  - MFA, Ministry of Foreign Affairs
  - FINNIDA, Finish International Development Agency
- France
  - AFD, *Agence Française Développement*
  - FSP, *Fonds de solidarité prioritaire*
  - MAE, *Ministére des Affaires Étrangéres*
  - Natexis, *Nateis Banque Populaire*
- Germany
  - BMZ, *Bundesministerium für Wirtschaftliche Zusammenarbeit und Entwicklung*
  - FO, Foreign Office
  - GTZ, *Duetsche Gesellschaft für Technische Zusammenarbeit*
  - KFW, *Kreditanstalt für Wiederaufbau*
  - LG, Federal States and Local Governments
- Ireland
  - DFA, Department of Foreign Affairs
- Italy
  - CA, Central Administration
  - DGCS, *Direzione Generale per la Cooperazione allo Sviluppo*
  - LA, Local Administration
  - MC, *Mediocrecito Centrale*
  - SACE, *Sezione Speciale per l'Assicurazione del Credito all'Esportazione*

- Japan
  - JBIC, Japan Bank for International Cooperation
  - JICA, Japan International Cooperation Agency
  - MOFA, Ministry of Foreign Affairs
- The Netherlands
  - MFA, Ministry of Foreign Affairs
- Norway
  - MFA, Ministry of Foreign Affairs
  - NORAD, Norwegian Agency for Development Cooperation
- Portugal
  - GP, Portuguese Government
  - ICP, Portuguese Cooperation Institute
- Spain
  - ECON, Ministry of Economy and Finance
  - EDUC, Ministry of Education and Science
  - ENV, Ministry of Environment
  - ICO, *Instituto de Credito Oficial*
  - MFA, Ministry of Foreign Affairs
- Sweden
  - SIDA, Swedish International Development Authority
- Switzerland
  - DDC, *Direction de Développement et de la Coopération*
  - SECO, *Secrétariat d'État á l'Économie*
- UK
  - DFID, Department for International Development
  - CDC, CDC Capital Partners PLC
- US
  - USAID, US Agency for International Development
  - STATE, US State Department
  - TDA, US Trade and Development Agency

Development bank – See '**World Bank**.'

Development bank (regional) – A multilateral institution that provides financing for development needs of a regional group of countries. Examples include: the African, Asian, Islamic, Caribbean and Inter-American Development Banks.

Development cooperation – A term often used synonymously with overseas development to indicate the interdependent nature of the development process and to emphasize the cooperation between poorer and richer countries.

Development round – WTO negotiations initiated in Doha, Qatar in 2001 that emphasize the need to eliminate trade protectionism (primarily in agriculture).

Diaspora – People who have been forced or induced to settle outside of their traditional homeland due to man-caused or natural disasters, being dispersed throughout other parts of the world, and the ensuing developments in their dispersal and culture. (MW; WP) See '**Refugee**,' '**Environmental refugee**.'

Diffuse pollution – Pollution from widespread activities and not necessarily from a single or discrete source, for example acid rain, pesticides, urban runoff, etc. (EEA)

Digital divide – The digital divide is a social/political issue referring to the socio-economic gap between communities that have access to computers and the internet and those that do not. The term also refers to gaps between groups regarding their ability to use information and communications technologies effectively, due to differing levels of literacy and technical skills, as well as the gap between those groups that have access to quality, useful digital content and those that do not. (WP)

Dioxin – A man-made chemical byproduct formed during the manufacture of other chemicals and during incineration. Studies show that dioxin is among the most potent animal carcinogens ever tested, as well as the cause of severe weight loss, liver problems, kidney problems, birth defects and death. (NRDC)

Diplomacy – The art and skill of conducting negotiations between states or between a state and an international organization. A form of international dispute settlement that attempts to reconcile parties to a disagreement by use of negotiation, mediation or inquiry. (MW)

Diplomat (1) – An informal term for a government official who is a skilled negotiator for the position of a state. (MW)

Diplomat (2) – A rank entitling a representative of a state to certain privileges such as immunity from arrest and prosecution when on official status or performing official duties. (MW)

Diplomat (3) – A rank reserved for the head of an international organization, generally carrying the same privileges and immunities as a diplomat of a state. (MW)

Diplomatic bag – See '**Diplomatic pouch**.'

Diplomatic corps – The body of the highest-ranking foreign diplomats in a given country. The title 'Dean' of the Corps is usually accorded to the longest serving diplomat in that post (rank/country). The Dean may represent the Corps in collective dealings with host country officials on matters of a ceremonial or administrative character affecting the Corps as a whole. (eD)

Diplomatic immunity – An exemption from local taxation and court action in a foreign country granted by international law to members of a diplomatic service above a negotiated rank (depending on the country and/or international organization) and their families. The purpose of these privileges and immunities is not to benefit individuals but to ensure the efficient and effective performance of their official missions on behalf of their governments or organizations. Most of these privileges and immunities are not absolute in that law enforcement can pursue diplomats who break the law, with the perpetrators usually deported to their home country for prosecution depending on the type of infraction claimed by the host country or actually committed by the diplomat. (UN; USDOS)

Diplomatic pouch – A sealed mail pouch used to carry communications between an embassy or international organization and its home office, the contents of which have diplomatic immunity to search and/or seizure. (WP)

Diplomatic privilege – See '**Diplomatic immunity**.'

Diplomatic Quartet – See '**Middle East Quartet**.'

Diplomatic Rank – (in order of precedence):

- Ambassador Extraordinary and Plenipotentiary
- Ministers Plenipotentiary
- Ministers
- Chargé d'Affaires ad hoc or pro tempore
- Chargé d'Affaires ad interim
- Minister-Counselors
- Counselors (or Senior Secretaries in the absence of Counselors)
- Army, Naval and Air Attachés
- Civilian Attachés
- First Secretaries
- Second Secretaries
- Assistant Army, Naval and Air Attachés, Civilian Assistant Attachés
- Third Secretaries and Assistant Attachés

Direct contribution – A term generally used to indicate a cash contribution to a program or project. Debt relief or restructuring, earmarked grant moneys or other financial tools resulting in 'effective cash' are also considered as direct contributions. (UN; WB) See '**Debt relief**,' '**Donor conference**,' '**In-kind contribution**.'

Direct use value – An economic value derived from the direct use or interaction with a resource or resource system. (GBA)

Direction de Développement et de la Coopération (DDC) – The principal agency through which Switzerland delivers technical assistance and distributes foreign aid.

Direzione Generale per la Cooperazione allo Sviluppo (DGCS) – The principal agency through which Italy delivers technical assistance and distributes foreign aid.

Directorate General for Development Cooperation (DGIS) – The principal agency through which The Netherlands delivers technical assistance and distributes foreign aid.

Directorate General for International Cooperation (DGIC) – The principal agency through which Belgium delivers technical assistance and distributes foreign aid.

Disaster – A singular event in space and time in which loss of life, damage to property or loss of livelihood occurs. (EES)

Disaster management – A collective term employed to encompass all aspects of planning for and responding to disasters. (PAHO)

Disaster mitigation – Long-term measures to reduce the scale and/or the duration of adverse effects of hazards on a society or community that is at risk, by reducing the vulnerability to its people, structures, services and economic activities. (OAS, 1987)

Disaster prevention – Measures aimed at reducing the chances of occurrence of a hazard event and/or preventing or reducing the impact of the disaster. (DFID)

Discharge (or flow) – The rate of water movement past a reference point, measured as volume per unit time (usually expressed as cubic feet or cubic meters per second). (SFWMD)

Disincentives – In the environmental context, a mechanism that internalizes the costs of the use of and/or damage to environmental resources, and in so doing provides economic incentives to reduce the use of or damage to the environment. Examples include user fees, non-compliance fees, fines for damages and cleanup, liability rules, performance bonds, etc. (AM)

Disinformation – erroneous material intentionally promoted to confuse, distract and otherwise make it more difficult to determine the truth. (WP)

Dissolved oxygen – Amount of gaseous oxygen (O_2) actually present in water expressed in terms either of its presence in the volume of water (milligrams of O_2 per liter) or of its share in saturated water (percentage) commonly used as an indicator of water 'health' or quality. (EEA; USEPA)

Division for the Advancement of Women (DAW) – DAW was established in 1946 as the 'Section on the Status of Women, Human Rights Division, and Department of Social Affairs' of the UN. In 1972, the section was upgraded to the 'Branch for the Promotion of Equality for Men and Women' and in 1993, it was moved to New York as a part of the Department for Policy Coordination and Sustainable Development (DPCSD), which, in 1996 became the Department of Economic and Social Affairs (DESA). DAW acted as the substantive secretariat for the Fourth World Conference on Women in Beijing (1995), the largest conference in the history of the United Nations. (CEDAW)

D-level staff – A term used to categorize director-level/professional level staff (and salary/benefit package) in the UN and OAS systems, starting at D1 and rising to D2. These staff members carry a red *Laissez-Passer* travel document. (UNDP)

DNA – Deoxyribonucleic acid – comprising molecules that carry the genetic information necessary for the organization and functioning of most living cells and control the inheritance of characteristics.

Doha Ministerial Declaration – The final document of the World Trade Organization's fourth ministerial conference (November 2001) in which the 142 members of WTO decided to launch a new three-year round of negotiations (the Doha Development Agenda) based on further trade liberalization and commitments to build capacity in developing countries. It also approved the accession of China and Taiwan to the WTO.

Domestic benefits – The benefits that accrue to a country from a GEF project aimed at achieving global environmental benefits. The country bears the expenditure for the domestic benefits. (GEF)

Donor conference – A gathering called by a competent authority (normally a country or international organization) to receive and/or formalize pledges of support for a specific activity, cause or crises. Pledges of support can take the form of direct (cash or earmarked grant funds), indirect (debt relief, concessionary loans) or in-kind (non-cash such as office space, transportation services, information, etc.) support. Normally the type and level of support have either been decided by a donor or negotiated prior to the conference and only formal and public announcement of what has been already negotiated is presented. (UN)

Donor country – A nation that participates in the direct transfer/contribution of funds, expertise or equipment through grants or low interest loans to developing countries.

Donor fatigue – A state in which donors no longer contribute to a cause because they have become tired of receiving urgent or repeated appeals for donations, either for a particular cause or in general terms.

Doomsday vault – A massive seed bank housing specimens from all known crops built deep in a sandstone mountain on the island of Svalbald, Sweden high above the Arctic Circle and meant to safeguard crop diversity in the event of a global catastrophe. (UNW) See '**Frozen Ark**.'

Double majority – A double majority requires a majority to be maintained both on the basis of one vote per country, as well as on the basis of financial contributions to a fund. (Gupta, 2002) See '**Qualified "double" majority voting**.'

Double weighted majority system – System used in the formal vote procedure; it is an affirmative vote representing both a 60 percent majority of the total number of participants and 60 percent majority of the total contributions. (GEF)

Draft agenda – A proposed program of work not yet formally approved by a meeting.

Draft annotated agenda – See '**Annotated agenda**.'

Drafting group (or committee) – Group established by the chair or president to facilitate negotiations and to prepare text. Normally, observers may not attend meetings of the drafting groups.

Drainage basin – An area of the Earth's surface from which surface drainage all flows to a single outlet stream (a watershed in North America).

Driving Forces, Pressures, States, Impacts and Responses (DPSIR) – The EU framework for describing/addressing interactions between society and the environment. (EEA)

Drought – A period of deficient precipitation or runoff extending over an indefinite number of days, but with no set standard by which to determine the amount of deficiency needed to constitute a drought. Thus, there is no universally accepted quantitative definition of drought; generally, each investigator establishes his or her own definition. (USGS)

Drought derivative – See '**Aid insurance**.'

DSA – See '**Daily subsistence allowance**.'

Dublin Principles/Statement – The Dublin Statement on Water and Sustainable Development adopted at the International Conference on Water and the Environment (ICWE), held in Dublin, Ireland, January 1992. The ICWE was attended by over 500 participants from more than 100 countries and 80 international governmental organizations and NGOs. The four resulting principles have served as a baseline for nearly all water meetings held since that time: (i) fresh water is a finite and vulnerable resource, essential to sustain life, development and the environment, (ii) water development and management should be based on a participatory approach, involving users, planners and policy-makers at all levels, (iii) women play a central part in the provision, management and safeguarding of water, and (iv) water has an economic value in all its competing uses and should be recognized as an economic good.'

Duty Officer – Responsible party for embassy business during non-business hours.

Duty Station – See '**Post**, **Posting**.'

Duty to interfere – An obligation that falls to all nation-states to provide assistance at the request of the supranational authority. Obviously, this notion is the closest to the original concept of humanitarian intervention. It is also soundly rejected by the Member States of the United Nations, who see this notion as an unacceptable infringement on their prerogatives. (WP) See '**Humanitarian intervention**,' '**Right to interfere**.'

Dynamics – The behavior of a system in time. Changes with time are the essence of complexity; a static system is merely a snapshot within an evolutionary continuum, however interesting it may be in its own right. (CSG)

Dysergy – See '**Negative sum**.'

Ee

E3 – See 'EU3,' 'EU3+.'

E6 – See 'EU6.'

E9 – Education Ministers from the nine high-population countries (Bangladesh, Brazil, China, Egypt, India, Indonesia, Mexico, Nigeria and Pakistan), comprising more than 50 percent of the world's population, meet regularly to discuss the Education For All (EFA) initiative of UNESCO and the UN Decade for Education for Sustainable Development. (UN)

E-waste – Discarded or recycled computers and other electronic equipment and materials.

Earmark(ed) – Refers to the pre-commitment of taxes or other public funds to support pre-specified expenditure items. These revenues are generally channeled through the general budget or may be paid directly to a dedicated fund. (MW)

Earth Charter – An initiative to create an instrument that would set forth fundamental principles for sustainable development called for in 1987 by the United Nations World Commission on Environment and Development and in 1994 by the Earth Council and Green Cross International with support from the Dutch government. An Earth Charter Commission was formed in 1997 to oversee the project and an Earth Charter Secretariat was established at the Earth Council in Costa Rica. (EC)

Earth Council, The – The Earth Council is an international NGO that was created in September 1992 to promote and advance the implementation of the Earth Summit agreements. It is led by a body of 18 Members, drawn from the world's political, business, scientific and nongovernmental communities. (EC)

Earth Negotiations Bulletin – A reporting service for environment and development negotiations published by the International Institute for Sustainable Development. (IISD)

Earth Summit – A common name for the 1992 UN Conference on Environment and Development (UNCED), held in Rio de Janeiro, from which came five major documents: the Rio Declaration, *Agenda 21*, A Framework Convention on Climate Change, A Framework Convention on Biological Diversity and a Statement of Principles on Forests.

Earth Summit +5 – See 'UNGASS.'

Earth system – The Earth regarded as a unified system of interacting components, including geosphere (land), atmosphere (air), hydrosphere (water and ice), and biosphere (life). (NASA)

EC-Ecolabel® (ECE) – The 1992 ECE scheme was designed to identify products that are less harmful to the environment than equivalent brands. Eco-labels may be awarded to products that do not contain chlorofluorocarbons (CFCs), to those products that can be recycled, or to those that are energy efficient based on EC criteria. These cover the whole life-cycle of a product, from the extraction of raw materials, through manufacture, distribution, use and disposal. (EEA) See '**Sustainability assessment measures**,' '**Cradle to cradle certification**.'

Eco-centrism – See '**Biocentrism**.'

Eco-certification – Process leading to a production unit being awarded a certificate by an independent body, confirming that quality criteria for management of natural resources and other environmental quality criteria have been met. Eco-certification works on a voluntary basis: companies that desire to have a good environmental image are free to take part in this process. For the consumer, the visible part of eco-certification is an 'eco-label' on the finished product, which is recognized as a guarantee of management quality.

Eco-development – Concept attributed to economist Jeffrey Sachs (1976) that combined basic needs and environmental strategies inspired in large part by the 1972 UN Stockholm Conference on the Human Environment. Eco-development is directed at the rural poor and embraces an environmentally conservative doctrine.

Eco-efficiency – The delivery of competitively priced goods and services that satisfy human needs and improve quality of life, while progressively reducing ecological impacts and resource use. (WBCSD, nd)

Eco-fund '92 – An independent, non-profit organization for mobilizing private funds to finance nongovernmental activities in support of UNCED preparations.

Eco-hydrology – Describes relationships between hydrological processes and biotic dynamics at the catchment scale. (UNESCO)

Eco-Management and Audit Scheme (EMAS) – The result of a European Union directive for a framework to implement and police 'green' labeling schemes in EU member states. (DFID)

Eco-regions – See '**Ecological regions**.'

Eco-terrorism (1) – Any crime, including property damage, vandalism and personal injury committed in the name of defending nature. (USDOS)

Eco-terrorism (2) – A term often described as 'monkeywrenching' or resistance to the destruction of natural diversity and wilderness. These activities are not directed against human beings or other forms of life, but rather aimed at machines, tools and property (public and/or private) used to 'destroy' or otherwise impact public or private natural resources to a degree considered unacceptable by its proponents. (GP) See '**Monkeywrenching**.'

Ecological corridor – See '**Biological corridor**.'

Ecological debt (day, month, year) – A theoretical concept implying that beyond a certain date, a city, region, country or the world is living beyond its environmental means for the remainder of the year (month, year), or the point at which the consumption of resources exceeds the ability of the planet to replace them (during the same time frame). While it may be possible to determine that point for a specific indicator, for example fish harvesting for a given species in a given year, there is no agreement in the scientific community on the suite of indicators that would have to be measured to actually determine a specific date to declare any political entity to be in 'ecological debt.' See: '*Gaia* **"revenge" hypothesis**.' (ENN)

Ecological economics – A branch of economics that takes account of ecological principles and examines economic values of non-market products and services. (BCHM; AM)

Ecological energetics – See '**Bioenergetics**.'

Ecological envelope – The range within a single target or a range of targets resulting from scientific study that meet criteria or legally established limits within an acceptable confidence range and within a specified time period. (EES)

Ecological footprint – See '**Environmental footprint (individual)**,' '**Environmental footprint (industry)**.'

Ecological regions – A land area that varies in size from a few hectares to thousands of square kilometers and has a unified climate, geology, topography, soil, potential natural vegetation and predominant land-use. (EES)

Ecology – The scientific discipline that is concerned with the relationships between organisms and their past, present and future environments. (ESA)

Economic development – The process of improving the quality of human life through increased per capita income, reduced poverty, enhanced individual economic and educational opportunities, better health and nutrition, resource conservation and a cleaner environment. (DFID)

Economic efficiency – The allocation of a resource in an economy yielding an overall net gain to society as measured by a cost–benefit ratio. (MW)

Economic growth – An increase in a country's total output. It may be measured by the annual rate of increase in a country's gross national product (GNP) or gross domestic product (GDP) as adjusted for price changes. (DFID)

Economic valuation – A method of giving economic value to environmental factors and considerations, which helps give weight to such considerations where they might otherwise not be taken into account.

Economies in transition – See 'Countries with economies in transition.'

Ecosystem – A dynamic complex of plant, animal and microorganism communities and their non-living environment interacting as a functional unit. Ecosystems boundaries are not fixed and their parameters are set according to the scientific, management or policy question being examined.

Ecosystem approach – For the purposes of the CBD, the 'ecosystem approach' is a strategy for the integrated management of land, water and living resources that promotes conservation and sustainable use of the components and processes of an ecosystem. It recognizes that humans, with their cultural diversity, are an integral component of ecosystems. (CBD)

Ecosystem health – See the essay, p20.

Ecosystem restoration – See the essay p21.

Ecosystem services – If any aspect of ecosystem structure and function has a value, known or unknown, to its inhabitants, it can be classified as an ecosystem service. For example, photosynthesis, a natural ecosystem process, provides food and fiber, and storage of high water by wetlands provides a flood control service. Ecosystem services may have economic, social or cultural values and, therefore, they are important to current human activities; they may have scientific values and are important for future development; and they may control ecosystem functioning and are, therefore, important to a sustained flow of other goods and services. Such services are variously named in the literature as 'natural services,' 'nature's services' and 'natural or system functions.' (OAS, 1987)

Ecotax – A generic term describing a tax with a potentially positive environmental impact, for example energy taxes, transport taxes and taxes on the 'right' to pollute or impact natural resources. Also called an environmental tax.

Ecotone – A boundary area or buffer zone between two adjacent ecosystems, such as a tract of savanna between grasslands and forest. (EES)

Ecotourism – Travel and travel services undertaken to visit sites or regions of unique natural or historic quality.

Ecotoxicology – The science of poisons and toxic substances occurring in the environment and their effects. (EEA)

Edge of chaos (EOC) – Point between chaos and stasis where evolution is most likely to occur. The tendency of dynamic systems to self-organize to a state roughly midway between globally static (unchanging) and chaotic (random) states. (CSG)

EDUN project – EDUN is a socially conscious clothing company launched in spring 2005 by singer Bono and his spouse Ali Hewson with New York clothing designer Rogan Gregory. The company's mission is to help increase trade and create sustainable employment for developing areas of the world with an emphasis on Africa, providing a business model that others can replicate.

Effective cash – See '**Direct contribution**.'

Efficiency – Achievement of a goal at the lowest cost. (MW)

Effluent – Treated wastewater released from a water treatment facility.

EIONET – The European Environment Information and Observation Network is a collaborative network of the European Environment Agency and its member countries, connecting national focal points in the EU and accession countries, European topic centers and national reference centers. These organizations jointly provide information used for making environmental decisions in Europe and making EU policies more effective. EIONET is both a network of organizations and an electronic network (e-Eionet). (EEA)

El Niño – A climatic event occurring irregularly, but generally every 3–5 years, so named because it first became evident during the Christmas season at the surface of the eastern tropical Pacific Ocean in part created by seasonal changes in the direction of the tropical winds over the Pacific and abnormally warm ocean surface temperatures. Although most intense in the Pacific region, changes can disrupt weather patterns throughout the tropics and to higher latitudes.

Embassy – The official residence and/or office of an ambassador more formally referred to as the 'embassy office' and the 'embassy residence.' (MW)

Emerald Network – A network of areas of special conservation interest (ASCI), established in the territory of the contracting parties and observer States to the Bern Convention, including central and east European countries and the EU Member States. (EEA)

Emergence – System properties that are not evident from those of the parts. Higher-level phenomena that cannot be reduced to that of the simpler constituents and need new concepts to be introduced. (CSG)

Emerging countries/economies – An informal designation based on growth rates and economic projections, as well as consumption patterns and development indictors classifying certain countries in between being classified as either developed or developing including, among others, Brazil, Chile, China, India, Mexico and Venezuela. These countries will likely reach the economic and development threshold to be viewed as developed or donor nations in the coming decade. (UNW) See '**Transition countries**.'

Emission permit – A non-transferable, non-tradable allocation of entitlement by a government to an individual firm to emit a specified amount of a substance. (EM)

Emissions – The release of greenhouse gases and/or their precursors into the atmosphere over a specified area and period of time. (UNFCCC)

Emissions cap – A legislated or negotiated limit on the amount of greenhouse gases that a company or country can legally emit. (NRDC)

Emissions standards – The maximum amount – either rate or concentration – of a particular pollutant that may legally be released into the air from a single pollutant source.

Emissions trading – Emissions trading is a regulatory program that allows firms the flexibility to select cost-effective solutions to achieve established environmental goals. With emissions trading, firms can meet established emissions goals by: (a) reducing emissions from a discrete emissions unit; (b) reducing emissions from another place within the facility; or (c) securing emission reductions from another facility. Emission trading encourages compliance and financial managers to pursue cost-effective emission reduction strategies and oftentimes catalyzes emitting entrepreneurs to develop the means by which emissions can inexpensively be reduced. (CF)

Empowerment – The expansion of people's capacities and choices; the ability to exercise choice based on freedom from hunger, want and deprivation; and the opportunity to participate in, or endorse, decision making that affects their lives. (UNEP) The expansion of freedom of choice and action, generally a participatory process that places or transfers decision-making responsibility and the resources to act into the hands of those who will benefit. This can include (i) capacity building for stakeholder organizations; (ii) strengthening the legal status of stakeholder organizations; (iii) stakeholder authority to manage funds, hire and fire workers, supervise work, and procure materials; (iv) stakeholder authority to certify satisfactory completion of a project and establish monitoring and evaluation indicators; and (v) support for new and spontaneous initiatives by stakeholders. (WB)

Enabling activities – Pre-project activities that include inventories, information gathering, policy analysis and the development of strategies and action plans that can provide a basis for making decisions regarding funding through the Global Environment Facility. (WB)

Enabling environment – Conditions surrounding an activity or system that facilitate the fulfillment of the potential of that activity or system. A policy document concerned with the preconditions for sustainable human development, including supportive laws and regulations, adequate resources and skills, broad understanding and acceptance of the differing roles of the state, private sector and civil society in sustainable human development, a common purpose and trust. (UNDP)

End-of-pipe solutions – Technologies such as scrubbers on smokestacks and catalytic converters on automobile tailpipes that reduce emissions of pollutants after they have formed. (EEA)

Endangered (species) – IUCN category of plant and animal taxa in danger of extinction and whose survival is unlikely if the causal factors continue operating. Included are taxa whose numbers have been reduced to a critical level or whose habitats have been so drastically reduced that they are deemed to be in immediate danger of extinction. In 2006, the IUCN estimated that the number of species in danger of extinction had reached 16,000 including one third of the planet's amphibians, 25 percent of the world's coniferous trees and a similar percentage of the world's mammals and nearly one in eight birds. (IUCN)

Endemic – Restricted to a specified region or locality. (GBS)

Energy efficiency – Technologies and measures that reduce the amount of electricity and/or fuel required to do the same work, such as powering automobiles, homes, offices and industries. (NRDC)

Enhanced Structural Adjustment Facility (ESAF) – A facility to provide medium term balance of payments assistance to countries facing protracted balance of payments difficulties.

Enrolled bill – A US term to indicate the final, certified bill sent to the president for signature and implying that House and Senate versions match exactly. (NRDC)

Entente – Denotes a close understanding between nations. It can be agreed orally or in writing, but as a concept is generally less binding than a treaty. (eD)

Entry into force – Multilateral treaties provide for a fixed number of states to express their consent and/or ratify an agreement, convention or treaty for entry into force. Other conditions are a fixed amount of time elapsed or a given percentage of states falling within a defined category. When these conditions are met a treaty enters into force for those states that gave the required consent. (VC)

Environment – See the essay p15.

Environment (human) – The compendium of natural, social and cultural values existing in a given place and moment that influences the material and psychological life of man. (PL)

Environment Fund – A voluntary fund of UNEP established to provide additional financing for environmental programs under the guidance of its Governing Council. (UNEP)

Environmental assessment – A term used almost interchangeably with environmental impact assessment, environmental appraisal and environmental analysis that refers to a formal procedure structured to ensure that selected environmental issues are considered in the early stages of the project cycle.

Environmental auditing – A process of assessing the impacts of existing developments, policies and projects, as opposed to environmental assessments that apply to new or greatly modified developments.

Environmental awards – There are literally hundreds of different local, national, regional and international environmental awards conferred throughout the world. We note a few of the most prominent.

- **Asahi Blue Planet Prize** – In 1992, the Asahi Glass Foundation established an award recognizing individuals and organizations that have made major contributions to solving global environmental problems. The prize was so named in the hopes that our blue planet will be a shared asset capable of sustaining human life far into the future. Areas of recognition include: environmental problems such as global warming, acid rain, ozone depletion, tropical rainforest destruction, destruction of ecosystems and species extinction, desertification, water pollution and environmentally induced afflictions; and environmental issues related to energy, population, food, water, environmental ethics, policies, disease caused by environmental change, waste treatment and recycling. Each year, two award recipients receive a certificate of merit, a commemorative trophy, and a supplementary award of JP¥50 million (about US$450,000).
- **King Hassan II Great World Water Prize** – An international award jointly established by the Government of the Kingdom of Morocco and the World Water Council, in memory of his Majesty King Hassan II. This award

recognizes cooperation and sound management in the development and use of water resources by an individual or organization. It is presented every three years at the opening ceremony of the World Water Forum and carries a stipend of US$100,000, a commemorative trophy and a certificate.

E

- **Kyoto World Water Grand Prize** – This award was created during the Third World Water Forum in March 2003 in Kyoto, Japan. This prize is funded by Soroptimist International of Kyoto, the Municipality of Kyoto and the World Water Council in recognition of an individual or organization whose grassroots-level activities addresses critical water needs of communities and regions including sustaining safe drinking water and preventing water contamination. The prize of JP¥5,000,000 (approximately US$45,000) is awarded every three years.

- **Nobel Peace Prize** – Although not an environmental prize, the Nobel Peace Prize was awarded to an environmental activist for the first time in 2004, when the Nobel Panel recognized the work of Dr Wangari Maathai of Kenya for her 'contribution to sustainable development, democracy and peace.' In addition, it should be noted that many Nobel laureates in other categories (physics, chemistry, medicine or physiology, literature and economics) have been recognized for work that has clear connection to improving and managing the environment. Each prize consists of a medal, personal diploma and monetary award (in 2006 Sek10 million, approximately US$1.3million). The Nobel prize(s) awarded annually since 1901 are recognized as the first and foremost international award.

- **Prince Sultan Din Abdulaziz International Prize for Water** – This international scientific prize is a significant contribution from the Kingdom of Saudi Arabia to global water issues and is intended to acknowledge special achievements by innovative scholars and scientists as well as applied organizations in the realm of water resources worldwide. The monetary award (one million Saudi Riyals, approximately US$266,000) is accompanied by a gold medallion, trophy and certificate in five thematic areas: creativity, surface water, groundwater, alternative (non-traditional) water resources, and water resources management and protection.

- **Stockholm Water Prize** – The Stockholm Water Prize is a global award presented annually to an individual, organization or institution for outstanding water-related activities in the fields of aid, awareness building and education, technology, management or science. The Stockholm Water Prize was founded by Swedish and international companies in collaboration with the City of Stockholm and first presented in 1991. The award includes a US$150,000 stipend and a crystal sculpture.

- **UNEP Global 500 Environmental Award** – Each year the UN Environment Programme (UNEP) names an unspecified number of individuals and organizations to receive the UNEP Global 500 Environmental Award for environmental achievement in helping to protect and better manage our natural resources.

- **UN Sasakawa Environment Prize** – The UNEP Sasakawa Environment Prize is one of the most prestigious environmental awards in the world. This international environment prize was recommended at the United Nations Conference on the Human Environment in Stockholm in 1972. This prize, then known as the Pahlavi Prize, was first awarded in 1976. In 1982, the UNEP Governing Council accepted an endowment of US$1 million from the Japan Shipbuilding Industry Foundation to finance this award in perpetuity. Since that time, the endowment has been administered by UNEP. Now known as the UNEP Sasakawa Environment Prize, it is awarded annually to leading environmentalists and recognizes the work of 'individuals or groups who have made outstanding global contributions to the management and protection of the environment'. The Prize aims to encourage achievement in any environmentally related field. Two awards of $200,000 are granted annually.

- **Volvo Environment Prize** – The Volvo Environment Prize was formally instituted in May 1988 by the Volvo shareholders with the objective of promoting research and development across the environmental spectrum, by acknowledging people who have made an outstanding contribution to understanding or protecting the environment through scientific, socio-economic or technological innovation or discovery of global or regional importance.

- **Zayed International Prize for the Environment** – The prize was founded by General H. H. Sheikh Mohamed Bin Rashid Al Maktoum, the Crown Prince of Dubai and Defense Minister of the United Arab Emirates in appreciation of the achievements of H. H. Sheikh Zayed Bin Sultan Al Nahyan, President of the United Arab Emirates and Governor of Abu Dhabi. The aim of the US$1 million prize is to recognize and promote pioneering contributions in the field of the environment in accordance with the philosophy and vision of H. H. Sheikh Zayed Bin Sultan Al Nahyan, and in support of *Agenda 21*. The Zayed Prize is presented every two years.

Environmental determinism – A view that the physical environment, rather than social conditions, determines culture. Those who believe this view say that humans are strictly defined by stimulus-response (environment-behavior) and cannot deviate. (WP)

Environmental diplomacy – The art of negotiating a shared way forward or a settlement to a dispute based on environmental issues that transcend countries and even continents and require international cooperation to solve. Addressing environmental problems such as global climate change, ozone depletion, ocean and air pollution, and resource use and degradation are frequently cited as issues requiring environmental (scientific) and diplomacy skills. These negotiations normally lead to an agreement or other mechanism defining the problem, identifying milestones or indicators of progress, and outlining a framework to facilitate ongoing discussions and/or monitor progress. (USDOS)

Environmental economics – A market-based approach to achieving a sustainable economy that integrates long-term economic growth, environmental quality and social fairness through innovative taxes, tax incentives, auctioned permits and other market-based mechanisms. (PPRC)

Environmental equity – Equal protection from environmental hazards afforded to individuals, groups or communities regardless of any social or economic conditions or status. (USEPA)

Environmental ethics – A theoretical and applied field of study that seeks a reunification of humans with nature. (EES)

Environmental footprint (individual) – An environmental footprint is a subjective measure aimed at determining how our individual actions impact the Earth based on a number of criteria including renewable and non-renewable resources. It is considered a subjective measure because of the infinite number of criteria that can be measured and the individuality of how acceptable impact and quality of life are defined. (WP)

Environmental footprint (industry) – For an industrial setting, this is a subjective measure of a company's environmental impact determined by a comparison of the amount of depletable raw materials and nonrenewable resources it consumes to make its products, with the quantity of wastes and emissions that are generated in the process. Traditionally, for a company to grow, the footprint had to get larger. Today, finding ways to reduce the environmental footprint is a priority for leading companies. (WP; UNEP) See '**Life-cycle approaches.**'

Environmental governance – Process that links and harmonizes policies, institutions, procedures, tools and information to allow participants (public and private sector, NGOs, local communities) to manage conflicts, seek points of consensus, make fundamental decisions, and be accountable for their actions. (IDB)

Environmental impact assessment (EIA) – A process of evaluating and suggesting management and mitigation scenarios for the impacts arising for a new development at the various stages of the project cycle.

Environmental indicators – Environmental indicators both quantify and simplify complex scientific information. The approach is to identify a single measure or a small number of measures of environmental pressure, state and response for a limited set of issues. For example, UNEP and OECD use climate change with greenhouse gas emissions as a pressure indicator, concentrations of GHGs as a pressure as a state indicator and environmental measures as a response indicator. Other issues for which indicators have been developed include ozone depletion, eutrophication, acidification, toxic contamination, urban environmental quality, biodiversity and waste. The World Bank categorizes issues into source indicators (agriculture, forest, marine resources, water and subsoil assets); sink or pollution indicators (climate change, acidification, eutrophication, toxification); life support indicators (biodiversity, oceans, special lands such as wetland); and human impact indicators (health, dependence on water and air quality as well as occupational exposure, food security and quality, housing, waste and natural disasters). (AM)

Environmental Integrity Group (EIG) – A coalition working within the UNFCCC that includes Mexico, the Republic of Korea and Switzerland.

Environmental justice – A social science term used to describe injustices in the way natural resources are used. Environmental justice is considered a holistic effort to analyze and overcome the power structures that have traditionally thwarted environmental reforms. (WP)

Environmental law – A body of law, which is a system of complex and interlocking statutes, common law, treaties, conventions, regulations and policies that seeks to protect the natural environment that may be affected, impacted or endangered by human activities. Some environmental laws regulate the quantity and nature of impacts of human activities: for example, setting allowable levels of pollution. Other environmental laws are preventive in nature and seek to assess the possible impacts before the human activities occur (environmental impact assessment). Groups and individuals seeking environmental protections for general public benefit practice environmental law in the public interest, but it is mostly practiced in the private interest, by groups and individuals that undertake polluting or environmentally destructive activities, and who seek to avoid violating environmental laws in the process. (WP)

Environmental management – The mobilization of resources and the use of government to control the use, improvement or conservation of both natural and economic goods and services in such a way that conflicts created by that use, improvement or conservation are minimized. (OAS, 1987)

Environmental Management Group (EMG) – An institution established by the UN General Assembly that focuses on the linkages between environment and development. Chaired by the Executive Director of UNEP, the goal of the EMG is to coordinate and promote joint action within the United Nations in the areas of environmental management and human settlements. (UNEP)

Environmental mitigation – Measures taken to reduce the impact of a potential risk or after a natural hazard to reduce the chances of it occurring again. (EES)

Environmental protection – Actions at the international, national and local levels to prevent and ameliorate deterioration of human environments. Such actions include conservation efforts, recycling, waste reduction and disposal, and the development of cleaner and safer technologies.

Environmental quality – The relative capacity of an environment to satisfy the needs and wants of the individual or society 'surrounded' by that environment. (OAS, 1987)

Environmental refugee – People who are forced to leave their home, temporarily or permanently, because of a potential environmental hazard (naturally occurring or man-induced) or a disruption in their life-supporting ecosystems. (UNEP) See '**Diaspora**,' '**Refugee**,' '**Environmental security**.'

Environmental risk – Likelihood, or probability, of injury, disease, or death resulting from exposure to a potential environmental hazard.

Environmental security – A complex issue that involves societal efforts to protect the health and productivity of ecological systems, to render their future secure, and to ensure their stability in terms of the goods and services they provide. It also involves repercussions of the state of the environment upon national and international strategic issues. It is generally defined in terms of eight broad issues: population growth rates; mortality, disease and hunger; national debt and world commodity prices; despoliation of regional (transboundary) environments and resources; political decision making and environment; natural resource conflicts; military security; and management of the global commons and extraterritorial claims. (EES)

Environmental stressor – Any environmental factor whose presence, absence or abundance is the main factor restricting the distribution, numbers or condition of an organism. (EES)

Environmental sustainability – Sustainability of the ecological services on which humans depend, directly and indirectly. (AM)

Environmental Sustainability Index (ESI) – A measure of the overall progress towards environmental sustainability developed by the World Economic Forum. The annual ESI ranking evaluates countries based on 22 core indicators each of which combines two to six variables for a total of 67 underlying criteria. (WEF) See '**Sustainability assessment measures**.'

Environmental terrorism – See '**Eco-terrorism**.'

Environmental toxicology – Concerns the identification and quantification of possible adverse effects on living organisms as a result of exposure to environmental contaminants. (EES)

Envoy – A senior diplomat. (MW)

Epidemic – A very fast spreading disease. (MW)

Epistemic community – As defined by Haas (1992), an epistemic community is a 'network of professionals with recognized expertise and competence in a particular domain and an authoritative claim to policy-relevant knowledge within that domain or issue area. They can be identified by a shared set of normative and principled beliefs, shared causal beliefs, shared notions of validity, and a common policy enterprise.'

Equal per capita concept – A concept that implies that the total national 'right to emit' carbon is based on population size and a basic per capita emissions quota.

Equity (1) – Impartial or just treatment, requiring that similar cases be treated in similar ways.

Equity (2) – In the environmental sense, the planned location of toxic or waste facilities in regions throughout the socio-economic strata. (NRDC)

Equity principle – A principle relating to burden sharing and the distribution of costs and benefits that can be temporal (intergenerational) or spatial (among countries and communities).

Erga omnes – 'Toward all,' wrongful acts that harm everyone and not simply one injured party. (BLD)

Estuary – A bay or inlet, often at the mouth of a river, in which large quantities of freshwater and seawater mix together. (NRDC; MW)

Ethical trading initiative – A UK initiative linking NGOs, private sector companies, trade unions and other investors aimed at improving corporate codes of practice to ensure that the supply chain working conditions for products produced in developing countries for the UK market. (WP)

Ethical values – Statements of ethical principles that inform the private and social valuation of biological resources. (GBA)

EU3 – An informal coalition comprising Britain, France and Germany that has taken stands on issues of importance to the EC, including security, trade and environment. As the EU's three largest economies, this grouping has substantial influence at both the EC and world scales. (EU) See '**G3**.'

EU3+ – The EU3 plus the United States, Russia and China who become involved when issues of importance to the EC are also important to one or more of the other countries or regions. (EU)

EU6 – An informal grouping including Italy, Germany, France, Spain, Belgium and Luxembourg that are perceived by some to have the strongest commitment to preserving a common European policy process.

EU-Rio Group – Established in 1986, the EU-Rio Group is a key forum for political dialogue among foreign ministers from the EU and Latin American regions and one of the main platforms through which EU–Latin American relations are enhanced, and the direction of the relationship discussed. (EU)

Euro (€) – The official currency of 12 of the original 15 EU Member States, which replaced national currencies in all countries except Britain, Denmark and Sweden on 1 January 2002. Several Member States admitted in 2004 are examining the possibility/process of adopting the euro as their national currency. Slovenia adopted the euro in January 2007, with an effective date for circulation of the currency in mid-2007. Bulgaria is planning to switch to the euro in 2009 or 2010.

European Bank for Reconstruction and Development (EBRD) – A major multilateral donor located in Luxembourg.

European Blue Flag® – An EC Eco-label awarded to beaches and marinas. The award of the Blue Flag is based on 27 specific criteria for beaches and 16 specific criteria for marinas as applied to four aspects: water quality, environmental education and information; environmental management; and safety and services. The Blue Flag Campaign is owned and run by the independent non-profit organization Foundation for Environmental Education (FEE). (EEA)

European Blue Plan – The European Blue Plan has several meanings: a process of reflection on the Mediterranean region in all its vastness and complexity; a research center where this reflective process is carried out; and the infrastructure of a non-profit organization for administration of the Plan. (EEA)

European Commission (EC) – Regarded as the executive branch of the

EU, this group of appointed Commissioners deals with the Union's leadership on a daily basis. The EC ensures that the Member States adhere to EU laws, and intervenes directly whenever a State fails to abide by those laws. A politician appointed by the Council of Ministers heads the EC, which can be dissolved by the European Parliament. (EU)

European Commission Presidency – The President of the Commission is selected by consensus among members of the European Council and must subsequently be approved by the European Parliament, along with the remainder of the Commission. Thereafter, the president is accountable to Parliament, who may dismiss the Commission with a vote of no confidence. (EU) See '**European Council Presidency**.'

European Constitution – The Treaty establishing a Constitution for Europe, commonly referred to as the European Constitution, is an international treaty intended to create a constitution for the European Union. Representatives of the Member States of the Union signed it in 2004. Its main aims are to replace the overlapping set of existing treaties that comprise the Union's current constitution, and streamline decision making. (EU)

European Council (EC) – Leaders of the member national governments, and the elected President of the European Commission. The Council is the EU's main decision-making body established by the founding treaties in the 1950s. It represents the Member States and its meetings are attended by one minister from each of the EU's national governments depending on the agenda. If, for example, the Council is to discuss environmental issues, the meeting will be attended by the Environment Minister from each EU country and it will be known as the 'Environment Council.' The EU's relations with the rest of the world are dealt with by the 'General Affairs and External Relations Council,' but as the Council configuration also has wider responsibility for general policy issues, its meetings are attended by whichever Minister or State Secretary each government chooses. Altogether, there are nine different Council configurations: General Affairs and External Relations; Economic and Financial Affairs (ECOFIN); Justice and Home Affairs (JHA); Employment, Social Policy, Health and Consumer Affairs; Competitiveness; Transport, Telecommunications and Energy; Agriculture and Fisheries; Environment; and Education, Youth and Culture. (EU)

European Council Presidency – This position rotates every six months as each EU country in turn takes charge of the Council agenda and chairs all the meetings for a six-month period, promoting legislative and political decisions and brokering compromises between the Member States. If, for example, the Environment Council is scheduled to meet during the term when Finland holds the Council Presidency, it will be chaired by the Finnish Minister for the Environment. (EU) See '**European Commission Presidency**.'

European Currency Unit (ECU) – The European currency unit was an artificial 'basket' currency that was used by the Member States of the European Union (EU) as their internal accounting unit. The ECU was conceived on 13 March 1979 by the European Economic Community (EEC), the predecessor of the European Union, as a unit of account for the currency area called the European Monetary System (EMS). The ECU was also the precursor of the new single European currency, the euro, which was introduced on 1 January 1999. (Antweiler, 2006)

European Development Fund – A development fund committed to under the Lomé Convention. (UNT)

European Environment Information and Observation Network (EIONET) – A collaborative network of the European Environment Agency and its member countries, connecting national focal points in the EU and accession countries, European topic centers and national reference centers. These organizations jointly provide information that is used for making decisions for improving the state of the environment in Europe and making EU policies more effective. (EEA)

European Environmental Agency (EEA) – The aim of the EEA, which was formally established in April 1999, is to establish a seamless environmental information system to assist the Community in its attempts to improve the environment and move towards sustainability, including the EU's efforts to integrate environmental aspects into economic policies. (EEA)

European Investment Bank (EIB) – A financial institution of the European Community that provides long-term lending to the member states of the European Union, approximately 50 percent of which is to the private sector. (EU)

European Monetary System (EMS) – A 1979 agreement that forced the nations of the EEC to bring their economies into a single-market community by 1986 with the signing of the Single European Market Act. The euro (€) became the official currency on 1 January 2002 in 12 of the original 15 EU Member States, with three exceptions in Britain, Denmark and Sweden. Several Member States admitted in 2004 are currently examining the possibility/process of adopting the Euro as their national currency. Slovenia became the 13th EU member to adopt the Euro in January 2007. (EU) See '**Euro**.'

European Nature Information System (EUNIS) – EUNIS has two main aims: to facilitate use of data by promoting harmonization of terminology and definitions, and to be a reservoir of information on environmentally important matters. EUNIS consists of a central unit integrating data models on species, habitats and sites; several secondary databases that are managed by different partners; and an increasing number of satellite databases. (EEA)

European Parliament (EP) – The only part of the EU governmental structure directly chosen by the electorate as representatives of their national parliamentary parties. There are 732 members of the EP. The number of MEPs that a nation can elect is based on population. The EP normally meets in Brussels, but as a result of political demands by France, meets one week each month in Strasbourg. (EU)

European Topic Centers (ETC) – Institutions/organizations contracted by the EEA to execute tasks identified in the multi-annual work program. They are designated by the management board after a competitive expertise/capacity selection process. Guiding principles for selection should be the cost-efficient use of existing and potential capacities in the member countries and avoidance of duplication of work and capacities. (EEA)

European Union (EU) – The EU was the dream of a group of French and German politicians aimed at avoiding war and increasing unity. In 1951, Belgium, France, Germany, Italy, Luxembourg and The Netherlands signed the Treaty of Paris. In 1957, the Treaty of Rome strengthened this commitment to cooperation when the EEC was created. In 1973, Denmark, Ireland and the United Kingdom joined the EEC, with Spain, Portugal and Greece following shortly after. The EU was formalized in the European Union Treaty, more commonly referred to as the Treaty of Maastricht (The Netherlands), in 1993. Sweden, Finland and Austria joined in 1995, bringing the total number of EU Member States to 15. In May of 2004, 10 new States, mostly from the former Warsaw Pact bloc joined the EU including Cyprus, Czech Republic, Estonia, Hungary, Malta, Lithuania, Latvia, Poland, Slovakia and Slovenia, bringing the total number of Member States to 25. Bulgaria and Romania entered the Union in January 2007, bringing the total number of Member States to 27. In October 2005 EU members initiated negotiations with Turkey and Croatia, potentially leading to their accession into the EU although no specific timetables were approved. (EU)

European Union Directive(s) – A European Union term indicating a mutually binding, collective decision made by the Member States, acting through their National Government Ministers, in the Council of the EU and the Parliament. A Directive is only binding in any Member State when it has been transposed into national law. For example the EU Drinking Water Directive (98/83/EC) of 3 November 1998, concerning the quality of water intended for human consumption is intended to protect human health by laying down healthiness and purity requirements, should be matched by drinking standards by all Member States. (EEA)

European Union law – The EU is unique among international organizations in having a complex and highly developed system of internal law which has direct effect within the legal systems of its Member States. There are three primary souces of EU law: (1) treaties (primary legislation); (2) regulations directives, decisions and recommendations and opinions made by the Union's institutions in accordance with existing treaties (secondary legislation); and (3) decisions by the European Court of Justice. (EEA, WP) See '**European Constitution**.'

European Union recommendation – A non-binding instrument of indirect action aiming at preparation of legislation in Member States, differing from the Directive only by the absence of obligatory power. (EEA)

European Union regulations – The most powerful form of EU law, regulations are directly and immediately applicable in all Member States. (EEA)

European Union, three pillars of – The Treaty of Maastricht, which established the EU, divided EU policies into three areas, called 'pillars': the first or Community pillar concerns economic, social and environmental policies; the second or Common Foreign and Security Policy (CFSP) pillar concerns foreign policy and military matters; and the third or Police and Judicial Cooperation in Criminal Matters (PJCC) pillar concerns cooperation in the fight against crime. (EEA; EU)

European Union Treaty – Europe's constitutional law; treaties comprising its primary legislation. (EEA; WP)

Euroscience – A pan-European association, founded in 1997, and including individuals interested in constructing a 'scientific Europe' from the bottom-up. It represents European scientists of all disciplines in order to: (1) provide an open forum for debate on science and technology; (2) strengthen the links between science and society; (3) contribute to the creation of an integrated space for science and technology in Europe; and (4) influence science and technology policies throughout the continent. (ES)

EU Troika – Generally a grouping of three high level officials from the EU system and/or Member States who are empowered to represent the EC in addressing a particular issue. (EU)

Eutrophic – An aquatic environment enriched with nutrients, usually associated with high plant productivity and low oxygen levels. (SFWMD)

Eutrophication – The nutrient enrichment of waters that results in the stimulation of an array of symptomatic changes, among which increased production of algae and macrophytes, deterioration of water quality and other symptomatic changes, are found to be undesirable and interfere with water uses. (UNESCO) A process by which a body of water becomes enriched in dissolved nutrients (as phosphates) that stimulate the growth of aquatic plant life usually resulting in the depletion of dissolved oxygen. (MW)

Evapotranspiration – The process by which water is released to the atmosphere by evaporation from a water surface or movement from a plant surface (more specifically known as transpiration). (SFWMD)

E-waste – Discarded computers, printers, copying machines, fax machines, mobile phones and other electronic equipment. (EU)

Ex propio motu – On its own accord. (BLD)

Exalted rank – Refers to a non-elected person who receives his/her title from blood lines (inherited) or marriage (appointed). (MW)

Ex-ante environmental evaluation – A forward-looking assessment of the likely future effects of a given environmental policy or decision. (eD; EEA)

Ex aequo et bono – Literally, in justice and fairness. Something to be decided *ex aequo et bono* is something that is to be decided by principles of what is fair and just. Most legal cases are decided on the strict rule of law. For example, a contract will be normally upheld and enforced by the legal system no matter how 'unfair' it may prove to be. But a case to be decided *ex aequo et bono* overrides the strict rule of law and requires instead a decision based on what is fair and just given the circumstances. (BLD)

Excellency – A title generally reserved for a Head of State or Cabinet-level Minister. (MW)

Exclusive economic zone (EEZ) – Exclusive Economic Zone as defined in the Law of the Sea. Within this zone (which may extend to 200 nautical miles under UNCLOS III), the state has jurisdiction and control over the exploration, exploitation, management and conservation of the natural resources of the waters, seabed and subsoil. Ships and aircraft enjoy high seas freedoms of navigation and over flight unless they infringe upon the coastal state's economic rights within the EEZ.

Excursion (in water quality) – A constituent concentration that is of potential concern as an exceedance and possible violation of a water quality criterion. 'Excursion' indicates some uncertainty in the interpretation of the reported constituent concentration requiring further evaluation of background conditions, ancillary data, quality assurance and historical data. (SFWMD)

Executing agency – Within the GEF, the organization that actually carries out the project work in the field with a team of national counterparts. (GEF) See '**Implementing agency**.'

Ex gracia – Something that is done as a gesture of goodwill and not on the basis of an accepted legal obligation. (eD)

Exhaustible resources – See '**Non-renewable resources**.'

Existence value – The value of knowing that a particular species, habitat or ecosystem does and will continue to exist. It is based on the perceived value of the environmental asset unrelated to current or future use.

Exotic species – Species of plants or animals that are not naturally found in a region (non-indigenous). (SFWMD)

Expert group – A group of academics, scientists and government representatives from specialized ministries or departments and NGOs convened to address specific issues without regard to political interest.

Exploitable water resources – That part of the water resource that is considered to be available for development under specific technical, economic and environmental conditions. (FAO)

Ex-post evaluation – An evaluation of a completed project carried out either immediately after project completion or at a later time when the project impacts are fully developed. (WB)

***Ex-situ* collection** – A collection of plant genetic resources for agriculture that are maintained outside their natural habitat. (CBD)

***Ex-situ* conservation** – The conservation of plant genetic resources for food and agriculture outside their natural habitats. (CBD)

External forcing – Influence on the Earth system (or one of its components) by an external agent such as solar radiation or the impact of extra-terrestrial bodies such as meteorites. (NASA)

Externality – An external effect; interactions between economic agents not involving market transactions. By way of their production or consumption activities, economic agents may unintentionally generate positive or negative effects for the well-being of other agents. Externalities may be negative: an industry whose waste pollutes a river might affect the welfare of fishermen. Conversely, conservation of local plant varieties by farmers, who are not remunerated for this, is a positive externality. The costs (or benefits) imposed on one individual or firm by the actions of another, for which the latter does not pay (or receive) compensation. (WB)

Extinct – IUCN category *Ex* for taxa that are no longer known to exist in the wild after repeated searches of their type localities and other known or likely places. (CBD)

Extractive Industries Review (EIR) – A process that the World Bank Group has launched to discuss its future role in the extractive industries with concerned stakeholders. The aim is to produce a set of recommendations that will guide involvement of the World Bank Group in the sectors of oil, gas and mining. (WB)

Extractive reserve – The main idea behind extractive reserves is that local communities own and control the harvesting of forest (wetland, savannah, etc.) products. In theory, much of the natural cover remains while people continue to live in the area. Rather than fence people away from the forest, extractive reserves are supposed to permit people to manage the forest without destroying it. (EES)

Extrabudgetary – Funding outside of the core or regular funds of an agency or organization. (IDB)

Extraterritoriality – The exercise by one nation, as the result of a formally concluded agreement, of certain sovereign functions within the territory of another nation. For example, at times The Netherlands represents the interests of Luxembourg in certain international fora. (eD)

Extreme poverty – A situation in which a person or household lacks the resources to consume a certain minimum amount of food judged to be necessary for adequate nutrition, even in the case when all resources are devoted to food.

Extrinsic value – A form of judgment that allows a continuum of possibilities, that is a measure of goodness or presence. (CSG)

Ff

Factor 4/Factor 10 – The concept that, in order for sustainability to be reached and maintained during a period when human populations are likely to double in size and average living standards to increase significantly, industry should increase its resource conversion efficiency by a minimum factor of 4 (i.e. resource productivity should grow fourfold). Put another way, the amount of wealth extracted from one natural resource unit should be quadrupled. Since industrialized societies typically consume 20–30 times more than less developed ones, some people are calling for a factor 10 increase in conversion efficiency in the developed world. (RMI; Wu)

Factor 10 – Refers to a number of European countries that met for the first time in 1992 in Carnoules, France because of mounting concerns over the role of human-induced global material flows, and the ecological ramifications of their unchecked growth. Their aim is to draw attention to the need for substantially reducing global material flows in a timely manner. (EEA)

Fair-trade – A system of international commerce based on equitable relationships between producers and consumers. The goal is for producers, often farmers in impoverished areas, to receive more of what consumers pay for the goods. Specifically, a fair trade organization pays producers more than the market rate, provides credit to the producers, builds long-term relationships with them, encourages them to form democratic co-ops, encourages ecologically sustainable production and bypasses intermediaries between producers and consumers. (WP) See '**Certification**.'

FAO – See '**United Nations Food and Agriculture Organization**.'

FAO Code of Conduct for Responsible Fisheries (1995) – This Code sets out principles and international standards of behavior for responsible practices with a view to ensuring the effective conservation, management and development of living aquatic resources, with due respect for the ecosystem and biodiversity. The Code recognizes the nutritional, economic, social, environmental and cultural importance of fisheries and the interests of all those concerned with the fishery sector. The Code takes into account the biological characteristics of the resources and their environment and the interests of consumers and other users. (FAO)

Fast track authority – In the US it is the authority given to the president by the Congress that allows the president to send to the Congress completed international trade agreements for a vote of 'yes' or 'no.' Under fast track authority, Congress is not allowed to alter or amend the agreements. (USAID)

Fast tracking – The process of reducing the number of sequential relationships and replacing them typically with parallel relationships, usually to achieve shorter overall durations but often with increased risk.

Fauna – All the animal species found in a given area. (MW)

Feedback – A linking of the output of a system back to the input. Traditionally this can be negative, tending to return the system to a wanted state, or positive tending to diverge from that state. (CSG)

Feed-in law – Refers to the legal requirement, in some parts of the world, requiring a public utility to purchase electricity generated from renewable private sources and incorporate it into the grid available to their subscribers. (USEPA)

Fertility rate – The average number of children that would be born alive to a woman during her lifetime if she were to bear children at each age in accord with prevailing age-specific rates. (UNCHS)

Filibuster – A strategy used to delay or stop a vote by making long speeches and encouraging unending debate. (MW)

Final act – A formal summary statement, drawn up (and sometimes witnessed or signed by the participants) at the conclusion of a meeting.

Final Act of the Uruguay Round for Establishing the World Trade Organization – A report that includes a section on 'Decision on Trade and Services and the Environment' that outlined the need to negotiate issues of trade and their relationship with the environment within a sustainable development context. These issues are being discussed at the regional and sub-regional levels in a variety of fora as a means of informing the WTO. The Uruguay Round Agreement also formally established the Trade and Environment Committee.

Financial mechanism – A mechanism of the UNFCCC that enables the transfer of funds and technology to developing countries on a grant or concessional basis, under the guidance of the COP. (UNFCCC)

Finnish International Development Agency (FINNIDA) – The principal agency through which Finland provides technical assistance and delivers foreign aid.

First World – A term referring to developed (in general OECD) countries.

Fiscal year – The 12-month period for which the annual budget is developed and implemented and which does not necessarily correspond to the calendar year. (MW)

Fisheries management – The management of fish and shellfish resources. It includes the setting of rules for how fishing can be carried out, the protection and enhancement of fish resources, the development of fisheries and the mediation of conflict between stakeholders. (EES)

Fission – The process whereby the nucleus of a particular heavy element splits into (generally) two nuclei of lighter elements, with the release of substantial amounts of energy. (NRDC)

Flemming principle – A set of criteria that defines the terms and conditions (salaries, allowances, fringe benefits) of employing general service (administrative) staff in the UN system and monitored by the International Civil Service Commission and the various staff committees in UN system organizations and other organizations using the UN system. In general terms, it means that the conditions of service should be among the best, without being the best. (UN) See '**Noblemaire Principle**.'

Flexibility mechanisms – A term that refers to the three cooperative implementation mechanisms under the Kyoto Protocol (Joint Implementation, International Emissions Trading and Clean Development Mechanism) and which includes the notion of differentiated commitments. (EM)

Flora – All the plant species found in a given area. (MW)

Fluorocarbons – Carbon-fluorine compounds that contain other elements such as hydrogen, chlorine or bromine. Common fluorocarbons include chlorofluorocarbons (CFCs), hydrochlorofluorocarbons (HCFCs), hydrofluorocarbons (HFCs), and perfluorocarbons (PFCs).

Focal area (also thematic area) – The four main areas that the GEF works in. They are climate change, biological diversity, international waters and ozone layer depletion. (GEF)

Focal point (1) – An arrangement whereby a national entity reflects an international public interest.

Focal point (2) – A formal representative nominated by a government to receive and distribute communications on a given topic as well as to participate in meetings on the subject on its behalf.

Foggy Bottom – A colloquial term originally referring to the marsh area near the Washington DC's Potomac River and now commonly used to refer to the US State Department. (USDOS)

Food chain – A sequence of organisms each of which uses the next to its benefit, primarily as a food source. (USEPA)

Food security – Concept that discourages opening the domestic market to foreign agricultural products on the principle that a country must be as self-sufficient as possible for its basic dietary needs. (WTO)

Force majeure – Literally, 'greater force'; a clause designed to protect against failures to perform contractual obligations caused by unavoidable events beyond the party's control, such as natural disasters or wars. (UN; MW)

Force multiplier (1) – The tendency by an invading or occupying force to consider aid and other humanitarian workers as automatically supporting their role, particularly when such force is authorized by the UN Security Council or viewed as being supported by the Member States. (USDOS)

Force multiplier (2) – The assumption (by the invading or occupying force) or perception (by those being invaded or occupied) that aid and other humanitarian workers and organizations support the goals of an invading or occupying force when such agencies receive direct financial support from such sources. (USDOS)

Foreign direct investment (FDI) – The act of building productive capacity directly in a foreign country. Investment in one country by firms owned in another country.

Forest certification – A process of certifying and labeling wood that has been harvested from a well-managed forest including social, cultural, marketing and chain of custody aspects as components of the overall management of the resource. (NRDC) See '**Forest Stewardship Council**,' '**Certified wood**,'.

Forest landscape restoration (FLR) – A planned process implemented to restore a specific forest type and enhance human well-being in deforested or degraded forest landscapes that requires choices at a landscape scale where overall landscape benefits are more important than choices relating to individual forest stands or sites.

Forest management – The practical application of biological, physical, quantitative, managerial, economic, social and policy principles to the regeneration, utilization and conservation of forests to meet specified goals and objectives while maintaining the productivity of the forest. (IUFRO)

Forest Principles – The non-legally binding authoritative statement of principles to guide the management, conservation and sustainable development of all types of forests agreed to by nearly 180 governments at UNCED in 1992. (UNCED; UNT)

Forest Stewardship Council (FSC) – An international, non-profit organization that offers forest certification internationally.

Forum – A medium of open discussion or expression of ideas. (MW)

Fossil fuel – Any hydrocarbon deposit that can be burned for heat or power, such as petroleum, coal and natural gas (or any fuel derived from them). (NASA)

Fossil water – See '**Non-renewable natural resources**.'

Founex Report – The written product of a meeting in Founex, Switzerland called to prepare for the 1972 Stockholm Conference that discussed the links between development and environmental protection in the Third World. (CIPA)

Fourth World – This term refers to peri-urban poor living in unplanned, informal and/or unauthorized settlements without the benefits of public services such as electricity, water and sewage/sanitation. They are referred to as the 'fourth world' as they are generally not covered by the social net, operate in a parallel economy, and are not counted or included in government statistical surveys or records; implying that they are even worse off than those from the Third World.

Fragile ecosystem – See the essay p20.

Fragile states – A 2006 World Bank classification of 26 States at risk of political or economic collapse. (WB)

Fragmentation – The breaking up of extensive landscape features into disjunctive, isolated, or semi-isolated patches as a result of land-use changes. (BCHM)

Framework – A broad overview, outline or skeleton within which details can be added. (GEF)

Framework convention – Agreements under which protocols can be developed to address specific subjects that require more detailed and specialized negotiations. (UNFCCC)

Free market-oriented reforms – See '**Structural adjustment loans**.'

Free trade – Trade in which goods can be imported and exported without barriers in the forms of tariffs, quotas or other restrictions. (WTO)

Free-rider problem – In debate of the UNFCCC the 'free-rider problem' refers to the possibility that some parties may take advantage from climate action by others without themselves accepting commitments or taking action.

Friends of the chair (president) – A few prominent negotiators invited by the chair/president to help informally in developing consensus on issues. (UNFCCC)

Friends of the Earth International (FoEI) – FoEI was founded in 1971 by four organizations from France, Sweden, England and the US. Today's federation of 66 groups grew from annual meetings of environmentalists from different countries who agreed to campaign together on certain crucial issues, such as nuclear energy and whaling. In 1998, the combined number of members and supporters of Friends of the Earth groups was close to 1 million, and the FoEI umbrella united almost 5000 local activist groups. The combined annual budget of FOE groups was close to US$200 million, and together they employed close to 700 full-time staff members. (FOE)

Friends of the United Nations – Founded in 1985, Friends of the United Nations is an independent, non-partisan organization dedicated to increasing awareness of the United Nations' activities. They work with educational institutions, corporations, the media, the international governments and other organizations to inform and educate people about the UN's efforts on behalf of peace, human rights, the environment, children and responsible economic development. This NGO is committed to facilitating communication between economically and socially diverse world populations, and creating solutions to global problems. Many national chapters of the Friends of the UN have been established throughout the world. (UN)

Frozen Ark – A British-led program involving zoos, museums, captive breeding programs and laboratories from many countries that stores DNA samples from endangered animal species for scientific purposes including providing a source for genetic variation that otherwise might be lost. (The Frozen Ark, nd) See '**Doomsday vault**.'

F.S.O. – A US term referring to the role of a career diplomat; Foreign Service Officer. (USDOS)

Fugitive fuels – Fuel emissions that may or may not be fully controlled although in most cases they are not accidental. Examples of fugitive emissions are leaks from gas pipelines and valves, venting and flaring of gases, methane emissions from coal seams and vapor given off by petroleum stores. (UNFCCC)

Full powers – A document emanating from the competent authority of a State designating a person or persons to represent the State for negotiating, adopting or authenticating the text of a treaty, for expressing the consent of the State to be bound by a treaty, or for accomplishing any other act with respect to a treaty. (VC)

Gg

G3 – The UK, Germany and France. A group formed in 2005 to assist the IAEA in working through issues related to nuclear power development and operation in the Islamic Republic of Iran.

G4 – Originally established by the four countries with the greatest hope of winning permanent seats on the proposed revised UN Security Council (Japan, Germany, India and Brazil). The G4 countries proposed in 2005 that the 15 member Security Council of 5 permanent and veto-wielding members and the 10 non-permanent and non-veto wielding members be expanded to 25 members, including 9 permanent members and 16 non-permanent members. Early discussions surrounding expanding permanent membership to the Council ruled out granting immediate veto power to new members. In early 2006 Japan left the G4 with the intent of opening direct talks with the US Government on a seat on the Council. (UN)

G5 ('old') – The five permanent Member States of the UN Security Council holding veto power (the UK, China, France, Russia, the US). (UN)

G5 ('new') – Group of the five largest European economies (the UK, France, Germany, Italy and Spain). (UN)

G6 ('old') – A trade-negotiating block comprising six major industrialized countries (the US, Japan, Germany, France, Italy and the UK). (UN)

G6 ('new') – A group formed in late 2005 primarily to deal with the issue of Iran's aspirations/rights to develop its nuclear power industry and comprising the old G5 plus Germany. (UN)

G7 (old) – The group of the seven largest industrialized economies/democracies whose responsibilities include setting the policies of the IMF and the World Bank (the US, Japan, Germany, France, the UK, Italy and Canada).

G7 (new) – The 'New G7' is a term that first came into use as the preparations for the 2006 G7 meeting were being discussed. It recognizes one of the original organizing principles of the G7, that being membership for the world's largest economies, no longer applied, as China's economy was larger than several of the existing members (France, the UK, Italy and Canada). However, the debate about China's inclusion also revolved around the condition of members also being democracies. (CFR, TWN) See '**CIFIC.**'

G8 – Group of eight main (largest GDP) industrialized democracies (G7+ Russia). The criteria for membership include: a democratic regime; a large economy; a high level of economic and institutional development; a convertible currency; membership in the WTO, the OECD and the International Energy Agency; and dedication to the goals and principles of international cooperation. (UNW)

G8+ – The G8 plus China.

G8+ (new) – The term 'New G8+' includes the G8+ countries, plus potentially India and Brazil, among others that will undoubtedly be noted as economies grow and the original members of the G8 are displaced according to the original criteria. (TWN; UN)

G10 – A group comprising the central bankers of Belgium, Canada, France, Germany, Italy, Japan, Luxembourg, The Netherlands, Sweden, Switzerland, the UK and the US who meet for the purpose of maintaining a mechanism to match the banking institutions' equity capital with regard to their operations, and defining the risks they run with regard to those operations. The 1988 Basle Agreement guides their work.

G13 – A concept proposed in 2005 at the UN Summit by The Netherlands together with 12 other countries supporting radical reform of the UN system including the elimination of many specialized organizations and combining the remaining functions into three strong operational agencies (development, humanitarian affairs and environment) plus the creation of global centers of excellence that would be charged with developing norms and standards and providing a platform for international dialogue on issues such as health, labor standards and agriculture. It would also organize all country-level activities under a single UN team leader responsible for a unified UN program in a given country (The Netherlands, Belgium, Canada, Denmark, France, Finland, Germany, Ireland, Luxembourg, Norway, Sweden, Switzerland and the UK). (UN) See '**United Nations Reform Process**.'

G15 – Group of 15. A summit level group of developing countries organized in 1989 that provides a platform to promote South–South cooperation and North–South dialogue. The group now has 19 members (Algeria, Argentina, Brazil, Chile, Colombia, Egypt, India, Indonesia, Iran, Jamaica, Kenya, Malaysia, Mexico, Nigeria, Peru, Senegal, Sri Lanka, Venezuela and Zimbabwe).

G20 – An international forum of finance ministers and central bank governors representing 19 governments, the EU and the Bretton Woods Institutions (Argentina, Australia, Brazil, Canada, China, France, Germany, India, Indonesia, Italy, Japan, Korea. Mexico, Russia, Saudi Arabia, South Africa, Turkey, the UK, the US, and the EU, plus the World Bank and the IMF).

G21 – A group of developing countries that coalesced at the WTO round in Cancun, Mexico in mid-2003 and is dedicated to negotiating an elimination of subsidies in all sectors, and particularly those provided in developed nations to sectors (such as agriculture) that directly impact the ability of developing nations to compete in the international marketplace. (UN)

G33 – A grouping of 40 developing countries whose work was assumed by the G20 from 1999. Several earlier seminars of the Group of 33 addressed international financial architecture and was convened at the initiative of the finance ministers and central bank governors of the G7. (WP) See **'Non-Aligned Movement.'**

G77 + China – A coalition of 135 members that aims to collectively articulate and promote the economic interests of the group and to enhance its negotiating position on all major issues in the UN. The chair rotates annually between nations and regions. The coalition currently has a Rome Chapter (at FAO), Paris Chapter (at UNESCO), Nairobi Chapter (at UNEP), Washington Chapter (at IMF and World Bank) and a Vienna Chapter (at UNIDO).

G90 – A group of the poorest developing countries that maintain an informal relationship based on trade principles and which operates within the WTO context. The G90 is an umbrella body of the African, Caribbean and Pacific (ACP) Group, including all HIPIC countries, and is the largest sub-grouping of Members States in the WTO. (TWN)

Gaia **hypothesis** – The hypothesis advanced by British scientist, James Lovelock, that the Earth's atmosphere, biosphere and its living organisms behave as a single system striving to maintain a stability that is conductive to the existence of life. (NASA; EES)

Gaia **'revenge' hypothesis** – The theory that predicts that humankind's abuse of the Earth's support systems is now making the stabilizing mechanism work against us. In short, the theory holds that the Earth has passed the point of return specifically triggered by climate change and life on the planet will never again be the same. (NASA)

Gap analysis – Systematic application of goals and criteria to determine what resources or values are currently protected and what needs to be protected.

Gazette/Gazetted – An official publication of a government or other constituted body such as a Parliament or legislature, similar in nature to the US Congressional Record, and generally required before a law enters into force. (MW)

GEF – See **'Global Environment Facility.'**

GEFable – A term used to describe a project proposal that meets the terms and conditions for a GEF grant.

Gender – The socially determined roles played by women and men, which can de determined by historical, religious, economic, cultural and ethnic factors. (UNDP)

Gender-related Development Index (GDI) – The GDI measures achievements in the same dimensions and variables as the Human Development Index (HDI), but captures inequalities in achievement between women and men. The greater the gender disparity in basic human development, the lower a country's GDI compared with its HDI. (AM)

Gene – The functional unit of heredity: the part of the DNA molecule that encodes a single enzyme or structural protein unit. (GBS)

General Agreement on Tariffs and Trade (GATT) – Originally signed by 23 nations in 1947, GATT is an international body devoted to eliminating import quotas, lowering tariffs, and otherwise promoting free, nondiscriminatory international trade. The Uruguay Round created the WTO as an international body in 1995 to administer the GATT. (WTO)

General Assembly – The highest principle organ of an intergovernmental organization that consists of representatives of all its Member States.

General circulation model (GCM) – A global, three-dimensional computer model of the climate system that can be used to simulate human-induced climate change. GCMs are highly complex and they represent the effects of such factors as reflective and absorptive properties of atmospheric water vapor, greenhouse gas concentrations, clouds, annual and daily solar heating, ocean temperatures and ice boundaries. The most recent GCMs include global representations of the atmosphere, oceans and land surface. (NASA)

General support staff – See '**G-level staff.**'

Genetic diversity – Variation in the genetic composition of individuals within or among species. (GBS)

Genetic material – Any material of plant origin containing functional units of heredity. (CBD)

Genetic resources – Genetic material of actual or potential value including the genes of plants, animals or other organisms. (CBD, EES)

Genetically modified organism (GMO) – An organism whose genetic characteristics have been changed by inserting a modified gene or a gene from another variety or species. Genetically modified organisms may be plants, animals or microorganisms.

Genocide – The deliberate and systematic destruction of a racial, political, cultural or religious group. (UN)

Genuine progress indicator (GPI) – A concept in green and welfare economics suggested as a replacement for GDP as a metric of economic growth. (WP)

Geoengineering – Rearranging the Earth's environment on a large scale to suit human needs and promote habitability. Examples include shielding the Earth from sunlight to reverse the effects of global warming, reversing or diverting the flows of major rivers, cloud seeding on a massive scale, desalination on a scale that could affect arid zone productivity, creating humidity on a regional scale, using large amounts of ocean water to cool regions or sub-regions. See '**Planetary engineering**.'

Geographic balance – See '**Quota, geographical**.'

Geographic information system (GIS) – A computer based system that stores, manipulates and displays spatial information. (EES)

Geothermal – Literally, heat from the Earth; energy obtained from the hot areas under the surface of the Earth. (NRDC)

German Technical Cooperation Agency (GTZ) – The principal agency through which Germany provides technical assistance and delivers foreign aid.

Gillnets – Walls of netting that are usually staked to the sea floor. Fish become entangled or caught by their gills. (NRDC)

G-level staff – A term used to denominate and categorize General Service or Administrative Support staff (and salary/benefit package) in the UN and OAS systems, starting at G1 and rising to G8. These staff are normally recruited on a local basis and paid using prevailing local rates and conditions. (UN)

Global benefits – Environmental benefits accrued at the global level as opposed to those gained nationally or locally through the development efforts of a government. (GEF)

Global Biodiversity Forum (GBF) – Mechanism founded in 1993 by IUCN, WRI and UNEP that acts to encourage analysis, dialogue and partnership on the main ecological, economic, social and institutional issues related to biodiversity at the local, national, regional and international levels. (CBD)

Global civil society – A term implying an extension of civil society into the transnational realm, where it constitutes something along the lines of a 'regime' composed of local, national and global NGOs. (Lipschutz, 1999)

Global Climate Coalition (GCC) – A coalition of energy-based industries that oppose the UNFCCC. (GCC)

Global Compact (GC) – A network of five UN agencies (HCHR, ILO, KNOP, UNIDO, UNEP) with private sector companies and other organizations formed in 2000 and promoting acceptance of 10 principles in the broad areas of human rights, labor standards, environmental responsibility, and corruption and aimed at responsible corporate citizenship (UN)

Global commons – A component of the Earth–atmosphere system that is claimed by no one but has the potential to be used by everyone – which carries the potential that, over time, it would be overused and destroyed. (UN)

Global cooling – A decrease over time of the average temperature of Earth's atmosphere and oceans generally ascribed to an increase in air pollution, resulting in less sunlight reaching the Earth's surface. The theory posits an overall cooling of the Earth and perhaps the commencement of glaciation or even an ice age. The Earth is generally not considered to be heading toward a period of global cooling at this time. (UNFCCC; WP) See '**Global dimming**.'

Global currency unit (GCU) – A proposed global currency unit based on the inflation-adjusted real GDP of the major economies. Implementing this concept does not imply issuing a new currency note, but rather a method for valuing the real market value of any existing currency in the global economy based on production costs and demand for goods and services and not speculation against future movements. Governments would issue bonds denominated in GCUs and hold them in their reserves to use to make cross-border payments in their own currency with payments settled inside an international clearinghouse using the GCU as the base unit of measure. (IMF) See '**European currency unit**.'

Global Development Learning Network (GDLN) – The GDLN is a worldwide partnership of distance learning centers and other public, private and nongovernmental organizations committed to development learning and development dialogue for lasting poverty reduction. Offering a unique combination of distance learning technologies and methods, GDLN facilitates timely and cost-effective knowledge sharing, consultation, coordination and training. (WB; UNESCO-IHE)

Global dimming – A term that refers to the reduction in the amount of sunlight reaching the Earth's surface due to increased aerosol particulate matter, pollution and water vapor, which absorb the solar energy and reflect sunlight back into space. Global dimming creates a cooling effect that may have led scientists to underestimate the effect of greenhouse gases on global warming. (UNFCCC; WP) See '**Global cooling**.'

Global Environment Facility (GEF) – An intergovernmental institution supported by its members that offers grants to cover the additional costs to a country's own actions for sustainable development to maximize agreed global environmental benefits in the areas of biodiversity, climate change, international waters, ozone layer depleting substances, persistent organic pollutants, and land degradation, primarily desertification and deforestation. Its secretariat is housed in the World Bank and its primary implementing agencies are the World Bank, UNDP and UNEP. New Executing Agencies under expanded opportunities include UNIDO, UNFAO, the Regional Development Banks and IFAD. These agencies have direct access to GEF Project Development Funds. (GEF) See '**GEFable**.'

G

- GEF Mid-size Project – A GEF grant for one time of up to US$1,000,000.
- GEF Project – A GEF grant that has no set limit.
- GEF Trust Fund (GEFTF) – Fund set up with the World Bank as Trustee, which consists of contributions received from members of the GEF and is used to fund grants. (GEF)
- GEF Working Paper Series – A series of documents that provide general information on GEF's work and more specific information on methodological approaches; scientific and technical issues; and policy and strategic matters. (GEF)
- GEF-PDF 'Block A' – A GEF grant of up to US$25,000.
- GEF-PDF 'Block B' – A GEF grant of up to US$750,000.
- GEF-PDF 'Block C' – A GEF grant of up to US$1,000,000.

Global environmental benefits – Benefits that accrue to the global community, for example the reduction of greenhouse gas emissions. (GEF)

Global environmental governance scenarios – The WBCSD defines three broad scenarios for global environmental governance. WBCSD claims that the current world of GEOPolity is failing but can be redesigned to succeed by insisting on new norm-setting procedures and new institutions, including establishment of a global environment organization. A second path to a sustainable future is to implement Jazz to scale in the business world.

- The FROG (first raise our growth) scenario calls for the resolution of economic challenges first. FROG is a business-as-usual scenario, leading to huge environmental costs, even in the eyes of business leaders.
- GEOPolity is a success scenario in which sustainability is vigorously pursued. In this case, people turn to government to focus the market on environmental and social ends and rely heavily on intergovernmental institutions and treaties.
- Jazz refers to a spirit, a world of unscripted initiatives,

decentralized and improvisational. In this world, there is abundant information about business behavior; good conduct is enforced by public opinion and consumer behavior. Governments facilitate, NGOs are very active, and business sees strategic advantage in doing the right thing.

Global Fund for the Environment (GFE) – An outcome of the 1992 Earth Summit, the fund was established to help preserve global biodiversity.

Global Mechanism (GM) – Established under the Convention on Desertification, the GM is in charge of promoting actions for the mobilization and channeling of substantial financial resources, and for the transfer of technology, on a grant basis, and/or on concessional or other terms, to affected developing country parties. (CD)

Global Ministerial Environment Forum – According to GA Resolution 53/242 of 28 July 1999 it is an annual, ministerial level, global environmental forum that meets together with the UNEP Governing Council and, in alternate years, takes the form of a special session of the Governing Council. Participants review important and emerging policy issues with due consideration for the need to ensure the effective and efficient functioning of the governance mechanism of the United Nations Environment Programme, as well as possible financial implications, and the need to maintain the role of the Commission on Sustainable Development as the main forum for high-level policy debate on sustainable development. (UN)

Global parliament – A concept that gathered formal support from about mid-2005 to ensure greater levels of citizen participation in decisions affecting global economics and the quality of life. The concept has been endorsed by the UNSG, the President of the World Bank, the Managing Director of the IMF, the Director General of the WTO and other world leaders but a clear strategy as to how to implement this idea has yet to emerge. Formally considered a utopian idea, the idea is gaining strength because it can no longer be ignored that decisions taken in one country or region have direct impacts on the lives of others as a result of globalization trends including trade, foreign direct investment, and capital flows, all of which is dispersing political authority throughout the international order. See '**New world order**.'

Global Policy Forum (GPF) – An NGO founded in 1993 that monitors policy making at the United Nations, promotes accountability of global decisions, educates and mobilizes for global citizen participation, and advocates on vital issues of international peace and justice.

Global tax – A view held by some segments of society that the 0.7 ODA goal is a global tax in disguise, meant to provide additional discretionary funds to the UN, World Bank and other multilateral organizations.

See '**Nations, 0.7**,' '**Millennium Project**;' '**Official development assistance**,' '**International Finance Facility**.'

Global village (1) – A utopian concept implying a world without restrictions to hinder trade or development while requiring shared policing of drug trafficking, terrorism and arms control. (WP)

Global village (2) – A term, coined by communicator Marshall McLuhan, describing how electronic mass media collapse space and time barriers in human communication, enabling people to interact and live on a global scale. In this sense, the globe has been turned into a village by the electronic mass media and the explosion in ICT. (WP)

Global warming – A theory based on an increasing number of scientific studies relating to an increase in the Earth's temperature caused, in part, by the 'greenhouse' effect being created by emissions of GHGs associated with human activities.

Global warming superfund – A proposed fund that would be supported by polluters from wealthy countries and be used for researching and promoting various green technologies. (UNW)

Global Water Challenge – A World Bank initiative aimed at mainstreaming water as a prime driver of social and economic development. (WB)

Global Water Initiatives (GWIs) – Institutions whose fundamental purpose is to advance the knowledge base regarding the world's inland water and its management. Since the 1980s, the core aim of many GWIs has expanded to include an active social and policy component aiming to improve access to potable water and sanitation across the globe. The phenomenon reflects a post-World War II trend toward collective approaches to resolving multinational issues in general and common-pool resources in particular. (Varady and Iles-Shih, 2005)

Global Water Partnership (GWP) – A working partnership, established in 1996, among all those involved in water management: government agencies, public institutions, private companies, professional organizations, multilateral development agencies and others committed to the Dublin–Rio principles. The GWP's objectives are to: clearly establish the principles of sustainable water resources management; identify gaps and stimulate partners to meet critical needs within their available human and financial resources; and support action at the local, national, regional or river basin level that follows principles of sustainable water resources management.

Globalization (1) – The increasing worldwide integration of markets for goods, services and capital, that began to attract special attention in the late 1990s.

Globalization (2) – A term used to encompass a variety of changes that were perceived to occur at about the same time, such as an increased role for large corporations (MNCs) in the world economy and increased intervention into domestic policies and affairs by international institutions such as the IMF, WTO and World Bank. (AD)

Globalization (3) – A term used to describe the increasing flow of goods, services, capital, technology, information, ideas and labor at the global level, driven by liberalization policies and technological change considered by proponents to be an integrating and inclusive force. (UN)

Goal – A set general purpose and direction; the end result of ultimate accomplishment toward which an effort is directed. (MW)

Goldilocks economy – A reference to the World Economic Forum and economies that are not too hot or too cold, but just right.

Good governance – Governance is the process of making and implementing decisions in the conduct of public affairs and in the management of public resources. Good governance includes a lack of corruption, freedom from human rights abuses and a firm regard for the rule of law.

Good neighborliness (principle of) – A principle of international law that calls for a broad standard of respect and recognition and which obligates states, enterprises and individuals to respect the rights of others to participate in the social development process. (BLD)

Good offices (1) – An effort by a third State (literally via the intervention by or assistance of), or by an individual or an international body, designed to facilitate communications and/or stimulate the processes of dispute settlement between two other states. (eD)

Good offices (2) – A term used to describe a service provided by one State to another (e.g. receipt of official correspondence, facilitating a meeting, providing a temporary visa). (MW)

Goodwill Ambassador – An honorary title given to an individual who can help promote an ideal or concept and frequently used by the UN or its Specialized Organizations. Oftentimes internationally recognized artists or senior statesmen are accorded this title as their name recognition can assist in furthering understanding of a particular issue and thereby generate financial or political support. (UN)

'GOUTHE' of water – Global Observatory of Units for Teaching, Training and Ethics. A UNESCO-IHP initiative aimed at stimulating and structuring cooperation and networking on water-related issues. It will act as a platform and alliance for information and communication, extending geographically limited partners and facilitating new partnerships. (UNESCO)

Governance – Concept describing the way power is exercised in the management of a country's economic and social resources through application of responsibility, participation, information availability, transparency and the rule of law. Governance is not equal to government, which is the art of administration at a given level of power. Rather, it is the art of coordinating administration actions between different territorial levels – one of which may be global. 'Governance is the sum of the many ways individuals and institutions, public and private, manage their common affairs.' (CGG, 1995)

Governing Council, UNEP (GC) – The 58-member governing body of the UNEP established in December 1975. The UNEP/GC reports to the General Assembly through the Economic and Social Council. Its responsibilities and functions include:

G

- promotion of international cooperation in environmental matters;
- general policy guidance for the direction and coordination of environmental programs within the UN system;
- reviews of global environmental conditions to ensure that emerging problems of international significance receive appropriate and adequate consideration by governments;
- promotion of participation of relevant international scientific and other professional communities for the acquisition, assessment and exchange of knowledge and information, and technical aspects of environmental programs within the UN system;
- continuous review of national and international environmental policies and their impact on developing countries including the additional costs that they may incur in the implementation of environmental programs and projects, and that ensures that such programs and projects are compatible with the development plans and priorities of those countries; and,
- review and approval of use of the Environment Fund. (UN; UNEP)

Grameen bank/banking – A system initiated in Bangladesh to provide small loans to the poorest of the poor. More than 25 Grameen-like lending institutions and systems have been instituted. On average they enjoy a 98 percent payback rate. The Grameen Bank (and its founder, Dr Muhammad Yunus), received the Nobel Peace Prize in 2006. See '**Microcredit**.'

Grassroots – People or society at a local level rather than at the center of major political activity.

Gray water/issues – See '**Water**.'

Great green wall, concept of – The term applied to China's efforts to reverse encroaching deserts throughout the country by planting 12 billion trees in five years. The Badain Jaran desert in the northwest and the Tengger Desert in the northwest continue to grow in spite of these efforts, while the government announced in 2006 that for the first time in its history the Gobi Desert on the outskirts of Beijing showed signs of shrinking by an average of 1283 km^2 (797 sq miles) annually since 2001.

Greater Mekong Sub-region (GMSR) – The name referring to the Mekong River watershed including countries that are members of the Mekong River Commission (Cambodia, Laos, Thailand, Vietnam) and countries which are not members of the Commission (China, Myanmar).

Green accounting – Systematic presentation of data on environmentally important stocks and flows (e.g. stocks of life-sustaining natural resources, flows of pollutants), accompanying conventional economic accounts (e.g. measures of gross domestic product) with the ultimate objective of providing a comprehensive measure of the environmental consequences of economic activity. (EEA) See '**Sustainability assessment measures**.'

Greenbelt – An area of land between a city or town and the countryside designed to limit the encroachment of urban areas onto rural land. It acts as a buffer zone between city and rural landscapes. (AM)

Green chemistry – The utilization of a set of principles that reduces or eliminates the use or generation of hazardous substances in the design, manufacture and application of manufactured products. It is a revolutionary science philosophy that seeks to unite government, academic and industrial communities by placing more emphasis on environmental impacts at the earliest stage of innovation and invention processes. This approach requires an open and interdisciplinary view of materials design, applying the principle that it is better to not generate waste in the first place, rather than disposing or treating it afterwards. (CGC)

Green collar jobs – A play on the terms white collar (office) and blue collar (factory), jobs related to retro-fitting a traditional industrial economy to one that is able to address environmental problems and produce environmentally friendly goods and services.

Green Cross International® – Founded in 1993 by Mikhail Gorbachev, the mission of GCI is to help ensure a just, sustainable and secure future for all by fostering a value shift and cultivating a new sense of global interdependence and shared responsibility in humanity's relationship with nature. GCI promotes legal, ethical and behavioral norms that ensure basic changes in the values, actions and attitudes of government, the private sector and civil society, necessary to build a sustainable global community; prevents/resolves conflicts arising from environmental degradation; and assists people affected by the environmental consequences of wars and conflicts.

Green diplomacy – A brand of diplomacy that relates traditional economic development issues to topics of significant relevance globally such as climate change, biodiversity, desertification, renewable energy, etc. (EU)

Green economics – Green economics loosely defines a theory of economics by which an economy is considered to be a component of the ecosystem in which it resides. A holistic approach to the subject is typical, such that economic ideas are commingled with any number of other subjects, depending on the particular theorist. (WP)

Greenfield site – Land on which no urban development has previously taken place; usually understood to be on the periphery of an existing built-up area. (EEA)

Greenhouse effect – Any change in climate over time whether due to natural variability or because of human activity. (IPCC) See '**Climate change**.'

Greenhouse gases (GHG) – The gaseous constituents of the atmosphere (water vapor, carbon dioxide, methane, nitrous oxide, and hydrofluorocarbons, perfluocarbons and sulphur hexafluoride) both natural and anthropogenic, that absorb and re-emit infrared radiation. (UNFCCC)

Green infrastructure – A system of parks, refuges and extractive reserves, combined with land-use regulations, carbon credits and other land management policies aimed at stimulating sustainable production of a range of forest/wetland goods and services, green businesses, and creating a green economic counterweight to the global economic forces driving unregulated harvesting of tropical forests and other unsustainable land-use practices. (CI)

Green Party/green party – The distinction is made between the more generic 'green parties' (lowercase) in a general sense of emphasizing environmentalism, and specific organized political parties with the name 'Green Party' (uppercase) that have grown up around a statement of principles called the Four Pillars and the consensus decision-making process built on them: Ecology (ecological sustainability); Justice (social responsibility); Democracy (appropriate decision making); and Peace (non-violence). (WP)

Greenpeace International® – Greenpeace is a non-profit organization founded in 1971, with a presence in 40 countries across Europe, the Americas, Asia and the Pacific and a membership of approximately 300,000 individuals. Its international headquarters is in The Netherlands. To maintain its independence, Greenpeace does not accept donations from governments or corporations but relies on contributions from individual supporters and foundation grants. As a global organization, Greenpeace focuses on the most crucial worldwide threats to our planet's biodiversity and environment.

Green pricing (energy) – Refers to an optional utility service that allows customers of traditional utilities to support a greater level of utility investment in renewable energy by paying a premium on their utility bill to cover any above-market costs of acquiring renewable energy resources.

Green productivity – A strategy for enhancing productivity and environmental performance with a view to overall socio-economic development, involving the use of appropriate techniques, technologies and management systems to produce environmentally compatible goods and services. Green productivity can be applied to manufacturing, services, agriculture and the community. (APO)

Green products – Products that have been certified through a process of 'eco' or 'green' labeling, which insures that the product was handled, made or grown under conditions that meet standards of sustained use, pesticide application and harvesting as well as certain social and economic criteria for workers. (CGC)

Green revolution – Refers to a movement in the agricultural sector starting in the 1950s and involving the use of fertilizers, pesticides, intensive irrigation and production of cereal grains using hybrid seed varieties. Dr Norman Borlaug, the father of this movement, received the Nobel Prize in 1970 for his work in developing and applying this concept, particularly in developing countries.

Green sector – A catchall label for 'environmental' projects that cover issues related to forests, land, biodiversity and protected areas.

Green tax, reverse – A measure proposed by France in 2006 to be adopted by the EU that would tax goods and services from countries that have not ratified the Kyoto treaty (EU)

Green upgrades – A term referring to voluntary changes in personal lifestyle with the aim of neutralizing an individual's share of waste produced. See '**Carbon offsetting**.'

Green water/issues – See '**Water**.'

Greenway – Undeveloped linear open space usually in cities, set aside or used for recreation or conservation. A linear open space; a corridor composed of natural vegetation. Greenways can be used to create connected networks of open space that include traditional parks and natural areas. (NRDC)

GRID – UNEP's Global Resource Information Database (GRID) is a network of information centers that provides improved access to high-quality environmental information. There are currently 16 GRID centers operational worldwide. (UNEP)

Gross domestic product (GDP) – The measure of all output produced by the factors of production located in a country regardless of who owns these factors. (IMF) See '**Sustainability assessments**.'

Gross national income (GNI) – GNI takes into account all production in the domestic economy (i.e. GDP) plus the net flows of factor income (such as rents, profits and labor income) from abroad. (WB)

Gross national income World Bank Atlas method – The Atlas method smoothes GNI calculated exchange rate fluctuations by using a three-year moving average, price-adjusted conversion factor. (WB)

Gross national product (GNP) – The measure of total income earned by the citizens of a country (GNP equals GDP plus earnings from abroad). (IMF) See '**Sustainability assessments**.'

Gross village product (GVP) – The measure of total output produced by a delimited village area, the size and/or population of which as defined in the national or state law. (UN) See '**Barefoot College**.'

Groundwater – Water found beneath the Earth's surface.

GS-level staff – A term used to categorize administrative support staff (and salary/benefit package) in the UN and OAS systems, starting at GS1 and rising to GS7. (UN)

Guideline – A recommended or customary method of working to accomplish an objective. A guideline is not enforced but is generally followed. (MW)

G

Hh

H.E. – Abbreviation for Honorable Excellency or His/Her Excellency.

Habitat – The place where an organism lives and/or the conditions of that environment including the soil, vegetation, water and food. (EES)

HABITAT – The United Nations Centre for Human Settlements (UNCHS) was established in October 1978 as the lead agency with the United Nations system for coordinating activities in the field of human settlements. It is the focal point for the implementation of the Habitat Agenda – the global plan of action adopted by the international community at the Habitat II Conference in Istanbul, Turkey in June 1996. The mission of UNCHS is to promote socially and environmentally sustainable human settlement development and the achievement of adequate shelter for all. (UNCHS)

Habitat Agenda – The second United Nations Conference on Human Settlements, held in Istanbul, June 1996, also called the 'City Summit.' (UNCHS)

Half-life – The time required for a pollutant to lose half of its effect on the environment. For example, the biochemical half-life of DDT in the environment is approximately 15 years; of radium, 1580 years. (USEPA)

Hanover Principles – A set of nine principles that encourage the design professions to take sustainability into consideration. They are descriptive of a way of thinking, not prescriptions or requirements and take the form of a framework, based on the enduring elements of earth, air, fire, water and spirit in which design decisions may be reviewed and evaluated. The principles are meant to guide our creative acts in order to blend aesthetic concerns with ecological principles so that design becomes a didactic tool, demonstrating that sustainable thinking can be put into practice in the real world. (MBDC) See '**Cradle to cradle, concept of**,' '**Harmonious world, concept of**.'

Hard law – The body of binding and enforceable laws (precise, legally binding obligations and appropriate third party delegation) (UNT; BLD) See '**Soft law**.'

Harmonious world, concept of – A concept formally introduced by President Hu Jintao of China in 2005 at the UN 'World Summit 2005' and gaining validity in the intergovernmental arena. The concept includes the principles of multilateralism, mutually beneficial cooperation and the spirit of inclusiveness as vital components in realizing common security and prosperity goals held by the international community. Since this time, a number of Chinese officials have tied these concepts to economic development, peaceful globalization and issues of equity in terms of natural resource use in a number of UN and other international fora. (UN) See '**Hanover Principles**.'

Harmonization – The process of making procedures or measures applied by different countries – especially those affecting international trade – more compatible, as by effecting simultaneous tariff cuts applied by different countries so as to make their tariff structures more uniform. (WTO)

Hazardous waste – Refers to any material intended to be discarded or of no further use and exhibits characteristics or qualities that make it dangerous to humans or the environment, normally defined by four parameters each with its own criteria: ignitability, corrosiveness, reactivity and toxicity. (EES)

Haze – An atmospheric condition marked by a slight reduction in atmospheric visibility, resulting from the formation of photochemical smog, radiation of heat from the ground surface on hot days or the development of a thin mist. (NRDC) See '**Contrails**.'

Hearing – Testimony normally given under oath to a legislative body.

Heat island effect – A 'dome' of elevated temperatures over an urban area caused by the heat absorbed by structures and pavement.

Heavily Indebted Poor Countries (HIPC) – Forty-two of the world's poorest countries (34 in Africa, four in Latin America, three in Asia and one in the Middle East). The concept was proposed by the World Bank and IMF and agreed to by governments around the world in the fall of 1996 as the first comprehensive approach to reduce the external debt of the world's poorest, most heavily indebted countries, and represented an important step forward in placing debt relief within an overall framework of poverty reduction and sustainable development. (AD; WB) See '**HIPC G8 debt relief plan**.'

Helsinki Convention – The 1992 Convention on the Protection of the Marine Environment of the Baltic Sea Area, which entered into force on 17 January, 2000. (EEA; UNT)

Helsinki I Convention – See '**Convention on the Protection and Use of Transboundary Watercourses and International Lakes**.'

Herbicide – Chemical that kills plants. (USEPA)

HFCs – Hydrofluorocarbons. Chemicals composed of one or two carbon atoms and varying numbers of hydrogen and fluorine atoms and used as solvents and cleaners in the semiconductor industry that are generally felt to contribute to global warming many times greater than CO_2. (NRDC)

High Commissioner – A senior diplomat from one country to another with the rank and responsibility of an Ambassador. This term is generally used interchangeably with the term Ambassador in the Commonwealth System. (MW)

High-income country – A country having an annual gross national product (GNP) per capita equivalent to $9361 or greater in 1998. Most high-income countries have an industrial economy. There are currently about 28 high-income countries in the world with populations of 1 million people or more. Their combined population is about 0.9 billion, less than one-sixth of the world's population. (WB)

High-level (meeting) segment – Ministerial component of a technical meeting where the most significant outputs from the technical component are formally decided and/or signed. (UN)

High seas – The ocean areas outside the territorial seas and maritime zones of coastal states. They are open to use by all states for peaceful purposes. (USEPA)

HIPC G8 Debt Relief Plan – A 2005 G8 plan to ease the IMF and World Bank debt burden of the 18 poorest countries'– the so-called 'poorest of the poor (Benin, Bolivia, Burkina Faso, Ethiopia, Ghana, Guyana, Honduras, Madagascar, Mali, Mauritania, Mozambique, Nicaragua, Niger, Rwanda, Senegal, Tanzania, Uganda and Zambia) by US$1.5 billion annually. The total savings over the life of the proposed loan repayment schedules is estimated to be US$40 billion. (WB) See '**Heavily Indebted Poor Countries**.'

His/Her Royal Highness – A title generally reserved for a person of 'exalted rank' such as a king, queen, prince or princess. (MW)

Holdridge life zone system – See '**Life zone**.'

Homosphere – The biosphere modified by humans. (EES) See '**Anthropocene**.'

Host country – The term used for a nation where an embassy, office or convention secretariat is located. (UN)

Hot air – The quantity of tradable greenhouse gas emissions of a country equal to the difference between its actual emissions and its higher legally binding limit. (UNFCCC)

Hotspot (1) – An area particularly rich in endemic species that are endangered by land-use change. (CBD)

Hotspot (2) – Patterns in the 'global environment' of macro-instability in natural cycles, patterns, and frequency/intensity of 'natural events.' (UN-FCCC)

HQ – Referring to Headquarters, such as New York City as the headquarters for the UN Secretariat, Rome being the 'HQ' for UNFAO, Paris being the 'HQ' for UNESCO, Nairobi being the 'HQ' for UNEP. (UN)

H.R.H. – Abbreviation for His/Her Royal Highness. (MW)

Human development index (HDI) – The HDI measures the overall achievements in a country in three basic dimensions of human development: longevity, knowledge and decent standard of living. It is measured by life expectancy, educational attainment (adult literacy and combined primary, secondary and tertiary enrolment) and adjusted income. (ACCU; UNDP) See '**Sustainability assessment measures**.'

Human Development Report – An annual report produced by UNDP that reports development progress based on human development index criteria. (UN)

Human immunodeficiency virus (HIV) – A virus that steadily weakens the body's defense (immune) system until it can no longer fight off infections such as pneumonia, diarrhea, tumors and other illnesses. All of which can be part of AIDS (acquired immunodeficiency syndrome). Most HIV infections have been transmitted through unprotected sexual intercourse with someone who is already infected with HIV, by infected blood or blood products (as in blood transfusions), by the sharing of contaminated needles, and from an infected woman to her baby before birth, during delivery, or through breast-feeding. HIV is not transmitted through normal, day-to-day contact. (UN)

Human poverty index – A measure that reflects the distribution of progress and the backlog of deprivations that still exists. (UNDP)

Humanitarian Charter – See '**Sphere concept/project**.'

Humanitarian intervention – The interference in a sovereign state by another with the objective of ending or reducing suffering within the first state. That suffering may be the result of civil war, starvation or genocide. Humanitarian intervention should not annex the state, nor affect the state's territorial integrity but merely act to minimize the suffering of civilians in that state. The rationale behind such an intervention is the belief in a concomitant duty under certain circumstances to disregard a state's sovereignty to preserve our common humanity. (WP; Schnabel and Thakur, 2000). See '**Right to Interfere**,' '**Duty to Interfere**'

Human rights – The minimum social, economic and political standards that are generally considered acceptable. The advancement of human rights is often thought of as a requirement for human development and/or sustainable development. In that regard, the Universal Declaration of Human Rights calls for the prohibition of slavery, torture, other cruel and degrading treatment, arbitrary arrest, detention and exile, stating that everyone has the right to life, liberty and security of person. It calls for an end to all forms of discrimination, for fair trials and reasonable punishment, the right of persecuted people to asylum in other countries, and for freedom of thought, conscience, opinion, expression, association and religion.

Hydrocarbons – Compounds of hydrogen and carbon in various combinations that are present in petroleum products and natural gas. Some hydrocarbons are major air pollutants, some may be carcinogenic and others contribute to photochemical smog.

Hydrofluorocarbon – See '**HFCS.**'

Hydrogeology – The science that studies groundwater, its movement in the subsurface, the water-bearing properties of the earth materials and the geological relationships between surface and subsurface water. (EES)

Hydroinformatics – A mathematical model-based field of study of the flow of information and the generation of knowledge related to the dynamics of water in the real world, through the integration of information and communication technologies for data acquisition, modeling and decision support, and taking into account the consequences for the aquatic environment and society and for the management of water-based systems. (UNESCO-IHE)

Hydrological cycle – The hydrological cycle refers to the circulatory flux of water molecules at or near the Earth's surface. They take the gaseous form when evaporated into the air masses under the influence of climatic and meteorological phenomena. Subsequently, they are precipitated as rain or snow, and eventually they return to the oceans, rivers and glaciers, completing the cycle. (EES)

Hydrological poverty – A term first used by Lester Brown of the Earth Watch Institute to describe the millions of people who will be born into a 'world' that does not have sufficient water resources to meet the basic needs of its citizens, currently numbering in excess of 1.2 billion people. See '**Water stress**,' '**Water scarcity**.'

Hydrological warfare, context of – A situation in which rivers, lakes and aquifers become national security assets to be fought over or controlled through proxy armies and client states. (UNDP)

Hydrology – The science dealing with water and snow, including their properties and distribution. (EES)

Hydropattern – Depth, duration, timing and distribution of fresh water in a specified area. A consistent hydropattern is critical for maintaining various ecological communities in wetlands and other ecosystems. (SFWMD)

Hydroperiod – Period of time during which soils, water bodies and sites are wet. (USEPA)

Hydropower – Energy produced by moving water. (MW)

Hydro-solidarity – A term implying the existence of a reciprocating policy involving upstream and downstream water dependencies/users with compensation mechanisms and agreements of water entitlements including monetary and policy arrangements. (EU)

Hyogo Framework for Action – In January 2005, 168 UN Member States adopted a 10-year plan to make the world safer from natural hazards at the World Conference on Disaster Reduction, held in Kobe, Hyogo, Japan. The Framework is a global blueprint for disaster risk reduction efforts during the next decade. Its goal is to substantially reduce disaster losses by 2015 – in lives, and in the social, economic and environmental assets of communities and countries. (UN)

Hyper-developed countries – A somewhat derogatory reference to OECD countries, as compared to HIPC countries.

Hypoxia – The depletion of dissolved oxygen in water. A condition resulting from an over-abundance of nutrients of human or natural origin that stimulates the growth of algae, which in turn die and require large amounts of oxygen as the algae decompose. Large fish kills have been attributed to this phenomenon globally. (NRDC)

Ii

Iberian America – A diplomatic forum created in 2005 and headquartered in Madrid, Spain intended to promote relations between Latin America and the Iberian Peninsula. (IDB)

Iboamerican Group – An informal intergovernmental policy exchange network including Spain plus 20 Latin American and Caribbean Spanish and Portuguese speaking countries.

Ikea development – A term, derived from a reference to the 'do-it-yourself' store Ikea®, and used to describe a grassroots or local approach to development whereby communities solve their own problems with the materials at hand. A proactive approach to problem solving when a community does not wait for ODA to arrive, but rather solves their own problem, whether as a stopgap or more permanent solution. (UNW)

ILO Declaration on Fundamental Principles and Rights at Work – A declaration of the 80th session of the ILO in Geneva (June 1998) that all its Members, 'even if they have not ratified the Conventions in question, have an obligation arising from the very fact of membership in the Organization to respect, to promote and to realize, in good faith and in accordance with the Constitution, the principles concerning the fundamental rights which are the subject of those Conventions, namely:

- freedom of association and the effective recognition of the right to collective bargaining;
- the elimination of all forms of forced or compulsory labor;
- the effective abolition of child labor; and
- the elimination of discrimination in respect to employment and occupation.

IMO Conventions in the Field of Marine Safety and Prevention of Marine Pollution – A suite of some 33 conventions dealing with marine safety, marine pollution, and liability and compensation, and coordinated through a variety of institutional mechanisms and partnerships by the IMO.

Impermissibility principle – A principle from the Vienna Convention on Treaties that states that a reservation incompatible with the object and purpose of a convention signed and ratified by the country wishing to make the reservation shall not be permitted.

Implementing agency (IA) – Within the GEF, an IA is one of three agencies (UNDP, UNEP, WB) accountable to the GEF council for activities financed by the GEF. (GEF) See '**Executing agency**.'

Incremental costs – The additional cost that the GEF funds between the cost of an alternative project that a country would have implemented in the absence of global environmental concerns and a project undertaken with global objectives in mind. (GEF)

Independent state – A state that is sovereign; one that operates independently internationally.

Indeterminate – An IUCN category of taxa known to be Extinct, Endangered, Vulnerable, or Rare but where there is not enough information to say which of the four categories is appropriate. (IUCN; CBD)

Index of Sustainable Economic Welfare (ISEW) – An economic indicator intended to replace the GDP. Rather than simply adding together all expenditures like GDP, ISEW includes factors such as income distribution and costs associated with pollution and other societal expenses. (WP) See '**Genuine progress indicator**.'

Indicator – A qualified/quantified parameter that details the extent to which a project objective has been achieved within a given time frame and in a specified location. (UNDP)

Indicator species – A species whose status provides information on the overall condition of the ecosystem and of other species in that ecosystem. They reflect the quality and changes in environmental conditions as well as aspects of community composition. (IUCN)

Indigenous – Occurring naturally but not exclusively in a given area. (GBS)

Indigenous Peoples Development Plan (IPDP) – A plan prepared for any investment project that affects indigenous peoples that is designed in a culturally appropriate manner and is based on the full consideration of the options preferred by the indigenous people affected by the project. The plan also includes provisions that ensure that institutions responsible for government interaction with indigenous peoples should possess the social, technical and legal skills needed to carry out proposed development activities. Elements of an IPDP include an assessment of the legal framework; collection of baseline data; examination of land tenure; a strategy for local participation; design of mitigation measures and activities; assessment of institutional capacity; an implementation schedule and a system for monitoring and evaluation. (WB)

Industrial metabolism – A metaphor, borrowed from biology, to study flows of materials from the extraction of raw materials via (industrial) transformations into products that are consumed, perhaps recycled and finally disposed of as waste. (EES)

Industrialized countries – A term that is somewhat out of date but refers to nations whose economies are based on industrial production and the conversion of raw materials into products and services, mainly with the use of machinery as opposed to those whose economies are based on agricultural production and the sale of unaltered agricultural products or processing agricultural products using hand labor. Industrialized nations are generally located in the northern and western hemispheres and comprise the OECD countries. (NRDC)

Informal agreement – A common form of international cooperation that permit states to conclude mutually profitable bargains without the formality of treaties.

Informal consultation – An informal meeting not contemplated in the agenda that is called by the conference chair who upon receipt of the report of the consultation presents it to the plenary.

Informal contact group – On the instructions of the meeting's president or chair, delegates may meet in private to discuss specific matters in order to consolidate different views, reach a compromise, and produce an agreed proposal, often in the form of a written text.

Informal employment – The percentage of the employed population, men and women, whose activity is part of the informal sector. (UNCHS)

Informal group – A group called into being by one or more of the parties, for purposes of informal consultation to reach a compromise or to produce an agreed upon proposal. (UNFCCC)

Informal sector – Persons engaged in the production of goods or services with the primary objective of generating employment and incomes to the persons concerned. It includes unregistered commercial enterprises and all non-commercial enterprises that have no formal structure in terms of organization and operation. (UNCHS)

Informal-informal consultation – An informal consultation of parties and at times, observers, to discuss a specific point. The results of the consultancy may then be presented by a party in plenary, but without a formal request from the conference chair.

Information and communication technologies (ICTs) – Any equipment, or interconnected system(s) or subsystem(s) of equipment, that is used in the automatic acquisition, storage, manipulation, management, movement, control, display, switching, interchange, transmission or reception of data or information.

Information documents/docs – Documents that underpin or annotate meeting working documents. (UN)

Initiative – An intervention by a formal or informal group to meet a specific objective.

Initiative 2020 (2020 Initiative; 20:20 Compact) – The 1995 UN Social Development Summit informally agreed that a minimum of 20 percent of aid (ODA) and 20 percent of developing country budgets would go to basic social services. (UN)

Injection well – A well into which fluids are injected for purposes such as waste disposal, improving the recovery of crude oil, or solution mining. (USEPA)

Innovative learning (I-Learning) – An intelligent blend of (i) technology-based systems, simulation applications and other e-learning packages aimed at bridging distances through internet, video and teleconferencing technologies, and (ii) social-psychological methods that employ tacit and intuitive knowledge and the creative powers of professionals. (Ramsundersingh, 2003)

In-kind contribution – A term generally used to indicate a non-cash contribution to a project or program that may include office space, utility costs, personnel time, equipment, access, etc.

In-material-breach – A term used to indicate a demonstrable non-compliance by a Member State with an approved resolution of the UN Security Council or the UN General Assembly.

Insecticide – A chemical that kills insects. (USEPA)

In-situ conservation – The conservation of ecosystems and natural habitats and the maintenance and recovery of viable populations of species in their surroundings and, in the case of domesticated or cultivated plant species, in the surroundings where they have developed their distinctive properties. (CBD)

Institute@WSIS E-Strategies – An initiative of the Smithsonian Institute and UNDP to promote sustainable development and launched at the WSSD in Johannesburg. It consists of a network of volunteers who deliver short courses in which practical skills and appropriate technologies are transferred directly to participants. (UNDP)

Institutional development – The process of enabling and facilitating an organization to develop and increase its capacities and capabilities so as to meet its desired objectives. (UNDP)

Instrument – A term used to refer to the tools used for certain types of work, which may be physical such as those used in surveying, or notional such as used in establishing law. (UNT)

Integrated area management (IAM) – A management approach whereby a specific area is zoned and regulated for a variety of uses, including research, species protection, tourism, harvesting, cutting of trees, hunting, or fishing that are compatible with the management goals for the area. (BCHM)

Integrated conservation development projects (ICDP) – An approach to biodiversity conservation that reconciles the management of protected areas with the social and economic needs of the allied or nearby local populations. This is usually done by the involvement of these communities in management of the protected areas and by ensuring that their social and economic needs are considered through the development of economic activities. (GEF)

Integrated development planning – A three-part technique for bringing about beneficial social and economic change: (1) diagnosis of principal problems and potentials; (2) preparation of a development strategy; and (3) formulation of a coordinated package of infrastructure, production, and service projects (including conservation) within an action plan for implementing the strategy. (OAS, 1987)

Integrated pest management (IPM) – A management system that uses all suitable techniques and methods in as compatible a manner as possible to maintain pest populations at levels below those causing economic injury. (USEPA)

Integrated Water Resource Management (IWRM) – A process that promotes the coordinated development and management of water, land and related resources in order to maximize the resultant economic and social welfare in an equitable manner without compromising the sustainability of vital ecosystems. (Global Water Partnership, 2003)

Integration – The action in which smaller and different units are brought together into a larger unit to form a satisfactory and working whole.

Intellectual property – A term generally referring to patents, copyrights, scientific discoveries or new theories, trademarks and trade secrets. This term also includes creative ideas and expressions (original art, writings, music, etc.) that have commercial value and receive the legal protection of a property right. (BCHM)

Intellectual property rights – A right enabling an inventor or discoverer to exclude imitators from the market for a limited time and generally related to national or international patent laws. Intellectual property rights, patents and trademarks enable owners to determine who can have access to and use their property, while protecting it from unauthorized use. (BCHM)

Inter alia – Among other things.

Inter-American Biodiversity Information Network (IABIN) – An initiative of the Summit of the Americas to provide greater and more useful access to biodiversity information throughout the western hemisphere. (OAS, 1998)

Inter-American Development Bank (IDB) – The IDB was established in December of 1959 to help accelerate economic and social development in Latin America and the Caribbean. Its principal functions are to utilize its own capital, funds raised in financial markets, and other available resources, for financing the development of the borrowing member countries; to supplement private investment when private capital is not available on reasonable terms and conditions; and to provide technical assistance for the preparation, financing and implementation of development plans and projects. Current lending priorities include poverty reduction and social equity, modernization and integration and the environment. (IDB)

Inter-American Water Resource Network (IWRN) – A network founded in 1993 whose purpose is to strengthen water resource partnerships among nations, organizations and individuals. (OAS)

Intergenerational equity – A core proposition of some definitions of sustainable development, which suggests that future generations have a right to an inheritance (capital bequest) sufficient to allow them to generate a level of well-being no less than that of the current generations. (GBA)

Intergovernmental Negotiation Committee (ING) – A formal group of representatives from different interested governments established to negotiate a draft convention or treaty.

Intergovernmental Oceanographic Commission (IOC) – The IOC was established by the General Conference of UNESCO in October of 1961 to promote scientific investigation with a view to learning more about the nature and resources of the oceans through the concerted action of its members. Current membership includes 136 nations. (WP)

Intergovernmental Panel on Climate Change (IPCC) – A group of approximately 2000 scientists established by the World Meteorological Organization and UN Environment Programme (UNEP) in 1988 to assess the state of knowledge on climate change. The IPCC prepares periodic assessments of the scientific basis for understanding global climate change and its consequences. It currently has three Working Groups and two Task Forces: Working Group I assesses the scientific aspects of the climate system and climate change; Working Group II addresses the vulnerability of socio-economic and natural systems to climate change, negative and positive consequences of climate change, and options for adapting to it; Working Group III assesses options for limiting greenhouse gas emissions and otherwise mitigating climate change; the Task Force on National

Greenhouse Gas Inventories oversees the National Greenhouse Gas Inventories Program; and the Task Group on Scenarios for Climate Impact Assessment. Although the IPCC advises the COP/UNFCCC, it is not an institution of the Convention. (IPCC)

Internal rate of return (IRR) – A decision-making criterion that assesses the amount and timing of project benefits and which is based on a discount rate that reduces the net present value of a project to zero. If the IRR is larger than the discount rate, the action is acceptable from an economic point of view. This criterion is often used by development banks to determine credit worthiness of a proposed project.

Internally displaced person – Someone that has been forced to leave his home due to a natural or man-made disaster/situation but who has remained within the borders of his country. (UN) See '**Refugee**,' '**Environmental refugee**.'

International Centre for Settlement of Investment Disputes (ICSID) – A part of the World Bank Group established in 1966 and including 140 member countries, which provides facilities for the conciliation and arbitration of disputes between member countries and foreign investors. (WB)

International Centre for Water Hazard and Risk Management (ICHARM) – An initiative of the Japanese government together with the Division of Water Sciences of UNESCO aimed at promoting sustainable development of river basins. The center, which was approved by UNESCO's General Conference in 2005, and serves as an international hub for specific water sector problems based on the objectives of the IHP relating to risk management. The center is located in Tsukuba, Japan.

International Civil Service Commission (ICSC) – A subsidiary body of the UNGA established in 1974 to regulate the conditions of service for all UN common system staff. (UN)

International Committee of the Red Cross, Red Crescent (and Red Crystal) Societies (ICRC) – See '**International Federation of the Red Cross, Red Crescent (and Red Crystal) Societies (IFRC)**.'

International community – A broad, generic term used to represent UN Member States, any recognized sub-group of UN Member States, any international or regional grouping, and/or any group of organizations from civil society (governmental, nongovernmental or private sector) recognized by the UN and/or involved in international governance or development. (UN)

International Conference on Financing for Development (ICFD) – Also known as the 'Monterrey Conference.' A meeting of more than 50 heads of State and senior government officials held in Monterrey,

Mexico in March, 2002, which may be considered as part of the run-up to the September 2002 World Summit on Sustainable Development. The meeting adopted the Monterrey Consensus and pledges were made by a number of developed countries to increase ODA to a level of 0.7 of GDP. See **'Monterrey Consensus,' 'Global tax.'**

International Conference on Population and Development – A conference sponsored by the United Nations to discuss global dimensions of population growth and change in Cairo, Egypt in September, 1994. The conference marks the achievement of a new consensus on effective ways to slow population growth and improve quality of life by addressing root causes of unwanted fertility.

International Court of Justice (ICJ) – The ICJ is one of the six principle organs of the UN System and the judicial organ of the UN with the power to hear two kinds of cases: (1) cases between states, and (2) any cases requested by specialized agencies of the UN. The Court's function is to settle legal disputes within the boundaries of international law submitted to it by states and also to give advisory opinions regarding legal questions referred to it by authorized international organs and agencies. The ICJ replaced the Permanent Court of International Justice in 1945 and operates under a Statute largely similar to this predecessor. The Court, located in The Hague, The Netherlands, is composed of 15 judges who serve nine-year terms of office. (UN)

International Criminal Court (ICC) – The ICC, established in 2002, is *not* jurisdictionally nor institutionally related to the UN. It is the first-ever permanent, treaty based, international criminal court established to promote the rule of law and ensure that the gravest international crimes do not go unpunished. It is a complimentary body to national criminal jurisdictions and is governed by the 'Rome Statute.' (WP) See **'Rome Statute,' 'Complimentarity, principle of.'**

International Development Association (IDA) – The World Bank Group's concessional lending window established in 1960 and including 165 member countries. The IDA provides long-term loans at zero interest to the poorest of the developing countries defined as those countries having a per capita income in 2002 dollar values of less than US$875.00 and lack the financial ability to borrow from the IBRD. In 2004 the IDA provided US$9 billion in loans to recipient countries. (WB)

International Energy Agency (IEA) – Formed in 1974, the IEA is an autonomous agency based in Paris that acts as the energy forum for the OECD. Members take joint action to meet oil supply emergencies, share energy information, coordinate their energy policies and cooperate in the development of rational energy programs. (IEA)

International environmental law – The body of law that concerns the protection of the global environment. There are many legally binding international agreements concerning the protection of the environment, but in this area of international law, 'soft law' is more common. Some basic principles of international environmental law are: the precautionary principle, the polluter pays principle, the principle of sustainable development and environmental procedural rights. (WP) See '**Soft law**.'

International Federation of the Red Cross, Red Crescent (and Red Crystal) Societies (IFRC) – The IFRC, and its Federation of 183 societies, is the world's largest nongovernmental humanitarian organization, providing assistance without discrimination as to nationality, race, religious beliefs, class or political opinions and regardless of the source or type of disaster that has befallen any group of people. Given the religious connotations that are at times associated with the cross and crescent symbols of the IFRC, the Government of Switzerland convened a meeting in December of 2005 that approved an additional symbol, the 'crystal' – a red frame in the form of a square standing on one of its points against a white background. It is equal in every way to the red cross and red crescent emblems and will reinforce its humanitarian mission and provide an additional protective device for the medical services of armed forces and Red Cross and Red Crescent humanitarian workers in conflicts where the existing emblems cannot always provide protection because of perceptions of political, religious or other cultural connotations.

International Finance Corporation (IFC) – A part of the World Bank Group established in 1956 and including 176 Member States that assists economic development by promoting growth in the private sector. (WB)

International Finance Facility (IFF) – A UK-proposed mechanism to increase development assistance based on allowing a beneficiary country to borrow money against future aid flows or by supporting increased assistance through instituting an international taxing arrangement such as an airline tax that would be earmarked for specific development-related objectives. It was first proposed at the 2005 G8 summit. See '**Global tax**.'

International Flood Initiative (IFI) – An inter-agency (UNESCO, WMO, UNU, UNISDR, UNISDR-PPEW, IAHS) initiative launched in 2005 by UNESCO aimed at minimizing loss of life and reducing damage caused by floods. The secretariat is located in the International Centre for Water Hazard and Risk Management (ICHARM) hosted by the Public Works Research Institute in Tsukuba, Japan. (UNESCO)

International Fund for Agricultural Development (IFAD) – The IFAD is a specialized agency of the UN established as an international financial institution in 1977 as a result of the 1974 World Food Conference that was organized in response to the food crises of the early 1970s. IFAD was created to mobilize resources on concessional terms for programs that alleviate rural poverty and improve nutrition. (IFAD)

International Heritage Convention (IHC) – A UNESCO-led convention that aims to protect the intangible heritage of the world including practices, expressions and representations of oral traditions; traditional music,
dance and theatre; social practices, rituals, and festive events; knowledge
and practices regarding nature and the universe; and traditional craftsman-
ship. The IHC entered into force in April, 2006. (UNESCO)

International law – The body of rules that govern the relationships of
states with each other. International treaties are a part of international law.
Sources of international law (from Article 38 of the Statute of the International Court of Justice) include: international conventions of general or
particular nature; international custom, as evidence of a general practice
accepted as law; and the general principles of law recognized by civilized
nations.

International Monetary Fund (IMF) – The IMF is an international organization of 182 member countries, established to promote international
monetary cooperation, exchange stability, and orderly exchange arrangements; to foster economic growth and high levels of employment; and to
provide temporary financial assistance to countries to help ease balance of
payments adjustment. (IMF)

International Office of Epizootics – Office that deals with international
standards concerning animal health. (WTO)

International organization (IO) – Organizations with global mandates,
generally funded by contributions from national governments. Examples
include the International Committee of the Red Cross and Red Crescent,
the International Organization for Migration, the Organization of American States and United Nations agencies. (UN)

International Pollinators Initiative (IPI) – The International Initiative
for the Conservation and Sustainable Use of Pollinators is a crosscutting
initiative within the program of work on agricultural biodiversity. (CBD)

International public good – Goods that will tend, in an international
market economy, to be provided in quantities that are too low from the
point of view of social efficiency. They are characterized by non-rivalry
and non-excludability. If, for example only the Annex I countries would
carry out global greenhouse strategies, the non-Annex countries would
benefit at no cost for themselves. The Annex I countries cannot prevent the
non-Annex countries from taking advantage of their greenhouse strategies,
nor can they force them to pay for their investments. This may lead to a
situation wherein a too low amount of the good – international commitments – will take place. (DFID)

International Seabed Authority – The UN Convention on the Law of
the Sea establishes a comprehensive legal framework to regulate all ocean

space, its uses and resources. It contains, among other things, provisions relating to the territorial sea, the contiguous zone, the continental shelf, the exclusive economic zone and the high seas. It also provides for the protection and preservation of the marine environment, for marine scientific research and for the development and transfer of marine technology. One of the most important parts of the Convention concerns the exploration for and exploitation of the resources of the seabed and ocean floor and subsoil thereof, beyond the limits of national jurisdiction (the Area). The Convention declares the Area and its resources to be 'the common heritage of mankind.' The International Seabed Authority, established by the Convention, administers the resources of the Area. (UN)

International Sediment Initiative (ISI) – The ISI was launched in 2002 as a major activity of Phase VI (2002–2006) of UNESCO's IHP and renewed in Phase VII (2008–2013). ISI studies issues concerning sediment management, thus making a valuable contribution to sustainable water resources development on a global scale. Its mission directly relates to the commitments of the international community expressed in major documents such as the Millennium Development Goals, the Rio Declaration of Sustainable Development, the World Water Assessment Programme, and the World Water Development Reports. (UNESCO)

International Standards Organization (also known as the International Organization for Standardization) (ISO) – ISO is a nongovernmental network of the national standards institutes of 146 countries, on the basis of one member per country, with a Central Secretariat in Geneva, Switzerland, that develops and coordinates technical standards. Its members are not, as is the case in the UN system, delegations of national governments. (ISO)

International Tribunal for the Law of the Sea – The International Tribunal for the Law of the Sea is an independent judicial body established by the Convention to adjudicate disputes arising out of the interpretation and application of its terms. The Tribunal is composed of 21 independent members, elected from among persons enjoying the highest reputation for fairness and integrity and of recognized competence in the field of the Law of the Sea. (UN)

International Tropical Timber Organization (ITTO) – An institution of producers formed in 1987 to promote conservation and sustainable development of tropical forests. (ITTO)

International Union for the Conservation of Nature (IUCN) – See 'World Conservation Union.'

International Water Association (IWA) – As the world's largest professional water organization, IWA integrates the leading edge of professional thought on research and practice, regulators and the regulated, across national boundaries and across the drinking water, wastewater and storm-water disciplines. IWA was founded in September, 1999, by the merger of the International Association of Water Quality (IAWQ) and the International Water Supply Association (IWSA). Its headquarters are in the UK. (WP)

International Water Convention – See 'Convention on the Law of the Non-Navigational Use of International Watercourses.'

International Water Management Institute (IWMI) – One of 16 centers supported by the Consultative Group on International Agricultural Research (CGIAR). Headquartered in Colombo, Sri Lanka, IWMI's mission is to improve water and land resources management for food, livelihoods and nature.

International waters – One of the seven focal areas of GEF defined as the seas, shared river and lake basins, shared estuaries and wetlands, and shared groundwater aquifers. The distinguishing feature is that more than one nation has access to or makes use of them. (GEF)

International Whaling Commission (IWC) – The IWC was established under the International Convention for the Regulation of Whaling, which was signed in Washington DC on 2 December, 1946. Its purpose is to provide for the proper conservation of whale stocks and support the orderly development of the whaling industry. It reviews and revises as necessary the measures laid down in the Schedule to the Convention, which governs the conduct of whaling throughout the world. These measures provide for the complete protection of certain species; designate specified areas as whale sanctuaries; set limits on the numbers and size of whales that may be taken; prescribe open and closed seasons and areas for whaling; and prohibit the capture of suckling calves and female whales accompanied by calves.

Inter-Parliamentary Union (IPU) – The IPU is the world's oldest multilateral political organization established in 1889 and including members of the parliaments of sovereign states. The Union is the focal point for worldwide parliamentary dialogue and works for peace and cooperation among peoples and for the firm establishment of representative democracy. For the first time in its history, the 2006 gathering of IPU members focused on the issue of environmental management as a fundamental component of sustainable development.

Interpretation – A term referring to translating the written or spoken word into other languages. (MW)

Interpretation, active – Refers to interventions permitted in any of the officially recognized working languages of an international or intergovernmental meeting that is subsequently translated into all of the working languages of that particular meeting simultaneously. (UN)

Interpretation, full – Questions and answers permitted/given in *any of the official languages* of a given organization. For example: **UN** – simultaneous translation into all six official UN languages: English, Spanish, French, Mandarin Chinese, Russian and Arabic; **Government of Canada** – simultaneous translation into English and French; **OAS** – simultaneous translation into English, French, Spanish and Portuguese; **EU** – simultaneous translation into all the languages of the Member States. (UN; OAS; EU; WP)

Interpretation, passive – Refers to interventions in any of the officially recognized languages of an international or intergovernmental body but translation into only the principle *working languages of a given organization.* For example: in a UNESCO meeting held in Paris and providing passive translation, a delegate could ask a question in any of the official UN languages, but it would only be translated (question and response) into French and English, the principle working languages at UNESCO headquarters. (UNESCO)

Interpretation, simultaneous – Translating the spoken word into a second language as it is spoken. (UN)

Inter-sessional meeting – An official meeting between regularly scheduled meetings.

Intervention scenario – Intervention scenarios/informed predictions (in the context of environmental studies) depict the future consequences of policy interventions. In other words, they describe the future state of society and the environment under influence of directed environmental policies. Intervention scenarios are also known as 'pollution control', 'mitigation' or 'policy' scenarios. (EEA)

Intra fauces terra – Literally, 'in the jaws of the land.' A principle for defining territorial seas. (BLD)

Intrinsic value – A form of judgment that takes into account all the values present in the system, an holistic valuation or fitness measurement of the whole. (CSG)

Introduced species – A species occurring in an area outside its historically known natural range as a result of intentional or accidental dispersal by human activities.

Invasive alien species – A species of plant, animal or other organism that is (1) non-native (or alien) to the ecosystem under consideration and (2) whose introduction causes or is likely to cause economic or environmental harm or harm to human health. (CBD)

Ipso facto – By the fact (or act) itself. (BLD)

Irreversibility of environmental damage – A situation resulting in permanent loss of environmental assets or environmental quality, requiring preventive or alternative actions rather than restoration or clean-up. For example, quarrying of rock is often cited as an irreversible environmental change as the original geologic formations can never be replaced in a human time frame. (EEA)

Island biogeography – The study of the relationship between island area and species number and between isolated continental areas, which are, effectively, islands for many species. (EES)

ISO generic management systems – ISO 9000 and ISO 14000 series are among ISO's most widely known standards, having been implemented by nearly 800,000 organizations throughout the world. ISO 9000 has become an international reference for quality management requirements in business-to-business dealings, and ISO 14000 is aimed at enabling organizations to meet their environmental challenges. 'Generic' means that the same standards can be applied to any organization, large or small, whatever its product including whether its product is actually a service in any sector of activity, and whether it is a business enterprise, a public administration, or a government department. 'Management system' refers to the organization's structure for managing its processes that transform inputs of resources into a product or service that meet the organization's objectives, such as satisfying the customer's quality requirements, complying to regulations or meeting environmental objectives. (ISO)

ISO 9000 standards – The ISO 9000 family is primarily concerned with quality management, referring to what the organization does to fulfill the customer's quality requirements and applicable regulatory requirements, while aiming to enhance customer satisfaction, and achieve continual improvement of its performance in pursuit of these objectives. (ISO)

ISO 14000 standards – The ISO 14000 family is primarily concerned with environmental management, referring to what the organization does to minimize harmful effects on the environment caused by its activities, and to achieve continual improvement of its environmental performance. (ISO)

Isolationism – A diplomatic or political policy whereby a nation seeks to avoid alliances with other nations. Most nations are not in a political position to maintain strict isolationist policies for extended periods of time, even though most nations have historical periods when isolationism was popular. (WP)

Iteration – A loop that uses the current value of a system to derive its future value by reinserting it into the equations controlling the system dynamics. (CSG)

IUCN – See 'World Conservation Union.'

Jj

Jakarta Mandate – The Jakarta Mandate on Marine and Coastal Biological Diversity is a global consensus on the importance of marine and coastal biological diversity and is a part of the Ministerial Statement on the implementation of the CBD, as adopted by the COP/CBD held in Jakarta, Indonesia, in November, 1995. Through its program of work, adopted in 1998, the Convention focuses on integrated marine and coastal area management, the sustainable use of living resources, protected areas, mariculture and alien species. (BCHM)

Japan International Cooperation Agency (JICA) – The principal agency through which Japan provides technical assistance and delivers foreign aid.

Johannesburg Declaration – The Johannesburg Declaration is one of the two documents agreed to at the 2002 World Summit on Sustainable Development. It reviews the current global challenges and the progress made in sustainable development from 1992 to 2002, commits its signatories to sustainable development, emphasizes the importance of working on a multilateral basis, and emphasizes the need to complete the work outlined in the WSSD 'Plan of Implementation.'

Johannesburg setting – A term used to identify ministerial level consultations and negotiation.

Joint contact group – Two contact groups created separately and brought together to resolve differences between them. (Gupta, 2002)

Joint Convention on the Safety of Spent Fuel Management and on the Safety of Radioactive Waste Management (2001) – This non-binding Convention seeks to achieve and maintain a high level of safety worldwide in spent fuel and radioactive waste management through the enhancement of national measures and international cooperation; to ensure that during all stages of spent fuel and radioactive waste management there are effective defenses against potential hazards so that individuals, society and the environment are protected from the harmful effects of ionizing radiation now and in the future; and to prevent accidents with radiological consequences and to mitigate their consequences if they occur during any stage of spent fuel or radioactive waste management.

Joint implementation (JI) – A project-based activity in which one country can receive emission reduction credits when it funds a project in another country where the emissions are actually reduced. (UNFCCC)

Joint working group – Two working groups, each convened by a different body, brought together to work on crosscutting issues. (Gupta, 1997)

Jus civile – Law created within each country. (BLD)

Jus cogens – Compelling law. Peremptory principles of international law that cannot be overridden by specific treaties between countries; norms that are binding on all states at all times. (BLD)

Jus inter gentes – Law among peoples, nations. (BLD)

JUSSCANNZ – A coalition of the non-EU developed countries (and other invited countries) that acts as an information sharing and discussion forum. The acronym stands for Japan, US, Switzerland, Canada, Australia, Norway and New Zealand.

J

Kk

Kareze – See 'Qanat.'

Key – A term that typically means an item, idea or concept that is a deciding factor, that is, is critical, instrumental or central to arriving at some determination.

Keystone species – A species that plays an important role in determining the overall structure and dynamic relationships within a biotic community. A keystone species presence is essential to the integrity and stability of a particular ecosystem.

Kimberley Process Certification Scheme – In May 2000, responding to a growing grassroots movement on 'blood diamonds,' governments and the diamond industry came together in Kimberley, South Africa to combat the trade in diamonds from conflict zones. The result of these negotiations was the Kimberley Process Certification Scheme, an internationally recognized certification for rough diamonds establishing national import/export standards. In November 2002, 52 governments ratified and adopted the Kimberley Process, which came into force in August 2003. (GPF)

Knock-on impacts – A term used primarily in the UK to mean secondary impacts.

Kyoto forest – The Kyoto Protocol and the Marrakech Accords allow industrial countries to discount their greenhouse gas emissions by implementing/investing in certain land-use change and forestry activities, including reforestation, sometimes called a 'Kyoto forest.' To qualify as a 'Kyoto Forest,' strict criteria apply including parcel size, species composition, canopy and under-story height and density, stocking levels and projected growth rates. (EEA; IPCC)

Kyoto mechanisms – Formerly known as 'flexibility mechanisms,' the Kyoto mechanisms are based on market principles that Parties to the Kyoto Protocol can use in an attempt to lessen the potential economic impacts of GHG emission-reduction requirements. They include Joint Implementation (Article 6), the Clean Development Mechanisms (Article 12), and Emissions Trading (Article 17). (IPCC)

Kyoto Protocol (KP) – In 1997 at COP-3 in Kyoto, Japan the parties adopted a protocol to the UNFCCC that entered into force in February, 2005. The Kyoto Protocol calls for a reduction in GHG emissions by the industrialized nations and the nations with economies in transition (Annex I countries) of at least 5 percent below 1990 levels (and in some cases 1995 levels) in the period 2008–2012. (IPCC) See '**Asia Pacific Partnership on Clean Development and Climate**,' '**United Nations Framework Convention on Climate Change**.'

K

Ll

L.docs – In-session documents that contain draft reports and texts for adoption by a COP or a subsidiary body. (UNFCCC)

Lacunae – Holes in the law; a gap or blank in a written document. (BLD)

Laissez-Passer – UN travel document, commonly referred to as an 'LP' or 'UN passport' and issued in two forms: Red for D-level staff and above, Blue for all other staff with travel responsibilities – General Service (G-level) and Professional (P-level). (UN)

Laissez faire – Free enterprise. The doctrine or system of government non-interference in the economy except as necessary to maintain economic freedom. (AD)

Land-based Sources Protocol (LBS) – The protocol concerned with land-based sources of pollution and polluting activities in the Wider Caribbean adopted 6 October, 1999 in Oranjestad, Aruba as part of the Framework Plan of the Cartagena Convention. (UNEP)

Landfill – A disposal area where waste is piled up and eventually covered with dirt and topsoil. (NRDC) See '**Sanitary landfill**.'

Land mapping unit (LMU) – The smallest area of land that can be delineated on a map of a particular scale.

Landsat – The Landsat ('land satellite') program, launched in 1972, is the longest running enterprise for acquisition of imagery of Earth from space. The instruments on the Landsat satellites, which have acquired millions of images, are archived in the US and at Landsat receiving stations around the world. Together they are a unique resource for global change research and applications in agriculture, geology, forestry, regional planning, education and national security. The program was called the Earth Resources Observation Satellites Program when it was initiated in 1966, but the name was changed to Landsat in 1975. (EEA)

Landscape amnesia, concept of – Forgetting how different the surrounding landscape looked in the past because the change from year to year has been so gradual. (Jared, 2005) See '**Creeping normalcy**'; '**Boiled-frog syndrome**.'

Land subsidence – Sinking of the topographic surface resulting directly or indirectly from human action or natural phenomenon. (EES)

Land tenure – Land tenure refers to the many rights and responsibilities associated with the possession or holding of a parcel of land. These rights *may* include the right of access to the land, the right to control products from the land (surface or subsurface), the right of succession, the right of transfer and the right to determine changes in land-use, and the right to use of riparian surface waters. Land tenure also implies obligations on the part of the owner or tenant to maintain the land as per existing zoning and land-use laws. (EES)

Land use – The way in which land is used, especially in agricultural, conservation and city planning processes. (NRDC)

Language(s), official – An official language(s) is something that is given a unique status in countries, states and other territories. It is typically the language(s) used in a nation's legislative bodies, though the law in many international organizations and nations requires that documents be produced in other languages as well. **Examples of official languages: UN Secretariat and specialized agencies** – English, Spanish, French, Mandarin Chinese, Russian and Arabic; **Government of Canada** – English and French; **OAS** – English, French, Portuguese and Spanish; **EU** – Czech, Danish, Dutch, English, Estonian, Finnish, French, German, Greek, Hungarian, Irish, Italian, Latvian, Lithuanian, Maltese, Polish, Portuguese, Slovak, Slovene, Spanish and Swedish; **ASEAN and APEC** – English. (EU; OAS ; UN; WP)

Language(s), post – The language(s) that are commonly used in normal day-to-day communication (not necessarily the local language) and which is normally required of all personnel assigned to that UN office (or the office of any international organizations). (UN)

Language(s), working – A working language(s) also known as a procedural language(s), is given a unique legal status in a state or international organization as its primary means of communication. It is primarily the language(s) of the daily correspondence and conversation, since the organization usually has members with differing language backgrounds. By definition, a working language is not equal to an official language, unless specifically noted by the organization, as is the case in the UN. Examples of working languages: **UN Secretariat** – English, Spanish, French, Mandarin Chinese, Russian and Arabic; **UNESCO** – English and French; **OAS** – English and Spanish; **Government of Canada** – English and French; **EU** – English, French and German; **ASEAN and APEC** – English. (EU; OAS; UN; WPWP)

La Niña – A period of stronger-than-normal trade winds and unusually low sea-surface temperatures in the central and eastern tropical Pacific Ocean; the opposite of *El Niño*. (NASA)

Large country – A country that is large enough for its international transactions to affect economic variables abroad, usually for its trade to matter for world prices. (AD)

Law – An act or bill that has become part of the legal code through passage by a legislative body and if required signed or endorsed by the elected Head of State.

LDC Fund – The LDC fund is intended to support the work program for the lesser-developed countries that 'shall include, *inter alia*, National Adaptation Programmes of Action (NAPAs).' (UNFCCC)

Leachate – Liquid that has seeped through solid waste in a landfill, farming area or feedlot and has extracted soluble dissolved or suspended materials (normally contaminants) in the process. (USEPA)

LEAD – An international network of professionals committed to sustainable development. Established in 1991 by the Rockefeller Foundation, LEAD's 'aim is to create and sustain a global network of emerging and working leaders ready and willing to address environment and development challenges in different countries.' (LEAD)

Lead reviewer – An individual designated from a list of experts generally nominated by parties because of their knowledge and experience in the topic to be covered in a report or other document to evaluate its accuracy and comprehensiveness.

League of Arab States – The Arab League or League of Arab States (Arabic: جامعة الدول العربية), is an organization of 21 Arab states from the Middle East and the Palestine Authority, founded in 1945. It is similar to the Organization of American States, the Council of Europe, or the African Union, in that its aims are primarily political. All of these organizations can be considered to be regional versions of the UN. (WP)

League of Nations – A world organization established in 1920 to promote international cooperation and peace. It was first proposed in 1918 by President Woodrow Wilson, although the US never joined the League. It was officially dissolved in 1946 and replaced by the United Nations System. (UN)

Leapfrogging – A process by which, through technology transfer, developing countries adopt technologies designed and tested in industrialized countries without bearing the costs of research and development or experiencing the relatively slow stages of development that characterized the introduction of these technologies in the industrialized world. (UNEP)

Least developed countries (LDCs) – As defined by the UN, 40–50 poor and vulnerable countries with an annual per capita income of less than US$1.00 per day; increasingly they work together as a coalition to defend their interests in international forums.

Least-cost alternative – An economic criterion applied in cost–benefit analysis in situations in which the benefits of projects or actions are equal. It then compares the net present value of the costs of the different projects. The alternative that has the lower present value of costs is preferred.

Legitimacy – The degree to which a government's procedures for making and enforcing laws are acceptable to the people. (UNDP)

Leipzig Declaration (1) – The full title is 'The Leipzig Declaration on Conservation and Sustainable Utilization of Plant Genetic Resources for Food and Agriculture', which was made in Leipzig in 1996 at a conference organized by FAO. The meeting attended by delegates from 150 countries reached a consensus on urgent actions needed to protect the world's dwindling plant genetic resources for food and agriculture, funding and the issue of Farmers' Rights. (FAO)

Leipzig Declaration (2) – A declaration made by a group of independent scientists researching atmospheric and climate problems concerned about the then upcoming climate conference in Kyoto, Japan in 1997 because it would impose 'on citizens of the industrialized nations, but not on others – a system of global environmental regulations that include quotas and punitive taxes on energy fuels.' (UNFCCC)

Less developed country (LDC) – A country where the annual per capita income is between \$300 and \$700. (UN)

Lessons learned – The notation and analysis of the achievements and errors of an activity that result in success or failures of material, timing or other mistakes, so that future similar activities may be improved.

Lex posterior derogat priori – More recent law prevails over (abrogates, overrules, trumps) an inconsistent earlier law. (BLD)

Liability and redress – A term describing the duty of reparation for damage when three conditions are met: (1) a breach of a legal obligation; (2) the breach can be attributed to an actor; and (3) causality can be established. There are at least two regimes: responsibility and liability. Under the first, the duty to repair exists only when a wrongful act is committed, and where wrongfulness is defined. Under the second, liability falls on the institution or person who benefits from or controls the activity even if there is no wrongfulness. Compensation may be paid by the liable actor through obligatory insurance, by a financial pool created by companies, and by the state of origin.

Life-cycle approaches – Strategies that help evaluate and address environmental issues and opportunities holistically with the aim of designing product service systems and reducing potential environmental impacts over the entire life-cycle. (UNEP)

- Life-cycle assessment – An objective process for evaluating the environmental burdens associated with a product, process or activity by identifying the energy and materials used and wastes released to the environment, and to evaluate and implement opportunities to effect environmental improvements. (SETAC)
- Life-cycle management – An integrated framework of concepts, techniques and procedures to address environmental, economic, technological and social aspects of products and organizations, in order to achieve continuous environmental improvement from a life-cycle perspective. (SETAC)
- Design for environment – The systematic integration of environmental and social considerations into product and process design. (NRCC)
- Product service systems – A marketable mix of products and services that jointly fulfill client needs with less environmental impact. (UNEP)
- Integrated product policy – A process of working to stimulate each part of each phase of a product or service life-cycle to improve its environmental performance, from natural resources extraction through design, manufacture, assembly, marketing, distribution, sale, use, recycling (partial or complete) and disposal. (EU)

Life zone – The two principle life zone classification systems in use today include the following definitions of a life zone: (a) in the *Merriam system*, a subdivision of the Earth's surface along lines conforming to particular magnitudes of temperature selected to account for differences in the distribution of organisms, and (b) in the *Holdridge system*, a unit of climatic classification involving three weighted climatic indices based on heat, precipitation and atmospheric moisture. (EES)

Limiting factor – An abiotic condition that controls the growth of a species. For most terrestrial plants this condition is the supply of the nutrient nitrogen in the soil. (EEA)

Lisbon Agenda – In March 2000, the EU Council of Ministers met in Lisbon, Portugal to enact a set of socio-economic and fiscal reforms aimed at making the EU more competitive on a global scale while maintaining environmental quality by 2010. (EU)

Lithosphere – The solid inorganic portion of the Earth (composed of rocks, minerals and elements). It can be regarded as the outer surface of the solid Earth. (EES)

Little Ice Age – A cold period that lasted from about AD 1550 to about AD 1850 in Europe, North America and Asia.

Littoral zone – The part of the shoreline that is submerged at high tide and exposed at low tide. (EES; USEPA)

Living modified organisms (LMOs) – All organisms produced through the use of recombinant DNA technology, with a wider range of modifying technologies relevant when considering living modified prokaryotes and yeast. (CBD)

Loading (water) – The amount of material carried by water into a specified area, expressed as mass per unit of time.

Locum tenens – A diplomatic term best translated as that of a placeholder in the absence of a superior. (WP)

Logic of collective action, concept of – A shared interest in a commonly held and used resource in which all users exercise restraint so as to avoid the collapse of the resource base. (Jared, 2005) See 'Tragedy of the Commons'; '**Sunk-cost effect, concept of.**'

Lomé Convention – An agreement originally signed in 1975 committing the EU to programs of assistance and preferential treatment for the ACP Countries. The Cotonou Agreement replaced the Lomé Convention in June, 2000. (AD)

London Club – An *ad hoc* forum for restructuring negotiations concerning debt owed to commercial banks. The forum is formed at the initiative of the debtor country and is dissolved when a restructuring agreement is signed. London Club 'Advisory Committees' are chaired by a leading financial firm and include representatives from a cross-section of other exposed firms.

Lose–lose options – See '**Negative sum**.'

Low-income country – A country having an annual gross national product (GNP) per capita equivalent to $760 or less in 1998. The standard of living is lower in these countries; there are few goods and services; and many people cannot meet their basic needs. There are currently about 58 low-income countries with populations of 1 million or more. Their combined population is almost 3.5 billion. (WB)

Mm

Maastricht Treaty – See '**European Union**'.

Make Poverty History® – A UK-based global campaign, which, with its North American partner the ONE® campaign, coordinates the NGO development community to help educate the general public about global poverty and exerts pressure on G8 countries to forgive bilateral and multi-lateral debt to the poorest countries. (TWN) See '**Heavily Indebted Poor Countries**.'

Mainstreaming – A term originally coined in the 1970s to describe education for students with disabilities although now, in terms of GEG, it has come to mean 'inclusive' (i.e. 'mainstreaming environment' means to include environmental protection measures or environmental management considerations in the policies and programs of an institution more or less on the same level as economic and social considerations).

Majority – A number greater than half of a total.

Majority vote (MV-EU) – See '**Qualified "double" majority voting**.'

Malmö Declaration – A ministerial level declaration (May 2000) that focuses on the major environmental challenges of the 21st century, the private sector, civil society and a 10-year review of the UN Conference on Environment and Development.

Malthusian – Based on the theories of British economist Thomas Robert Malthus (1766–1834), who argued that population tends to increase faster than food supply, with inevitably disastrous results, unless the increase in population is checked by moral restraints or by war, famine and disease. (NRDC)

Man and the Biosphere Programme (MAB) – An interdisciplinary program guided by UNESCO dedicated to research and training intended to develop the basis for the rational use and conservation of the resources of the biosphere.

Mandates – A legal term referring to Territories noted in the Charter of the League of Nations and requiring international protection/management in the years after World War I. The Mandates became United Nations Trust Territories with the formation of the UN. (UN) See '**United Nations Trusteeship Council**'.

Mangroves – Salt tolerant trees or shrubs that grow between near mean sea level and the high spring tide mark in accretive shores, where they form distinct communities. (EES; USEPA)

Manifest destiny – A 19th-century belief that the US had a divinely inspired mission to expand, particularly across the North American frontier towards the Pacific Ocean. (WP)

Manila Declaration – The full name for this declaration is 'The Manila Declaration Concerning the Ethical Utilization of Biological Resources', which was developed at the ASOMPS meeting in Manila, Philippines in February, 1992. (BCHM)

Mare clausum – Closed seas as opposed to *mare liberum* (freedom of the seas). (BLD)

Mare liberum – Freedom of the seas as opposed to *mare clausum* (closed seas). (BLD)

Mariculture – Mariculture is the cultivation of marine organisms for food, either in their 'natural environment,' or in seawater in ponds or raceways. (WP)

Market-based environmental instruments – Market-based environmental instruments seek to address the market failure of 'environmental externalities' either by incorporating the external cost of production or consumption activities through taxes or charges on processes or products, or by creating property rights and facilitating the establishment of a proxy market for the use of environmental services. (EEA)

MARPOL Convention – The Convention for the Prevention of Pollution from Ships is the main international convention covering prevention of pollution of the marine environment by ships from operational or accidental causes.

Marsh – Wetland, swamp or bog, saturated with water constantly or recurrently and dominated by herbaceous vegetation. Marshes may be fresh or saltwater, tidal or non-tidal. (NRDC)

Matrix – A non-negotiated reference and informational tool consisting of economic and technical solutions outlining best practices and lessons learned regarding relevant environmental and social actions. (EEA)

Maximum sustainable yield – The maximum amount of a product that can continuously be taken from a stock under existing environmental conditions. (USEPA)

MDIAR agreement – An EU agreement governing the monitoring-data-information-assessment-reporting chain that functions as the main filter for flow of data and information from national monitoring to European reporting systems. See '**Chain of custody**.'

Mediation – Bringing about a peaceful settlement or compromise between parties to a dispute through the benevolent intervention of an impartial third party.

Mediterranean Action Plan (MAP) – The Mediterranean Action Plan, formally the 'Barcelona Convention for the Protection of the Marine Environment and the Coastal Region of the Mediterranean,' strives to protect the environment and to foster sustainable development in the Mediterranean basin. It was adopted in Barcelona, Spain in 1975 by 16 Mediterranean States and the EC, under the auspices of the United Nations Environment Programme (UNEP). Its legal framework comprises the Barcelona Convention adopted in 1976 and revised in 1995, and six protocols covering specific aspects of environmental protection. A Mediterranean Commission for Sustainable Development was also established by MAP in 1995 to facilitate the participation of all stakeholders in the Mediterranean area. (EEA)

Medium-sized projects – Medium-sized projects require no more than US\$1 million in GEF financing for preparation and implementation. Most GEF projects average \$5.5 million per project and take several years to implement. As the GEF has gained experience in implementing projects, it has been recognized that smaller projects could benefit from expedited procedures so that they could be designed and executed more quickly and efficiently. (GEF)

Meeting of the Parties (MOP) – Whereas the Conference of the Parties carries with it the sense of 'association' or 'members' and is reserved for conventions, 'meeting of the parties' is meant to convey the sense of an encounter and is reserved for a meeting of the parties to a protocol.

Mekong River Commission (MRC) – A commission established in 1995 by the governments of Cambodia, Laos, Thailand and Vietnam to help manage the 4880km river. Myanmar and China are not members, although the river flows through their territories.

Member states (1) – Governments that officially participate in an intergovernmental organization or are a 'party' to a convention.

Member states (2) – Members of the UN General Assembly and/or its subsidiary bodies and specialized organizations, an international or intergovernmental body. (UN)

Memorandum of Understanding (MOU) – An agreement defining the roles and responsibilities of all parties in relation to the other parties on an issue of interest to each (often made between international organizations). (UNT)

MERCOSUR – The 'common market of the South,' created by the 1991 Treaty of Asunción (Paraguay). MERCOSUR originally included Argentina, Brazil, Paraguay and Uruguay. Chile and Bolivia became associate members in 1996 and 1997, respectively. Venezuela became a member in mid-2006. (AD) See '**South American Community of Nations**.'

Meteorology – The science of the Earth's atmosphere aimed at understanding the processes by which every state of the atmosphere is created, matures and is ultimately dissipated. (EES)

Methane – A hydrocarbon with four hydrogen atoms attached to each carbon atom (CH_4).

Microclimate – The climatic conditions on the scale of a vegetation or crop canopy, together with the immediately adjacent atmosphere and underlying soil layers. It has a vertical measure of approximately 1 meter for crops and between 10–30 meters for forest canopies. (EES)

Microcredit – A small loan to a client made by a bank or other institution, offered, often without collateral, to an individual or through group lending. Microcredit came to prominence in the 1980s, although early experiments date back 30 years in Bangladesh, Brazil and a few other countries. The important difference of microcredit is that it has avoided the pitfalls of an earlier generation of targeted development lending, by insisting on repayment, by charging interest rates that could cover the costs of credit delivery, and by focusing on client groups whose alternative source of credit is the informal sector. Emphasis shifted from rapid disbursement of subsidized loans to prop up targeted sectors to build local, sustainable institutions to serve the poor. Microcredit has largely been a private (non-profit) sector initiative that avoided becoming overtly political or bureaucratic, and has outperformed virtually all other forms of development lending in terms of repayment success. In recent years, development banks have also initiated similar programs. (UN) See '**Microfinance**,' '**Grameen banking**.'

Microfauna – That part of an animal population too small to be clearly distinguishable without the use of a microscope, including protozoan and nematodes. (USEPA)

Microfinance – Microfinance refers to loans, savings, insurance, transfer services and other financial products targeted at low-income clients. Microfinance means providing very poor families with very small loans (microcredit) to help them engage in productive activities or grow their tiny businesses. Over time, microfinance has come to include a broader range of services (credit, savings, insurance, etc.) as we have come to realize that the poor and the very poor who lack access to traditional formal financial institutions require a variety of financial products. (UN) See '**Microcredit**.'

Microflora – That part of a plant population too small to be clearly distinguishable without the use of a microscope, including antinomycete, bacteria and some algae and fungi. (USEPA)

Micronationalism – Division of larger states or regions along ethnic, linguistic, cultural and/or religious lines. Civil unrest, ethnic, linguistic, cultural and religious tensions, terrorism, factionalism and separatism have conjointly created a new texture of political boundaries and friction in contemporary society. (CW) See '**Balkanization**.'

Microvending – Selling small amounts of products such as is practiced by street vendors throughout the world. See '**Grameen banking**,' '**Microfinance**,' '**Microcredit**.'

Middle East Quartet – An informal group comprising the UN, EU, the Russian Federation and the US formed in 2004 and dedicated to working with Palestinians and Israelis to resolve land, water and security/access issues among others in that region. (UN)

Middle-income country – A country having an annual GNP per capita equivalent to more than $760 but less than $9360 in 1998. The standard of living is higher than in low-income countries, and people have access to more goods and services, but many people still cannot meet their basic needs. There are currently about 65 middle-income countries with populations of 1 million or more. Their combined population is more than 1.5 billion. (WB)

Millennium +5 Summit (MDG +5) – In September 2005, the UN held a high-level plenary meeting – also referred to as the MDG+5 or the World Summit 2005 – to review the implementation of the Millennium Declaration (2000), and the integrated follow-up to the major UN conferences and summits in the economic and social fields. Member States at the Summit also deliberated the Secretary-General's March 2005 report on the implementation of the Millennium Development Goals as well as issues related to peace and security, and his proposals for UN reform. (UN)

Millennium Challenge Account (MCA) – A US$5 billion annual grant program of the US Government created in 2002 that developed out of a World Bank research project showing that aid money is most effectively spent in countries that are governed well. This program links financial assistance to 16 objectively measured social and economic criteria including reform initiatives promoting democracy, government transparency, civil liberties, immunization rates and trade policy. (USAID)

Millennium Challenge Corporation (MCC) – A US Government corporation charged with managing the MCA and designed to support innovative strategies and to ensure accountability for measurable results. (USAID)

Millennium Declaration – The United Nations Millennium Declaration was adopted at the Millennium Summit in September 2000 by 147 heads of State and Government, and the then 191 Member States of the UN. The Declaration spells out values and principles, as well as goals in the priority areas of peace, development (reducing global poverty by half and creating universal primary education by the year 2015), the environment, human rights, protecting the vulnerable, the special needs of Africa and strengthening the UN. (UNMD)

Millennium Development Goals (MDGs) – The *Millennium Declaration*, adopted by the UN Member States in 2000, established eight Millennium Development Goals to be reached by the year 2015:

- eradicate extreme poverty and hunger;
- achieve universal primary education;
- promote gender equality and empower women;
- reduce child mortality;
- improve maternal health;
- combat HIV/AIDS, malaria and other diseases;
- ensure environmental sustainability;
- develop a global partnership for development.

The goals detail 18 specific development targets, each of which has a time frame and indicators designed to monitor degree of achievement. The cost to attain these goals is between $40–$60 billion each year in additional development assistance. See Appendix 1. (UN)

Millennium Ecosystem Assessment (MA) – A program modeled on the IPCC as a multi-scale, interdisciplinary assessment of biodiversity to meet the scientific needs of the Ramsar Convention on Wetlands, the CBD and the Convention to Combat Desertification. It is a scientifically based roadmap for how we could slow or reverse ecosystem degradation as an important step in the sustainable development process. The final published volume of the Millennium Ecosystem Assessment, the four-year, landmark report on the state of the world's ecosystems, was released in January 2006. The MA was commissioned by the UN and involved 1300 scientists from 95 countries. (UN)

Millennium gap – The growing gap between ODA pledges and actual disbursements.

Millennium Project – The UN Secretary-General and the Administrator of the UNDP launched the Millennium Project in 2000 to recommend the best strategies for achieving the MDGs. The Millennium Project's research focused on the operational priorities, organizational means of implementation, and financing structures necessary to achieve the MDGs. Ten thematically orientated task forces undertook the research and comprised representatives from academia, the public and private sectors, civil society organizations, and UN agencies under the leadership of Professor

M

Jeffrey Sachs of Columbia University. The Millennium Project submitted its report *Investing in Development: A Practical Plan to Achieve the Millennium Development Goals* to the UN Secretary-General and the Administrator of the UNDP in January, 2005. Among other recommendations, it called for industrialized nations to dedicate 0.7 percent of GDP to ODA activities in support of the MDGs. In September 2005 a summit was held to review the progress on achieving the MDGs. (UNDP) See '**Millennium +5 Summit**.'

Millennium village – A concept that tangible steps towards realizing the MDGs are most effective if undertaken at the village level with small inputs of targeted funding and under the control of village leadership. The UN has stated that this model brings reality to the oft-cited slogan 'think globally, act locally.' (UNW)

Minister (1) – A high officer of a state entrusted with management of a division of government activities. (MW)

Minister (2) – A diplomatic representative ranking below an ambassador. (MW)

Ministerial (meeting) segment – See '**High-level (meeting) segment**.'

Misc. docs – Miscellaneous documents issued on plain paper with no masthead: they generally contain views or comments submitted as received from a delegation without formal editing.

Mission (1) – Official travel for an administration, representational or technical purpose. (UN)

Mission (2) – Used interchangeably with 'embassy,' when the representative, often carrying the rank and title of ambassador is accredited to an international organization rather than the office of the ambassador, accredited to a country, which is referred to as the embassy. (UN)

Mitigation – Actions taken during the planning, design, construction and operation of works and undertakings to alleviate the potential adverse effects of those activities on other interests. (USEPA)

Modality – A ceremonial form, protocol or condition that surrounds formal agreements or negotiations. (DC)

Model United Nations (MUN) – A simulation education activity focusing on civics, communications, globalization and multilateral diplomacy. In MUN, secondary or college level students take on roles as foreign diplomats and participate in a simulated session of an intergovernmental organization. Participants research a country or accredited NGO, take on a role as a diplomat, investigate international issues, debate, deliberate, consult, and then develop solutions to world problems. (WP) See '**C8 for kids**.'

Modus vivendi – An instrument recording an international agreement of temporary or provisional nature intended to be replaced by an arrangement of a more permanent and detailed character. It is usually made in an informal way, and never requires ratification. (UNT)

Monitoring – A continuous process of collecting and analyzing information to measure the progress of a project toward expected results. Monitoring provides managers and participants with regular feedback that can help determine whether a project is progressing as planned. (UNDP)

Monitoring and evaluation (M&E) – The periodic evaluation of management activities to determine how well objectives were met and how management practices should be adjusted.

Monkeywrenching – A term coined to illustrate 'economic warfare' by sabotage, often by illegal means, used to slow down or halt an undesired government-sanctioned activity, particularly in natural or protected areas such as forests and parks. In the US the term is most often used in the context of eco-defense from one political point of view to eco-terrorism or ecotage on the other extreme. Monkeywrenching is therefore the destruction of equipment such as bulldozers, logging equipment and road-building machinery. It also includes the removal of road survey markers, billboards and certain bridges, power lines, power poles and towers, and roads. The term 'monkeywrenching' comes from Edward Abbey's novel *The Monkey Wrench Gang* published in 1975. (WP)

Monterrey Consensus – The primary document resulting from the International Conference on Financing for Development (ICFD) that has as its goal to 'eradicate poverty, achieve sustained economic growth and promote sustainable development' that looks toward a 'fully inclusive and equitable global economic system.' Actions are to treat the issues of the mobilization of domestic financial resources for development; mobilization of international resources for development, foreign direct investment and other private flows; international trade as an engine for development; the augmentation of international financial and technical cooperation for development; external debt; and economic issues, and the coherence and consistency of international monetary, financial and trading systems in support of development.

Montevideo Programme – A long-term strategic program of UNEP that provides the foundation for the development of environmental law. Its achievements include the development of global conventions on the ozone layer, transboundary movements of hazardous wastes, biological diversity and information exchange on hazardous chemicals.

Montreal Process – An international working group established to identify and define criteria and indicators for the sustainable management of temperate and boreal forests. (UNT)

Montreal Protocol (on Substances that Deplete the Ozone Layer) – The principal international agreement under which ozone-depleting compounds are regulated. Established in 1987 and entered into force on 1 January (1992), it has subsequently been adjusted and amended. (UNT)

Moratorium – A legislative (Parliamentary or Congressional) action that prevents a law or policy from being implemented. (MW; NRDC)

Morbidity – The number of sick persons in relation to a specific population pool. (MW)

Mortality – The number of deaths in relation to a specific population pool. (MW)

MOSAICC – A voluntary code of conduct developed to facilitate easy access to, and international circulation of, microbial genetic resources for the benefit of science and worldwide sustainable development in the framework of the CBD. (BCHM)

Most favored nation clause – A principle that guides progress towards trade liberalization within GATT and WTO whereby any advantage granted by one signatory country to another must be extended to all the other signatory countries. (AD)

Multidimensional (problem solving) – A term that gained prominence internationally in 2005 at the Davos, Switzerland World Economic Forum to describe a system in which states and state-based multilateral organizations work with businesses and civil society through a dense web of international and interdisciplinary networks to solve complex problems requiring coordinated responses not only across geographic borders, but also across professional ones. Examples cited include terrorism, the proliferation of weapons of mass destruction, corporate fraud involving multinational companies, pandemics, environmental disasters, poverty, spread of technology, intellectual property management and the interdependence of markets. (WEF)

Multifunctionality – The idea that agriculture has many functions in addition to producing food and fiber, e.g. environmental protection, landscape preseravation, rural employment, food security, etc. (WTO)

Multilateral – Negotiations, agreements or treaties that effect or are between three or more parties, countries or other civil society organizations. (MW)

Multilateral Agreement on Investments (MAI) – The Multilateral Agreement on Investments is the result of negotiations within the Organisation for Economic Co-operation and Development and is designed to eliminate nearly all barriers to international trade by liberalizing international trade laws and protecting foreign investments. Its basic provisions are to open most economic and natural resource sectors to foreign ownership; treat foreign firms fairly and equally; remove restrictions against the movement of capital; allow individual firms to sue foreign governments before an international mediation panel; and give full and proper compensation for expropriation. It was never adopted. (TWN)

Multilateral aid – Aid channeled through multilateral institutions for use in, or on behalf of, aid recipient countries.

Multilateral institutions – International institutions with governmental membership, spanning several regions, including financial institutions such as the World Bank and IMF, UN agencies and regional groupings.

Multilateral Investment Guarantee Agency (MIGA) – A component of the World Bank Group established in 1988 and including 164 member countries that assists economic development through loan guarantees to foreign investors. (WB)

Multistakeholder (MS) – Term used to describe the case where there are a number of parties interested in the outcome of a decision; *Agenda 21* lists women, youth, Indigenous Peoples, NGOs, business and industry, workers and trade unions, science and technology, farmers and local authorities as being the major stakeholders that should be included in environment/development discussions. (UNED)

Multi-stakeholder dialogue – Meetings that enable direct interactions between governments and major groups on specific topics and as part of the official intergovernmental process rather than taking place on the margins. The dialogues allow major groups to discuss their concerns, experiences and proposals in specific areas in detail with governments. (WSSD)

Mutates mutandis – The necessary changes having been made; having substituted new terms; with respective differences taken into consideration.

Mutually coherent policies – Policies that are related to one another such that they are consistent, cohesive and understandable.

My wonderful world campaign – In mid-2006 the National Geographic Society, the United Nations Foundation and leaders from the business, non-profit and education communities initiated a public-engagement campaign designed to give students tools to become more informed global citizens by aiming to improve geographic and environmental literacy about the world they will inherit. (UNW)

M

Nn

Nation – A stable, historically developed community of people with a territory, economic life, distinctive culture, and language in common. (MW) See **'Country,' 'State,' 'Territory.'**

National delegation – One or more officials who are empowered to represent and negotiate on behalf of their government. (BCHM)

National Environment Action Plan (NEAP) – A plan that identifies key environmental problems, sets priorities for dealing with them and leads to a comprehensive national environmental policy and programs to implement the policy. (GEF)

National income accounts – A system of accounting used to measure a nation's economy, the results of which are often given in terms of GNP or GDP.

National interest, concept of – A concept that identifies interests of one country that are distinct from or even contrary to those of another.

National park – A reserve of land, usually owned by a national government, that is protected from most development activities. Hunting, logging, mining, commercial fishing, agriculture and livestock grazing are all controlled within national parks, as is industrial activity. (IUCN; UNEP) See **'Protected Area Management Categories.'**

National Strategies for Sustainable Development (NSSD) – According to an agreement produced at the UN Rio+5 Conference, the NSSD are a plan of national action developed to achieve sustainable development goals.

Nations, 0.7 – Those countries meeting the standard of designating 0.7 percent or greater of GDP for ODA-supported activities. See **'Millennium Project;' 'Global tax.'**

Native species – Plants, animals, fungi and microorganisms that occur naturally in a given area or region.

Natura 2000 – EU network of sites designated by Member States under the birds and habitats directives. (EEA)

Natural capital – Mineral, plant and animal formations of the Earth's biosphere when viewed as a means of producing natural goods and services such as oxygen, water filter services, and soil stabilization. It is one approach to ecosystem valuation, an alternative to the traditional view of all non-human life as passive natural resources, and to the idea of ecological health. (WP)

Natural hazards – A naturally occurring geophysical condition that threatens life or property usually involving the risk of extreme events in which phenomena in the atmosphere, hydrosphere, lithosphere or biosphere differ substantially from their mean values. For example, excessive rainfall may give rise to floods, while a lack of precipitation may lead to drought. The main natural hazards include: earthquakes, tsunamis, volcanic eruptions, floods, drought, hurricanes (typhoons, tropical cyclones), tornadoes, lightning and severe thunderstorms, hailstorms, avalanches, glacier hazards, snow storms, frost hazards, soil erosion, desertification, landslides, land subsidence, soil heave and collapse, coastal erosion, wildfires and dam disasters. (EES)

Natural law – A theory based on the premise that there are certain normative principles that are 'self-evident' and which exist independently of their codification or enforcement by human beings. (ECO)

Natural persons – People, as distinct from juridical persons such as companies and organizations. (WTO)

Natural resource – A term describing anything that is provided by nature, such as minerals deposits, forests, water, wildlife, etc. The term is being replaced by 'natural' or 'ecosystem services.'

Natural Step, concept of – Dr Karl-Henrik Robert, one of Sweden's leading oncologists, developed the Natural Step program as a method of reaching consensus about sustainable futures. The Natural Step model is a simple, scientifically based approach to sustainable development that encourages environmental systems thinking within corporations, governments and academic institutions founded on basic science principles and the principal that humanity cannot tolerate continual degradation of the environment. (NS)

Navigable waters – Traditionally, waters sufficiently deep and wide for navigation by all or specified vessels. (USEPA)

Negative sum – The idea, from game theory that agents combine in such a way that both lose or that the total change is a reduction in overall fitness, sometimes called dysergy or 'lose–lose' when referring to a situation that solutions proposed do not serve the interests of any of the parties involved in a disagreement.

Negotiated science – Conclusions of government appointed scientists

N

that are criticized by nongovernmental scientists as representing compromises rather than pure scientific findings.

Negotiating state – A state that took part in the drawing up and adoption of the text of a treaty. (VC)

Negotiation – A process whereby two or more people who begin with conflicting positions attempt to reach an agreement by modifying their original positions or by developing new proposals that reconcile the interests underlying them. The preliminary discussions leading up to the adoption of an agreement.

Neoclassical economics – A system of economics that seeks the optimum allocation of resources through market competition in which the well-being of one individual cannot be increased without that of another being diminished.

Neoliberalism – A business-government philosophy based on the primacy of the individual with only a minimal role for government. Neoliberal policies recommend solutions based on free movement of goods, services and capital, with reliance on market forces to allocate resources.

Net present value (NPV) – An economic criterion used to evaluate whether a project is economically viable or not where the discounted value of the expected costs of an investment is deducted from the discounted value of the expected benefits of the same investment. If the NPV is positive, the project or action is usually considered worthwhile. Likewise the NPVs of more than one project can be compared to isolate the one that would theoretically be preferred.

Never Again, Principle of – See 'Responsibility to Protect, the Doctrine of.'

New Europe – A rhetorical term to describe the bloc of Easter European post-Communist countries including Bulgaria, Czech Republic, Estonia, Hungary, Latvia, Lithuania, Poland, Romania, Slovakia and Slovenia. (WP)

New Partnership for Africa (NPfA) – A voluntary, independent anti-corruption mechanism including an inspectorate that can assess whether a government is seeking to run itself in an honest and accountable way. The inspectorate, including experts from other countries, verifies a government's claims against 40 criteria by examining documents and conducting in-depth interviews with government leaders, opposition leaders, civic and religious groups and NGOs active in the country.

New world order – This term refers to the dramatic changes in world political thought and the balance of power after the collapse of the Soviet

Union and based on the notion of a Western-led post-Cold War structure of global power. (WP) See 'Global parliament.'

Niche – The place occupied by a species in an ecosystem and its role: where it lives, what it feeds on, and when it performs its activities. (EES)

NIMBY, principle of – See 'Not in my backyard, principle of.'

Nitrogen oxides – Gases that contribute to acid rain and global warming emitted as a byproduct of fossil fuel combustion. (NRDC)

Noblemaire Principle – A concept dating from 1921 and the League of Nations and adopted by the UN when it was formed that provides that salaries of staff at the professional and higher categories in the UN system be set by reference to the highest paid national civil service. For that, the US Federal Civil Service has been used as the comparator. The margin is the average percentage difference between the pay of UN staff in New York and that of the US federal service. In addition to the UN system, there are 13 other international and regional organizations that subscribe to this principle, but in practice the salaries of staff of many international or regional organizations, such as the development banks, exceed those called for in this principle by substantial amounts. (UN) See 'Base floor salary scale,' 'Post adjustment index,' 'P-level staff,' 'D-level staff.'

No net loss – A working principle that strives to balance unavoidable habitat losses with habitat replacement on a project-by-project basis.

No-regrets measures – Decisions and actions taken that can reduce greenhouse gas emissions but which merit implementation purely on a financial basis.

Non-Aligned Movement (NAM) – A group of 114 developing countries and an important lobbying group in global affairs. Since its inception in 1961, the movement has played a highly visible role in representing the interests of developing countries, particularly in the eradication of colonialism, supporting struggles for liberation and self-determination, the pursuit of world peace and the search for a more equitable and just global order including addressing environmental issues of regional or global interest. (UNW)

Non-consumptive value – A value assigned to a resource that is not diminished by the use of that resource.

Nongovernmental actor – The full range of NGOs and civil society including the major groups identified at UNCED.

Nongovernmental organization (NGO) – A non-profit group or association organized outside of institutionalized political structures to realize particular social objectives or serve particular constituencies. (GBS)

Nongovernmental organization consultative status (with ECOSOC) – The authority granted to an NGO to be formally accredited to a UN meeting or conference and have formal 'voice' (without vote). Today more than 2600 NGOs enjoy this status. Article 71 of the UN Charter provided the arrangements for formal consultation with nongovernmental organizations. The consultative relationship with ECOSOC is governed today by ECOSOC resolution 1996/31, which outlines the eligibility requirements for consultative status, rights and obligations of NGOs in consultative status, procedures for the withdrawal or suspension of consultative status, the role and functions of the ECOSOC Committee on NGOs, and the responsibilities of the UN Secretariat in supporting the consultative relationship. Consultative status is granted by ECOSOC upon recommendation of the ECOSOC Committee on NGOs, which comprises 19 Member States. (UN)

Non-group – Under circumstances of extreme reluctance to enter into negotiation, non-groups can be called into being by the chair in order to encourage communication without the pressure of negotiations. (Gupta, 1997)

Non-linear – A term used to describe systems that behave in unexpected ways and that do not change proportionally to a change in input. The change may sometimes go down when expected to go up, do nothing instead, or change drastically with only minor changes to the input. (CSG)

Non-methane volatile organic compounds (NMVOC) – Compounds generally emitted from combustion sources that can combine with other pollutants to produce photochemical smog.

Non-papers – In-session documents issued informally to facilitate negotiations; they do not have an official document symbol or number although they may have an identifying number or the name of the author(s). (CBD)

Non-party – A state that has not ratified a convention but may attend meetings of a COP, MOP or their subsidiary bodies as an observer.

Non-point source pollution (NPSP) – Pollution emanating from diffuse sources and caused by rainfall or snowmelt moving over and through the ground. (USEPA)

Non-reimbursable grant – That part of a pre-investment study (pre-feasibility or feasibility study) or loan package that is not required to be repaid by the borrowing or beneficiary country even if the project proves to have an internal rate of return that does not support the loan. (WB)

Non-renewable natural resources – The term refers to natural resources found in the ground or in the sea with a finite stock that can only be replaced or increased in a geologic time frame. Examples include oil, coal, natural gas, mineral rock and, in certain circumstances, freshwater when it is removed from aquifers that are not being recharged (fossil water). (EES)

Non-state Actor – An individual, private company or NGO that has suf-ficient influence to impact a decision taken in an intergovernmental body. (Suskind 2006)

Noosphere – The realm of the human mind interconnected and interacting through communication and a manifestation of the most advanced life form on this planet, *homo sapiens*. It is the realm of human possibility that distin-guishes humans from all other life forms. (EES)

North American Agreement on Environmental Cooperation (NAAEC) – Established by the governments of Canada, Mexico and the US, the Agreement aims to: (a) foster the protection and improvement of the environment in the territories of the parties for the well-being of present and future generations; (b) promote sustainable development based on co-operation and mutually supportive environmental and economic policies; (c) increase cooperation between the parties to better conserve, protect and enhance the environment, including wild flora and fauna; (d) support the en-vironmental goals and objectives of the NAFTA; (e) avoid creating trade dis-tortions or new trade barriers; (f) strengthen cooperation on the development and improvement of environmental laws, regulations, procedures, policies and practices; (g) enhance compliance with, and enforcement of, environ-mental laws and regulations; (h) promote transparency and public participa-tion in the development of environmental laws, regulations and policies; (i) promote economically efficient and effective environmental measures; and (j) promote pollution prevention policies and practices. (NAFTA) See '**Com-mission on Environmental Cooperation**.'

N

North American Biodiversity Information Network (NABIN) – An initiative of Mexico, the US and Canada to provide greater access to biodi-versity information.

North American Commission for Environmental Cooperation (NACEC) – Canada, the US and Mexico forged a trilateral commission made up of Canada's Minister of Environment, Mexico's Secretary of the Environment and the Administrator of the USEPA to address regional en-vironmental concerns, help prevent potential trade and environmental con-flicts, and promote effective enforcement of environmental law. The Agree-ment, which was established under the terms and objectives of NAAEC complements the environmental provisions of the North American Free Trade Agreement (NAFTA). See '**North American Agreement on En-vironmental Cooperation (NAAEC)**.'

North American Free Trade Agreement (NAFTA) – An agreement implemented in 1994 committing Canada, the US, and Mexico to the elimi-nation of all tariffs, quotas, and other trade barriers between them before 2009. See '**North American Agreement on Environmental Coop-eration**,' '**Commission on Environmental Cooperation**.'

Northern countries – High-income or developed countries.

North–South (1) – A term indicating collaboration or technology sharing between a 'northern' country and one from the 'south.'

North–South (2) – North referring to developed countries; South referring to developing countries.

Norwegian Agency for Development Cooperation (NORAD) – The principal agency through which Norway provides technical assistance and distributes foreign aid.

Not in my backyard, principle of (NIMBY) – The so-called 'NIMBY principle' is a broad concept that includes any organized movement against any proposed development or investment, implying that while the proposed development may or may not be important, it should not be constructed where it is proposed. See '**PIMBY, principle of.**'

Notification – A formality through which a state or an international organization communicates certain facts or events of legal importance. Instead of opting for the exchange of documents or deposit, states may be content to notify their consent to the other party or to the depositary. (VC)

Nuclear club – A term commonly used to indicate those nations having uranium conversion capabilities, either for nuclear energy or arms production. There are currently seven states known to be nuclear weapons states; an internationally recognized status conferred through a verification process by the Treaty on the Non-Proliferation of Nuclear Weapons (NPT). In order of acquisition of nuclear weapons they are: the US, Russia, the UK, France, the People's Republic of China, India and Pakistan. Several other nations have either claimed or are suspected to possess uranium conversion capabilities and/or possess nuclear weapons without having had such claims verified, including Israel and North Korea. (UNIAEA)

Nuclear energy – Energy or power produced by nuclear reactions – fusion (a process in which two nuclei join, forming a larger nucleus and releasing or absorbing energy) or fission (when the nucleus splits into two or more smaller nuclei releasing substantial amounts of energy). (NRDC; WP)

Nuclear Threat Initiative – An initiative of Ted Turner of the UN Foundation, former US Senator San Nunn and entrepreneur Warren Buffett who together pledged US$50 million to the IAEA to create a uranium stockpile. The aim is to supply low-grade fuel for nuclear power plants around the world and discourage countries from developing their own nuclear programs. (UN)

Nutrients – Organic or inorganic compounds essential for the survival of an organism. In aquatic environments, nitrogen and phosphorus are important nutrients that affect the growth rate of plants. (SFWMD)

Oo

Objection – Any signatory or contracting state has the option of objecting to a reservation, *inter alia*, if, in its opinion, the reservation is incompatible with the purpose of the treaty. (VC)

Observer – A state or other institution such as the specialized agencies of the UN, other international organizations, and qualified governmental and nongovernmental organizations that are accredited to attend the meetings of COP, MOP and their subsidiary bodies, and having 'voice' at the discretion of the president of the meeting, but never having a direct 'vote' from the floor. (UN)

Ocean desert – A portion of the sea floor that is barren of obvious forms of life.

OECD – See '**Organisation for Economic Co-operation and Development.**'

Official assistance (OA) – Similar to ODA but is intended for countries in the OECD-DAC Part II list – countries in transition. (OECD)

Official development assistance (ODA) (1) – The amount that a nation expends through grants and other development assistance programs calculated as a percent of GNP. A net ODA target of 0.7 percent of GNP for developed nations was agreed to at the 1990 UN General Assembly and reiterated at various summits such as the UN Conference on Environment and Development (UNCED) in 1992. A net ODA target for the least developed beneficiary countries (HIPC or LLDC) of 0.15 percent of GNP was agreed to at the 1981 UN Conference on LLDC. The World Bank estimated that ODA totaled US\$106.5 billion in 2006. (UN; WB) See '**Remittances.**'

Official development assistance (ODA) (2) – Flows of grant moneys to OECD-DAC Part I aid recipients administered with the promotion of the economic development and welfare of developing countries as its main objective. This aid is concessional in character and conveys a grant element of at least 25 percent (calculated at a discount rate of 10 percent). (OECD) See '**Organisation for Economic Co-operation and Development – Development Assistance Committee Part I List.**'

Official development assistance, bilateral – ODA that is administered and sent to the recipient country by the donor country. It may pass through an NGO provided that it remains under the control of the donor country. (OECD)

Official development assistance, multilateral – ODA consists of donations made by OECD member countries through regional groupings such as the EU, or grants by development banks to international organizations working in development. (OECD)

Official UN languages – See 'Language(s), official.'

Offsetting effect – Increased consumption resulting from actions that increase efficiency and reduce consumer costs. One example would be a home insulation program that reduces heat loss by 50 percent but does not bring about an equal reduction in energy consumption, because residents can then afford to keep their homes warmer more cheaply. (VTPI)

Offshore – Away from the shoreline; refers largely to the expanse of submerged continental shelf on the ocean side of the shoreline but may also refer to areas nearer the ocean edge of the shelf. Used also to refer to the area beyond the three nautical miles territorial waters. (EEA)

Oil Spills Protocol – The protocol concerning cooperation in combating oil spills in the Wider Caribbean Region that was adopted and entered into force concurrently with the Cartagena Convention. (UNEP-CAR/RCU)

Old Europe – Traditionally a term referring to Western European nations and members of NATO. In January 2003, the term Old Europe was used out of its normal context by US Government officials to refer to those European countries that did not support the 2003 invasion of Iraq. (WP)

Omnibus spending bill – A US legislative term meaning a bill combining the appropriations for several federal agencies. (NRDC)

ONE – See 'Make Poverty History.'

Open-ended Intergovernmental Group of Ministers or their Representatives (IGM) – The group of ministers mandated in Decision 21/21 of the UNEP Governing Council (February 2001) to undertake a comprehensive policy-oriented assessment of existing institutional weaknesses as well as future needs and options for strengthened international environmental governance, including the financing of UNEP. (UNEP)

Operational focal point – A focal point charged with coordinating GEF operational matters within a country. See 'Political focal point.'

Opportunity cost (1) – The value of goods or services foregone, including ecosystem goods and services.

Opportunity cost (2) – The value of that which must be given up in order to achieve something else. (MW)

Organization – A social group with a structure designed to achieve collective goals. (UNDP)

Organisation for Economic Co-operation and Development (OECD) – An intergovernmental organization that includes most of the world's industrialized, market economies (Australia, Austria, Belgium, Canada, Czech Republic, Denmark, Finland, France, Germany, Greece, Hungary, Iceland, Ireland, Italy, Japan, Korea, Luxembourg, Mexico, The Netherlands, New Zealand, Norway, Poland, Portugal, Slovak Republic, Spain, Sweden, Switzerland, Turkey, the UK, and the US).

Organisation for Economic Co-operation and Development Convention on Combating Bribery of Foreign Public Officials in International Business Transactions – Adopted by OECD members in 1997 (and entered into force in 1999), the Convention imposes criminal sanctions on those convicted of bribing foreign officials and provides for monitoring and evaluation through country peer reviews. In a complimentary action, OECD published *Risk Awareness Tool for Multinational Enterprises in Weak Governance Zones*, which addresses risks and ethical dilemmas that companies are likely to face in particular countries with weak institutions. (OECD)

Organisation for Economic Co-operation and Development – Development Assistance Committee Part I List (OECD-DAC Part I list) – A list of the world's developing countries classified as least developed countries, low-income countries, lower middle income countries, upper middle income countries. (OECD)

Organisation for Economic Co-operation and Development – Development Assistance Committee Part II List (OECD-DAC Part II list) – Countries classified as being 'in transition' to market economies and developed country status by the OECD-DAC. (OECD)

Organization of African Unity (OAU) – The Organization of African Unity was established in 1963 to promote self-government, respect for territorial boundaries, and social progress throughout the African Continent. Membership is open to all independent African countries. The OAU was replaced in 2001 by the African Union.

Organization of American States (OAS) – A western hemisphere organization established in 1890 (as the Pan American Union) to provide a forum for political, economic, social and cultural cooperation among its 35 member and 54 observer states. The OAS Charter was opened for signature in 1948 and entered into force in 1950. (OAS)

Organization of Eastern Caribbean States (OECS) – The OECS came into being in June 1981, when seven eastern Caribbean countries signed a treaty agreeing to cooperate with each other and promote unity and solidarity among the Members. The Treaty became known as the Treaty of Basseterre, so named in honor of the capital city of St. Kitts and Nevis where it was signed. The OECS is now a nine-member grouping comprising Antigua and Barbuda, Commonwealth of Dominica, Grenada, Montserrat, St. Kitts and Nevis, St. Lucia, and St. Vincent and the Grenadines. Anguilla and the British Virgin Islands are associate members of the OECS.

Oslo Convention – See '**Convention for the Prevention of Marine Pollution by Dumping from Ships and Aircraft**.'

OSPAR Convention – The Convention for the Protection of the Marine Environment of the North-East Atlantic was opened for signature at the Ministerial Meeting of the Oslo and Paris Commissions in Paris on 22 September, 1992 and entered into force on 25 March, 1998. (EEA)

Our Common Future – The final report of the UN World Commission on Environment and Development published in 1987. See '**Sustainable development**.'

Outfall – The point of discharge of wastewater.

Overarching role – A term variously used to mean the 'preponderant,' 'strategic,' and/or 'overriding' objective or theme of an institution that may include a sense of a high degree of formal and informal influence.

Oxfam – A British NGO formed in 1942 as a development, relief and campaigning organization dedicated to finding lasting solutions to poverty and suffering around the world. (Ox)

Ozone – Technically, the triatomic, allotropic form of oxygen, with the formula O_3. What is important for humanity is that ozone is the most chemically active form of oxygen and over time spans of several months is only semi-stable. In the terrestrial environment it has two sources and two areas of concentration: (a) in the stratosphere it is a normal natural product of solar radiation, but is subject to accelerated destruction by anthropogenic release into the atmosphere of certain chlorine and nitrogen compounds; and (b) at the Earth's surface in urban environments as a product of urban pollution in photochemical smog. (EES)

Ozone depleting substances – A compound that contributes to stratospheric ozone depletion. (EES)

Ozone hole – A sharp seasonal decrease in stratospheric ozone concentration that occurs over Antarctica in the spring. First detected in the late 1970s, the ozone hole continues to appear because of complex chemical reactions in the atmosphere that involves CFCs. (EEA)

Ozone layer – Very dilute atmospheric concentration of ozone found at an altitude of 10–50km above the Earth's surface. (EEA)

Pp

P staff – See '**P-level staff**.'

P5 (1) – The highest rank for professional/technical staff in the UN personnel classification system. See '**P-level staff**.'

P5 (2) – The five permanent and veto-wielding members of the UN Security Council (China, France, Russia, the UK and the US). (UN)

Pacta sunt servanda – The doctrine that agreements must be observed (that is: honored, and obeyed). (BLD)

Pan American Health Organization (PAHO) – A specialized organization of the Organization of American States and a regional agency of the World Health Organization founded in 1902. It provides technical assistance to Latin America and the Caribbean in environmental health and sanitation; water supply, wastewater, control of air, water and soil pollution and hazardous wastes. (PAHO)

Pan American Union – The predecessor to the OAS and the world's oldest regional organization dating to the First International Conference of American States held in Washington, DC from October 1889 to April 1890. (WP)

Pandemic – Widespread throughout an area, nation or the world. (MW)

Parent material – The mineral material from which soil forms.

Paris Club – A group of 19 governments that hold claims on other governments either directly or through their government institutions. Created to maintain strict standards for negotiating debt-restructuring arrangements with bilateral creditors. The following countries are permanent members: Austria, Australia, Belgium, Canada, Denmark, Finland, France, Germany, Ireland, Italy, Japan, The Netherlands, Norway, Russian Federation, Spain, Sweden, Switzerland, the UK and the US.

Paris Conference for Global Ecological Governance – The so-called 'Citizens of the Earth Conference' was held in Paris in early 2007 to receive the IPCC report on global warming. At that Conference President Jacques Chirac of France called for the establishment of a UN Organization to deal with global environmental issues such as climate change. Some 45 countries signed a letter of intent to support such an initiate.

Parliament – A body of individuals to whom the people have entrusted the responsibility of representing them by laying down the legal framework within which society shall be governed and seeing to it that these legal conditions are implemented in a responsible manner by the Executive and through the creation of laws. (IPU)

Participation – A process through which stakeholders influence and share control over development initiatives and the decisions and resources that affect them. It is a process that can improve the quality, effectiveness and sustainability of projects and strengthen ownership and commitment of government and stakeholders. (WB)

Participatory urban governance – The relative degree to which citizens are involved in local policy development, planning, programming, budgeting, service delivery and monitoring. (UNCHS)

Particulate matter – In the form of small liquid or solid particles, particulate matter is suspended in either a gas or a liquid medium. (EES)

Partnership (1) – A relationship resembling a legal partnership and usually involving close cooperation between parties having specified and joint rights and responsibilities. (MW)

Partnership (2) – Two or more parties combining knowledge, skills and means to achieve a common goal. (UNESCO)

Parts per million/billion – The number of 'parts' by weight of a substance per million or billion parts of air or water and normally used to record pollution concentrations.

Party – A state that has consented to be bound by the treaty and for which the treaty is in force. (VC)

Patent – An incorporeal statutory right that gives an inventor, for a limited period, the exclusive right to use or sell a patented product, method or process. (MW)

PDF A, PDF B – See '**Project Preparation and Development Facility**.'

Peacekeeping – The deployment of a UN presence in the field, with the consent of all the parties concerned, normally involving UN military and/ or police personnel and frequently civilians as well. Peacekeeping is a technique that expands the possibilities for both the prevention of conflict and the making of peace. A decision of the Security Council is often considered to be a necessary step prior to deployment of troops. (UN)

Peacemaking – Action to bring hostile parties to agreement, essentially through such peaceful means as those foreseen in Chapter VI of the Charter of the United Nations. (UN)

Peak level – Level of airborne pollutant contaminants much higher than average or occurring for short periods of time in response to sudden releases or intense climatic occurrences.

Pelagic species – Fish that live at or near the surface of the water. (NRDC)

People–planet–profit – See '**Triple bottom-line**.'

People's Summit – A series of meetings held in Rio de Janeiro in 1992 to coincide with the meetings of UNCED attended by thousands of private citizens, and representatives from NGOs, indigenous peoples, businesses, scientific and spiritual groups from all over the world.

Per diem – See '**Daily subsistence allowance**.'

Perm-5 – A reference to the five permanent members of the UN Security Council – China, France Russia, the UK and the US. (UNW)

Perm-5 'convention' – An unwritten, customary practice whereby the five permanent members of the Security Council are allowed to serve on any UN body they choose, in exchange for rarely seeking the leadership of those entities. It is argued that the presence of the permanent five on any UN body makes it more serious and more likely to succeed over the long term, but at the same time can be viewed as too heavy-handed by other Member States. (UNW)

Permafrost – Ground that remains frozen at or below 0°C for at least two consecutive years. (EES)

Persistent organic pollutants (POPs) – Chemical substances that bio-accumulate through the food web and pose a long-term risk to human and environmental health.

Persona non grata – An individual who is unacceptable to or unwelcome by a government.

Perverse environmental subsidies, concept of – Large sums of money that governments pay to support industries that might be uneconomic without the subsidies, but which may be considered strategic to the welfare of a community or a country. For example, support to North Atlantic fisheries, sugar growing in the US or cotton growing in Australia. (Jared, 2005)

Pesticides – Chemical agents used to destroy pests. (NRDC)

Philanthropreneurs – A new generation of philanthropists who believe that donating a portion of their wealth to selected charities can positively impact the development process. See '**Billanthrophy**.'

pH scale – A measure for the degree of acidity of a particular substance on a 0–14 scale. A measure of 14 indicates that the substance is extremely alkaline, a measure of 0 indicates pure acid.

PIC Convention – The PIC Convention (The Rotterdam Convention on the Prior Informed Consent Procedure for Certain Hazardous Chemicals and Pesticides in International Trade) was opened for signature in 1998 and will come into force when ratified by 50 countries. The Convention will allow monitoring and control of international trade in various health-threatening chemicals. Importing countries will decide which chemicals they want to receive and to exclude those they cannot safely manage. (PIC)

PIMBY, principle of – See 'Please in my backyard, principle of.'

Pinochet principle/concept – The term refers to international attempts by a number of countries to pursue justice against the former President of Chile for crimes against citizens of Chile committed during his administration. The concept refers to individual responsibility for international crimes as defined by UN principles and practices, in addition to those of a number of countries and regional entities with a common body of law such as the EU. While the term has generally been applied to human rights violations, reference has been made to the concept in pursuing responsible parties for other 'crimes' in transboundary environmental pollution or boundary violation cases. (IPS; UN) See 'Universal jurisdiction cases,' 'International Criminal Court.'

Plan of action – An official document that outlines the goals, objectives, mandates, partnerships, coordination and management processes, time frame and funding mechanisms of an initiative, project or program.

Plan of Implementation – The Plan of Implementation is one of two documents signed at the 2002 World Summit on Sustainable Development. It is a framework for action for implementation of the UNCED commitments and includes an introduction and chapters on poverty eradication; consumption and production; the natural resource base; health; SIDS; Africa as a priority area for ODA investment; other regional initiatives; means of implementation; and an institutional framework.

Planetary engineering – The application of technology for the purpose of influencing the global properties of a planet. The goal of this theoretical task is to make the world more suitable for supporting life, or other worlds habitable for life. (WP) See 'Geoengineering.'

Plant Genetic Resources for Food and Agriculture (PGRFA) – Any material of plant origin, including reproductive and vegetative propagating material, as well as the genetic parts and components, containing functional units of heredity, of actual or potential value for food and agriculture. (FAO)

Please in my backyard, principle of – The so-called 'PIMBY principle' is the counter to the 'NIMBY principle' and implies support for a proposed development or investment on the part of a citizens' group who consider themselves as partners or stakeholders in the process. See '**NIMBY, principle of**.'

Pledging conference – See '**Donor conference**.'

Plenary – An open session of the entire Conference of the Parties to a convention or to any of the subsidiary bodies where all formal decisions are made. (BCHM)

Plenipotentiary – A person who has full power to do something. The person authorized by an instrument of full powers to undertake a specific treaty action. (UNT) In international law, a senior diplomatic officer commissioned to act for his or her government. A *minister plenipotentiary* is one who by custom ranks immediately below an ambassador and is of the same rank as an envoy extraordinary.

P-level staff – A term used to categorize professional level staff (and salary/benefit package) in the UN and OAS systems, starting at P1 and rising to P5; similar to most civil service ranking systems..

PM10, 20, 30, etc. – Particulate material less than 10 microns in diameter. (NRDC)

Point of order – A challenge from a participant with 'voice rights', via the chair, to the procedure that is being followed or to the germaneness of an amendment or intervention being offered at a meeting. (eD)

Point-source pollution (PSP) – Pollution discharged directly from a specific site such as a municipal sewage treatment plant or an industrial outfall pipe. (USEPA)

Political focal point – A focal point responsible for coordination matters related to GEF governance. See '**Operational focal point**.'

Political will – Having the fortitude and determination to take a decision on a controversial issue and the willingness to accept the political fallout or ramifications from such a decision. Taking the route of minimum conflict. See the essay p24.

Politically correct – A term used to describe language that appears calculated to provide a minimum of offense, particularly to the racial, cultural or other identity groups being described or discussed. (WP)

Polity – A specific form of political organization. (MW) The form of government of a nation, state or organization or the political organization itself, such as a nation.

Polluter pays principle (PPP) – The concept that the cost of measures needed to improve a polluted environment to an acceptable state should be reflected in the cost of the goods and services whose production (or consumption) caused the pollution. (EES)

Pollution offsets – A concept whereby emissions from a proposed new or modified stationary source are balanced by reductions from existing sources to stabilize total emissions. (USEPA)

Pollution prevention – The use of processes, practices, materials, products or energy that avoid or minimize the creation of pollutants and waste, and that reduce the overall risk to human health or the environment. Pollution prevention and cleaner production both focus on a strategy of continuously reducing pollution. (EC)

Population – A group of individuals with common ancestry that are much more likely to mate with one another than with individuals from another such group. (GBS)

Population at risk – Certain populations who are more likely to experience increased risks of diseases, injuries, attack or the effects of natural or man-induced disasters as a result of biologic, social and/or economic characteristics such as age, race, genetic susceptibility, language, literacy, culture, historic rivalries, living conditions and low income. (UN)

Portfolio – The area of official responsibility or duties of an individual, office or institution; the collection of programs and projects belonging to a given theme.

Portuguese Cooperation Institute (ICP) – The principal agency through which Portugal provides technical assistance and distributes foreign aid.

Positive sum – The idea, from game theory that when agents interact they can both benefit, the whole being greater than the sum of the parts; also called synergy or 'win–win.' (CSG)

Post/Posting – An official career assignment (position)/location of assignment. (UN)

Post adjustment index – A formula that when applied measures living conditions of UN staff in a given location compared with costs, based on a basket of goods and services, in New York on a specific date. Post adjustment is a supplement to base pay and is calculated as a percentage of net base pay. (UN)

Potable water – Water that is suitable for human consumption – drinkable and safe. 'Drinkable' water means it is free of unpleasant odors, tastes and colors, and is within reasonable limits of temperature. 'Safe' water means it contains no toxins, carcinogens, pathogenic microorganisms or other health hazards. (EES)

Poverty, relative – A term, normally legally defined at a national or regional level, as the minimum income required to maintain a lifestyle considered acceptable by community (nationally or regionally) standards, and including such measures as shelter, sustenance, access to health services, education, transportation, etc.

Poverty, subjective – A term defining 'poverty' that is based on individual perceptions of income levels required to maintain an acceptable standard of living.

Precautionary Principle – A principle adopted by the 1992 UN Conference on Environment and Development (Rio principle 15) stating: (1) that environmental protection measures should be applied where threats of serious or irreversible environmental damage can be seen even though there is a lack of full scientific certainty of the threat, and (2) that this lack of certainty should not be used to postpone cost-effective actions to prevent environmental degradation. Used for the first time at the 1990 Bergen Conference, which stated: 'when confronted with serious or irreversible environmental threats, the absence of absolute scientific certainty should not serve as a pretext for delaying the adoption of measures to prevent environmental degradation.' Also referred to as the 'precautionary approach.' (UNFCCC)

Precision – The degree of reproducibility of a measurement. Low precision yields high scatter in data. (SFWMD) See '**Accuracy**.'

Preemptive intervention, concept of – A concept, as yet unaccepted by the international community, under which a State (or group of States) take a unilateral decision to intervene in the affairs of another State (or group of States) for vested interests (strategic, political, economic, etc.) or humanitarian or altruistic goals. (The Aspen Institute, 1996) See '**Humanitarian intervention**.'

Preparatory committee (PrepCom) – A committee established as an administrative step in the process to develop an international conference in order to achieve consensus on issues and pre-negotiated documents that world leaders are to approve.

President (1) – Elected individual who presides over a meeting or assembly. For example, a person, generally a senior official or minister from the state or region hosting the meeting elected by the COP to preside over that meeting. (MW)

President (2) – An elected official having the position of both head or chief of state and chief political executive in a republic having a presidential government. (MW)

President (3) – An elected official having the position of head or chief of state, but with only minimal or ceremonial political powers in a republic having a parliamentary government. (MW)

Presidium – An executive committee of a legislative or organizational body that acts for the larger group when it is not in session (WP)

Preventive diplomacy – Action to prevent disputes from arising between parties, to prevent existing disputes from escalating into conflicts and to limit the spread of the latter when they occur. (UN)

Primary forest – A forest largely undisturbed by human activities.

Primary productivity – The rate at which new plant biomass is formed by photosynthesis. Gross primary productivity is the total rate of photosynthetic production of biomass; net primary productivity is gross primary productivity minus the respiration rate. (NASA) The transformation of chemical or solar energy to biomass. Most primary production occurs through photosynthesis. (GBS)

Primary sewage treatment – Removal of floating solids and suspended solids, both fine and coarse, from raw sewage. (USEPA)

Primary treatment – Treatment of urban wastewater by a physical and/or chemical process involving settlement of suspended solids, or other processes in which the BOD and total suspended solids of the incoming wastewater is reduced to predetermined levels before discharge. (EEA)

Prime Minister – The chief political executive in a republic having a parliamentary government.

Principle of subsidiarity – A general principle embodied in the EU Environmental Directives that states that a decision should be taken at the 'lowest possible level' or by the population most directly affected. The idea is that more practical decisions are taken in this manner. (EU)

Principles for responsible investment (PRI) – A set of six principles formally endorsed by the UN in 2006 encouraging institutional investors worldwide in ways that protect the planet and meet social responsibilities. The principles, strictly voluntary, will support sustainable development, allowing the world to develop economically without destroying natural habitats or increasing poverty. (UNW)

Prior informed consent, principle of (PIC) – A principle established to help participating countries know the characteristics of potentially hazardous chemicals that may be shipped to them. The aim is to promote a shared responsibility between exporting and importing countries to protect human health from the harmful effects of certain hazardous chemicals that are traded internationally. (PIC)

Private sector – In a mixed economy, the part of the economy not under government control that functions within the market; private enterprise. (UNDP)

Privatization – Policies that allow the change of a business, industry, activity or institution from public to private control or ownership. (AD)

Procedural equity, principle of – A principle that refers to how decisions are made: (a) equity implies that those who are affected by decisions should have some say in the making of these decisions and (b) equity must ensure equal treatment before the law.

Procedural language – See 'Language(s), working.'

Process indicators – Monitoring tools that can provide information about where interventions are needed. (UNFPA)

Product Red – A Bono-founded project, Product Red is not a charity but rather a money generating venture. Companies donate a percentage of profits on RED brand products to the Global (AIDS) Fund and in turn gain access to an expanded customer base and the 'halo' effect of doing good for society. (UNW)

Program (1) – A coherent and interactive set of proposals and projects that are synchronized within a planning and implementation scheme.

Program (2) – A portfolio of projects that aims to achieve a strategic goal of an organization, planned and managed in a coordinated way.

Programme of Action of the International Conference on Population and Development (IPCD) – The ICPD was held from 5–13 September 1994 in Cairo, Egypt. ICPD delegates considered the interconnectedness of population, poverty, gender, patterns of production and consumption and the environment. The 1994 Program of Action recommended a set of important population and development objectives, including: sustained economic growth in the context of sustainable development; education, especially for girls; gender equity and equality; infant, child and maternal mortality reduction; and the provision of universal access to reproductive health services, including family planning and sexual health care.

Programme of Action of the Special Session of the General Assembly to Review and Appraise the Implementation of *Agenda 21* (UNGASS) – The 19th special session of the UNGA convened in June,

P

1997 (Earth Summit +5) to review the outstanding issues not fully resolved at the UNCED including finance, climate change, freshwater management and forest management. This session adopted the Programme for the Further Implementation of *Agenda 21* (A/RES/S-19/2). It assessed progress since UNCED, examined implementation, and established the CSD's work program for the period 1998–2002, leading up to WSSD.

Project – A planned and goal-oriented socio-economic development activity requiring financial investment or human participation over a given time.

Project cycle – An ordered series of activities that include planning, approval, execution, monitoring and evaluation.

Project Preparation and Development Facility (PDF) – Facility that grants money to the implementing agencies for developing project concepts in three blocks: Block A (up to $25,000), Block B (up to $750,000) and mid-size or Block C (up to $1 million). Block A funds are for pre-project activities at national level. Block B funds are for obtaining information to complete project proposals. Block C funds are a one-time GEF grant for completing technical design and feasibility studies for large-scale projects to be funded by another entity. Four Regional Development Banks (AfDB, ADB, EBRD and IDB), FAO, UNIDO and IFAD can access PDF-B resources under the expanded opportunities executing agencies. (GEF)

Project screening – A World Bank project classification method prepared by the project team and based on its potential environmental impact and therefore the level of environmental assessment required: category A – EA is normally required as the project may have significant environmental impacts; category B – a more limited EA is appropriate as the project may have specific environmental impacts; category C – EA is normally not necessary as the project is unlikely to have significant environmental impacts. (USEPA; WB)

Protected area – A geographically defined area (land or sea) that is designated or regulated and managed to achieve specific conservation objectives (CBD). Some definitions suggest that the area needs to be legally designated. (WRI)

Protected Area Management Categories (IUCN – World Conservation Union) – A set of management objectives assigned to ten different classifications of protected areas:

- Category I: *Scientific Reserve/Strict Nature Reserve.* To protect nature and maintain natural processes in an undisturbed state in order to have ecologically representative examples of the natural environment available for scientific study, environmental monitoring, education, and for the maintenance of genetic resources in a dynamic and evolutionary state.

- Category II: *National Park*. To protect natural and scenic areas of national or international significance for scientific, educational and recreational use.
- Category III: *Natural Monument/Natural Landmark*. To protect and preserve nationally significant natural features because of their special interest or unique characteristics.
- Category IV: *Managed Nature Reserve/Wildlife Sanctuary*. To assure the natural conditions necessary to protect nationally significant species, groups of species, biotic communities, or physical features of the environment where these require specific human manipulation for their perpetuation.
- Category V: *Protected Landscape or Seascape*. To maintain nationally significant natural landscapes which are characteristic of the harmonious interaction of man and land while providing opportunities for public enjoyment through recreation and tourism within normal lifestyle and economic activity of these areas.
- Category VI: *Resource Reserve*. To protect resources of the area for future use and prevent or contain development activities that could affect the resource pending the establishment of objectives which are based upon appropriate knowledge and planning.
- Category VII: *Natural Biotic Area/Anthropological Reserve*. To allow the way of life of societies living in harmony with the environment to continue undisturbed by modern technology.
- Category VIII: *Multiple-Use Management Area/Managed Resource Area*. To provide for the sustained production of water, timber, wildlife, pasture and outdoor recreation, with the conservation of nature primarily oriented to the support of economic activities (although specific zones may also be designed within these areas to achieve specific conservation objectives).
- Category IX: *Biosphere Reserve*. These are part of an international scientific program, the UNESCO Man and the Biosphere (MAB) Program, which is aimed at developing a reserve network representative of the world's ecosystems to fulfill a range of objectives, including research, monitoring, training and demonstration, as well as conservation roles.
- Category X: *World Heritage Site*. The Convention Concerning the Protection of the World Cultural and Natural Heritage (which was adopted in Paris in 1972 and came into force in December, 1975) provides for the designation of areas of 'outstanding universal value' as World Heritage Sites, with the principal aim of fostering international cooperation in safeguarding these important sites. (IUCN)

Protectionism – An international trade philosophy that favors the creation of barriers against the importing of goods to shelter domestic industries from foreign competition. (WP)

Pro tempore – A term that best translates to 'for the time being' in English.

This phrase is most often used in politics or international diplomacy to describe a person who acts as a *locum tenens* (placeholder) in the absence of a superior. See '***Ad interim.***' (WP)

Protocol (1) – An international agreement supplementary to a convention that adds to or changes some provision of the convention only for the states parties who adopt the protocol. (VC)

Protocol (2) – In science, a series of prescribed steps for conducting an experiment or for protecting the integrity of samples or data collected. (USEPA)

Prototype Carbon Fund (PCF) – World Bank funding of US$145 million to Uganda, Chile and Latvia for these and other developing countries to adapt to climate impacts and develop emissions reducing technologies. Under this fund, the World Bank will buy carbon dioxide emissions reductions for up to $3.9 million over 15–20 years.

Provinciality effect – Increased diversity of species because of geographical isolation. (IUCN)

Public – One or more natural or legal persons, and, in accordance with national legislation or practice, their associations, organizations or groups. (UNECE)

Public authority – A government at the national, regional or other level; natural or legal persons performing public administration functions under national law, including specific duties, activities or services; other natural or legal persons having public responsibilities or functions, or providing public services; and the institutions of any regional economic integration organization. (UNECE)

Public concerned – The public affected or likely to be affected by, or having an interest in, environmental decision making. Nongovernmental organizations promoting environmental protection and meeting any requirements under national law shall be deemed to have an interest. (UNECE)

Public consultation – The process of engaging affected people and other interested parties in open dialogue through which a range of views and concerns can be expressed in order to inform decision making and help build consensus. (WB)

Public good – A good that is impossible to keep anyone from using and where one person's consumption of that good does not reduce the quantity available for use by someone else.

Public land – Land owned in common by all and represented by a governmental jurisdiction (e.g. village, town, country, state or nation). (NRDC)

Public participation – A process by which the views and concerns of the public are identified and incorporated into decision making by public institutions. Participation is a process through which stakeholders influence and share control over development initiatives and the decisions and resources that affect them. Includes access to information, access to process and access to justice.

Public sector – The part of the economy that is not privately owned, either because it is owned by the state or because it is subject to common ownership. Includes the national government, local authorities, national industries and public corporations. (UNDP)

Punta del Este Declaration – A 1986 declaration from the parties to the General Agreement on Tariffs and Trade (GATT) written to launch the Uruguay Round of multilateral trade negotiations. (AD)

Purchasing power parity (PPP) – The number of units of a country's currency needed to purchase the same amount of goods and services in a different country. PPP GNI is measured in current *international* dollars, which, in principle, have the same purchasing power as a dollar spent on GNI in the US economy. Because PPPs provide a better measure of the standard of living of residents of an economy, they are the basis for the World Bank's calculations of poverty rates at US$1–2 a day. The GNI of developing countries measured in PPP terms generally exceeds their GNI measured using market exchange rates. (WB)

P

Qq

Qanat – An underground system tapping subsurface water, constructed by tunneling into a cliff, scarp or base of a mountainous area, following a water-bearing formation. The water is not brought up to the surface but rather out to the surface via tunnels that are roughly horizontal, with a slope to allow water to drain out. (UNESCO)

Qualified 'double' majority voting (QMV-EU) – A system utilized in the European Council of Ministers that replaced the 'majority vote' system (vote weighted by the number of people living in a given country. Thus a 'yes' vote by Poland would have more weight than a 'no' vote by smaller Luxembourg). The new system is defined as 'at least 55 percent of the members of the Council, comprising at least 15 of them and representing Member States comprising at least 65 percent of the population of the EU.' In other words, a proposal is accepted when at least 55 percent of the representatives of the national governments in the Council of Ministers, and at least 15 nations represented in *that* Council vote in favor. Those 15 nations (or votes) must also represent 65 percent of the entire EU population. (EU) See '**Double majority**.'

Qualified majority – The raising of the simple majority requirement of '50 percent plus one' to a higher level, in order to protect the rights of the minority; thus, a system of weighted votes. For example for certain decisions in the EU, Member States' votes are weighted based on their population and corrected in favor of less-populated countries.

Quality assurance/quality control (QA/QC) – The process of strengthening research outcomes by applying rigorous and systematic approaches to planning and conducting scientific investigations. (USEPA)

Quality of life – Quality of life is largely a matter of individual preference and perception and overlaps the concept of social well-being. Generally, the emphasis is on the amount and distribution of public goods, such as health care and welfare services, protection against crime, regulation of pollution, preservation of landscapes and historic and cultural aspects of a region. (MW)

Quick win – In the international development context, a concept that an injection of ODA or grant money for a very specific purpose (i.e. mass distribution of insecticide-treated bed nets to combat malaria or home water purification kits to treat dysentery) will have an immediate and measurable impact on solving a particular problem. (UN)

Quod hoc – On this matter.

Quorum – The minimum number of people/governments/institutions required to formally open a meeting.

Quota, financial – See '**Assessed contribution**.'

Quota, geographical – A term used to describe a policy of most international organizations to try to balance the numbers of staff from any given nation employed in that organization. It is based on a formula using variously population, GDP per capita and assessed contribution, among other criteria. Generally, this policy applies to internationally recruited professional staff and not to locally recruited general service or administrative support staff. (UN)

Q

Rr

R2P – See 'Responsibility to Protect, the doctrine of.'

Radioactive waste – The byproduct of nuclear reactions that gives off (usually harmful) radiation. (NRDC)

Radioactivity – The spontaneous emission of matter or energy from the nucleus of an unstable atom. (NRDC)

Rainforest – A tropical or temperate woodland with an annual rainfall of at least 254cm and marked by lofty, broad-leaf evergreen trees forming a continuous canopy. (EES; MW)

Ramsar Convention – Convention on Wetlands of International Importance especially as Waterfowl Habitat, signed at Ramsar, India on 2 February, 1971. It came into force on 21 December, 1975. (RC)

Rapid assessment procedures (RAP) – A term indicating a methodology permitting a rapid assessment of a given situation (commonly applied in the health, environment and human rights fields).

Rapporteur – The officer specifically charged with keeping the minutes and writing the draft final report of each session of a meeting. Subsequent to final comments from meeting participants, the *rapporteur* compiles and edits the final report.

Rare – An IUCN category (R) of taxa with small world populations that are not at present Endangered or Vulnerable, but are at risk. These taxa are usually localized within restricted geographical areas or habitats or are thinly scattered over a more extensive range. (IUCN)

Ratification – An international act whereby a state, through congressional or parliamentary approval, indicates its consent to be bound to a treaty if the parties intended to show their consent by such an act (VC).

REACH – An EU program to register substances manufactured or imported in volumes greater than 1 ton per year with the European Chemicals Agency. Unlike US regulations, REACH would also apply to 'articles' (objects composed of substances and/or preparations, with a specific shape, surface or design), whose contents or composition could be released during normal and foreseeable use. The Proposal also contemplates pre-market authorization of the use of chemicals of 'very high concern,' and places the burden of proof (risk analysis) on businesses seeking to put these chemicals to new uses. (EU) See '**Rotterdam Convention**.'

Rebound effect – See '**Offsetting effect**.'

Recharge – The process by which water is added to a zone of saturation or accumulation, usually by percolation from the soil surface. (USEPA)

Recipient – See '**Beneficiary**.'

Reclaimed materials – Reprocessed or regenerated materials that provide a useable product or 'new' raw material (lead from spent batteries, reprocessed oil, paper or plastics). (EES)

Recommendation – A determination that is weaker than a decision or a resolution and not binding on parties.

Recyclable materials – Materials that can be reprocessed to provide a secondary material for human use. (EES)

Red Book/List species – A publication of the IUCN listing the conservation status of different taxa in a given geographic area (e.g. region, country, world). This series provides an inventory on the threat to rare plants and animal species. Information includes status, geographical distribution, population size, habitat and breeding rate. The books also contain the conservation measures, if any, that have been taken to protect the species. There are five categories of rarity status: 'endangered species;' 'vulnerable organisms,' which are those unlikely to adapt to major environmental effects; 'rare organisms,' which are those at risk because there are few of them in the world, such as plants that only grow on mountain peaks or on islands; 'out of danger species,' which were formerly in the above categories, but have had the threat removed because of conservation actions; and 'indeterminate species,' which include plants and animals probably at risk, although not enough is known about them to assess their status. (IUCN)

Red Cross and Red Crescent Societies – See '**International Federation of the Red Cross, Red Crescent (and Red Crystal) Societies (IFRC)**.'

Referendum (1) – A question or measure proposed by a legislative body or popular initiative and put to the voters for a decision. (MW)

Referendum (2) – A note from a diplomat asking for government instructions on a particular issue. (MW)

Reforestation – The action of renewing or improving forest cover by planting seeds or seedlings on land that had been previously forested.

Refugee – A person who, owing to well-founded fear, or fact, of being persecuted for reasons of race, ethnicity, religion, nationality, membership of a particular social group or political opinion, is outside the country of his/her nationality and is unable or, owing to such fear, is unwilling to avail him/her self of the protection of that country; or who, not having a nationality and being outside the country of former habitual residence as a result of such events, is unable or, owing to such fear, is unwilling to return to it. (UNDP) See '**Internally displaced person,**' '**Diaspora,**' '**Environmental refugee.**'

Refugee fatigue – See '**Asylum fatigue.**'

Regime – An institutional arrangement formally or informally established to study and support a common property issue area (atmosphere, oceans, biodiversity, Antarctica, outer space, etc.).

Region – An area of territory that can be defined for spatial analysis and planning purposes as distinct and coherent. Planning regions can be administrative following the borders of particular jurisdictions within countries; or functional, which follow the boundary of the issue subject to the planning process, for example, river catchment areas and travel to work areas.

Regional Economic Integration Organization – An organization constituted by sovereign States of a given region, to which its member States have transferred competence in respect of matters governed by this convention and which has been duly authorized, in accordance with its internal procedures, to sign, ratify, accept, approve or accede to it. (CBD)

Regional group – One of five regional groupings within the UN system that meet to discuss issues and nominate bureau members and other officials (Africa, Asia, Central and Eastern Europe (CEE), Latin America and the Caribbean (GRULAC), and WEOG, the Western Europe and Others Group.

Regional Seas Conventions and Action Plans – A series of 19 regional conventions and action plans administered by the UNEP (six programs) and other independent partner organizations (13 programs). Those under direct UNEP management include:

- Barcelona Convention for the Protection of the Marine Environment and the Coastal Region of the Mediterranean (1976);
- Abidjan Convention for Cooperation in the Protection and Development of the Marine and Coastal Environment of the West and Central African Region (1981);
- East Asian Seas Convention and Action Plan (1981);
- Cartagena Convention for the Protection and Development of the Marine Environment of the Wider Caribbean Region (1983);
- Nairobi Convention for the Protection, Management and

Development of the Marine and Coast Environment of the Eastern
Africa Region (1985).

Those administered by other intuitions include:

- Helsinki Convention on the Protection of the Marine Environment
  of the Baltic Sea Area (1992);
- OSPAR Convention for the Protection of the Marine Environment
  of the North-East Atlantic (Oslo and Paris conventions, adopted
  1974, revised and combined 1992);
- Arctic Council for the Protection of the Arctic Marine Environment
  (1992);
- Antarctic Treaty System: Convention for the Conservation of
  Antarctic Marine Living Resources (1982) and Madrid Protocol on
  the Protection of the Antarctic Environment (1991);
- Kuwait Regional Convention for Co-operation on the Protection of
  the Marine Environment from Pollution (1978);
- Lima Convention for the Protection of the Marine Environment and
  Coastal Area of the South-East Pacific (1981);
- Jeddah Regional Convention for the Conservation of the Red Sea
  and Gulf of Aden Environment (1982);
- Noumea Convention for the Protection of Natural Resources and
  Environment of the South Pacific Region (1986);
- Convention and Action Plan for the Caspian Sea and Bucharest
  Convention on the Protection of the Black Sea Against Pollution
  (1992);
- North-West Pacific Action Plan (1994);
- North-East Pacific Action Plan (1995);
- South Asian Seas Action Plan (1995).

Regional Seas Programme – The Regional Seas Programme was initiated in 1974 as a global program implemented through regional components. The Program at present includes 13 regions involving more than 140
coastal States and Territories. (UNEP)

Regular funds/budget – Assessed contributions from member states of an
international organization. (UNDP)

Regulations – Rules or orders issued by an executive authority or regulatory agency of a government and having the force of law.

Reimbursable grant – That part of a pre-investment study (pre-feasibility or feasibility study) or loan package that is required to be repaid by the
borrowing or beneficiary country if the proposed project proves to have an
internal rate of return that justifies the (repayment of the) loan. (WB)

Remittances – Private money transfers normally from someone earning
a convertible currency to a family member in a developing country. The

R

World Bank estimated that remittances totaled US$230 billion in 2006, more than twice the amount of all ODA estimated at US$106.5 billion in 2006. (UNW)

Renewable energy – Energy derived from a variety of natural resources including sun, wind, tide, wave, geothermal and biomass (if the latter is planted at a greater rate than it is utilized). (EES)

Renewable natural resources – Any natural resource that replaces itself or is replenished within a human time frame, including forestry, fisheries and wildlife resources, as well as air, water and soil resources. However, they are only renewable in an economic/anthropogenic sense if the rate of replacement is equal to or greater than the rate of utilization. The term 'renewable' dos not imply 'inexhaustible.' (EES)

Renewables – Energy sources that are, within a short time frame relative to the Earth's natural cycles, sustainable, and include non-carbon technologies such as solar energy, hydropower, geothermal, wave and wind as well as carbon-neutral technologies such as biomass. (IPCC)

Replenishment – A contribution to a fund such as those managed by a development bank or to a granting agency by third parties and normally based on an agreed-to or negotiated plan. (GEF) See '**Tranche**,' '**Donor conference**.'

Report of the World Food Summit (2002) – This report summarized the progress made in reaching the goals of the Rome Declaration on World Food Security and the World Food Summit POA. In all aspects it is one of the most criticized meetings ever held under the auspices of the UN.

Report of the World Summit for Social Development (WSSD) – In the WSSD, held in March 1995 in Copenhagen, governments reached a new consensus on the need to put people at the center of development. In the final report governments pledged to make the conquest of poverty, the goal of full employment and the fostering of social integration overriding objectives of development.

Request for proposal (RFP) – A document issued by one organization to another organization (or to several other organizations) describing work that the issuer wishes to have undertaken by the recipient(s) and inviting the recipient(s) to respond with a proposal.

Res. Rep. – See '**United Nations Resident Representative**.'

Reservation – A unilateral statement, however phrased or named, made by a State, when signing, ratifying, accepting, approving or acceding to a treaty, whereby it purports to exclude or to modify the legal effect of certain provisions of the treaty in their application to that State. (VC)

Reservoir (1) – A component or components of the climate system where a greenhouse gas or a precursor of a greenhouse gas is stored. (UNFCCC)

Reservoir (2) – A body of water created artificially by the construction of a dam across a flowing river or stream.

Resolution – A formal action such as a recommendation that does not normally become part of the body of decisions that guide the work of a COP. They are directives that guide rather than permanent legal acts. Formal resolutions of a general assembly are binding decisions.

Resolution 47/191 – A resolution of the UN General Assembly adopted in 1992 relative to the creation of the UN Commission on Sustainable Development (CSD). The resolution presents the terms of reference, make-up, guidelines for NGO participation, organization of work, relations with other UN bodies and Secretariat agreements for the CSD.

Resolution 55/199 – A resolution of the UN General Assembly adopted in December 2000 that calls for a ten-year review of UNCED (September of 2002) at the summit level to reinvigorate global commitment to sustainable development. The review was to focus on accomplishments, identify areas requiring further efforts to implement *Agenda 21* and other UNCED outcomes, lead to action-oriented decisions, and result in renewed political commitment to achieve sustainable development.

Resource recovery – The process of obtaining matter or energy from discarded materials. (USEPA)

Responsibility to Protect, the Doctrine of – Instead of challenging the legitimacy of State sovereignty, the Responsibility to Protect Doctrine challenges sovereign states to embrace a deeper, socially responsible concept of sovereignty. The International Commission on Intervention and State Sovereignty (ICISS) of the UN calls upon all Member States to accept their responsibility to protect the ultimate sovereigns – *the people* – as the prime obligation of state sovereignty. If a nation fails to fulfill this responsibility so horribly so as to 'shock the conscience of humanity,' and based on six 'threshold criteria' (just cause, right intention, last resort, proportional means, reasonable prospects and right authority) other sovereign states must assume that responsibility in its place. (UN) See '**R2P**,' '**Never again, Principle of.**'

Restoration – In ecosystem management restoration is the return of that system to some previous desired state or earlier successional state in terms of its principle components of species and functions. (EES)

Results – A broad term used to refer to the effects of a project. The terms 'outputs,' 'outcomes' and 'impact' describe more precisely the different types of results: (GEF)

R

- *Outputs*: tangible products (including services) of a project that are necessary to achieve its objectives.
- *Outcomes*: results of a project relative to its immediate objectives that are generated by the project outputs.
- *Impact*: results of a project that are assessed with reference to the development objectives or long-term goals of that project; changes in a situation, whether planned or unplanned, positive or negative, that a project helps to bring about.

Retroactivity, the concept of – See '**Preemptive intervention, concept of**.'

Retrospective terms adjustment – A term used in the World Bank to indicate a revision of the conditions of a loan. (WB) See '**Debt relief**.'

Reversible effect – An effect that is not permanent; especially adverse effects that diminish when exposure to a toxin is deceased or stopped. (USEPA)

Rich man's club – A somewhat pejorative reference to OECD countries.

Rider – A US Congressional or Legislative term referring to unrelated provisions tacked onto an existing Congressional bill. Since bills must pass or fail in their entirety, riders containing otherwise unpopular language are often added to popular bills. (NRDC)

Right to development – According to the 1986 UNGA 'Declaration on the Right to Development,' the right to development 'is an inalienable human right by virtue of which every human person and all peoples are entitled to participate in, contribute to, and enjoy social, cultural and political development, in which all human rights and fundamental freedoms can be fully realized.' Development, as a 'right' is not accepted by all states.

Right to environment – A phrase that generally relates to the Rio Declaration and its principles, which defined the rights and responsibilities of people to a clean and safe environment. The 18 principles included in the Declaration provide substantial detail as to what the right includes and what responsibilities it implies. (UNCED)

Right to interfere – The right of one or many nations to violate the national sovereignty of another state, when a mandate has been granted by a supranational authority. (WP) See '**Duty to interfere**,' '**Humanitarian intervention**.'

Right to participation – A right generally referring to Articles 19, 20 and 21 of the Universal Declaration of Human Rights of December 1948 which recognized an individual's right to freedom of opinion and expression, assembly and decisions affecting the future of one's country including elections of representatives. (UN)

Right to water – In 2002 the UN Committee on Economic, Social and Cultural Rights affirmed the right of all people to clean and 'sufficient quantities' of 'safe and acceptable' fresh water, which is both 'physically accessible' and 'affordable' as a precondition for the realization of human rights. (OECD; UN)

Rio Declaration on Environment and Development – The formal outcome of the UNCED meeting in Rio de Janeiro in 1992 that summarizes a consensus of principles for sustainable development.

Rio Group – The Rio Group is an international organization of Latin American states. It arose in 1986 as an alternative body to the Organization of American States during the Cold War, since that body was, in the opinion of some, dominated by the US. The Rio Group does not have a secretariat or permanent body, and instead relies on yearly summits of heads of states. (WP)

Rio Principles – A statement of 27 principles produced by the UNCED in Rio de Janeiro in 1992, which define the rights and responsibilities of nations as they pursue human development and well-being. See Appendix I. (UNCED)

Riparian rights – Entitlement of a land owner to certain uses of water on or bordering his property, normally including the right to prevent diversion or misuse of upstream waters, but with the same responsibilities to downstream users. (USEPA)

Riparian zone – The area adjacent to a stream that is subject to direct influence of the water in the stream. It forms the ecotone between the terrestrial and aquatic ecosystems. (EES)

Risk – The probability of an undesirable outcome. (MW)

Risk analysis/assessment – A detailed examination performed to understand the nature of unwanted, negative consequences to human life, health, property or the environment: to provide information regarding undesirable events; and to quantify the probabilities and expected consequences for identified risks.

River basin – A geographical area (catchment area) generally determined by the watershed limits of a water system, including surface and underground water that flow into a common terminus.

Road map – A term that refers to a strategy or strategic plan of work that includes a timetable and milestones, and which came into common usage in about 2003.

Robert's Rules of Order – Robert's Rules of Order is a handbook of

R

parliamentary procedure that is often used as the parliamentary authority by deliberative bodies, as part of their overall rules of order. (WP)

Rome Declaration on World Food Security and the World Food Summit POA (1996) – The Summit was hosted by the UN Food and Agriculture Organization (UNFAO) in Rome in November, 1996. The meeting Declaration signed by 187 heads of State and Governments reaffirmed the right of everyone to have access to safe and nutritious food, consistent with the fundamental right of everyone to be free from hunger. These officials pledged their political will and made commitments to eradicate hunger and to reduce the number of undernourished people by half, no later than 2015. The Plan of Action identifies seven major commitments, presents objectives and outlines actions that need to be taken by developed and developing countries in order to achieve these objectives.

Rome Statute – The Rome Statute of July 1998 established the International Criminal Court when 120 States participating in the 'United Nations Diplomatic Conference of Plenipotentiaries on the Establishment of an International Criminal Court' adopted the Statute. The Statute entered into force on 1 July, 2002. Anyone from an Acceding State who commits any of the crimes covered under the Statute after this date will be subject to arrest in any of the Acceding States and liable for prosecution by the Court. (UN)

Rotterdam Convention – In 1998, governments decided to strengthen the 'Prior Informed Consent' (PIC) procedure by adopting the Rotterdam Convention, which makes PIC legally binding. The Convention establishes a first line of defense by giving importing countries the tools and information they need to identify potential hazards and exclude chemicals they cannot manage safely. If a country agrees to import chemicals, the Convention promotes their safe use through labeling standards, technical assistance and other forms of support. It also ensures that exporters comply with the requirements. The Rotterdam Convention entered into force on 24 February, 2004. (EU) See '**REACH**.'

Round – As used in international parlance, one of a series of meetings (as in the Uruguay Round or the Doha Round of the WTO negotiations). (MW)

Rovaniemi Process (AEPS) – An extensive international Arctic cooperative program (the Arctic Environmental Protection Strategy) adopted by the eight Arctic countries: Russia, the US, Canada, Greenland/Denmark, Iceland, Norway, Sweden and Finland in 1991. Other countries and international organizations have observer status. Its objectives are to protect Arctic ecosystems; provide for the protection, enhancement and restoration of natural resources; recognize the traditional and cultural needs, values and practices of the indigenous peoples; review regularly the state of the Arctic environment; and identify, reduce and eliminate pollution.

Rule of law – Equal protection (of human as well as property and other economic rights) and punishment under the law. The rule of law reigns over government, protecting citizens against arbitrary state action, and over society generally, governing relations among private interests. It ensures that all citizens are treated equally and are subject to the law rather than to the whims of the powerful. The rule of law is an essential precondition for accountability and predictability in both the public and private sectors. The establishment and persistence of the rule of law depend on clear communication of the rules, indiscriminate application, effective enforcement, predictable and legally enforceable methods for changing the content of laws and a citizenry that perceives the set of rules as fair, just or legitimate, and that is willing to follow it. (UNDP)

Rules of procedure – The rules that govern the organization and proceeding of a COP or other subsidiary body, including the procedures for decision-making, voting and participation. They may (and often do) vary somewhat between institutions and meetings.

R

Ss

Safeguard policies – Policies of the World Bank requiring that potentially adverse environmental impacts and selected social impacts of Bank investment projects be identified, avoided or minimized where feasible, and mitigated and monitored. These policies provide guidelines for Bank and borrower staff in the identification, preparation and implementation of programs and projects in support of environmentally and socially sustainable development. Specific safeguard policies are provided for environmental assessment, natural hazards, pest management, involuntary resettlement, indigenous peoples, forests, safety of dams, cultural property, projects on international waterways and projects in disputed areas. (WB)

Safety-net aid, concept of – Financial assistance given directly by a government or NGO donor to those who implement actions on the ground rather than through a government agency. This practice has become commonplace by donors providing assistance to governments considered to be either too disorganized or corrupt to ensure that aid reaches those who need it. (UNW)

Sahel – The tropical, semi-arid region along the southern margin of the Sahara desert that forms large parts of six African countries (Mauritania, Mali, Niger, Chad, Somalia and Sudan) and smaller parts of three more (Senegal, Burkina Faso and Ethiopia). (EES)

Salinity – The measure of saltiness of water frequently expressed as parts of salt per thousand parts of water. (USEPA)

Salinization/salination – The impregnation of soils by various salts that precipitate from the groundwater by percolating vertically through capillary action under the influence of evapotranspiration during periods of drought and not from the evaporation of stagnant water on impermeable soils. The process by which drinkable water becomes undrinkable brackish or salt water. (EES)

Saltwater intrusion – The invasion of fresh surface or groundwater by salt water.

Salvage harvesting – A forest management technique in which standing but damaged (disease, fire, etc.) or downed (wind storm, flood, etc.) tress are harvested before they lose market value or further damage the remaining healthy stand. (USEPA)

Sanctions (in the UN context) – A coercive measure(s) approved by the UN Security Council requiring a nation to undertake an action based on international law, normally enforced through punitive economic sanctions and/or diplomatic measures. (UN)

Sanitary landfill – A method of refuse disposal on land without creating nuisance to public health or safety by using the principles of engineering to confine refuse to the smallest practicable area, to reduce it to the smallest volume, and to cover it with a layer of earth at the conclusion of each day's operation, or at more frequent intervals if necessary. Byproducts are either collected and safely disposed of (leachate) or utilized for other purposes such as heat or electricity generation (gases). (EES)

Sasia – A name coined by the South Asia Foundation for what could become a common South Asian currency, similar to the euro in Europe. The Foundation feels the Sasia could become the anchor of economic stability and regional cooperation.

Scenario – A plausible description of how the future may develop, based on a coherent and internally consistent set of assumptions about key relationships and driving forces. (IPCC)

Scientific and Technical Advisory Panel (STAP) – An independent advisory body to the GEF, established by UNEP in consultation with UNDP and the World Bank. It advises the GEF on the issues of global environmental management; develops and maintains a Roster of Experts; reviews selected projects; cooperates and coordinates with the scientific and technical bodies of the various MEAs; and provides a liaison between the GEF and the wider scientific and technological communities. (UNEP)

Scientific philanthropy – A term widely attributed to the large and directed donations of American magnates Andrew Carnegie and John D. Rockefeller Sr. whose giving focused on education and health issues nearly a century ago. Since that time others such as Ted Turner, Bill and Melinda Gates and Warren Buffet have followed this trend. While generally praised, this type of directed private philanthropy has been criticized for its impact on the global agenda and for suplanting national development/investment priorities. (UNW)

Scoping – A procedure for attempting to ensure that an environmental assessment focuses on the key environmental issues associated with a project, omitting irrelevant material. (EEA)

Sea level rise – An increase in the mean level of the ocean. (USEPA)

Sea level rise, eustatic – A change in global average sea level brought about by an alteration to the volume of the world ocean. (UNFCCC)

Sea level rise, relative – A net increase in the level of the ocean relative to local land movements and average high tide recordings. (UNFCCC)

Second Assessment Report (SAR) – The second report of IPCC also known as 'Climate Change 1995.' Its conclusion (written and reviewed by some 2000 scientists) was that 'the balance of evidence suggests that there is a discernible human influence on global climate' and confirmed the availability of 'no-regrets' options and other cost-effective strategies for combating climate change. (UNFCCC)

Second super power – A term referring to the power of global public opinion (expressed through communication media, mass demonstrations, political pressure, etc.) to influence the decisions or actions of the US, frequently referred to as the world's only 'super power.' (IPS)

Secondary forest – Natural forest growth after some major disturbance (e.g. logging, serious fire or insect attack).

Secondary sewage treatment – Primary sewage treatment plus biochemical oxidation of biodegradable substances in wastewater.

Secretariat – An institution of an MEA that undertakes the day-to-day activities of coordinating the implementation of the MEA and makes arrangements for the annual meetings of the COP or periodic meetings of its subsidiary bodies.

Secretary General – The chief administrative officer of an organization. (MW)

Sector – A sociological, economic or political subdivision of society: economically as the primary, secondary and tertiary sectors; and socially and politically to indicate any division of human activity (or any interest group) that provides for the protection or promulgation of its interests.

Sector loan – A loan made by the World Bank, IMF or a regional development bank to fund a particular set of productive activities and at times requiring adjustments and policies of that sector, such as agriculture, fisheries, forestry, health, education, etc. (WB) See '**Structural adjustment loans**.'

Sectoral – Pertaining to a sector.

Security Council – See '**United Nations Security Council**.'

Sedimentation – A general term referring to the suspension, transport and deposition of sediments. (EES)

Selected harvesting/thinning – A forest management technique in which selected trees (species, age, health, market demand, etc.) are removed from a forest stand. (USEPA)

Self-contained convention – An Agreement that works using annexes and appendices and, although they may be revised periodically by the COP, requires no other protocols. (CITES)

Senior Statesman – An informal 'title' normally referring to a retired senior official who undertakes specific tasks for a government or an international organization on a periodic basis. (WP)

Seoul Millennium Declaration – The declaration of the 1999 Seoul 'Millennium' Conference of NGOs. The Conference was attended by more than 10,000 participants representing some 1400 NGOs from at least 107 countries. The declaration addresses several major themes including environment, gender equality, social and economic development, education for all and human rights. (CONGO)

Sequestration – Opportunities to remove atmospheric CO_2, either through biological processes (e.g. plants and trees), or geological processes through storage of CO_2 in underground reservoirs. (PEW)

Seventh floor – A US term referring to the top floor in the US Department of State and the location of the offices of the most senior staff (Secretary of State and senior aides). (USDOS)

Sewage treatment – A multi-stage process designed to clean wastewater before it re-enters a body of water (EES)

Shadow pricing – A technique sometimes used to attribute a value to a commodity or service that has no market price (or of which the market price does not reflect the true economic value) due to market failures (externalities) or market distortions.

Sherpas – A somewhat irreverent name given to those G8, behind-the-scenes civil servants who do the so-called 'heavy lifting' of preparing and revising a seemingly infinite number of background and final meeting documents required for formal meetings of Heads of State.

Shifting cultivation – A process of removing primary or secondary forest cover on a periodic basis, planting crops on that cleared land and then allowing forest cover to regenerate. This practice is variously known as slash-burn agriculture, swidden agriculture or subsistence agriculture. (EES; FAO)

Sick building syndrome – A human health condition where infections linger, caused by exposure to contaminants within a building as a result of poor ventilation. (NRDC)

S

Side event – In the UN context, a presentation open to all, normally held during the lunch period or after normal meeting hours, that is related to the issues being negotiated during an intergovernmental meeting.

Signatory – A term that usually refers to a state that has signed an agreement or convention. (UNT)

Signature – Usually signifies that a state has consented to be bound by the treaty especially in bilateral treaties. For multilateral treaties, however, the signature is as a rule not definitive, meaning that the treaty is subject to ratification, acceptance or approval in order to enter into force (VC).

Signature *ad referendum* – A term meaning that an agreement may be signed by a representative of a state but the agreement only becomes binding once the signature is confirmed by the responsible organ. (VC)

Silviculture – Management of forest land for timber.

Simple majority – Fifty percent of delegates in attendance and official proxies plus one vote.

Simultaneous translation/interpretation – Refers to the spoken word. (MW)

Sine qua non – Without which not. An indispensable condition, a prerequisite. (BLD)

Sink – Any process, activity or mechanism that removes a greenhouse gas, an aerosol or a precursor of a greenhouse gas from the atmosphere. (UNFCCC)

Six, The – See 'G6 (new).'

Sixth floor – A US term referring to the floor in the US Department of State where regional and Assistant Secretaries of State have their offices. (USDOS)

Slash-burn agriculture – See '**Shifting cultivation**.'

Small Grants Programme (SGP) – A program administered by the UNDP that provides grants of up to $50,000 to grassroots groups and NGOs to demonstrate community-based strategies and technologies that address global environmental concerns. (GEF)

Smog – A dense, discolored radiation fog containing large quantities of soot, ash and gaseous pollutants such as sulfur dioxide and carbon dioxide. (NRDC)

Social business – A new category of corporation that would be neither profit-maximizing nor nonprofit in line with the principles of the Grameen Bank. Such institutions could bring health care, information technology, education and energy to the poor without requiring infusions of aid.

Social capital – Features of social organization – such as networks and values, including tolerance, inclusion, reciprocity, participation and trust – that facilitate coordination and cooperation for mutual benefit. Social capital inheres in the relations between and among actors. (UNDP)

Social cost – The cost to society of any economic activity. (MW)

Social issues – Issues arising due to differential access to land and other resources; conflicting demands on the same resources for conservation and economic development of traditional users; marginalization of women; religious or ethnic tensions; winners and losers in privatization and reform programs; structural exclusion of a social group; poor governance, adverse social impacts, etc. (WB)

Soft law – Non-legally binding agreements. Though they may be signed by governments, they are less precise than hard law instruments and have less stringent obligation and weaker delegation. Compared to hard law instruments, they are easier to achieve, provide strategies for dealing with uncertainty, infringe less on sovereignty and facilitate compromise among differentiated actors. (Abbott and Snidal, 2000) See '**International environmental law**.'

Solar energy – Energy generated by converting sunlight into useful energy and normally divided into three categories: active and passive building modifications, solar thermal collectors, and photovoltaic cells. (EES)

Solar water disinfection system (SODIS) – A simple means of purifying water using clear plastic bottles made from standard polyethylene terephthalate (PETE or PET) that are filled with water and exposed to natural sunlight for six hours.

Solid waste – Any solid or semi-solid material discarded from industrial, commercial, mining, agricultural operations or household sources, including garbage, construction debris, commercial refuse, sludge from water supply or waste treatment plants, or air pollution control facilities and other discarded materials. (MW)

Source – Any process or activity that releases a greenhouse gas, an aerosol or a precursor of a greenhouse gas into the atmosphere. (UNFCCC)

Source Principle – The environmental damage should preferably be prevented at the source, rather than by using the 'end-of-pipe technology.' This principle also implies a preference for emission standards rather than

S

environmental quality standards, especially to deal with water and air pollution.

South – Another name for the low- and middle-income countries as a group.

South American Community of Nations (SACN) – A continent-wide free trade zone conceived to unite two free trade organizations, MERCOSUR and the Andean Community of Nations (CAN), eliminating tariffs on non-sensitive products by 2015 and sensitive products by 2020. Representatives of the 12 South American nations signed the Cuzco (Peru) Declaration in December 2004 formally establishing SACN and signaling their intention to model the organization on the EU model including a common constitution, currency, parliament and passport. In mid-2006, Venezuela announced its intentions to leave the CAN because two of its members had signed trade agreements with the US, endangering the rationale for the SACN. (SACN) See '**Andean Community of Nations**.'

South Centre – An intergovernmental body of developing countries established on 31 July, 1995, the Centre currently has 46 members and draws its strength from networking so as to carry out the designated work in cooperation with other institutions and individuals of the South. Its work is to promote solidarity, consciousness and mutual understanding among the countries and peoples of the South; promote South–South cooperation and action, South–South networking and information exchange; and developing country participation in international forums dealing with South–South and North–South matters and global concerns. It fosters convergent views and approaches among countries of the South with respect to global economic, political and strategic issues and contributes to better mutual understanding and cooperation between the South and the North on the basis of equity and justice for all.

South–North – A term indicating collaboration or technology sharing/transfer from a 'South' nation to a 'North' nation.

South Pacific Regional Environment Programme (SPREP) – Headquartered in Apia, Samoa, SPREP is the Pacific Region's main environmental organization with 26 members including the US, Australia, New Zealand and France. Its mandate is to promote cooperation in the South Pacific Region, provide assistance in order to protect and improve its environment and ensure sustainable development for present and future generations.

South–South – A term indicating collaboration or technology sharing between low income and/or middle income developing countries. (UNT)

Sovereignty – This difficult concept has both emotional and rational components and is often a matter of perception. It relates to the state's monopoly on the use of force and its position as final authority over matters within its territory. State sovereignty is diminished with the rise of international corporations, multinational organizations and transnational forces like religion, ethnicity and culture.

Specific funds – Monies donated for a specific purpose but within the overall mandate of an organization but normally in addition to regular funds.

Sphere concept/project – The Sphere Project was launched in 1997 by a group of humanitarian NGOs and the Red Cross and Red Crescent Societies. Sphere is based on application of The Humanitarian Charter and its two core beliefs: first, that all possible steps should be taken to alleviate human suffering arising out of calamity and conflict and, second, that those affected by disaster have a right to life with dignity and therefore a right to assistance.

Spoils – Dirt or rock removed from its original location resulting in an altered soil structure and composition as in strip mining or dredging. (USEPA)

Square brackets [ ] – Symbols used during treaty negotiations to indicate that a section of text is being discussed but has not yet been agreed upon. One would state: 'put it in square brackets for the time being and we can revisit it later.' Fiona McConnell's 1996 explanation of square brackets in *The Biodiversity Convention: A Negotiating History*, identifies six rationales for their use:

- Alternative brackets comprise alternative text for the same issue and may revolve around a substantive disagreement, but tend to be similar wording for the same issue.
- Contentious brackets are there because of fundamental disagreement over a particular section.
- Suspicious brackets are used when one group thinks the other is up to something with a section or a phrase and therefore the brackets are put in until it becomes clearer.
- Tactical or trading brackets may be put in by one country to enable them to trade with another bracket in another section or in another area.
- Uncertain brackets are put where no one was quite sure what the proposed text meant or why the brackets were placed there in the first place.
- Waiting brackets are inserted when governments are waiting for instructions from the capital on what to do.
- Weary brackets are usually included when negotiations go on into the early morning and when people get too tired to negotiate effectively.

SRES scenarios – A suite of emissions scenarios developed by the IPCC to explore a range of potential future greenhouse gas emissions pathways over the 21st century and their subsequent implications for global climate change. (PEW)

Stability – Unchanging with time. This can be a static state (nothing changes) or a steady state (resource flows occur). (CSG)

Stage (water) – The height of a water surface above an established reference point.

Stakeholder – An institution, organization, or group that has some interest in a particular sector or system or outcome of a project, program or policy initiative. (EEA)

State (1) – The set of political institutions whose specific concern is with the social and political organization and management, in the name of the common interest, within a determined territory. (UNDP)

State (2) – The power or authority represented by a body of people politically organized under an independent government within a territory having defined boundaries and constituting the basis for civil government. (MW). See '**Country**', '**Nation**', '**Territory**.'

State of the World Forum (SWF) – Formed in 1995, SWF is a non-profit organization dedicated to 'establishing a global network of leaders, citizens and institutions committed to discerning and implementing the principles, values and actions necessary to guide humanity wisely as it gives shape to an increasingly global and interdependent civilization.' (SWF)

Statement of Forest Principles (United Nations Conference on Environment and Development – UNCED) – The 'Non-legally Binding Authoritative Statement of Principles for a Global Consensus on the Management, Conservation and Sustainable Development of all Types of Forests' was agreed to at UNCED in 1992 and addresses issues related to sustainable forest management. This was the first global consensus on forests that attempted to deal with people who want to protect forests for environmental and cultural reasons together with those who depend on trees and other forest life for economic development. The hope is that these principles will form the basis of further negotiations toward a binding agreement.

Stockholm Convention – An international legally binding instrument (opened for signature on 22 May, 2001) for implementing international action on twelve persistent organic pollutants (POPs) grouped into three categories: (1) Pesticides: aldrin, chlordane, DDT, dieldrin, endrin, heptachlor, mirex and toxaphene; (2) industrial chemicals: hexachlorobenzene (HCB) and polychlorinated biphenyls (PCBs); and (3) unintended byproducts: dioxins and furans. The Convention will come into force when 50 parties have ratified.

Stockholm Declaration on the Human Environment – The Declaration produced at the first United Nations Conference on the Human Environment that met at Stockholm from 5–16 June, 1972, which supports a common outlook and principles to inspire and guide the peoples of the world in the preservation and enhancement of the human environment. See Appendix I.

Straddling stock – A population of organisms that travels between the exclusive economic zones of two or more countries, or between them and the high seas. (BCHM)

Strange attractors – Areas around which behaviors and interactions tend to occur.

Stormwater treatment area – A large, constructed wetland designed to remove pollutants, particularly nutrients from stormwater runoff using natural processes.

Strategic Ambiguity, concept of – A term referring to a country's decision to neither confirm nor deny the existence of a particular infrastructure or policy. This term was first used in 2004 by certain countries in reference to nuclear sites and the existence or non-existence of nuclear weapons, the ability to manufacture nuclear weapons and/or being in possession of the raw materials or technology to do so. (UNIAEA)

Strategic environmental assessment (SEA) – A technique similar to environmental impact assessment (EIA) but normally applied to policies, plans, program and groups of projects. There are two main types of SEA: Sectoral, which is applied when many new projects fall within one sector and Regional, which is applied to cover development within a region. (EEA)

Strategy – A framework guiding those choices that determine the nature and direction to attain the objective.

Stratosphere – The upper portion of the atmosphere, approximately 11–50km above the surface of the earth. (NRDC)

Straw vote – An unofficial vote used to predict how an election might turn out.

Strip mining – A mining technique in which the land and vegetation covering the mineral being sought are stripped away by huge machines, usually permanently altering the land and limiting subsequent uses. (NRDC)

Structural adjustment loans – Large loans made by the World Bank, IMF or regional development banks to developing countries that may carry strict financial and budgetary obligations or required policy reforms intended to open recipient countries to private investment and increase the recipient's

S

competitiveness in the global economy. Reforms are usually orientated towards liberalization of trade rules, privatization of State-held assets, and a reduction in government expenditures. (WB)

Sub-Saharan – Of or relating to or situated in the region south of the Sahara Desert. (UN)

Subsidiarity, principle of – A hierarchical form of government where decision making is made at the level of authority most responsive to the public. (UNCHS). A principle that recognizes that actions will occur at different levels of jurisdiction depending on the nature of the issue. It assigns priority to the lowest jurisdictional level consistent with effectiveness. (IISD)

Subsidiary Body for Implementation – Assists the Conference of the parties (COP) in the assessment and review of the effective implementation of a convention. (UNFCCC)

Subsidiary Body on Scientific, Technical and Technological Advice (SBSTTA) – The SBSTTA is a body of the Conference of the Parties (COP) that reports regularly on its assessments of the status of the subject matter of the Convention; the measures taken by the parties in accordance with the provisions of the Convention; and, it responds to questions put to it by the COP. (CBD; UNFCCC)

Subsidy – A direct or indirect benefit granted by a government for the production or distribution (including export) of a good.

Subsistence agriculture – See '**Shifting cultivation**.'

Succession – The more or less predictable changes in the species composition on a given site over time. (EES)

Sui generis – A Latin term meaning unique or peculiar, in a class of its own.

Summit of the Americas Process – A series of formal Summits of the Americas (Miami, US December 1994; Santiago, Chile April 1998; Quebec City, Canada April 2002; and Mar de Plata, Argentina November 2005), and one specialized Summit of the Americas on sustainable development (Santa Cruz, Bolivia December 1996). The next Summit of the Americas will be held in Trinidad and Tobago in late 2008 or early 2009. The Summit of the Americas is the first step in developing policies, declarations and plans of action for Inter-American cooperation in a wide range of topics including trade, education and environment. The Inter-American system, led by the Organization of American States, its institutional partners, and civil society organizations, play fundamental roles in the debate leading to the definition of hemispheric policies. Through Summit Implementation Review Group (SIRG) meetings, participating governments meet an average of three times a year to discuss official Summit documents, namely the declaration and the Plan of Action. (OAS, 2001; UNCED)

Sunk-cost effect, concept of – A psychological term that implies an unwillingness to abandon a policy or course of action in which so much has already been invested. (Jared, 2005) See '**Tragedy of the Commons**;' '**Logic of collective action, concept of**.'

Sunset clause – A statement added to the end of a measure, agreement, *ad hoc* committee creation/assignment, legislation, etc. that causes the same to 'sunset' or become ineffective, null and void after a certain date.

Supplementarity, principle of – A term referring to whether or not the Parties of The Kyoto Protocol, which use flexibility mechanisms such as emissions trading to lower greenhouse gas mitigation costs, also institute adequate domestic energy and other policies to achieve long-term greenhouse gas reduction goals.

Sustainability – Sustainability is an economic, social and environmental concept. It is intended to be a means of configuring civilization and human activity so that society and its members are able to meet their needs and express their greatest potential in the present, while preserving biodiversity and natural ecosystems, and planning and acting for the ability to maintain these ideals indefinitely. Sustainability affects every level of organization, from the local neighborhood to the entire planet. See the essay pp3–38.

Sustainability assessment measures – The traditional measures of growth such as GDP have been criticized as inappropriate measures for human and ecosystem well-being as they register income but not its distribution and do not distinguish between sustainable and unsustainable activities. For example, crime, forest fires, disease, natural disasters all add to the GDP because in confronting them money is exchanged. Therefore, a number of indices or assessment measures have been developed within a sustainable development context providing another point of view as to what constitutes 'progress' in the context of human and ecosystem health, including: the *Human Development Index*, which measures factors such as life expectancy, education, GDP per capita, etc. (www.undp.org/hdr), *Environmental Sustainability Index* measuring environmental systems, reducing environmental stress, reducing human vulnerability, global stewardship, etc. (www.ciesin.org/indicators/ESI), *Living Planet Index* measuring the health of animal species in a variety of ecosystems (www.panda.org/livingplanet), *Ecological Footprint*, which reports on a variety of impacts in productive sectors (www.panda.org/livingplanet), *Compass of Sustainability*, which examines the well-being of humans based on several measures of nature, economy and society (www.iisd.org), *Dashboard of Sustainability*, which measures institutions active in environment, economy and society (www.iisd.ca/cgsdi/dashboard), and *Well Being Assessment/Barometer of Sustainability*, which looks at ecosystems and people and a variety of indicators (www.iucn.org/

info_and_news/press/wonback.doc). See '**Commitment to Development Index**.'

Sustainability indicator – A variable, a pointer, an index of a complex phenomenon. Its fluctuations reveal the variations in components of the ecosystem, the resource or the sector. The position and trend of the indicator in relation to the criteria indicate the present state and dynamics of the system. Ideally, composite indicators are needed, the position and trajectory of which, within a system of reference of related criteria, would allow simple holistic assessment of sustainability. One can distinguish indicators of the state of the system, pressure (or stress, driving forces) on the system, and response (reflecting action taken to mitigate, reduce, eliminate or compensate for the stress). (EEA) See '**Sustainability assessment measures**.'

Sustainability, principle of – A principle that implies a relationship between the rate and type of use of natural resources and the ability to support a defined lifestyle. (RFF)

Sustainable community – Fosters healthy people and biodiversity, and the linkages between them; continuously invests in capacities, institutions and partnerships that protect, restore and enhance natural, social and economic capital; actively monitors and disseminates knowledge and know-how; promotes inclusive, collaborative, stakeholder-driven planning and adaptive action in response to changing conditions; prefers local products and services that result in triple bottom-line profits – social, economic and environmental; and has increasing options and opportunities because its citizens choose to internalize the local, regional, global and inter-generational impacts of their decisions and actions. (SNW)

Sustainable consumption – The consumption of services and products that respond to basic needs and bring a better quality of life, while minimizing use of natural resources and toxic materials as well as the generation of wastes and pollutants over the life-cycle of a product or service, so as not to jeopardize the needs of future generations. (CSD)

Sustainable development – There are literally hundreds of definitions of sustainable development. Perhaps the most famous is that included in the Bruntland Commission report, *Our Common Future*, stating that sustainable development is development that meets the needs of the present without compromising the ability of future generations to meet their own needs. It contains within it two key concepts: the concept of 'needs', in particular the essential needs of the world's poor, to which overriding priority should be given; and the idea of 'limitations' imposed by the state of technology and social organization on the environment's ability to meet present and the future needs. However, it must be remembered that the Bruntland Commission did not invent the term sustainable development. Others including the IUCN had used the term for years prior. The Commission undoubtedly used the term in the context of the time and based on the understanding of the meetings held in relation to producing its final report. (UNCED) See the text: '*Our Common Future.*' (World Commission on Environment and Development, 1987)

Sustainable enterprise – A concept that the production and sale of goods and services must incorporate the role of and impact on nature and society; pursues triple bottom-line profits – economic, social and environmental; practices eco-efficiency and commits to moving toward eco-effectiveness (i.e. where the byproducts of production are inputs for other processes – zero waste); builds a strong customer base and expands market share by helping consumers consume less, serving their true needs; and engenders loyal shareholders and employees. (SNW)

Sustainable forest management – Forest management activities that benefit people and the resource base today, but do not compromise the resource for future generations. (USFS). The stewardship and use of forests and forest lands in a way, and at a rate, that maintains their biodiversity, productivity, regeneration capacity, vitality and their potential to fulfill, now and in the future, relevant ecological, economic and social functions, at local, national and global levels, and that does not cause damage to other ecosystems. (UNFF)

Sustainable human development (SHD) – A paradigm of development that puts people and their ongoing needs and aspirations at the center of its concerns; that not only generates economic growth but distributes its benefits equitably; that regenerates the environment; that empowers people; and that, because of their existing position of fewer opportunities, gives priority to the poor, enlarging their choices and opportunities and providing for their participation in decisions that affect their lives. UNDP's core mission, focused on building human and institutional capacity for poverty elimination, livelihood and job creation, the advancement of women and environmental protection. SHD differs from human development concepts by more attention towards the factor of time. (UNDP)

Sustainable livelihood – A livelihood is sustainable when it can cope with and recover from stresses and shocks while maintaining or enhancing its capabilities and assets.

Sustainable use (of biodiversity) – The use of components of biological diversity in a way and at a rate that does not lead to the long-term decline of biological diversity, thereby maintaining its potential to meet the needs and aspirations of present and future generations. (CBD)

Sustained yield – The yield that a renewable resource can produce continuously at a given intensity of management.

Swedish International Development Agency (SIDA) – The principal

S

agency through which Sweden provides technical assistance and delivers foreign aid.

Swidden agriculture – See '**Shifting cultivation**.'

Symbiosis – Association of two organisms in which the relationship is mutually beneficial. (USEPA)

Symbols – Symbols commonly used in United Nations documents. See '**Units of measurement**.'

- b — billion
- ¢ — cents
- © — copyright
- € — euro
- F — French Franc (replaced by euro in 2002)
- fte — full-time equivalent(s) referring to staff members
- g — giga
- ha — hectare (2.47 acres; 10,000 square meters)
- ac — acre (2.47 acres; 43,560 square feet, 405 hectares)
- k — kilo
- l — liter
- £ — British pound
- m — meter
- m^2 — square meter
- m^3 — cubic meter
- Mm^3 — millions of cubic meters
- Mm^3a^{-1} — millions of cubic meters per annum
- masl — meters above sea level
- M — mega
- M — million
- ppb — parts per billion
- ppm — parts per million
- ESP — Spanish Peseta (replaced by euro in 2002)
- [ ] — square brackets, text under discussion
- ® — registered
- s — second
- T — tera
- t — ton
- ™ — trademark
- US$ — US dollar
- ¥ — Japanese yen
- < — less than
- > — greater than
- @ — at (in electronic mail addresses)
- % — percentage
- ‰ — parts per thousand

Synergy – The result of a combined action or operation of two or more parties, systems, or parts, in which the results are greater than they would be acting separately.

Systemic insecticide/pesticide – An insecticide or pesticide that is absorbed into plant sap and/or a root system and is lethal to insects and pests feeding on the treated plant. (USEPA)

S

Tt

Table – A term that, depending on who is using it, can mean to either take up or halt debate on an issue. To place on the agenda or to remove (as a parliamentary motion) from consideration indefinitely.

Tacit knowledge – The accumulated portion of experiences and skills within people gained through cognition in one's lifetime. (Nonaka and Takeuchi, 1995)

Tailings – See '**Spoils**.'

Tailor-made economies – A term that came into common use in mid-2006 to indicate small-scale, locally developed economic reform strategies as opposed to 'big bang' institutional changes such as structural/sector reform policy packages advocated by development banks. The four-point agenda proposed for HIPC and other low income countries includes: fostering active trade and production sector policies for economic diversification; improving the trade environment; opening up more space for counter-cyclical macroeconomic policies; and ensuring sustained levels of public spending. (UNW) See '**Cyclical macro-economic policies**,' '**Ikea development**.'

Take-back effect – See '**Offsetting effect**.'

Tallberg Forum – An international forum involving global leaders started in 1980 to enhance understanding of transformational leadership, values and institutional change. (WP)

Target groups – The main stakeholders of a project that are expected to gain from the results of that project; sectors of the population that a project aims to reach in order to address their needs based on gender considerations and their socio-economic characteristics.

Technocentrism – A belief that constant generation of new technology is a panacea for humanity's problems. (EES)

Technological colonialism – A term that can be traced to the role of large ICT companies and their strategies for developing and marketing software and hardware for use in developing countries. The argument is made that developing countries are forced (by cost, availability, patent protections and technical internet access configurations) to accept ICT developed by a few large multinational companies, which in turn indebts them socially and economically to the values of developed nations. In essence they are frozen out of effective competition in the ICT marketplace and dominated by outside firms. See '**Digital divide**.'

Technology transfer (1) – The transfer of knowledge or equipment to enable the manufacture of a product, the application of a process, or the rendering of a service. (BCHM)

Technology transfer (2) – The process of developing practical applications for the results of scientific research. (WP)

Territorial sea – Littoral zone waters regarded as being under jurisdiction of the state: commonly, those waters measured from the shoreline of a sovereign state where the laws of that state are applicable. These waters commonly extend to 12 nautical miles (22km) from the coast, as per the terms of the United Nations Convention on the Law of the Sea. (WP)

Territory – The land and water controlled by a country, nation or state.

Terrorism – The intentional use of, or threat to use, violence against civilians or against civilian targets, in order to attain political aims. (USDOS) See '**Eco-terrorism**,' '**Monkeywrenching**.'

Tertiary sewage treatment – Primary and secondary treatment plus a final stage involving a number of alternate treatments aimed at raising the effluent quality to the standard required before it is discharged to the receiving environment (sea, river, lake, ground, etc.) (WP)

The Nature Conservancy (TNC) – Incorporated in 1951 in the US, TNC is one of the largest conservation NGOs in the world. Its mission is to help preserve plants, animals and natural communities that represent the natural diversity of life on Earth by protecting the lands and waters they need to survive. Its headquarters are in Arlington, Virginia, US.

Third state – A state not a party to the treaty. (VC)

Third World – A term referring to the areas of the world that are the least developed, which consists of large parts of Latin America, Africa and South and East Asia.

Third World Academy of Sciences (TWAS) – An association of more than 600 eminent scientists, largely from the South. Its principle aim is to promote scientific capacity and excellence for sustainable development in the South. It supports scientific research in more than 90 countries by providing promising scientists with research facilities necessary for the advancement of their work. (TWAS)

Third World Network of Scientific Organizations (TWNSO) – A nongovernmental alliance of 154 scientific organizations in the South, including ministers of science, technology and higher education, science

T

academies, and research councils. TWNSO's primary goals are to help build political and scientific leadership in the South for science-based economic development and to promote sustainable development through South–South and South–North partnerships in science and technology. (TWNSO)

Third World Organization for Women in Science (TWOWS) – An independent NGO, established with the assistance of TWAS in 1993, it is the first international forum designed to unite eminent women scientists from the South for the purposes of strengthening their role in sustainable development and promoting their representation and leadership in science and technology. (TWOWS)

Thirty percent club – Countries who have signed the Protocol to the 1979 Convention on Long-Range Transboundary Air Pollution. This Convention calls for reductions of at least 30 percent in sulphur emissions or their transboundary fluxes. (AM)

Threatened species (1) – Species that are genetically impoverished, of low fecundity, dependent on patchy or unpredictable resources, extremely variable in population density, persecuted or otherwise prone to extinction in human dominated landscapes. (GBA)

Threatened species (2) – A classification referring to a species that is likely to become endangered within the near future, throughout all or a significant portion of its range. (IUCN)

Three pillars of sustainable development – A commonly accepted idea that sustainable development is based on the sustainability of its three components: economical sustainability, social sustainability, and 'ecological' or 'environmental' sustainability.

Tied aid – Aid is said to be 'tied' when one of the conditions for granting it is that the money given or loaned will be used to buy goods and services from the donor country or another specified country. Donor countries in the OECD-DAC are committed to untying aid for the least developed countries. (OECD)

Top-up funds – Funds that are in addition to those requested for a project for the purposes of enabling the project to move forward.

Top-up projects – Enabling projects that are different from, but necessary for, the success of projects designed to meet a specific goal.

Total allowable catch – The quantity of fish that can be taken from each stock each year.

Total dissolved solids (TDS) – The dry weight of all material in water or wastewater that *passes through* a series of calibrated standard filters. (USEPA; WP)

Total maximum daily load – The maximum allowed level of pollutant loading for a water body, while still protecting its uses and maintaining compliance with established water quality standards.

Total suspended solids (TSS) – The dry weight of the suspended solids in wastewater, effluent or water bodies *trapped by* a series of calibrated standard filters. (USEPA; WP)

Tour – See '**Post/Posting**.'

Tour D'Horizon – A diplomatic discussion covering most subjects of current and common concern among the parties. (eD)

Toxic waste – Refuse or other unwanted material posing a significant hazard to the health of humans or other organisms when improperly handled. (WP)

Track 1 diplomacy – Government to government conversations or negotiations. (eD)

Track 2 diplomacy – Civil society to government or government to civil society conversations or negotiations. (eD)

Tradable emissions – An approach to limiting the global discharge of greenhouse emissions by allowing polluters to 'trade' the costs of emissions for proactive conservation initiatives in related sectors. An example would be carbon emissions from a power station 'traded' for support to carbon sequestration in forestry. (UNFCCC)

Traditional resource rights (TRR) – Similar to intellectual property rights, but the term denotes broader 'bundles of rights' that include human rights, land rights, religious rights and cultural property. (BCHM)

TRAFFIC – A wildlife trade-monitoring group sponsored by IUCN and WWF.

Tragedy of the Commons – A book published by Dr Garrett Hardin in 1968, which explored the issue of carrying capacity of natural resources. The thesis of the book argued that in many situations, the self-maximizing gains by individuals ultimately destroy the resource, such that nobody wins. The utility of an additional item for the person is more than the disutility of the additional strain on resources (shared by everybody). This occurs with park usage, pollution, etc. Appeals to conscience will not be effective. In a sense, freedom must be restricted to retain the resource.

Tranche (1) – A work program that contains a timetable, project component and funding level. (GEF)

Tranche (2) – A disbursement/payment of funds based on an agreed-to timetable and tied to milestones or products in a project workplan. (GEF)

Transboundary – Describes collaboration activities or any system or externality extending beyond one jurisdiction, region or nation state at any scale (cross-border, inter-regional, transnational) and is thus a generic term for collaboration extending over national borders.

Transboundary diagnostic analysis (TDA) – A study undertaken to identify and evaluate the major environmental problems and their root societal and economic causes responsible for the deterioration of international waters. Further, the TDA is a mechanism to define priority actions and co-operative efforts between GEF and countries/participants. The study includes natural and social scientists and economists as well as representatives of the area's stakeholders. (GEF)

Transboundary Freshwater Dispute Database (TFDD) – The world's largest searchable database on freshwater conflict prevention and dispute resolution. The database, housed in the Department of Geosciences at Oregon State University, has become an increasingly important source of information for negotiators and contains five elements: the Atlas of International Freshwater Agreements, the International Freshwater Treaties Database, the Transboundary Freshwater Spatial Database, the International Freshwater Event Database, and the International River Basin Register. (TFDD)

Transboundary governance – A term referring to either a formal or informal framework to manage a natural resource or to address an environmental problem shared between two or more jurisdictions. (OAS, 2001)

Transboundary pollution – Polluted air and water, or any other contaminated waste that is generated in one jurisdiction and transmitted to others. (EEA)

Transformational diplomacy – A USDOS term defined in 2006 as working with partners around the world to build and sustain democratic, well-governed states that will respond to the needs of their people and conduct themselves responsibly in the international system. Transformational diplomacy is rooted in partnership, not paternalism, in doing things with other people, not for them, to help foreign citizens to better their own lives, to build their own nations, and to transform their own futures. (USDOS)

Transition countries – A term referring to a class of 24 countries from the former Soviet Union (Commonwealth of Independent States) and the former Warsaw Pact. See '**Emerging countries/economies**.'

Transitional waters – Bodies of surface water in the vicinity of a river mouth that are partly saline in character as a result of their proximity to coastal waters but which are substantially influenced by freshwater flows. (EES)

Translation – A term referring to translating the written or spoken word into other languages.

Trans-national Actor – See '**Non-state Actor**.'

Transparency – A policy of sharing information and acting in such a way so as to allow stakeholders to gather information that may be critical to uncovering abuses and defending their interests. Transparent systems have clear procedures for public decision making and open channels of communication between stakeholders and officials, and make a wide range of information accessible. (UNDP)

Transparency International (TI) – Formed in 1993 and based in Berlin, Transparency International is a nongovernmental organization dedicated to increasing government accountability and curbing both international and national corruption. It works to ensure that the agendas of international organizations give high priority to curbing corruption. Both the TI Secretariat and TI National Chapters around the world actively monitor the implementation of the anti-corruption instruments of the OECD, the Council of Europe, the EU and the Organization of American States. (TI)

Treaty – An international agreement concluded between States in written form and governed by international law, whether embodied in a single instrument or in two or more related instruments and whatever its particular designation. (VC)

Treaty of Basseterre – The treaty establishing the Organization of Eastern Caribbean States. See '**Organization of Eastern Caribbean States**.'

Treaty of Nice – The Treaty of Nice (France) was adopted by the European Council to amend the two founding treaties of the EU: – the Treaty on European Union, or Maastricht Treaty, which introduced the euro and the institutional structure of the EU; and the Treaty of Rome, which established the European Economic Community and the European Atomic Energy Community. It entered into force on 1 February, 2003. (EU; WP)

Treaty on European Union – See '**European Union**.'

Tripartite Agreement – An agreement of 28 October, 1991, formally signed by the heads of the World Bank, UNDP and UNEP to establish and operate the GEF.

T

Triple bottom-line (1) – Expanding the traditional company reporting framework from one that is exclusively financial to one including social, environmental and economic factors. (WP)

Triple bottom-line (2) – The whole set of values, issues and processes companies must address in order to minimize the harm resulting from their activities and to create economic, social and environmental value. The three bottom lines represent society, the economy and the environment. Society depends on the economy and the economy depends on the global ecosystem, whose health is the ultimate bottom line. (UNEP)

Trophic level(s) – One of the hierarchical strata of a food web characterized by organisms that are the same number of steps removed from the primary producers. A predator species represents one or more trophic levels higher than the species being consumed. (EES)

Tropical forest – The natural and semi-natural tropical or subtropical forest ecosystems, whether primary or secondary, whether closed or open forests, in both dry and humid areas found within the tropics and subtropics delimited by the 30th northern and southern parallels. (EEA)

Trust funds – Extra-budgetary program resources that help meet the objectives of UNEP that are negotiated between UNEP and the donor (or several donors) and form separate accounts. (UNEP)

Trust Fund for the Convention on Biological Diversity – An institution established by the COP-CBD to administer funds for the administration of the convention including the functions of the Secretariat. The Trust Fund is financed from contributions made by Parties to the Conventions based on a set scale, additional contributions by the parties, contributions from States not Parties to the Convention and governmental, intergovernmental and nongovernmental organizations. (CBD)

Tsunami – A sea wave of local or distant origin that results from large-scale seafloor displacements associated with large offshore earthquakes, major submarine slides or erupting underwater volcanic islands. (UNDP)

Tundra – A zone between the perpetual snow and ice of Arctic regions and the tree line (boreal taiga), having a permanently frozen sub-soil and supporting low-growing vegetation such as lichens, mosses, dwarf shrubs and stunted trees. (EES)

Turbidity – A measure of water clarity. (USEPA)

Turner Foundation – See '**United Nations Foundation**.'

Turtle excluder device (TED) – A net modification used on shrimp boats that enables incidentally caught sea turtles to escape. (NRDC)

Twinning arrangements – Arrangements made to facilitate sharing of knowledge and technology transfer between institutions having similar mandates in different countries.

Type 1 Outcome – A tangible outcome of a conference, generally a treaty.

Type 2 Outcome – A tangible outcome of a conference, generally partnerships.

Uu

U4 Resource Center – The U4 Utstein Anti-Corruption Resource Centre is a web-based resource center established by the Utstein Group to strengthen their partnership for fighting corruption in support of international development. See '**Utstein Group Partnership**.'

Umbrella convention – A stand-alone convention that can foster other conventions (primarily regional conventions) that helps to meet its objectives. (CMS)

Umbrella group – A coalition of like-minded governments established for purposes of voting within the UNFCCC (Japan, the US, Iceland, Canada, Australia, Norway, New Zealand, Russian Federation and Ukraine).

Unanimity – A decision having the agreement and consent of all participants.

Uncertainty – Distinguished from risk by the fact that there is no scientific basis upon which to formulate any probabilistic argument.

UN Dispatch – A daily summary of UN-related 'blog' commentary (website where comments can be posted). www.undispatch.com/

UNESCO Category I Water Institute – An integral part of UNESCO addressing a particular theme or priority of the organization. See '**UNESCO-IHE Institute for Water Education**.'

UNESCO Category II Water Institutes – One of the four pillars of UNESCO's Water Program. The Category II water institutes (national thematic water centers but collaborating with UNESCO through the Division of Water Sciences) include the following: the International Research and Training Centre on Erosion and Sedimentation (IRTCES) in China, Water Centre for the Humid Tropics of Latin America and the Caribbean (CATHALAC) in Panama, Regional Humid Tropics Hydrology and Water Resources Centre for Southeast Asia and the Pacific (HTC) in Malaysia, Regional Center on Urban Water Management (RCUWM) in Iran, Regional Center for Training and Water Studies of Arid and Semi-Arid Zones (RCTWS) in Egypt, International Research and Training Center on Urban Drainage (IRTCUD) in Serbia, International Center on Qanats and Historic Hydraulic Structures (ICQHHS) in Iran, International Centre for Water Hazard and Risk Management (ICHARM) in Japan, Water Centre for Arid and Semi-Arid Regions of Latin America and the Caribbean (CAZALAC) in Chile, IHP-HELP Centre for Water Law, Policy and Science in

Scotland, the European Regional Centre for Ecohydrology in Poland, and the Regional Centre on Urban Water Management for Latin America and the Caribbean in Colombia (CINARA).

UNESCO Centre University of Ulster – A university research center that concentrates on the themes of education for pluralism, human rights and democracy in local, national and international contexts.

UNESCO–IHE Institute for Water Education – One of the four pillars of UNESCO's Water Program. Located in Delft, The Netherlands, UNESCO-IHE is a Category I (an integral part of UNESCO) postgraduate training institute in water sciences, engineering and policy that aims to contribute to the education and training of professionals and to build the capacity of sector organizations, knowledge centers and other institutions active in the fields of water, environment and infrastructure in developing and transition countries. (UNESCO)

UNESCO–IHE Partnership for Water Education and Research (PoWER) – A network of eighteen autonomous collaborating centers in all regions of the developing world that aims to conduct and disseminate research into all aspects of integrated water resource management and capacity building. (UNESCO)

UNESCO–IHP International Hydrological Programme – One of the four pillars of UNESCO's Water Program. UNESCO's intergovernmental scientific cooperative program in water resources is a vehicle through which Member States can upgrade their knowledge of the water cycle and thereby increase their capacity to better manage and develop their water resources. IHP aims at the improvement of the scientific and technological basis for the development of methods for the rational management of water resources, including the protection of the environment. (UNESCO)

UNESCO 'Water Family' – An informal union of the Division of Water Sciences of UNESCO Headquarters, UNESCO-IHP (chairs, networks and centers), the World Water Assessment Programme (WWAP), and UNESCO-IHE that collaborate on water-related issues aimed at achieving the goals of the 'UN Decade for Action: Water for Life' and the UN Millennium Development Goals. (UNESCO)

UNESCO World Water Assessment Programme (WWAP) – One of the four pillars of UNESCO's Water Program (together with IHP, UNESCO Category II Centers, and UNESCO-IHE). WWAP focuses on assessing the developing situation with regard to freshwater throughout the world. The primary output of the WWAP is the periodic World Water Development Report (WWDR). (UNESCO)

UNese – A slang term referring to the array of jargon and acronyms used by UN insiders, making full understanding by outsiders very difficult.

U

UNGASS (Earth Summit +5) – The 19th special session of the UNGA convened in June, 1997, to review the outstanding issues not fully resolved at the UNCED including finance, climate change, freshwater management and forest management. This session adopted the Programme for the Further Implementation of *Agenda 21* (A/RES/S-19/2). It assessed progress since UNCED, examined implementation, and established the CSD's work programme for the period 1998–2002, leading up to WSSD.

UNspeak – See 'UNese.'

UN Watch – A nongovernmental organization based in Geneva that monitors activities of the UN based on the Charter and other Agreements and Resolutions emanating from the General Assembly. (UN)

UN Water (Family) – An inter-agency structure of 24 agencies in the UN system with activities related to water in all its aspects. This group is responsible for steering the World Water Assessment Program and its principle output, the World Water Assessment Report, and serves as an action forum to provide a multistakeholder mechanism for engagement with extra UN bodies through the World Water Implementation Program. The United Nations System Chief Executive Board for Coordination (CEB), on the recommendation of its High-level Committee on Programs (HLCP), endorsed UN Water in 2003 as the new official United Nations system-wide inter-agency mechanism for follow up of the water-related decisions reached at the World Summit on Sustainable Development 2002 and the Millennium Development Goals.

UNWire – A daily summary of major world news and how it affects or is being affected by the UN system, including its specialized organizations. un.wire@smartbrief.com (UNW)

United Nations – The United Nations Conference on International Organization opened in San Francisco on 25 April, 1945 where delegates of 50 nations discussed and modified the original Dumbarton Oaks proposals. On 26 June the United Nations Charter was completed and signed. By 24 October, 1945, the required number of nations had ratified the charter and the United Nations came officially into existence. Trygve Lie, foreign minister of Norway, was elected the first secretary-general. The UN presently includes 192 Member States. With the exception of the Holy See, the sole permanent Observer State, all internationally recognized independent countries are members. Other political entities, notably the Republic of China, Taiwan; (Taiwan of China; Taiwan, China); Saharawi Arab Democratic Republic (Western Sahara); and Palestine, have *de facto* independence and/or some international diplomatic recognition from selected states, but are not full UN members.

United Nations Association(s) – The mission of the World Federation of United Nations Associations is to inform, sustain and energize a global network of more than 100 national UN associations to support the principles and programs of the UN system and to help shape its agenda. See **Friends of the United Nations**.'

United Nations Capital Development Fund (UNCDF) – The UN-CDF was established by the UNGA in 1966 as a semi-autonomous unit within UNDP that develops new solutions for poverty reduction in least developed countries.

United Nations Central Emergency Response Fund – A $500 million fund established in late 2005 by the UN General Assembly, providing the UN with a cash on-hand account to be able to respond immediately following a natural disaster to the most urgent rescue and relief needs. (UN) See 'Web Relief.'

United Nations Centre for Human Settlements (UNCHS) – UNCHS (Habitat), located in Nairobi, Kenya, was established in 1978, two years after the UN Conference on Human Settlements held in Vancouver, Canada. The Centre serves as the lead agency for UN's human settlement development activities, as well as for the global exchange of information about human settlements, conditions and trends.

United Nations Charter – The UN Charter is the founding document of the UN, which was opened for signature in June 1945 and entered into force in October 1945.

United Nations Commission on Human Rights (UNCHR) – The United Nations Commission on Human Rights, composed of 53 States, met each year in regular session in March/April for six weeks in Geneva until it was disbanded in mid-2006 and replaced by the UN Human Rights Council. During its regular annual session, the Commission considered resolutions, decisions and chairperson's statements on matters of relevance to individuals in all regions and circumstances. (UN) See '**United Nations Human Rights Council**.'

United Nations Conference on Environment and Development (UNCED) – The United Nations Conference on Environment and Development was held from 3 June through 14 June, 1992, in Rio de Janeiro, Brazil. Five major agreements on global environmental issues were signed. Two of these, The Framework Convention on Climate Change and The Convention on Biological Diversity are formal treaties whose provisions may eventually be binding on the parties. The other three UNCED agreements are non-binding statements on the relationship between sustainable environmental practices and the pursuit of social and socio-economic development: *Agenda 21* is a wide-ranging assessment of social and economic sectors with goals for improving environmental and developmental impact of each; the *Rio Declaration* summarizes consensus principles of sustainable development, and the *Statement on Forest Principles* pledges parties to more sustainable use of forest resources.

U

United Nations Convention Against Corruption (UNCAC) – The convention sets standards for the prevention and criminalization of corrupt acts and spells out terms of increased international cooperation and for the recovery of the proceeds of corruption. The Convention entered into force in December 2005. (UN)

United Nations Convention on Biological Diversity (CBD) – Signed by 150 government leaders at the 1992 Rio Earth Summit, the Convention on Biological Diversity is dedicated to promoting sustainable development. Conceived as a practical tool for translating the principles of *Agenda 21* into reality, the Convention recognizes that biological diversity is about more than plants, animals and microorganisms and their ecosystems – it is about people and our need for food security, medicines, fresh air and water, shelter and a clean and healthy environment in which to live. (UNEP)

United Nations Convention on the Control of Transboundary Movements of Hazardous Wastes and their Disposal (UNT) – See '**Basel Convention**.'

United Nations Convention on the Law of the Sea (UNCLOS) – UNCLOS provides a global framework for the protection and management of the marine environment and the conservation and management of its living and non-living resources. It became operational in November 1994. See '**International Seabed Authority**.'

United Nations Convention to Combat Desertification (UNCCD) – As the question of how to tackle desertification was still a major concern at the time of UNCED, *Agenda 21* supported a new, integrated approach to the problem emphasizing action to promote sustainable development at the community level. It also called on the UNGA to establish an Intergovernmental Negotiating Committee to prepare, by June 1994, a Convention to Combat Desertification. In December 1992, the General Assembly agreed by adopting Resolution 47/188. The Committee completed its negotiations in five sessions and the Convention was adopted in Paris on 17 June, 1994. It entered into force on 26 December, 1996.

United Nations Decade(s) – A ten-year period during which a particular theme is given priority in terms of funding (regular and extra budgetary) such as the 'UN Decade of Education for Sustainable Development' (2005–2014); The 'UN Decade for Action: Water for Life' (2005–2014). (UN)

United Nations Decade 'Education for Sustainable Development (2005–2014)' – The United Nations Decade of Education for Sustainable Development (DESD) was officially launched at UN Headquarters in New York on 1 March, 2005, by UNESCO's Director General Koïchiro Matsuura. The Decade aims to see Education for Sustainable Development implemented in thousands of local situations on the ground, involving the integration of the principles of Sustainable Development into a multitude of different learning situations.

United Nations Decade for Action: Water for Life (2005–2014) – The 'Water for Life' Decade, launched on World Water Day (22 March) 2005, calls upon the international community to strengthen efforts to increase access to water and sanitation for all. The decision to establish this Decade was made by the General Assembly during its 58th annual session (A/RES/58/217). This is the second international decade on water-related issues under the auspices of the UN. The first, the International Decade on Drinking Water Supply and Sanitation, was held from 1981 to 1990.

United Nations Development Group – A consortium of the heads of all UN development funds, programs and departments headed by the Administrator of the UNDP.

United Nations Development Programme (UNDP) – Established in 1965, the United Nations Development Programme (UNDP) is one of the largest multilateral sources of grant technical assistance in the world. Head-quartered in New York City, this voluntarily funded organization provides expert advice, training and limited equipment to developing countries, with increasing emphasis on assistance to the least developed countries in priority areas of governance, poverty reduction, crises prevention and recovery, energy and environment, and HIV/AIDS. (UN)

United Nations Economic and Social Council (ECOSOC) – One of the six principle organs of the UN system. It is established by chapter 10 of the UN Charter and has 54 (18 before 1965) member nations elected annually for three-year terms by the General Assembly. The council undertakes investigations of international economic and social questions and reports its conclusions and suggestions to the General Assembly and other organs of the UN for action. The council also coordinates the activities of the Functional Commissions, Regional Commissions, and Specialized Agencies/Organizations of the UN and arranges for consultations with international nongovernmental organizations as listed below. (UN)

- Functional Commissions
  - Commission for Social Development (UNCSD)
  - Commission on Human Rights (UNHCR); Replaced by the UN Human Rights Council (2006)
  - Commission on Narcotic Drugs (UNCND)
  - Commission on Crime Prevention and Criminal Justice (UNCCPCJ)
  - Commission on Science and Technology for Development (UNCSTD)
  - Commission on Sustainable Development (UNCSD)
  - Commission on the Status of Women (UNCSW)
  - Commission on Population and Development (UNCPD)
  - Statistical Commission (UNSC)

U

- Regional Commissions
  - United Nations Economic Commission for Europe (UNECE)
  - United Nations Economic Commission for Africa (UNECA)
  - United Nations Economic Commission for Latin America and the Caribbean (UNECLAC)
  - United Nations Economic and Social Commission for Asia and the Pacific (UNESCAP)
  - United Nations Economic and Social Commission for Western Asia (UNESCWA)
- Specialized Agencies. The Specialized Agencies are autonomous organizations working with the UN and each other through the coordinating machinery of the Economic and Social Council.
  - International Labour Organization (ILO)
  - International Atomic Energy Agency (IAEA)
  - Food and Agriculture Organization (FAO)
  - United Nations Educational, Scientific and Cultural Organization (UNESCO)
  - World Health Organization (WHO)
  - International Monetary Fund (IMF)
  - International Civil Aviation Organization ((ICAO)
  - International Maritime Organization (IMO)
  - International Telecommunication Union (ITO)
  - Universal Postal Union (UPU)
  - World Meteorological Organization (WMO)
  - United Nations Development Programme (UNDP)
  - United Nations Environment Programme (UNEP)
  - World Intellectual Property Organization ((WIPO)
  - International Fund for Agricultural Development (IFAD)
  - United Nations Industrial Development Organization (UNIDO)
  - International Refugee Organization (eliminated in 1952)
  - International Narcotics Control Board (INCB)
  - World Bank Group
    - International Bank for Reconstruction and Development (IBRD)
    - International Development Association (IDA)
    - International Finance Corporation (IFC)
    - Multilateral Investment Guarantee Agency (MIGA)
    - International Centre for Settlement of Investment Disputes (ICSID)
- Other Entities
  - United Nations Forum on Forests
  - Sessional and Standing Committees Expert, *ad hoc* and related bodies

United Nations Economic Commission for Europe (UNECE) – The UNECE was instituted in 1947 as a forum at which the countries of North America, Central and Eastern Europe and Central Asia come together to strengthen economic cooperation. UNECE focuses on economic analysis, environment and human settlements, statistics, sustainable energy, trade, industry and enterprise development, timber and transport.

United Nations Economic Commission for Latin America and the Caribbean (ECLAC) – ECLAC was established in February 1948 as a regional agency of the UN to cooperate with the governments of Latin America in the economic and social development of the region; the scope of its activities was subsequently expanded to include the countries of the Caribbean. ECLAC carries out studies and programs in collaboration with the governments of the region in integration, foreign trade, agricultural production, industrial development, transport and communications, statistics, natural resources, the environment, science and technology, and transnational corporations. (ECLAC)

United Nations Educational, Scientific, and Cultural Organization (UNESCO) – UNESCO was founded on 16 November, 1945 and presently includes 192 Member States. Its headquarters are in Paris, France with 73 field offices and units in different parts of the world. The main objective of UNESCO is to contribute to peace and security in the world by promoting collaboration among nations through education, science, culture and communication in order to further universal respect for justice, for the rule of law and for human rights and fundamental freedoms.

United Nations Environment Programme (UNEP) – UNEP was created as a consequence of the 1972 Stockholm Conference on the Human Environment. Its mission is to be the leading environmental authority within the UN system that sets a global environmental agenda; promotes the coherent implementation of the environmental dimension of sustainable development; serves as an authoritative advocate for the global environment; and encourages international cooperation and action, based on the best scientific and technical capabilities available. UNEP has had five Executive Directors including: Maurice Strong (1973–1974, Canada), Mustafa Tolba (1975–1992, Egypt), Elizabeth Dowdeswell (1992–1997, Canada), Klaus Toepher (1998–2005, Germany), and Achim Steiner (2006–, Germany). (UN)

United Nations Environment Programme Blue Plan – A UNEP think tank established in 1996 to address environmental policy issues for the promotion of sustainable development in the Mediterranean basin. (UNEP)

United Nations Environmental Management Group (UNEMG) – Created in 1999 as a UN system-wide mechanism, the UNEMG convenes 28 UN agencies, convention secretariats and Bretton Woods institutions under the chairmanship of the Executive Director of UNEP. The goal of the UNEMG is to 'promote inter-linkages, encourage timely and relevant exchange of data on information of specific issues and compatibility of different approaches to finding solutions to those common problems, and to contribute to the synergy and complimentary among activities of

U

its members in the field of environment and human settlements.' Members include: UNDESA, UNRWA, UNIDO, UNCHS, UNHCR, WHO, UNESCO, WFP, ILO, WTO, IBRD, ICAO, IMO, UPU, UNFCCC, UNFPA, UNICEF, UNCTAD, UNDP, UNDCP, UNITAR, WMO, OCHA, FAO, IFAD, ITU, WIPO, IAEA. (UNEP)

United Nations Food and Agriculture Organization (FAO) – FAO was founded in 1945 with a mandate to raise levels of nutrition and standards of living, to improve agricultural productivity, and to better the condition of rural populations. It is one of the largest specialized agencies in the UN system and the lead agency for agriculture, forestry, fisheries and rural development. An intergovernmental organization, FAO has 183 member countries plus one member organization, the EC. (FAO)

United Nations Forum on Forests (UNFF) – The UNFF is a subsidiary body of ECOSOC established to promote the management, conservation and sustainable development of all types of forests. Its purpose is to: promote the implementation of internationally agreed actions on forests at the national, regional and global levels; provide a coherent, transparent and participatory global framework for policy implementation, coordination and development; and carry out principal functions, based on the Rio Declaration, the Forest Principles, Chapter 11 of *Agenda 21*, and the outcomes of the IPF and the IFF.

United Nations Foundation – In 1997, businessman and philanthropist Ted Turner made a historic gift of US$1 billion in support of UN efforts to address global issues. He chose to channel his global commitment through the UN because of its vital role as the primary forum for international cooperation recognized by all nations. The UN Foundation's mission is to support the goals and objectives of the UN and its Charter, in order to promote a more peaceful, prosperous and just world – with special emphasis on the UN's work on behalf of pressing health, humanitarian, socio-economic and environmental challenges of the 21st century. (UN)

United Nations Foundation/Club of Madrid Task Force on Climate Change – A task force formed in 2006 that will develop an international plan for tackling global warming after the Kyoto Treaty expires in 2012. The task force will make recommendations to the Dialogue on Climate Change, Clean Energy and Sustainable Development, which is part of UN's Framework Convention on Climate Change. (UNW)

United Nations Framework Convention on Climate Change (UNFCCC) – The UNFCCC was signed in 1992 at the Earth Summit in Rio de Janeiro by more than 150 countries. It consists of a Preamble, 26 Articles and two Annexes and has as its objective to achieve the stabilization of greenhouse gas concentrations in the atmosphere at a level that would prevent dangerous anthropogenic interference with the climate system within a time frame sufficient to allow ecosystems to adapt naturally to climate change, to ensure that food production is not threatened and to enable economic development to proceed in a sustainable manner. The treaty took effect in March 1994 upon the ratification of more than 50 countries; some 186 nations have now ratified. (UNFCCC)

United Nations General Assembly – One of the six principle organs of the UN system comprising all of the Member States. It meets annually under an elected president from the Member States. (UN)

United Nations Global Alliance for Information and Communications Technologies for Development (UNG@ID) – A 2006 initiative of the United Nations bringing together a wide variety of interested participants as part of broader international efforts to harness technological advances for use in the fight against poverty within the context of the MDGs. The Alliance will organize thematic global forums on core issues related to the role of ICT in economic development and the eradication of poverty, focusing on health, education, gender issues and youth, as well as disabled and disadvantaged segments of society. (UN) See '**Technological colonialism**;' '**Digital divide**.'

United Nations Global Compact – See '**Global Compact**.'

United Nations Global Youth Leadership Summit – A UN initiative designed to bring together young leaders in their efforts to accelerate the achievement of the Millennium Development Goals (MDGs). The first summit was held in October 2006 at UN Headquarters in New York. (UN)

United Nations, hard – A term referring to the political mediation and peacekeeping roles of the UN. See '**United Nations, soft**.'

United Nations High Commissioner for Refugees (UNHCR) – The UNHCR was established in 1951 and is mandated to lead and coordinate international action for the worldwide protection of refugees and the resolution of refugee problems. Its primary purpose is to safeguard the rights and well-being of refugees and ensure that everyone can exercise the right to seek asylum, find safe refuge in another state and return home voluntarily.

United Nations Human Rights Council (UNHRC) – The Council was proposed as a replacement for the UN Commission on Human Rights in 2005 and approved by the General Assembly (GA) in March 2006. It formally replaced the Commission in June 2006. The 47-member body is elected by an absolute majority of the GA (96 Member States) for a three-year period (13 seats for Africa, 13 for Asia, 6 for Eastern Europe, 8 for Latin America and the Caribbean, and 7 for a block of mainly Western countries including Europe, the US and Canada). All Member States are eligible for membership but must 'uphold the highest standards in the promotion and protection of human rights,' fully cooperate with the Council and have their human rights records reviewed during the period of their term. The new Council may suspend any Member for 'gross and systematic violations

U

of human rights by a two-thirds majority of those Member states casting votes.' Any Member of the Council with the support of at least one-third of the Members can call a special session in order to get quick resolution to an emergency human rights situation. The work of the Council is overseen by the so-called Third Committee. (UN; UNW) See '**United Nations Commission on Human Rights**.'

United Nations Peace-building Commission – A 31-member body established in December 2005 as part of the UN Reform Process with the mandate to prevent countries emerging from war from falling back into chaos. The Commission acts only by consensus, proposing integrated strategies for stabilization, economic recovery and development, and providing recommendations for improving the coordination of the UN system in those efforts. Membership includes seven Security Council members, including the five permanent members, selected by the Council; seven members of ECOSOC elected from regional groups, five top contributors to UN budgets, funds, programs and agencies; five top providers of military personnel and civilian police to UN missions and seven additional members elected by the General Assembly, with special consideration for States that have experienced post-conflict recovery. (UN)

United Nations Reform Process – The reform effort provides a significant reshaping of the United Nations Organization to respond to the challenge of maintaining and improving multilateralism in the 21st century. Within six months of assuming office in 1997, Secretary General Kofi Annan consolidated the UN organizational structure to reduce overlapping functions and improve coordination and accountability, and created a cabinet of senior executives. Subsequently, the Secretary General led an overhaul of peacekeeping operations, and human rights advocacy was integrated into all major areas of UN work. New ways of involving civil society and the private sector in development and world affairs were also implemented. In 2002, the Secretary General launched a second major package of reforms aimed principally at ensuring that all activities of the UN are aligned with the priorities decided upon in the Millennium Declaration. In September 2005 at the Millennium +5 Summit (also known as the World Summit) meeting, other measures were proposed to restructure several departments and specialized organizations. Early in 2006, a debate was opened on two key issues of the reform process: (1) replacing the discredited UN Human Rights Commission with a revised UN Human Rights Council, and (2) establishing a UN Peace-building Commission to help countries emerging from war in their redevelopment process. Agreement on the UN Peace-building Commission was reached in December 2005 and on the Human Rights Council in March 2006. (UN) See '**Millennium +5 Summit**', '**G13**.'

United Nations Resident Representative/Coordinator (UNRR/UNRC) – Normally the UNDP Resident Representative (Res. Rep.) in a given country and the highest ranking UN official. (UN)

United Nations Resolution 'Towards the Sustainable Development of the Caribbean Sea for Present and Future Generations' (A/C.2/61/L.30) – Adopted in December 2006 by the UNGA, this resolution differs from previous UNGA resolutions in that its declared objectives are unequivocal in recognizing the Caribbean Sea as a special area in the context of sustainable development by the international community. (WC)

United Nations Revised Reform Plan 2007 – In 2007 UN Secretary General Ban Ki Moon revised the Reform Process introduced by his predecessor Kofi Annan. The planned merger of UN agencies dealing with political affairs and disarmament was dropped in favor of greater accountability after opposition from the Non-aligned movement, a powerful block of 118 developing countries. Additionally, UN Peacekeeping operations would be streamlined. (UNW)

United Nations Secretariat – One of the six principle organs of the UN System. It is headed by the United Nations Secretary General, assisted by a staff of international civil servants worldwide. It provides studies, information and facilities needed by UN bodies for their meetings. It also carries out tasks as directed by the UN Security Council, the UN General Assembly, the UN Economic and Social Council, and other UN bodies. The UN Charter provides that the staff be chosen by application of the 'highest standards of efficiency, competence and integrity,' with due regard for the importance of recruiting on a wide geographical basis. (UN; UNW)

United Nations Secretary General's Advisory Board on Water and Sanitation – A group of high-level experts appointed by UN Secretary General Kofi Annan in 2004 to consider ways to mobilize political support and financial resources to ensure that the world stays on track to meet the MDG development targets on water and sanitation. (UN)

United Nations Secretaries General – The secretary general (SG) is the senior most international civil servant and chief administrator of the UN System. The SG is formally chosen by the General Assembly, but must first be nominated by the Security Council and win the consent of all five of its permanent members. The SG serves a five-year term, which may be renewed once. The Security Council can nominate a candidate from any country, but it is tradition that the position rotates geographically, with a secretary general chosen from a new region after every two terms. In 1997 the General Assembly created the post of Deputy Secretary General (DSG appointed by the SG) to assist in the management of the Secretariat. Past secretaries general have come from various regions of the world, but it is an unwritten rule that they never should come from one of the most powerful countries. This tradition is a response to concerns that a secretary general selected from such a country would not be perceived by other nations as objective or neutral. There is also a fear that such a selection would give the world's most influential nations that much more power. Past secretaries general include Trygve Lie of Norway, who served from 1946 to 1953; Dag Hammarskjöld of Sweden, 1953–1961; U Thant of Burma, 1962–1971; Kurt Waldheim of

U

Austria, 1972–1981; Javier Pérez de Cuéllar of Peru, 1982–1991; Boutros Boutros-Ghali from Egypt 1992–1996; Kofi Annan from Ghana, 1997–2006 and Ban Ki-moon of South Korea, 2007–2011 (first five-year term). (UN)

United Nations Secretary General's Expert Panel on Water and Sanitation – A seven-member panel appointed by the secretary general in 2004 to provide expert advice on all aspects of water and sanitation, particularly those issues addressed in the Millennium Development Goals.

United Nations Security Council (UNSC) – A 15-member group consisting of five permanent members (China, France, Russia, the UK, and the US, all with a veto power) and ten non-permanent members who are elected by the General Assembly for a two-year period. The UN Security Council is responsible for maintaining international peace and security in the world. (UN)

United Nations, soft – A term referring to the social, humanitarian and economic development functions of the UN. See '**United Nations, hard**.'

United Nations Specialized Agencies/Organizations – Established by Article 57 of the UN Charter and defined as an Organization that conducts a program of importance for the UN, in a specific field of competence, under the general review of the General Assembly and of the Economic and Social Council, but with important scope of autonomy in matters of membership, program, personnel and finances. (UN) See '**United Nations Economic and Social Council**.'

United Nations System – Comprises six principle organs: UN General Assembly, UN Security Council, UN Economic and Social Council, UN Trusteeship Council, UN Secretariat, and the International Court of Justice. (UN)

United Nations Trusteeship Council – One of the principal organs of the UN System, the Council was established to help ensure that non-self-governing territories were administered in the best interests of the inhabitants and of international peace and security. The trust territories – most of them former mandates of the League of Nations or territories taken from nations defeated at the end of World War II – have all now attained self-government or independence, either as separate nations or by joining neighboring independent countries. The last was Palau, which became a member of the UN in 1994. Its mission fulfilled, the Trusteeship Council suspended its operation on 1 November, 1994, and although under the UN Charter, it continues to exist on paper, its future role and even existence is undetermined. (UN)

United Nations World Intellectual Property Organization (UN-WIPO) – Created in 1967, the Geneva-based UN body is one of the specialized agencies of the UN System. It administers 23 international treaties dealing with different aspects of intellectual property protection. Specialized terminology or laws, included in the treaties under WIPO administration, and increasingly used in GEG debates particularly relating to the CBD and the WTO, include:

- Copyright – An exclusive right conferred by a government for a specified period to the creator of a work or a discoverer of a new plant or animal species to exclude others from reproducing it.
- Digital Millennium Copyright Act (DMCA) – A 1998 US law that criminalizes the use of technology that can circumvent copyright protections.
- Discovery – To find or discover something new.
- European copyright directive – Includes the same prescriptions as the DMCA.
- Fair use or fair dealing – A complex legal doctrine that may allow limited use of copyrighted work without permission for criticism, comment, parody, satire, news reporting, teaching and research. The term 'fair use' is used in the US. The term 'fair dealing' is used in the EU and by some other States.
- First to file – A patent system in which the first inventor or discoverer to file an application for a specific invention or discovery is entitled to the patent. In most countries, the first person to file has priority over others claiming rights for the same invention or discovery.
- Intellectual property – See '**Intellectual property**.'
- Invention – The creation of a technical idea and the physical means to accomplish or embody it. To be patentable, an invention must be novel, have utility and differ from what skilled users might expect.
- License – Permission to use an intellectual property right within a defined time, context, market and/or State or Territory.
- Naming – The act of providing a label for a thing (such as a species name), person, place, product (as in a brand name), and even an idea or concept, normally used to distinguish one from another.
- Patent – A government-conferred right to exclude others from making, using or selling an invention. Patents do not protect ideas, only structures and methods that apply the ideas.
- Patent pool – An arrangement allowing the holders of several patents necessary for a product or process to license their rights at a single price.
- Open source – A movement in the computer programming and scientific communities to make program instructions free and available to anyone.
- Piracy – The unauthorized duplication of goods protected by intellectual property law.
- Public domain – The status of an invention or creative work that is not protected by intellectual property rights and is available for copying and use by anyone.
- Royalty – A payment to copyright or patent owners for the right to use their work.
- Trademark – A name or symbol used to identify and distinguish goods.

U

United States Agency for International Development (USAID)
– The principal agency through which the US provides technical assistance and delivers foreign aid.

Units of measurement (commonly used in UN and scientific reports). See '**Symbols**.'

- **Metric Unit Symbol – US Unit Equivalent**
    - meter m, ≡ yard 1.094yd
    - kilometer km, ≡ mile 0.6214mi
    - hectometer h, ≡ none 328ft
    - cubic meter m³, ≡ cubic yard 1.308yd³
    - square kilometer km², ≡ square mile 0.386sq mi
    - hectare ha, ≡ acres 2.477ac
    - cubic hectometer hm³, ≡ acre-foot; 810.68ac-ft.
    - gram g, ≡ ounce 0.035oz
    - kilogram kg, ≡ pound 2.205lb
    - metric ton (1000kg), ≡ mt ton 2,205lb
    - milliliter ml, ≡ fluid ounce 0.0338oz
    - liter L, ≡ quart 1.057qt
    - milligram/liter mg/L, ≡ part per million 1ppm = 1mg/L
    - microgram/liter μg/L, ≡ part per billion 1ppb = 1μg/L
    - nanogram/liter ng/L, ≡ part per trillon 1ppt = 1ng/L
- **Other common units:**
    - cfs – cubic feet per second
    - mgd – million gallons per day
    - ppm – parts per million
    - ppb – parts per billion
    - μmhos/cm – micromhos per centimeter
    - NTU – nephelometric turbidity unit

Universal Declaration of Human Rights – A declaration made by the UN General Assembly in 1948 that outlines a common standard for all people and all nations regarding the human rights and freedoms (See Appendix 2).

Universal jurisdiction cases – The principle and practice of one State or regional entity with a common body of law pursuing an individual(s) who has violated either UN or other shared laws and policies through court proceedings. (UN; IPS) See '**Pinochet principle/concept**,' '**Universal justice**.'

Universal justice (UJ) – A concept that allows one country to prosecute a citizen of another country for violations of international agreements. Most writings on this subject are related to human rights abuses, but legal specialists are also beginning to explore the implications of applying such principles in relation to international environmental treaties and malicious acts impacting the resources of another state or the global commons.

Neither the ICJ nor the ICC has yet endorsed this concept although national governments have held and prosecuted individuals in a manner consistent with UJ. (EU) See '**International Criminal Court**,' '**Pinochet principle**.'

Upcycling – The practice of recycling waste materials for use in higher value goods, such as the use of old tires for road beds or turning old lumber into furniture.

Urban heat island – Refers to the tendency for urban areas to have warmer air temperatures than the surrounding rural landscape due to the low albedo of streets, sidewalks, parking lots and buildings. These surfaces absorb solar radiation during the day and release it at night, resulting in higher night temperatures. (PEW) See '**Albedo**.'

Uruguay Round – The round of multilateral trade negotiations under the GATT that commenced in 1986 and was completed in 1994 with the creation of the WTO. (DC)

User-pays principle – A variation of the polluter-pays principle that calls upon the user of a natural resource to bear the cost of running down natural capital.

Usufructory right – A mechanism to convey a right to use a natural resource as opposed to owning the natural resource. (AM)

Utstein Group Partnership – The Utstein Group consists of the UK, Norway, Sweden, The Netherlands, Germany and Canada, whose international development ministers formed a partnership to coordinate development assistance policies. The partnership started in 1999 at Utstein Abbey in Norway, among the four female ministers of the original Utstein countries: UK, Norway, The Netherlands and Germany. Sweden and Canada joined the group in 2004, strengthening the network and contributing to secure the achievement of the MDGs. See '**U4 Resource Center**.'

U

Vv

Valuation – The process of determining the current worth of an asset or the estimated worth of a thing or process. It differs from price, which does not always afford a true criterion of value. (LLL)

Variety – Plant grouping, within a single botanical taxon of the lowest known rank, defined by the reproducible expression of its distinguishing and other genetic characteristics. (CBD)

Verbal note – In diplomacy, an unsigned note or memorandum sent as a notification or reminder of some matter and generally not of immediate importance.

Veto – An action taken by an empowered individual or body (e.g. President of a State or any of the five permanent UN Security Council Member States) rejecting an action that otherwise has received approval by a legislative or governing body. (UN)

Victim pays principle – A principle that suggests that victims affected by pollution should pay the polluter not to pollute, implying that property rights in environmental resources lie with the polluter rather than with those affected. (AM)

Vienna Convention of 1963 – The Vienna Convention on Civil Liability for Nuclear Damage (1963). This Convention preceded the adoption of the Protocol to Amend the 1963 Vienna Convention on Civil Liability for Nuclear Damage and the Convention on Supplementary Compensation for Nuclear Damage adopted in 1997.

Vienna Convention of 1969 – The Vienna Convention on the Law of Treaties was signed at Vienna, 23 May, 1969 and entered into force, 27 January, 1980. It is the source for definitions and principles that guide international treaties. Previously, treaty rules were based on customary international law or were a part of the general principles of law. The Vienna Convention codified these rules and now governs all the international treaties since it entered into force. Although the Vienna Convention does not apply to treaties concluded before its entry into force, it is *de facto* applied since it incorporates the customary rules that were applicable before this date.

Vienna Convention of 1985 – The Vienna Convention for the Protection of the Ozone Layer is a convention that gives priority to research, cooperation among countries, and exchange of information regarding substances and activities which may harm the ozone layer.

Vienna Convention of 1986 – The Vienna Convention on the Law of Treaties between States and International Organizations or between International Organizations (1986) reflects international customary law but it has yet to enter into force.

Vienna Convention on Civil Liability for Nuclear Damage – A UN Convention on liability and compensation for nuclear damage similar to the Paris Convention. It was recently revised by means of the 1997 Protocol and a new Convention on Supplementary Compensation was agreed to provide additional compensation, although this has not yet entered into force. The Vienna Convention and Paris Convention are linked by the Joint Protocol relating to the Application of the Vienna Convention and the Paris Convention.

Vienna Convention on Diplomatic and Consular Relations – An agreement that places the security of embassies and consular offices and their recognized staff in the hands of the host country.

Vienna setting – A negotiating format modeled after the final negotiations on the Cartagena Protocol on Biosafety that involves spokespersons from the major negotiating groups.

Virtual Water Credit/Debt Relief – An untested concept based on analyzing data from the World Water Exchange and the Water Poverty Index resulting in a water-health index. Water-health/poor countries would be ranked (water and health) and based on that ranking receive a virtual water credit (from donors such as the World Bank, regional development banks, ODA from specific countries by way of an 'earned grant') that could in turn be expended to import fruits and vegetables to help offset water-related health issues from a lack of such dietary inputs. See '**World Water Exchange**;' '**Water Poverty Index**;' '**Debt relief**;' '**Debt for nature swap**.'

Virtual water/issues – See '**Water**.'

Visa (1) – Written authority to enter a country for either temporary or permanent residence depending on its wording. (eD)

Visa (2) – A term commonly used in the UN system implying the required process of gaining approval of a letter, memo or report before it is sent for final signature; as in 'you will have to "visa" this letter before sending it for signature to the Secretary General,' or 'Has that text been "visa'd" yet?'

Voice, right of – Being recognized by the chair of a meeting and allowed to speak to a gathered audience. (UN)

Voice vote – A vote where members vote by saying out-loud either 'yes' or 'no' together, and after which the chair estimates which response is stronger; individual member's votes are not placed on record. (MW)

V

Voluntary agreement – A set of policy instruments introduced in several countries to prevent industrial pollution. Pollution reduction is reached through a contract between government and industry and may include regulation and taxation.

Voluntary contribution – Funds donated by a state in excess of its assessed contribution that may be based on a separate appeal or for a designated purpose. (UN)

Voluntary fund – A fund created for a specific purpose and to which countries are encouraged to contribute. (UN)

Vote (right of) – Being recognized by the chair as having the right to cast a ballot for or against a proposal. (UN)

Vulnerability – The propensity of a population group to experience substantial damage, disruption and casualties as a result of a hazard. (DFID) A condition characterized by higher risk and reduced ability to cope with shock or negative impacts. It may be based on socio-economic condition, gender, age, disability, ethnicity or other criteria that influence people's ability to access resources and development opportunities. Vulnerability is always contextual, and must be assessed in the context of a specific situation and time. Good practice in World Bank projects indicates that development interventions and support mechanisms should assess vulnerability, and target interventions to be appropriate and reduce risk for those deemed as vulnerable. (WB)

Vulnerable – An IUCN category of taxa believed likely to move into the Endangered category in the near future if the causal factors continue operating. Included are taxa of which most or all the populations are decreasing because of over-exploitation, extensive habitat or other environmental disturbance; taxa with populations that have been seriously depleted and whose ultimate security is not yet assured; and taxa with populations that are still abundant but are under threat from serious adverse factors throughout their range. (IUCN)

Vulnerable taxa – A classification referring to a species that is likely to become endangered within the foreseeable future, throughout all or a significant portion of its range. (IUCN)

Ww

Wadi Hydrology – A project initiated by UNESCO, through its International Hydrology Programme on 'Wadi Hydrology,' that focuses on the sustainable management of ephemeral rivers. The Arabic term 'Wadi' refers to a seasonal water source in the world's arid regions, which are an excellent and at times the only source of freshwater. (UNESCO)

Washington Consensus – A term describing a set of policy reforms that most official Washington financial institutions thought would be good for Latin America. The reforms include fiscal discipline, a redirection of public expenditure priorities toward primary health care, primary education, infrastructure, tax reform, interest rate liberalization, a competitive exchange rate, trade liberalization, privatization, deregulation and secure property rights. However, there are now other, often mutually exclusive, definitions of the term that complicate its use.

Waste – Unwanted materials left over from a manufacturing process or refuse from human or animal habitation. (USEPA)

Waste steam – Overall waste and waste disposal/treatment cycle of a given population.

Water –

- **Blue water/issues** – A term relating to surface and groundwater freshwater resources. (UN)
- **Black water/issues** – Refers to water that contains or is contaminated with faecal material, (sanitary engineers); fossil groundwater (hydrologists, geologists), water from swamps or other wetlands (wetland ecologists). (UN)
- **Brown water/issues** – A term referring to highly acidic waters normally produced in swamps, wetlands or wet environments with a low flow rate or near-stagnate condition (wetland ecologists); and to raw wastewater (sanitary engineers). (UNESCO-IHE)
- **Gray water/issues** – A term referring to wastewater from shower, laundry and other (household and industrial) cleaning activities that does not contain faecal material (sanitary engineers); and to treated wastewater for reuse (hydrologists). (FAO)
- **Green water/issues** – Water in the biosphere (soil) or water that supports all non-irrigated vegetation, including forests and

woodlands, grasslands and rain-fed crops or the water available in the root zone (FAO); all issues related to 'water for nature.' (UN)

- **Virtual Water (1)** – A term referring to water used for food production or for producing industrial products. This term has also been used to reflect the potential for producing new products that could be realized if more water was available or new investments were made to improve water resource management. (UN)

- **Virtual Water (2)** – The volume of water required to produce a commodity or service. When there is a transfer of products or services from one place to another, there is little direct physical transfer of water (apart from the water content of the product, which is generally quite insignificant in terms of volume). There is, however, a significant transfer of virtual water. By importing virtual water, water poor countries can relieve the pressure on their domestic water resources. (WFp; UNESCO-IHE)

- **White water/issues** – A term referring to water lost through evaporation, through interception or directly from the soil. (FAO); and to the oceans or rapids (recreationists). (USGS)

Water balance/budget – The amount of inflow vs. outflow of water per unit area or unit volume and time, taking into account net changes of storage. (FAO)

Water Cooperation Facility (WCF) – A UNESCO/World Water Council (WWC) initiative linking these two bodies together with other pivotal organizations, the Permanent Court of Arbitration (PCA), and the University Partnership for Transboundary Waters (UPTW) aimed at resolving transboundary water disputes and serving as a nexus for education and technical expertise in dispute resolution techniques and case studies. (UNESCO)

Water dependency ratio – Indicator expressing the part of the total renewable water resource originating outside of a given country. (FAO)

Water footprint – The water footprint of an individual, business or nation is defined as the total amount of freshwater that is used to produce the goods and services consumed by the individual, business or nation, and generally expressed in terms of the volume of water use per year. (WFp; UNESCO-IHE)

Water footprint, individual – The total water used to survive and for the production of the goods and services consumed by an individual. It can be estimated by multiplying all goods and services consumed by their respective virtual water content. (WFp)

Water footprint, national – The total amount of water used to produce the goods and services consumed by the inhabitants of the nation. The national water footprint can be assessed in two ways. The bottom-up approach is to consider the sum of all goods and services consumed multiplied by their respective virtual water content. In the top-down approach, the water footprint of a nation can be calculated as the total use of domestic water resources plus the net virtual water import. It should be noted that the virtual water content of a particular consumption good can vary as a function of the place and conditions of production. (WFp)

Water, hard – Any water that contains significant amounts of salts and/or magnesium. (USEPA)

Water Integrity Network (WIN) – A 2006 Transparency International led initiative to stimulate anti-corruption activities in the water sector worldwide based on accountability, transparency, integrity, honesty, mutual support and knowledge exchange among its members. WIN members will come from all sectors of society. Other founding partners include the International Water and Sanitation Center, Stockholm International Water Institute and the Swedish Water House. (TI; UNW)

Water nanotechnology – Water altering technologies that use 'nanotechnology' to render it suitable for human use without contributing to further pollution of the environment. (AIT)

Water Poverty Index – An interdisciplinary measure linking household welfare with water availability and indicating the degree to which water scarcity impacts on human populations. Such an index makes it possible to rank countries and communities taking into account both physical and socio-economic factors associated with water scarcity. (Lawrence et al, 2002)

Water quality – The chemical, physical and biological characteristics in respect to its suitability for a particular use or to meet a defined standard. ((FAO; USEPA)

Water quality criteria/standards – Legally mandated water quality levels based on specific scientific criteria.

Water scarcity (1) – A concept developed by Swedish hydrologist Malin Falkenmark to gauge current and future water needs against available supplies, which has gained wide acceptance internationally, although the specific measures are still being debated. When supplies drop below 1000 cubic meters per person per year, the country faces water scarcity for all or part of the year. (FAO)

Water scarcity (2) – The ratio of the total water footprint of a nation or region to the total renewable water resource. The national scarcity can be more than 100 percent if a nation consumes more water than domestically available. (WFp)

W

Water self-sufficiency – Denotes the national capability of supplying the water needed for the production of the domestic demand for goods and services. Self-sufficiency is 100 percent if all the water needed is available and taken from within its own territory. Water self-sufficiency approaches zero if the demand for goods and services in a country is largely met with virtual water imports or the use of imported water. (WFp)

Watershed – The divide separating one drainage basin from another. However, although 'drainage basin' is preferred, over the years, use of the term 'watershed' to signify a drainage basin or catchment area has come to predominate. Drainage divide, or just divide, is used to denote the boundary between one drainage area and another. Used alone, the term 'watershed' is ambiguous and should not be used unless the intended meaning is made clear. (USGS)

Water, soft – Any water that does not contain a significant amount of dissolved minerals such as salts of calcium or magnesium. (USEPA)

Water stress – A concept developed by Swedish hydrologist Malin Falkenmark to gauge current and future water needs against available supplies, which has gained wide acceptance internationally, although the specific measures are still being debated. A country is said to experience water stress when the annual water supplies drop below 1700 cubic meters per person per year. (FAO)

Water table – The level below the land surface at which the subsurface material is fully saturated with water. The depth of the water table reflects the minimum level to which wells must be drilled for water extraction. (USEPA; EES)

Water year – The 12-month period defining the length of the wet and dry seasons.

Web Relief – An electronic clearinghouse project of the UN Office for Coordination of Humanitarian Affairs established in 1996 to help the international community improve its response to emergencies. Specifically it aims to act as a main source of time-critical and reliable information for global humanitarian assistance; provide updated information on unfolding emergencies and natural disasters in order to support decision making on relief, logistics, funding and contingency planning; provide a guaranteed, central access point for humanitarian information, and encourage information sharing, coordination and standardization among the humanitarian community's information partners, both at headquarters and the field level. Web relief also provides country-related information on all pledges made and tracks compliance with payment of pledges by donor nations/organizations, and tracks disbursements to recipient or beneficiary countries of both direct and in-kind contributions as per the terms agreed to between the donor and recipient or as per the terms set by the UN and agreed to by all involved parties. (UNOCHA) See '**United Nations Central Emergency Response Fund**.'

WEHAB (Water, Energy, Health, Agriculture and Biodiversity) – Objectives articulated at WSSD including: water supply and sanitation; cleaner production and recycling; energy efficiency and conservation, renewable energy and clean coal technology; emergencies and disaster preparedness and response, including urban security; post shock and conflict restoration, rehabilitation and reconstruction; engaging engineers in decision making, policy making and planning.

Weighted majority – A majority where additional weight is given to some countries for varied specific reasons such as monetary contributions.

Well – A hole dug to the point where water can be extracted.

Westphalia Settlement of 1648 – The treaty that spelled out the conditions to end the Thirty Year War that is generally considered to be the origin of modern state order. This treaty recognized the absolute sovereignty and legal equality of states as the basis for international order.

W-E-T – A UNESCO-IHP Phase VI program that provides a coherent approach in the area of partnerships in water-related capacity building. Specifically it address four priority areas: unity of education and research in higher education, facilitation of high intensity networks, quality assurance and assessment, and raising public awareness as an obligation of water professionals and educators.

Wetlands – Areas of marsh, fen, peatland or water whether natural or artificial, permanent or temporary, with water that is static or flowing, fresh, brackish or salt, including areas of marine water the depth of which at low tide does not exceed six meters. See '**Ramsar Convention**.'

Whistleblower – A whistleblower is an employee or former employee of an organization who reports misconduct to people or entities that have the power to take corrective action. Generally the misconduct is a violation of law, rule, regulation and/or a direct threat to public interest – fraud, health, safety violations and corruption are a few examples. (WP) See '**Water Integrity Network**.'

White Helmets – In October 1993 the President of Argentina launched a global initiative for the creation of national volunteer groups, called 'White Helmets', whose objective would be to make men and women of good will available to the UN, with the aim of strengthening the reserve capacity of developing countries in support of UN activities in the field of emergency humanitarian assistance and the gradual transition from relief to rehabilitation, reconstruction and development. (UN)

W

White revolution – A counterpart term to that of the 'green revolution', but referring to the provision of milk and milk products as a fundamental component to improve the quality of life for the most undeveloped regions of the world.

White water/issues – See '**Water**.'

White water to blue water – A US government initiative launched at the WSSD in Johannesburg to promote integrated river basin management in the Caribbean.

WHO Health Policy for All in the 21st Century – A global health policy aimed at meeting the major challenges in health during the next decades. The policy was developed in consultation with all WHO national and international partners and evolved from the Health-For-All goal subscribed to in 1979.

Wilderness – There are many national and legislated definitions of wilderness, wild, natural and primitive areas used throughout the world. After the Fourth World Wilderness Conference (1987) the IUCN defined wilderness as 'an enduring natural area, legislatively protected and of sufficient size to protect the pristine natural elements which may serve spiritual and physical well-being. It is an area where little or no persistent evidence of human intrusion is permitted, so that natural processes may begin to evolve.' This definition is included here as it has been adapted by many countries and cited in several UN documents. (IUCN)

Willingness to accept – Refers to the amount of money a person would be willing to accept as compensation for suffering a loss. (AM)

Willingness to pay – The amount an individual is willing to pay to acquire some good or service. This may be elicited from stated or revealed preference approaches. (EEA)

Win–win options – In the context of multi-criteria analysis those options that have the highest scores on both selected criteria. Also more broadly used to characterize options with potential positive welfare implications for both parties involved.

Withdrawal – Termination of a party to a treaty, usually with 12 months' notice for multilateral treaties and automatically after a fixed period or when the projects they deal with are completed for some bilateral treaties. A party may withdraw from or denounce a treaty in accordance with the withdrawal or denunciation provisions of the treaty (article 54(a) of the 1969 Vienna Convention) or, with the consent of all parties to a convention (article 54(b) of the 1969 Vienna Convention). In the case of a treaty that is silent on withdrawal or denunciation, withdrawal is possible by giving at least 12 months' notice provided that it is established that the parties intended to admit the possibility of denunciation or withdrawal; or a right of denunciation or withdrawal may be implied by the nature of the treaty. (VC)

Without borders, concept of – An idea credited to a group of French doctors who in 1971 established Médecins Sans Frontières (abbreviated MSF; known as Doctors Without Borders in English) as a non-profit private organization founded in the belief that all people have the right to medical care and that their need is more important than national borders. MSF received the Nobel Peace Prize in 1999. Since its establishment, this 'without borders' concept of providing services via non-profit organizations to all people regardless of race, nationality, political or religious persuasion has been emulated by a vast number of technical and professional groups including engineers, architects, reporters, water specialists, teachers, nurses, etc. (WP)

Working documents/docs – Official documents of a meeting supported by information documents. (UN)

Working group – A group convened by a COP or one of the subsidiary bodies to work on large-scale issues. Its head, or chair, of the working group is designated by the president of the body that created it and its membership is open to all Parties to the MEA or subsidiary body. (Gupta, 1997)

World Bank (WB) – Established in 1945 to help Europe recover from the devastations of World War II, the World Bank is also known as the International Bank for Reconstruction and Development (IBRD). It is a specialized agency of the UN, consists of The World Bank and the International Development Association, and is the world's largest source of development assistance (over $20 billion in loans in FY 2004) to its 100 plus client countries. The IBRD is owned by 184 member countries. (WB)

World Bank Anticorruption Strategy – Adopted at the 2006 WB/IMF Annual Meeting held in Singapore, this new policy aims at confronting graft and corruption at the project, country and global levels:

- Project level – Identifying risky operations and ensuring upstream risk mitigation; establishing anticorruption teams to review project design, risk rating and anticorruption action plans; improving design and supervision methods and enhancing oversight and monitoring of Bank financed projects.
- Country level – In countries where governance is relatively good, the Bank's strategies will aim at greater flexibility. In countries where leadership is undertaking major governance and anticorruption reforms, the Bank will match such resolve with scaling-up technical and financial assistance. In countries where governance and corruption pose major problems, the Bank will make use of its anticorruption teams and anticorruption action plans in projects.

The Bank will engage with the private sector and civil society to address corruption and also support participatory and transparency initiatives.

- Global level – Promoting anticorruption initiatives with the IMF and other multilateral development banks and other donors; strengthening joint sanctions with other MDBs, making investigative rules and procedures more consistent; working closely with the private sector and civil society to promote change coalitions; and supporting implementation of key international anticorruption conventions. (WB)

World Bank Group – The World Bank Group consists of five closely aligned institutions: The International Bank for Reconstruction and Development (World Bank), the International Development Association, the International Finance Corporation, the Multilateral Investment Guarantee Agency, and the International Centre for Settlement of Investment Disputes. A sixth group, the Global Environment Facility (GEF) is also recognized as a semi-autonomous component of the World Bank Group. (WB)

World Bank Safeguard Policies – See 'Safeguard Policies.'

World Bank Voluntary Disclosure Program – A 2006 program forming a central component in the bank's anti-corruption campaign by offering conditional amnesty to companies that voluntarily admit to corrupt dealings on bank-funded projects. In return, the companies would agree to investigate thoroughly their past dealings with the bank, share this information with the bank, and appoint a bank-approved independent monitor to track internal compliance for the following three years. The companies will not be required to pay any fine, but will have to pay the cost of investigation and compliance. Companies that fail to come clean voluntarily but are caught by bank investigations will continue to be banned from participation in future projects. (WB)

World Business Council for Sustainable Development (WBCSD) – Formed in 1991, the World Business Council for Sustainable Development (WBCSD) is a coalition of 150 international companies (2002) united by a shared commitment to sustainable development via the three pillars of economic growth, ecological balance and social progress. Members are drawn from more than 30 countries and 20 major industrial sectors. Its mission is to provide business leadership as a catalyst for change toward sustainable development, and to promote the role of eco-efficiency, innovation and corporate social responsibility. (WBCSD)

World Charter for Nature – Ethical guidelines for the relationships between humans and the rest of nature that were accepted by the world community as UNGA resolution 37/7 (1982).

World Commission on the Social Dimension of Globalization – A commission of the ILO created in November of 2001 that is mandated to analyze the social dimensions of globalization and make proposals to correct any imbalances. The commission is made up of 26 internationally eminent persons. Reports on its findings and recommendations can be found at www.ilo.org/public/english/wcsdg/commission.htm.

World Conservation Monitoring Centre (WCMC) – The World Conservation Monitoring Centre of UNEP provides information services on conservation and sustainable use of the world's living resources, and helps others to develop information systems of their own. It was established in 2000 as the World Biodiversity Information and Assessment Center but has roots that go back to 1979 when IUCN established a Cambridge office to monitor endangered species. In 1988 the independent, non-profit World Conservation Monitoring Centre was founded jointly by IUCN, WWF and UNEP. (WCMC)

World Conservation Strategy (WCS) – The WCS is a report and long-range worldwide conservation plan sponsored by the IUCN, UNEP and WWF. Published in 1980, it was one of the first written and widely distributed calls for sustainable development.

World Conservation Union (IUCN) – The World Conservation Union was founded in 1948 and brings together 78 states, 112 government agencies, 735 NGOs, 35 affiliates, and some 10,000 scientists and experts from 181 countries in a unique worldwide partnership. Its mission is to influence, encourage, and assist societies throughout the world to conserve the integrity and diversity of nature and to ensure that any use of natural resources is equitable and ecologically sustainable. (IUCN)

World Court – See '**International Court of Justice**.'

World Declaration on Nutrition and the Plan of Action for Nutrition (1992) – The outputs of the 1992 UNFAO-sponsored meeting held in Rome to prepare for the World Food Summit.

World Economic Forum ('Davos Symposium') – The World Economic Forum, based in Switzerland, is an independent organization committed to improving the state of the world. Funded by the contributions of 1000 of the world's foremost corporations, the Forum acts in the spirit of entrepreneurship in the global public interest to further economic growth and social progress. The Forum serves its members and society by creating partnerships between and among business, political, intellectual and other leaders of society to define, discuss and advance key issues on the global agenda. Incorporated in 1971 as a foundation, the World Economic Forum is impartial and not-for-profit, and is tied to no political, partisan or national interests. In 1995, the Forum was awarded NGO consultative status with the Economic and Social Council of the United Nations. (WEF)

World Environment Day – World Environment Day (WED) was established by the United Nations General Assembly in 1972. WED is hosted every year by a different city and commemorated with an international exposition through the week of 5 June. The UN uses WED to stimulate awareness of the environment and enhance political attention and public action. (WP)

World Health Organization (WHO) – An international organization established in 1948 with the goal of improving human health. WHO assists countries in strengthening their health services, provides technical assistance in health emergencies, promotes disease prevention and control, and promulgates international food safety and medical standards. It currently has 192 member countries. (WHO)

World Heritage Alliance – A partnership between Expedia, Inc., UNESCO, and the UN Foundation that works to engage the travel and tourism industry in preserving World Heritage Sites for future generations to enjoy. (UNW)

World Heritage Convention (WHC) – The International Convention for the Protection of World Cultural and Natural Heritage (World Heritage Convention) was adopted in Paris under the auspices of UNESCO in 1972 and came into force in December 1975. It provides for the designation of both natural and cultural heritage deemed to have outstanding universal value. (UNESCO)

World Heritage Fund (WHF) – A special fund established by the WHC in 2006 to address the crucial need of funding endangered world heritage sites. Initially the fund will give special attention to Africa's world heritage sites designated by UNESCO. Of the world's 812 heritage sites (2006), only 66 are in Africa and 14 of them are on the World Heritage Endangered List as a result of lack of funding, or natural or man-induced disasters such as climate change, wars or unregulated tourism. (UNESCO)

World Heritage Site – Cultural and natural properties submitted by the States Parties to The Convention Concerning the Protection of the World Cultural and Natural Heritage and approved by the General Conference of UNESCO that are considered to be of outstanding universal value. (UNESCO)

World Heritage Trust – The World Heritage Convention recognizes that many sites cannot be adequately maintained and financed within some developing countries. To that end UNESCO maintains a list of priority sites and through the Trust (public and private solicitations) provides financial resources to these sites. (UNESCO)

World Resources Institute (WRI) – The World Resources Institute (WRI) is a policy research center created in late 1982 to help governments, international organizations, and private businesses understand how to meet basic human needs and nurture economic growth without undermining the natural resources and environmental integrity on which life, economic vitality, and international security depend. The Institute's current areas of policy research include forests, biological diversity, sustainable agriculture, energy, climate change, atmospheric pollution, economic incentives for sustainable development, and resource and environmental information. (WRI)

World Social Forum (WSF) – The World Social Forum is an open meeting place for reflective thinking, democratic debate of ideas, formulation of proposals, free exchange of experiences and inter-linking for effective action, by groups and movements of civil society opposed to neoliberalism, and domination of the world by capital and any form of imperialism. The WSF wishes to build a planetary society centered on the human person. It was originally organized as a counter forum to the World Economic Forum but has since developed an important role as an independent gathering to discuss social and ethical aspects of development. Annual meetings of the WSF have been held since 2001. (WSF)

World Summit 2005 – See 'Millennium +5 Summit.'

World Summit on Sustainable Development (WSSD) – A world meeting held from 26 August–4 September 2002, at the Sandton Convention Centre in Johannesburg, South Africa. According to UN General Assembly (UNGA) Resolution 55/199, the meeting's goal was to hold a ten-year review of the 1992 UN Conference on Environment and Development (UNCED) at the Summit level to reinvigorate global commitment to sustainable development. Over 21,000 participants from 191 countries attended and included representatives from intergovernmental and non-governmental organizations, the private sector, civil society, academia and the scientific community. The WSSD adopted two main documents: the Plan of Implementation and the Johannesburg Declaration on Sustainable Development. (WSSD)

World Trade Organization (WTO) – An organization based in Geneva set up in 1995 to implement and enforce the Uruguay Round Agreement. Replaces the General Agreement on Tariffs and Trade (GATT). WTO establishes the legal and institutional foundations of the international trading system. It determines government obligations in trade legislation and regulation, and specifies trade dispute resolution mechanisms. It currently has 142 member countries. (WTO)

World Water Council (WWC) – The World Water Council, formed in 1996, is the premier nongovernmental international water policy think tank dedicated to strengthening the world water movement for an improved management of the world's water resources and water services. Its mission is 'to promote awareness, build political commitment and trigger action on

W

critical water issues at all levels, including the highest decision-making level to facilitate the efficient conservation, protection, development, planning, management and use of water in all its dimensions on an environmentally sustainable basis for the benefit of all life on Earth.' The Council organizes and convokes the World Water Forum every three years. The WWC is headquartered in Marseille, France.

World Water Day – World Water Day or the 'World Day for Water' occurs each year on 22 March, as designated by United Nations General Assembly resolution. This day was first formally proposed in *Agenda 21* of the 1992 United Nations Conference on Environment and Development (UNCED) in Rio de Janeiro, Brazil. Observance began in 1993 and has grown significantly ever since.

World Water Exchange® – A private sector initiative of Next Level Banking and Rain Trust Climate Exchanges Ltd to: (i) manage an international water exchange that publishes a globally accepted price by listing a 'water index' for blue and green water; (ii) promote that index as the underlying value for cleared environmental financial products; (iii) determine the financial value of importing and exporting virtual water based on the water footprint of livestock products and crops; and (iv) manage an exchange mechanism (green e-Bay®) bringing technologies (patents), producers and distributors together in the most efficient manner. (van Woerden et al, 2006)

World Water Forum – The official meeting of the WWC – first forum in 1997 in Marrakech, Morocco; second forum in 2000 in The Hague, The Netherlands; third forum in 2003 in Kyoto and Osaka, Japan; fourth forum in 2006 in Mexico City, Mexico; fifth forum planned for 2009 in Istanbul, Turkey.

Worldwide Fund for Nature (WWF) – Formerly known as the World Wildlife Fund, the WWF is an independent conservation organization with almost 5 million supporters from five continents. Since 1985 its 28 National Organizations, 24 Programme Offices and 4 Associates have invested over US$1165 million in more than 11,000 projects in 130 countries. (WWF)

WSSD Plan of Implementation – A framework for action to implement the commitments agreed at UNCED. The plan of implementation has 11 chapters: introduction; poverty eradication; consumption and production; the natural resource base; globalization; health; small island developing States; Africa; other regional initiatives; means of implementation; and institutional framework. See '**World Summit on Sustainable Development**'.

Xx

X files – A term relating to a long-standing rumor within the UN system and referring to private files that the Secretary General supposedly maintains on confidential negotiations with Member States and/or on selected staff members.

Xenophile – One who is attracted to things foreign. (MW)

Xenophobe – One who is unduly fearful of things foreign. (MW)

Xeric – Habitat requiring only small amounts of moisture. (MW)

Xerophytic – Plants adapted for life in dry places and able to resist dessication. (USEPA)

Yy

Yellow pages – The generic name given to internal newsletters published in many UN offices.

Yellow rain – A yellow substance reported to occur as a mist or as spots on rocks and vegetation in Southeast Asia and variously held to be a chemical warfare agent used in the Vietnam War or as a naturally occurring substance similar to pollen or the feces of bees. (WB)

Zz

Zero sum – A term originating in game theory where the sum of wins and losses in a game always equals zero for each set of strategies chosen. In governance, it means that if one party wins, the other party loses.

Zero Waste Alliance (ZWA) – An initiative of the International Sustainable Development Foundation, based in Portland, Oregon, US, and aimed at introducing life-cycle responsibility and green chemistry principles into manufacturing processes.

Zonal discharge permit – A marketable permit based on zones (and trading rights within that zone, not across zones), preventing the occurrence of highly localized concentrations of pollutants. (AM)

Zoning – The arrangement or partitioning of land areas for various types and intensities of usage in natural or managed protected lands, cities, boroughs, townships or other political jurisdictions.

Acronyms and Abbreviations

A

A	Assembly (GEF)
AAAID	Arab Authority for Agricultural Investment and Development
AACCLA	Latin American Association of American Chambers of Commerce
AALCC	Asian-African Legal Consultative Committee
AAPA	American Association of Port Authorities
AARINENA	Association of Agricultural Research Institutions in the Near East and North Africa
AARS	Automatic Aircraft Reporting System
AAS	African Academy of Sciences
AAU	Assigned Amount Unit (UNFCCC)
ABC	Brazilian Cooperation Agency
ABCDE	Annual Bank Conference on Development Economics (World Bank)
ABM	Australian Bureau of Meteorology
ABS	Access to Genetic Resources and Benefit Sharing (CBD)
AC (1)	Accession Countries
AC (2)	Animal Committee (CITES)
AC (3)	Aårhus Convention
AC (4)	armed conflict
AC (5)	African Conservancy
AC(6)	Ad Hoc Committee
ACABQ	UN Advisory Committee on Administrative and Budgetary Questions
ACAL	Latin American Academy of Sciences (Venezuela)

ACAP	Agreement on the Conservation of Albatrosses and Petrels
ACC (1)	Administrative Committee on Coordination
ACC (2)	Cuban Academy of Sciences
ACCOBAMS	Agreement on the Conservation of Cetaceans of the Black Sea, the Mediterranean Sea and Contiguous Atlantic Area
ACCSWR	Administrative Committee on Coordination, Sub-Committee on Water Resources
ACCU	Asia/Pacific Cultural Centre for UNESCO
ACDA	Arms Control and Disarmament Agency
ACDI	American Cooperatives Development International (Brazil)
ACI	International Cooperative Alliance
ACIA	Arctic Climate Impact Assessment
ACMED	African Centre of Meteorological Applications for Development
ACP	Africa, Caribbean, and Pacific
ACP-EUWF	Africa, Caribbean, Pacific – European Union Water Facility
ACS	Association of Caribbean States
ACSAD	Arab Centre for the Studies of Arid Zones and Drylands
ACTS	African Centre for Technology Studies
ACTT	African Centre for Technology Transfer (GEF)
ACWP	African Conservancy for Wildlife Protection
ADA (1)	Austrian Development Agency
ADA (2)	Australian Development Agency
ADB (1)	African Development Bank (sometimes AfDB)
ADB (2)	Asian Development Bank (sometimes AsDB)
ADC (1)	Andean Development Corporation
ADC (2)	African Development Council
AdE	Water Academy of France
ADELA	Atlantic Community Development Group for Latin America
ADF	African Development Fund
ADI	acceptable daily intake
ADPC	Asian Disaster Preparedness Center
ADR	alternative dispute resolution
ADRC	Asian Disaster Reduction Center
AEC	African Economic Council
AECI	Spanish Agency for International Cooperation
AEGDM	ASEAN Experts Group on Disaster Management
AEPS	Arctic Environmental Protection Strategy
AERYD	*Asociación Española de Riegos y Drenajes*
AESN	*Agence de l'Eau Seine-Normandie* (France)
AETF	Australian Emissions Trading Forum Review
AEWA	Agreement on the Conservation of African-Eurasian Migratory Waterbirds

AEWS	accident emergency warning system
AFD	*Agence Française Développement*
AfDB	African Development Bank (sometimes ADB)
AFESD	Arab Fund for Economic and Social Development
AFLEG	African Forest Law Enforcement and Governance
AFOLU	Agriculture, Forests, and other Land Use (UNFCCC)
AFPPD	Asian Forum of Parliamentarians on Population and Development
AFSED	Arab Fund for Social and Economic Development
AFTA (1)	ASEAN Free Trade Area
AFTA (2)	Andean Free Trade Association
AFWC	African Forestry and Wildlife Commission
AG (1)	Assembly of Governors (IDB)
AG (2)	Australia Group
AG13	Ad hoc Group on Article 13 (UNFCCC)
AGBM	Ad hoc Group on the Berlin Mandate (UNFCCC)
AGCM	atmospheric general circulation model (WMO)
AGDP	agricultural gross domestic product
AGFUND	Arab Gulf Programme for the United Nations Development Organization
AGHCL	Advisory Group on Harmonization of Classification and Labeling (OECD)
AGIRS	Agriculture Investment Research Service (IBRD)
AGO	Australian Greenhouse Office
AGORA	Access to Global Online Research in Agriculture
AGR	Agriculture Department (WB)
AGR_{EMP}	percentage of labor force in agricultural sector
AHEG	Ad Hoc Expert Group
AHEG PARAM	UN Ad-hoc Group on Consideration with a view to Recommending the Parameters of a Mandate for Developing a Legal Framework on all Types of Forests
AHTEG	Ad Hoc Technical Working Group
AIA (1)	Advance Informed Agreement (Cartagena Protocol on Biosafety)
AIA (2)	American International Association for Economic and Social Development
AIACC	agricultural impact assessment of climate change
AIC	African Investment Association
AID	Agency for International Development (USA)
AIDA	International Association for Water Law
AIDIS	Pan-American Engineering Association for the Public Health and Environment
AIDS	acquired immune deficiency syndrome (UN)
AIH	American Institute of Hydrology
AIJ	Activities Implemented Jointly (UNFCCC)
AIMS	Atlantic, Indian Ocean, Mediterranean, and the South China Seas (SIDS grouping)

AIRC	Asia International Rivers Center (China)
AIRVIEW	Air Quality Visualization Instrument for Europe on the Web
AIT	Asian Institute of Technology (Thailand)
AIXG	Annex I Expert Group (UNFCCC)
ALA	EU's Assistance Programme in Asia and Latin America
ALADI	Latin American Institute for Integration and Development
ALALC	Latin American Association of Free Commerce
ALCORDES	Latin American Association of Regional Development Associations
ALESCO	Arab Centre for the Study of Arid Zones and Dry Lands (LAS)
ALIDE	Latin American Association of Development Finance Institutions
ALIDES	Central American Alliance for Sustainable Development
ALMAE	*Alliance Maghreb Machrek pour l'Eau* (Morocco)
ALTERRA	International Land Research Institute (Wageningen University, The Netherlands)
AMAP	Arctic Monitoring and Assessment Programme
AMCEN	African Ministerial Conference on the Environment
AMCOW	African Ministers' Council on Water
AMF	Arab Monetary Fund
AMH	Mexican Association of Hydraulics
AMNCA	*Alianza Mexicana par la Nueva Cultura del Aguas*
AMU	Arab Maghreb Union
ANA	National Water Agency (Brazil)
ANBO	African Network for Basin Organization
ANCEFN	National Academy of Exact, Physical and Natural Sciences (Argentina)
ANCYT	National Academy of Science and Technology (Peru)
ANEW	Africa Network of Civil Society Organizations
ANGO	Advocacy NGO
ANPED	Northern Alliance for Sustainability
AoA	Agreement on Agriculture (WTO)
AOAD	Arab Organization for Agricultural Development
AOML	Atlantic Oceanographic and Meteorological Laboratory
AONB	Areas of Outstanding Natural Beauty
AOSIS	Alliance of Small Island States
AP (1)	Alliance for Progress
AP (2)	associated program
APD	approved project document (IDB)
APE	assimilative potential of the environment
APEC	Asia-Pacific Economic Cooperation Forum
APELL	alert and preparedness for emergencies at local level
APEP	Alliance for Progress
APFC	Asia-Pacific Forestry Commission
APFED	Asia-Pacific Forum for Environment and Development

APFM	Associated Programme on Flood Management
APL	adaptable program lending
APO	Asian Productivity Organization
APPCDC	Asia-Pacific Partnership on Clean Development and Climate
APPP	annual participatory programming process
APR	Annual Programme/Project Report (GEF)
APS	ambient permit system
APWF	Asia Pacific Water Forum
AQUASTAT	Country Information on Water and Agriculture
AR	agricultural research
A/R	afforestation/reforestation
AR4	IPCC Fourth Assessment Report
ARC (1)	Agricultural Research Centre
ARC (2)	Agricultural Research Council
ARC (3)	Alliance to Rescue Civilization
ARD	afforestation, reforestation and deforestation
ARES	African Regional Environmental Strategy
ARF	ASEAN Regional Forum
ArgCapNet	Argentine Water Education and Capacity Building Network
ARI	Agricultural Research Institute
ARIDE	Assessment of the Regional Impact of Droughts in Europe
ASA	Association for Social Advancement
ASAL lands	arid or semi-arid lands (UN)
ASARECA	Association for Strengthening Agricultural Research in Eastern and Central Africa
ASCE	American Society of Civil Engineers
ASCOBANS	Agreement on the Conservation of Small Cetaceans of the Baltic and North Seas
ASD	Asian Development Bank
AsDB	Asian Development Bank
ASE	Alliance to Save Energy
ASEAN	Association of Southeast Asian Nations
ASG	Assistant Director General
ASIL	American Society of International Law
ASIP	Inter American Press Association
ASOEN	ASEAN Senior Officials on Environment
ASR	artificial storage and recovery
ASRWG-ICID	International Commission on Irrigation and Drainage, Asian Regional Working Group
ASSMAE	*Associacao Nacional de Servicios Municipais de Saneamiento* (Brazil)
ASTHyDA	analysis, synthesis and transfer of knowledge and tools on hydrological droughts assessment through a European network
ASWAF	Africa Safe Water Foundation (Nigeria)

ATL	technical cooperation loan (IDB)
ATO (1)	African Timber Organization
ATO (2)	Arab Towns Organization
ATS	Antarctic Treaty System
ATT	advanced treatment technology
ATTP	Advanced Technical Training Programme (UNESCO)
AU (1)	African Union
AU (2)	anti-bribery undertaking
AUDMP	Asian Urban Disaster Mitigation Program
AusAid	Australian Agency for International Development
AVHRR	advanced very high-resolution radiometer
AVU	African Virtual University
AWA	Australian Water Association
AWARENET	Arab Integrated Water Resources Management Network
AWB	Association of Water Boards (Germany)
AWC	Arab Water Council
AWEC	Annual Water Experts Conference
AWF	African Water Facility (AfDB)
AWG	Advisory Working Group (CHy of WMO)
AWGB	Ad Hoc Working Group on Biodiversity (GEF/STAP)
AWGGWE	Ad Hoc Working Group on Global Warming and Energy (GEF)
AWMC	Advanced Wastewater Management Centre (Australia)
AWP	Area Water Partnership (GWP)
AWRA	American Water Resources Association
AWTF	African Water Task Force

B

BA	beneficiary assessment
BAA	Bolivarian Alternative for the Americas
BACT	best available control technology
BADEA	Arab Bank for Economic Development in Africa
BAHC	biospheric aspects of the hydrological cycle
BAPA	Buenos Aires Plan of Action (UNFCCC)
BAS	Academy of Sciences (Bangladesh, Brazil)
BASD	Business Action for Sustainable Development
Basel	Basel Convention on the Control of Transboundary Movements of Hazardous Wastes and their Disposal
BAT	best available technology
BATNEEC	best available technology not entailing excessive cost
BAU	business as usual
BBC	British Broadcasting Corporation
BCA	benefit–cost analysis
BCH	Biosafety Clearing House (CBD)
BCHM	Belgium Clearing House Mechanism
BCIS	Biodiversity Conservation Information System

BCR	benefit–cost ratio
BCSD	Business Council for Sustainable Development
BCSR	Bahrain Centre for Studies and Research
BDC	biological data collection
BDDC	British Development Division – Caribbean
BDO	Buccament Development Organization
BE	Special Voluntary Trust Fund of the CBD
BEGIN	Basic Education for Growth Initiative (Japan)
BEP	best environmental practice
BGR	Federal Institute for Geosciences and Natural Resources (Germany)
BICC	Bonn International Centre for Conversion (Germany)
BINGO	Business and Industry NGO
BIONET	Biodiversity Action Network
BIT	Bilateral Investment Treaties
BKA	Federal Chancellery (Austria)
BLICC	Business Leaders Initiative on Climate Change
BLKALET	Block A Agreement Letter (GEF)
BMA	Federal Ministry of Foreign Affairs (Austria)
BMENA	Broader Middle East and North Africa
BMP	best management practice
BMU	German Federal Ministry of Environment
BMZ	German Federal Ministry for Economic Cooperation and Development
BNGO	Business NonGovernmental Organization
BNSC	British National Space Centre
BOD	biological oxygen demand
BOG	Board of Governors
BOO	build, own, operate
BOT	build, operate, transfer
BP	bank procedures (WB)
BPA	Barbados Plan of Action (SIDS)
BPDWS	Building Partnerships for Development in Water and Sanitation
BPEO	best practicable environmental option
BPM	best practicable means
BPOA	Barbados Plan of Action (SIDS)
BPP	Blue Planet Project
BPPE	Bureau for Programme Policy and Evaluation (GEF)
BRG	Genetic Resources Board (France)
BRGM	French Geological Survey and Bureau of Mines
BRIC countries	Brazil, Russia, India and China
BSE	bovine spongiform encephalopathy 'mad cow disease'
BSEC	Black Sea Economic Cooperation
BSH	basic systems in hydrology
BSWG	Open-ended Ad Hoc Working Group on Biosafety (CBD)
BTC	Belgian Technical Cooperation
BTWC/BWC	Biological and Toxin Weapons Convention

BUWAL	Swiss Agency for Environment, Forests and Landscape
BVI	British Virgin Islands
BWO	Basin Water Organization
BWP (1)	Bretton Woods Project
BWP (2)	Bangladesh Water Partnership
BY	Trust Fund for the Convention (CBD)
BZ	Special Voluntary Trust Fund to Facilitate Participation by the Parties to the Convention (CBD)

C

C&C	contraction and convergence
C&I	criteria and indicators
C2D	Contract for Debt Relief and Development
CA (1)	cooperating agency
CA (2)	cooperative agreement
CA (3)	Central Administration (Italy)
CA (4)	comprehensive assessment of water management in agriculture
CA (5)	Chamber of Accounts
CAA	Clean Air Act
CAADP	Comprehensive Africa Agriculture Development Programme
CABEI	Central American Bank for Economic Integration
CAC (1)	Central American Agricultural Advisory Board
CAC (2)	Codex Alimentarius Commission
CAC (3)	command and control
CAC&M	Central Asia, Caucasus and Moldova
CACAM	Central Asia, Caucasus, Albania and Moldova
CACILM	Central Asia Countries Institutions for Land Management
CACM	Central American Common Market
CAD	Administrative Commission of the Executive Directorate (IDB)
CAETS	International Council of Academies of Engineering and Technological Sciences
CAEU	Council of Arab Economic Unity
CAF (1)	Andean Development Corporation
CAF (2)	Conflict Analysis Framework (WB)
CAF (3)	Conserve Africa Foundation
CAFÉ	Clean Air for Europe Programme
CAFF	Conservation Council Conservation of Arctic Flora and Fauna
CAFTA	Central American Free Trade Agreement
CAI	Clean Air Initiative
CAMLR	Commission or the Conservation of Antarctic Marine Living Resources

CAMRE	Council of Arab Ministers Responsible for the Environment
CAN (1)	Andean Community of Nations (*Comunidad de las Naciones Andinas*)
CAN (2)	Climate Action Network
CAN (3)	Country Assistance Note
CANSA	Climate Action Network Southeast Asia
CANUS	Climate Action Network United States
CAP	Common Agricultural Policy
CAPAM	Commonwealth Association for Public Management
CAPNET	International Network for Capacity Building for Integrated Water Resources Management (GWP)
CAR	Central Asian Republics
CARA	Central American Water Resource Management Network
CARAPHIN	Caribbean Animal and Plant Health Information Network
CARDI	Caribbean Agricultural Research and Development Institute
CAREC	Regional Development Centre for Central Asia
CARIBANK	Caribbean Development Bank
CARICOM	Caribbean Community and Common Market
CARICOMP	Caribbean Coastal Marine Productivity Program
CARIFTA	Caribbean Free Trade Association
CARIRI	Caribbean Industrial Research Institute
CARIS	Chemical Accident Response Information System
CAS (1)	Academy of Sciences (Cameroon, Chile, China, Costa Rica)
CAS (2)	Country Assistance Strategy (WB)
CAS (3)	Commission for Atmospheric Sciences (WMO)
CAS (4)	complex adaptive systems
CASIN	Centre for Applied Studies in International Negotiations
CAT	Convention against Torture and other Cruel, Inhuman or Degrading Treatment or Punishment
CATAC	Central American Technical Committee (GWP)
CATEP	Certified Action on Tradable Emissions Permits
CATHALAC	Water Center for the Humid Tropics of Latin America and the Caribbean, Panama (UNESCO)
CATIE	Tropical Agriculture Training and Research Center
CATNIP	cheapest available technology not involving prosecution
CAWST	Centre for Affordable Water and Sanitation Technology
CAZALAC	Water Centre for Arid and Semi-Arid Regions of Latin America and the Caribbean, La Serena, Chile (UNESCO)
CAZRI	Central Arid Zone Research Institute (India)
CB	capacity building (UNDP)
CBD	Convention on Biological Diversity
CBDR	common but differentiated responsibilities

CBE	Centre for Built Environment
CBF	Chesapeake Bay Foundation
CBH	capacity-building in hydrology and water resources
CBI (1)	confidential business information
CBI (2)	Caribbean Basin Initiative
CBI (3)	cross-border initiative
CBNRM	Community Based Natural Resource Management
CBO	community-based organization
CBRST	Centre for Scientific and Technical Research (Benin)
CBS	Commission for Basic Systems (WMO)
CBW	chemical and biological weapons/warfare
CCs	collaborating centers
CCA (1)	Common Country Assessment
CCA (2)	Caribbean Conservation Association
CCA (3)	Coalition for Clean Air
CCA (4)	*Consejo Consultivo del Agua* (Mexico)
CCAD	Central American Commission for Environment and Development
CCAMLR	Convention on the Conservation of Antarctic Marine Living Resources
CCAP	Climate Change Action Plan
CCC	Caribbean Conservation Corporation
CCCC	Caribbean Climate Change Centre
CCCDF	Canada Climate Change Development Fund
CCCO	Committee for Climate Changes and the Ocean
CCD	Convention to Combat Desertification
CCF	Country Cooperation Framework
CCHRI	Centre for Community Health Research (India)
CCI (1)	Commission for Climatology (WMO)
CCI (2)	crosscutting issues
CCJ	Caribbean Court of Justice
CCL	Climate Change Levy
CCLM	Committee on Constitutional and Legal Matters (IU)
CCOHS	Canadian Centre for Occupational Health and Safety
CCOL	Coordinating Committee on the Ozone Layer (UNEP)
CCP	Copenhagen Consensus Project (Denmark)
CCPR	International Covenant on Civil and Political Rights
CCPR-OP1	Optional Protocol to the CCPR
CCRH	Central American Commission for Water Resources
CCS	capture, compression, and sequestration of CO_2
CCSM	Community Climate Systems Model (IPCC)
CCX	Chicago Climate Exchange (Market for GHG)
CD (1)	Conference on Disarmament
CD (2)	Convention to Combat Desertification
CD (3)	capacity development
CD (4)	Community of Democracies
CD4CDM	Capacity Development for Clean Development Mechanism

CDB	Caribbean Development Bank
CDC (1)	Conservation Data Center
CDC (2)	Center for Disease Control and Prevention (USA)
CDEF	Community Development Carbon Fund (WB)
CDERA	Caribbean Disaster Emergency Response Agency
CDF (1)	Comprehensive Development Framework (WB)
CDF (2)	Clean Development Fund (UNFCCC)
CDI	Capacity Development Initiative
CDIAC	Carbon Dioxide Information Analysis Center
CDM	Clean Development Mechanism (UNFCCC)
CDMS	Comprehensive Disaster Management Strategy
CDP	Carbon Disclosure Project
CDQs	community development quotas
CDRM	Comprehensive Disaster Risk Management
CE	Central Europe
CEA (1)	Cumulative Effects Assessment
CEA (2)	cost-effectiveness analysis
CEAC	Commission on Education and Communication (IUCN)
CEB	Chief Executive Board (UN)
CEC (1)	Commission of the European Communities
CEC (2)	Commission for Environmental Cooperation (NAFTA)
CEC (3)	Council on Environmental Quality (USA)
CECAL	European Committee for Cooperation with Latin America
CECLA	Special Coordination Committee for Latin America (UN)
CECODHAS	European Liaison Committee for Social Housing
CECON	Special Commission for Consultation and Negotiation
CEDARE	Centre for Environment and Development in the Arab Region and Europe
CEDAW	Convention on the Elimination of all Forms of Discrimination against Women
CE-DESD	China–Europe Dialogue and Exchange for Sustainable Development
CEE	Central and Eastern Europe
CEESP	Commission on Environmental, Economic, and Social Policy (IUCN)
CEETAC	Central and Eastern Europe Technical Advisory Committee (GWP)
CEFIC	European Chemical Industry Council
CEFTA	Central European Free Trade Agreement
CEH	Centre for Ecology and Hydrology (UK)
CEHI	Caribbean Environmental Health Institute
CEIP	Carnegie Endowment for International Peace (US)
CEITs	Countries with Economies in Transition
CEL (1)	Commission on Environmental Law (IUCN)
CEL (2)	Latin American Economic Community
CEM (1)	Country Economic Memorandum
CEM (2)	Commission on Ecosystem Management (IUCN)

CEM (3)	Committee on Economic Information and Market Intelligence (ITTA)
CEMDA	Mexican Center for Environmental Law
CENAREST	National Centre for Scientific and Technological Research (Gabon)
CENTO	Central Asian Treaty Organization
CEO (1)	Centre for Earth Observation
CEO (2)	Chief Executive Officer (GEF)
CEOP	Coordinated Enhanced Observing Period
CEOS	Committee for Earth Observation Satellites
CEP	Caribbean Environment Programme (UNEP)
CEPAT	Continuing Education Programme in Agricultural Technology
CEPES	European Centre for Higher Education (Bucharest, Romania) (UNESCO)
CEPREDENAC	Coordination Center for the Prevention of Natural Disasters in Central America
CEPS	Centre for European Policy Studies
CEQ (1)	Commission for Environmental Quality (NAAEC)
CEQ (2)	Council on Environmental Quality (USA)
CER (1)	Certified Emissions Reduction
CER (2)	Comprehensive Evaluation Report
CER (3)	Closer Economic Relations
CERD	International Convention on the Elimination of all Forms of Racial Discrimination
CERES	Coalition for Environmentally Responsible Economies
CERMES	Centre for Resource Management and Environmental Studies (UWI, Barbados)
CERN	Chinese Ecosystem Research Network
CERP	Comprehensive Environmental Restoration Plan
CERT	Committee on Energy Research and Technology and Working Parties (IEA)
CES	Compensation for Ecosystem Services
CESCR	International Covenant on Economic, Social and Cultural Rights
CESI	Committee for Environmental and Social Impacts (IDB)
CETA	Conventional Energy Technical Assistance
CF	*Caisse Française*, French Development Assistance Agency
CFA (1)	concessional finance arrangement
CFA (2)	Committee on Finance and Administration (ITTA)
CFAA	Country Financial Accountability Assessment (WB)
CFAW	Canadian Fund for Africa on Water
CFC	chlorofluorocarbon
CFDT	Committee on Forest Development in the Tropics (FAO)
CFI	Committee on Forest Industry (ITTA)
CFL	compact fluorescent lamp
CFP	Common Fisheries Policy (EEA)
CFR (1)	case fatality rate

CFR (2)	Council on Foreign Relations (USA)
CFS	Committee on World Food Security
CFT	Conservation Rainforest Trust
CFTC	Commonwealth Fund for Technical Cooperation
CFZA	Common Fisheries Zone Agreement
CG (1)	Canadian Government
CG (2)	Consultative Group (WB)
CG/HCCS	Coordinating Group for the Harmonization of Chemical Classification Systems (OECD)
CG-11	Central Group-11
CGC	Center for Green Chemistry (US)
CGD	Center for Global Development (US)
CGD/FP	Center for Global Development/Foreign Policy (Commitment to Development Index)
CGE (1)	Consultative Group of Experts (UNFCCC)
CGE (2)	Compatible General Equilibrium
CGG	Commission on Global Governance
CGIAR	Consultative Group on International Agriculture Research (IBRD)
CGIAR-CA	CGIAR Comprehensive Assessment of Water Management in Agriculture
CGIAR-CPWF	CGIAR Challenge Program on Water and Food
CGLU	United Cities and Local Governance (UN)
CGMW	Commission for the Geological Map of the World
CGP	Consultative Group to Assist the Poorest (IBRD)
CGRFA	Commission on Genetic Resources for Food and Agriculture
CH_4	methane
CHARM	see ICHARM
CHINATAC	China Technical Advisory Committee (GWP)
CHM	Clearing House Mechanism (SBD)
CHOGM	Commonwealth Heads of Government Meeting
CHP	combined heat and power
CHR	Commission on Human Rights
CHS	Commission on Human Security
CHy	Commission for Hydrology of WMO
CI (1)	Conservation International
CI (2)	Consumers International
CIAB	The Coal Industry Advisory Board (IEA)
CIAT	International Centre for Tropical Agriculture
CIC/Plata	Intergovernmental Coordination Committee of the Plata Basin Countries (OAS)
CICERO	Centre for International Climate and Energy Research, Oslo
CICI	International Conference on the Contribution of Criteria and Indicators for Sustainable Forest Management
CICR	Center for International Conflict Resolution
CIDA	Canadian International Development Agency

CIDH	Inter-American Human Rights Commission
CIDI	Inter-American Commission for Integral Development (OAS)
CIDIE	Committee of International Development Institutions on the Environment
CIDS	Inter-American Committee for Sustainable Development (OAS)
CIESIN	Consortium/Center for International Earth Science Information Network
CIFIC	Council for International and Economic Cooperation (CFR)
CIFOR	Center for International Forestry Research
CIGR	International Commission of Agricultural Engineering
CIHEAM	International Centre for Advanced Mediterranean Agronomic Studies
CILSS	Convention Establishing a Permanent Inter-States Committee for Drought Control in the Sahel
CI-K	contribution in-kind
CIMMYT	International Center for the Improvement of Maize and Wheat
CINARA	Regional Centre on Urban Water Management for Latin America and the Caribbean (Colombia)
CIP	International Potato Center
CIPAC	Collaborative International Pesticide Analytical Council
CIRA	*Centro Interamericano para Investigaciones de Recursos de Agua* (Mexico)
CIRAD	French Agricultural Research Centre for International Development
CIS	Commonwealth of Independent States
CITES	Convention on International Trade in Endangered Species of Wild Fauna and Flora
CITMA	Ministry of Science, Technology and Environment (Cuba)
CITO	Center for International Training and Outreach (University of Idaho, US)
CIVICUS	World Alliance for Citizen Participation
CK-Net	Collaborative Knowledge Network (Indonesia)
CLAEH	Latin American Center for Water Studies
CLAES	*Centro Latino Americano de Ecologia Social*
CLAPN	Latin American Committee for National Parks
CLC	Convention on Civil Liability for Oil Pollution
CLCS	Commission on the Limits of the Continental Shelf
CLEQM	Central Laboratory for Environmental Monitoring (Egypt)
CLI	Country-led Initiative
CLIVAR	Climate Variability Research Programme
CMA	critical marine area
CMAP	Climate Prediction Center Merged Analysis of Precipitation

CMC	Center for Marine Conservation
CMP (1)	Carbon Market Programme (UNFCCC)
CMP (2)	Conference of the Parties to the UNFCCC serving as the Meeting of the Parties to the Kyoto Protocol (UNFCCC)
CMS	Convention on the Conservation of Migratory Species of Wild Animals
CN (1)	conference notes
CN (2)	committee notes
CNA (1)	Climate Network Africa
CNA (2)	National Water Commission (Mexico)
CNE	Climate Network Europe
CNF	Canadian Nature Federation
CNMC	Committee on Non-Member Countries (IEA)
CNPPA	Commission on National Parks and Protected Areas (IUCN)
CNPq	Brazilian National Research Council
CNRS	National Centre for Scientific Research (France)
CNS	Center for Nonproliferation Studies
CO (1)	Country Office
CO (2)	carbon monoxide
CO_2	carbon dioxide
COA	Comité Operativo de las Américas
COAG	Committee on Agriculture (FAO)
COBSEA	Coordination Body on the Seas of East Asia
COCEF	Ecological Transboundary Cooperation Commission
COD	chemical oxygen demand
CoE	Center of Excellence
COFO	Committee on Forestry (FAO)
COHG	Conference of Heads of Governments of the Caribbean Community
COLCIENCIAS	Colombian Institute for Development of Science and Technology
COMESA	Common Market for Eastern and Southern Africa
COMEST	World Commission on the Ethics of Scientific Knowledge and Technology (UNESCO)
CONACyT	National Council for Science and Technology (Latin America)
CONAFOR	*Comisión Nacional Forestal* (Mexico)
CONAGUA	*Comisión Nacional de Agua* (Mexico)
CONCAUSA	Central America/United States Joint Accord
CONDESAN	Consortium for Sustainable Development in the Andean Region
CONF	conference (document identification)
CONGO	Conference of Non-Governmental Organizations in Consultative Relationships with the United Nations
CONICET	National Council of Scientific and Technical Research (Latin America)
CoP (1)	Community of Practice (WB)

COP (2)	Conference of the Parties to a Convention
COP (3)	Country Operational Programme (EU)
COPUOS	Committee on the Peaceful Uses of Outer Space (UN)
CORECA	Regional Council for Agricultural Cooperation in Central America, Mexico and the Dominican Republic
COREPER	Committee of Permanent Representatives (EU)
CORINE	Coordination of Information on the Environment in Europe (CEC)
CO/RSAT	Operations Committee/Technical Assistance Request Summary (IDB)
CO/RSP	Operations Committee/Loan Request Summary (IDB)
COW	Committee of the Whole
COWAR	Committee on Water Research (of the ICSU)
CP (1)	Conference of Parties (document identification)
CP (2)	press release (IDB)
CP (3)	Consulting Partners (GWP)
CPA (1)	Country Performance Assessment
CPA (2)	Loan Committee (IDB)
CPA (3)	Consolidated Plan of Action
CPACC	Caribbean Planning for Adaptation to Climate Change
CPAN	Circumpolar Protected Area Network
CPC	Climate Prediction Center
CPD	Commission on Population and Development
CPF	Collaborative Partnership on Forests
CPGR/CGR	Commission for Plant Genetic Resources/Genetic Resources (FAO)
CPI (1)	Corruption Perceptions Index
CPI (2)	Consumer Price Index
CPIA	Country Policy and Institutional Assessment (ADB)
CPLP	Community of Portuguese Speaking Nations
CPPF	Canadian Project Preparation Trust Fund (IDB)
CPR (1)	Committee of Permanent Representatives
CPR (2)	common pool resources
CPR (3)	Personnel Committee (IDB)
CPR (4)	Conflict Prevention and Reconstruction Unit (WB)
CPS	Cleaner Production Assessment
CPWC	Cooperative Programme on Water and Climate
CR	Country Report (GEF)
CRAMLR	Convention on the Regulation of Antarctic Mineral Resources
CRC (1)	Convention on the Rights of the Child
CRC (2)	Chemical Review Committee (Rotterdam Convention)
CRED	Centre for Research on the Epidemiology of Disasters
CREHO	RAMSAR Regional Centre for Training and Research on Wetlands in the Western Hemisphere
CRF (1)	common reporting format
CRF (2)	Committee on Reforestation and Forest Management (ITTA)

CRIC	Committee for the Review of the Implementation of the Convention to Combat Desertification
CRMI	Coastal Resources Management Initiative
CROP	Council of Regional Organizations in the Pacific
CRP	conference-room paper
CRRH	Regional Commission for Water Resources
CRS	Creditor Reporting System (OECD)
CRUESI	Research Centre for the Utilization of Brackish Water in Irrigation (Tunisia)
CSA (1)	cost sharing agreement
CSA (2)	Central Statistics Authority
CSAG	Civil Society Advisory Group
CSC	Commonwealth Council (UK)
CSCO	Caspian Sea Cooperation Organization
CSD	Commission on Sustainable Development
CSDS	Countries in Special Development Situations (UN)
CSD-WAND	Commission on Sustainable Development – Water Action and Networking Database
CSE	Centre for Science and Environment (India)
CSI	Environment and Development in Coastal Regions and Small Islands (UNESCO)
CSIR	Council of Scientific and Industrial Research (South Africa, India)
CSIRO	Commonwealth Scientific and Industrial Research Organization (Australia)
CSM	climate system model
CSME	CARICOM Single Market and Economy
CSMP	Center for the Study of Marine Policy (University of Delaware)
CSN	*Comunidad Sudamericana de Naciones*
CSO	Civil Society Organization
CSocD	Commission for Social Development (UN)
CSR	Civil Service Reform
CSRIO	Commonwealth Scientific and Industrial Research Organization
CST	Committee on Science and Technology (CCD)
CSW	Commission on the Status of Women
CTBT	Comprehensive Test Ban Treaty (IAEA)
CTE	Committee on Trade and Environment (WTO)
CTI (1)	Climate Technology Initiative (UNFCCC)
CTI (2)	Climate Technology Institute
CTIP	Climate Technology Implementation Plan (UNFCCC)
CTM	Center for Transdisciplinary Environmental Research (Sweden)
CTO (1)	Certified Tradable Offsets (UNFCCC)
CTO (2)	Caribbean Tourist Organization
CU (1)	conservation unit
CU (2)	country unit (IBRD)

CUCSD	China–US Center for Sustainable Development (US and Beijing)
CV	curriculum vitae
CVD	countervailing duties
CVI	Climate Vulnerability Index
CVM	contingent valuation method
CVPU	country valuation project unit (GEF but outdated)
CWC	Chemical Weapons Convention
CWIS	Center for World Indigenous Studies
CWP	Country Water Partnership (GWP)
CWRA	Canadian Water Resources Association
CWS	Cities without Slums
CY	calendar year
CZM	coastal zone management

D

D&FD	deforestation and forest degradation
DA	development assistance
DAC	Development Assistance Committee (OECD)
DADG	Deputy Assistant Director General
DALY	disability adjusted life year
DANCED	Danish Cooperation for Environment and Development
DANIDA	Danish International Development Agency
DATA	Debt, AIDS, Trade, Africa (UK)
DAW	Division for the Advancement of Women (UN)
DB	development business (WB)
Db	decibels
DC	developed country
DCA	Development Control Authority
DCI	Development Cooperation Ireland
DCS	data collection system
DDC (1)	*Direction de Développement et de la Cooperation* (Switzerland)
DDC (2)	Data Distribution Center
DDC (3)	Department of Development Cooperation (Austria)
DDG	Deputy Director General
DDT	dichlorodiphenyltrichloroethanne
DE	decentralized energy path
DEC	Division of Environmental Conventions (UNEP)
Dec	decision (document identification)
DEFRA	Department for Environment, Food and Rural Affairs (UK)
DENR	Department of Environment and Natural Resources
DEPHA	Data Exchange Platform for the Horn of Africa
DES	dietary energy supply
DESA	United Nations Department of Economic and Social Affairs

DESD	UN Decade of Education for Sustainable Development
DESIP	Demographic, Environmental, and Security Issues Project (UN)
DETS	emissions trading scheme
DEWA	Division of Early Warning and Assessment (UNEP)
DFA	Department of Foreign Affairs
DFID	Department for International Development (UK)
DG	Director General
DGCS	Directorate General for Development Cooperation (Italy)
DGD	decision guidance document
DGIC	Directorate General for International Cooperation (Belgium)
DGIS	Directorate General for Development Cooperation (The Netherlands)
DHF	dengue hemorrhagic fever
DHI	Danish Hydrological Institute of Water and Environment
DHS	Demographic Health Surveys
DIMP	Data and Information Management Panel (GTOS)
DINGO	Australian NGO
Distr.	distribution (document identification)
DIVERSITAS	International Programme of Biodiversity Science
DKKV	German Committee for Disaster Reduction
DL	distance learning
d-learning	distance learning
DM	Department of Management (UN)
DMC	Drought Monitoring Centre
DMF	Disaster Management Facility (WB)
DMFC	Disaster Mitigation Facility for the Caribbean
DMS	double majority voting system
DMT	Disaster Management Team
DMZ	demilitarized zone
DNA (1)	deoxyribonucleic acid
DNA (2)	Designated National Authority
DNH	National Water Directorate (France)
DNS	Debt for nature swap
DO (1)	Development Objective (GEF)
DO (2)	dissolved oxygen
DOD	Department of Defense (US)
DOE (1)	Department of Energy (US)
DOE (2)	Designated Operational Entity
DOEM	Designated Officials for Environmental Matters (UNEP)
DONGO	donor-organized NGO
DOS	Department of State (US)
DPA	Department of Political Affairs (UN)
DPCSD	United Nations Department for Policy Coordination and Sustainable Development
DPI	UN Department of Public Information
DPKO	Department of Peacekeeping Operations (UN)

DPM (1)	disaster preparedness and mitigation
DPM (2)	Deputy Prime Minister
DPPC	Disaster Prevention and Preparedness Commission (UN)
DPSIR	Driving Forces, Pressures, States, Impacts, Responses
DR/dr	discount rate
DRA	demand responsive approaches
DRB	Danube River Basin
DRI	disaster risk index
DRPC	Danube River Protection Convention
DSA	daily subsistence allowance (UN)
DSB	Dispute Settlement Body (WTO)
DSD	Division for Sustainable Development (ECOSOC)
DSDS	Delhi Sustainable Development Summit
DSM	demand-side management
DSPD	Division for Social Policy and Development (ECOSOC-UN)
DSS	data synthesis system
DSU	Dispute Settlement Understanding
DTIE	Division of Technology, Industry and Economics (UNEP)
DWC/CPWP	Dialogue on Water and Climate/Cooperative Programme on Water and Climate
DWD	Directorate of Water Development (EU)
DWF	Danish Water Forum
DWFE	Dialogue on Water, Food and the Environment
DWFNs	Distant-water Fishing Nations
DWSSD	(International) Drinking Water Supply and Sanitation Decade (1981–1990)

E

E (1)	English
E (2)	edited
E (3)	Executive
E7	Nine of the leading electric utilities from the G7 countries
E9	Nine high-population countries: Bangladesh, Brazil, China, Egypt, India, Indonesia, Mexico, Nigeria and Pakistan
E&D	expansion and divergence
E/D	environment/development
EA (1)	environmental assessment
EA (2)	Executing Agency (GEF)
EA-5	East Asia 5 (Indonesia, Korea, Malaysia, Philippines, Thailand)
EAC (1)	European Advisory Committee
EAC (2)	East Africa Community
EACC	East African Cooperation Community

EAEC	East Asian Economic Caucus
EAGs	Environmental Assessment Guidelines
EAP	Environmental Action Program
EARCSA	Rainwater Catchment System Association
Earth3000	Earth3000 (Germany)
EA-RWP	Eastern Africa Regional Water Partnership
EAS (1)	Economic Assessment of Natural Resources
EAS (2)	East Asia Seas
EASAC	European Academies' Science Advisory Council
EAS-RCU	East Asian Seas Regional Coordinating Unit (UNEP)
EATRR	European Agreement on the Transfer of Responsibility for Refugees
EAWAG	Swiss Federal Institute for Environmental Science and Technology
EB	Executive Board
EBRD	European Bank for Reconstruction and Development
EC (1)	European Community
EC (2)	European Commission
EC (3)	Commission of the European Communities
EC (4)	European Council
EC (5)	Earth Council
ECA (1)	United Nations Economic Commission for Africa
ECA (2)	Export Credit Agency
ECA (3)	Environment Canada
ECBA	economic cost–benefit analysis
ECBI	European Capacity Building Initiative
ECCAS	Economic Community of Central African States
ECE (1)	United Nations Economic Commission for Europe
ECE (2)	Evaluation Committee of Experts
ECECEP	United Nations Economic Commission for Europe Committee on Environmental Policy
ECEH	European Centre for Environment and Health
ECG	Ecosystem Conservation Group (UNEP, FAO, UNESCO, IUCN, UNDP, WWF)
ECHO	European Community Humanitarian Office
ECI	Earth Charter Initiative
ECLAC	United Nations Economic Commission for Latin America and the Caribbean
ECN (1)	Energy Research Centre of The Netherlands
ECN (2)	Environmental Change Network
ECO (1)	Earth Council Ombudsman (Earth Council)
ECO (2)	Pan American Center for Human Ecology and Health (PAHO)
ECO (3)	Ecological Citizens Organization
ECO (4)	Environmental Community Organization
ECO (5)	The Ombudsman Centre for Environment and Development
ECO (6)	Economic Cooperation Organization
ECOA	Ecoa and Pantanal Network

ECOLEX	Environmental Law Information System (UNEP, IUCN, FAO)
ECON	Ministry of Economy and Finance (Spain)
ECOSOC	United Nations Economic and Social Council
ECOWAS	Economic Commission of West African States
ECPF	Expert Consultation on the Role of Planted Forests (FAO)
ECPFO	Environmental and Consumer Protection Foundation (India)
ECU	European Currency Unit, replaced by euro (€)
ECX	European Climate Exchange
ED	Executive Director
EDF (1)	European Development Fund
EDF (2)	Environmental Defense Fund (US)
EDF (3)	Ecologic Development Fund
EDGI	Expert Group on Development Issues
EDI	Economic Development Institute (Now WBI)
EDSS	Educational Decision Support Systems
EDUC	Ministry of Education and Science (Spain)
EE&C	Environmental Education and Communication
EEA (1)	European Environment Agency
EEA (2)	European Economic Area
EEAD	Environmental Effects Assessment Panel
EEAS	Energy Efficiency Accreditation Scheme
EEB	European Environmental Bureau
EEOS	European Earth Observing System
EES	Encyclopedia of Environmental Science
EEWP	Energy Efficiency Working Party (IEA)
EEZ (1)	exclusive economic zone
EEZ (2)	economic exclusion zone
EF	Environment Fund (UNEP)
EF!	Earth First!
EFA	Education for All (UNESCO)
EFC	European Forestry Commission
EfE	Environment for Europe
EFF	Environment Forever Foundation (Bulgaria)
EFI	European Forest Institute
EFSD	Environmental Foundation for Sustainable Development (OAS)
EFTA	European Free Trade Association
EGM	Expert Group Meeting
EGTT	Expert Group on Technology Transfer
EHC	Environmental Health Criteria (IPCS)
EIA (1)	environmental impact assessment
EIA (2)	Environmental Investigation Agency
EIB	European Investment Bank
EIG	Environmental Integrity Group
EIIL	European Institute for Industrial Leadership
EINECS	European Inventory of Existing Commercial Chemical Substances

EIONET	European Environment Information and Observation Network
EIR	Extractive Industries Review
EIS	environmental impact statement
EIT	economies in transition
EJCW	Environmental Justice Coalition for Water
EKC	environmental Kuznets curve
ELANEM	Euro-Latin American Network for Environmental Assessment and Monitoring
ELC	Environmental Law Centre (IUCN)
ELCI	Environmental Liaison Centre International
e-learning	electronic learning
ELINCS	European List of Notified Chemical Substances
ELIIW	Environmental Law Institute and IW-LEARN
ELOSS	Encyclopedia of Life Support Systems
ELS	ecolabelling schemes
EMA	Emissions Marketing Association
EMAN	Ecological Monitoring and Assessment Network
EMAP	Environmental Monitoring and Assessment Programme (USA)
EMAS	Eco-Management and Audit Scheme (EU)
EMB	Environmental Management Bureau
EMDG	Emissions Market Development Group
EMEP	Co-operative Programme for Monitoring and Evaluation of the Long-Range Transmission of Air Pollutants in Europe
EMF	Environmental Management Foundation (The Netherlands)
EMG	Environmental Management Group
EMP	Euro-Mediterranean Partnership
EMS (1)	Environmental Management System
EMS (2)	European Monetary System
EMU	European Monetary Union
EMWIS	Euro-Mediterranean Information System
ENA	Europe and North Asia
ENB	Earth Negotiations Bulletin
ENCs	electronic navigational charts
ENCID	International Commission on Irrigation and Drainage
ENCORE	Eastern Caribbean Environment and Coastal Resources Management Project
ENDA-TM	Environment and Development Action in the Third World
ENGO	environmental non-governmental organization
ENN	Environmental Network News
ENRG	Environment and Natural Resources Group (UNDP)
ENRICH	European Network for Research in Global Change
ENSD	Earth Network for Sustainable Development
ENSO	*El Niño* Southern Oscillation
ENTRI	Environmental Treaties and Resource Indicators

ENV (1)	Environment Department (WB)
ENV (2)	Ministry of Environment (Spain)
ENVGC	Global Environment Coordination Division (WB)
EO	Earth Observation
EOS	Earth Observatory Satellite
EOSG	Executive Office of the Secretary General (UN)
EOU	Evaluation and Oversight Unit (UNEP)
EP (1)	environmental programme
EP (2)	European Parliament
EPA (1)	Environmental Protection Agency (many countries)
EPA (2)	Environmental Protection Act (UK)
EPC	European Patent Convention
EPD	Environmental Product Declaration
EPE (1)	European Partners for the Environment
EPE (2)	Environmental Programme for Europe
EPER	European Pollutant Emission Register
EPOCH	European Programme on Climatology and Natural Hazards
EPRC	Environment and Population Research Center
EPRG	Environmental Policy Review Group (EU)
EPS	emission permit system
EQS	Environmental Quality Standards
ERA	European Research Area
ERICAM	environmental risk internalization through capital markets
ERO	Expert Advisory Panel on Emergency Relief Operations (WHO)
EROS	US Geological Survey Earth Resources Observation Systems
ERP	Every River has its People Project
ERPA	Emissions Reduction Purchase Agreement
ERR	economic rate of return
ERSDAC	Earth Remote Sensing Data Analysis Center
ERT	expert review team
ERU	Emissions Reduction Unit (UNFCCC)
ES (1)	environmental statement
ES (2)	Euroscience
ESA (1)	European Space Agency
ESA (2)	Ecological Society of America
ESA (3)	environmental and social assessment
ESA (4)	Environmentally Sensitive Area
ESA (5)	economic stakeholder analysis
ESA (6)	ecosystem approach
ESAF	Enhanced Structural Adjustment Facility
ESAP	Environmental and Social Assessment Procedure
ESCAP	Economic and Social Commission for Asia and the Pacific (UN)
ESCWA	Economic and Social Commission for Western Asia (UN)
ESD (1)	Environmentally and Socially Sustainable Development Network (WB)

ESD (2)	Education for Sustainable Development
ESDG	Environmental Sustainable Development Group
ESE	environmental, social and ethical
ESI	Environmental Sustainability Index
ESIA	environmental and social impact assessment
ESM	Environmentally Sound Management
ESMP	Environmental and Social Management Plan (ADB)
ESP	environmental and social policy papers
ESPAR	Agricultural Research Group (WB)
EST&P	Environmentally Sound Technology and Products
ESTs	environmentally sustainable technologies
ESW	economic and sector work (WB)
E-TOOLS	electronic tools
ET	emissions trading (UNFCCC)
ETAP	Environmental Technology Action Programme (EU)
ETC	European Topic Center
ETC-ACC	ETC on Air and Climate Change
ETC-NPB	ETC on Nature Protection and Biodiversity
ETC-TE	ETC on Terrestrial Environment
ETC-WMF	ETC on Waste and Material Flows
ETFRN	European Tropical Forest Research Network
ETIC	Euphrates-Tigris Initiative for Cooperation
ETPA	education, training and public awareness (UNFCCC)
ETS (1)	emissions trading scheme
ETS (2)	effective temperature sum
ETUC	European Trade Union Confederation
EU (1)	European Union
EU (2)	European Community and its member states
EUFORGEN	European Forest Genetic Resources Programme
EUNIS	European Nature Information System
EUROBATS	Agreement on the Conservation of Bats in Europe
EUROPARL	European Parliament
EUROSTAT	Statistical Office of the European Communities
EUWF	European Union Water Facility
EUWI	European Union Water Initiative
EV	expected value
EVI	Environment Vulnerability Index (UNDP)
EWA	European Water Association (EU)
EWB	Engineers without Borders
EWI	Ecosystem Well-being Index
EWRI	Environmental and Water Resources Institute
EXC (1)	Executive Council (GEF)
EXC (2)	Office of the President (WB)
EXCOM	Executive Committee (Multilateral Fund for the Montreal Protocol)
EXCOP	Extraordinary Meeting of the Conference of the Parties
EXIM	Export–Import Bank of the United States

F

F2F	Face-to-face meeting, learning, etc. (WB)
FAJ	Forest Agency of Japan
FAN	Freshwater Action Network
FANCA	Freshwater Action Network – Central America
FANMEX	Freshwater Action Network of Mexico
FAO	Food and Agriculture Organization (UN)
FASRC	Federation of Arab Scientific Research Councils (Iraq)
FBA	Freshwater Biological Association (UK)
FBD	forest biodiversity
FBW	free basic water
FC	Facilitation Committee
FCB	fuel cell buses
FCCC	Framework Convention on Climate Change (also |UNFCCC)
FCM	Forest Concession Management
FCZ	fishery conservation zone
FDA	Food and Drug Administration (USA)
FDI	foreign direct investment
FEMIP	Facility for Euro-Mediterranean Investment and Partnership
FEPS	Final Executive Project Summary (GEF)
FEWS	Famine Early Warning Systems Network
FFA (1)	Forum Fisheries Agency
FFA (2)	Framework for Action (GWP)
FFC	Forum Fisheries Committee
FfD	Financing for Development (also FFD)
FFEM	French Fund for the Global Environment
FGRA	*Fundación Río Arronte* (Mexico)
FHI	Family Health International
FI	financial initiative (UNEP)
FIDA	Inter-American Forum on Environmental Law
FIDIC	International Federation of Consulting Engineers
FIELD	Foundation of International Law Development
FINNIDA	Finnish International Development Agency
FION	Federation for International Education in The Netherlands
FIS	International Seed Trade Federation
FishNet	Fisheries Information Network
FLACSO	Latin American Social Science Faculty
FLEG	Forest Law Enforcement and Governance
FLEGT	Forest Law Enforcement, Governance and Trade
FLR	forest landscape restoration
FMA	*Fundación* Miguel Alemán (Mexico)
FMCN	*Fundación para la Conservación de la Naturaleza* (Mexico)
FMESD	Ministry of Ecology and Sustainable Development (France)

FMSP	First Meeting of the States Parties
FMU	forest management unit
FN (1)	*Fundación Natura* (many Latin American Countries)
FN (2)	First Nations (Canada)
FO	Foreign Office
FOC (1)	Friends of the Chair
FOC (2)	Flag of Convenience
FoEI	Friends of the Earth International
FOEN	Federal Office for the Environment (Switzerland)
FOREM	Foundation of River and Watershed Environment Management (Japan)
FORNESSA	Forestry Research Network for Sub-Saharan Africa
FOSA	Forestry Outlook Study for Africa
FP	family planning
FPG	Finance Partners Group (GWP)
FRA	forest resource assessment
FRICS	Foundation of River and Basin Integrated Communication (Japan)
FRIEND	Flow Regimes from International Experimental and Network Data (UNESCO)
FROG	first raise our growth
FRW	Friends of the Right to Water
FSC	Forest Stewardship Council
FSO	Fund for Special Operations (IDB)
FSP	*Fonds de solidarité prioritaire* (France)
FSU	Former Soviet Union
FT	fuzzy thinking
FTA (1)	Free Trade Area of the Americas
FTA (2)	Free Trade Area
FTAA	Free Trade Area of the Americas
FTE	full-time equivalent
FTI	fast track initiative
FWCW	Fourth World Conference on Women
FY	fiscal year

G

G (1)	general distribution (document identification)
G (2)	Group of ... 3, 4, 5, ...
G3	UK, Germany and France
G4	Japan, Germany, India, Brazil
G5 (old)	UK, China, France, Russia and US
G5 (new)	UK, France, Germany, Italy and Spain
G6 (old)	US, Japan, Germany, France, Italy and UK
G6 (new)	UK, China, France, Russia, US and Germany
G7	US, Japan, Germany, France, UK, Italy and Canada
G8	G7 and Russia

G8+	G8 and China
G8+ (new)	G8+, plus India and Brazil
G10	A group of central bankers from 10 countries united under the 1988 Basle Agreement
G13	The Netherlands and 12 other nations supporting radical UN reform
G15	Summit level group of developing countries
G20	Finance ministers and central bank governors representing 19 governments, the EU and the Bretton Woods Institutions (WB, IMF)
G21	A group of developing countries that coalesced at the WTO
G77 + China	Group of 77 developing countries plus China (now includes nearly 150 governments)
G90	ACP and HIPC countries
GA	UN General Assembly
GAAS	Ghana Academy of Arts and Sciences
GAIM	Global Analysis and Modeling
GAS	Guarani Aquifer System
GATS	General Agreement on Trade in Services
GATT	General Agreement on Tariffs and Trade
GAW	Global Atmospheric Watch
GBA	Global Biodiversity Assessment
GBF	Global Biodiversity Forum
GBIF	Global Biodiversity Information Facility
GBS	Global Biodiversity Strategy
GC	Governing Council
GC/GMEF	Governing Council/Global Ministerial Environment Forum
GCA	Global Coalition for Africa
GCC (1)	global climate change
GCC (2)	Global Climate Coalition
GCC(3)	Gulf Cooperation Council
GCI	Green Cross International
GCM	general circulation model
GCOS	Global Climate Observing System
GCP	Government Cooperative Programme (FAO)
GCRIO	US Global Change Research Information Office
GCRMN	Global Coral Reef Monitoring Network
GCTE	Global Change and Terrestrial Ecosystems
GCU	global currency unit
GD	global deal
GDI	Gender-related Development Index
GDIN	Global Disaster Information Network (USDS)
GDLN	Global Development Learning Network (WB)
GDP	gross domestic product
GDP_{AGR}	percentage of GDP produced by agricultural sector
GDP_{CAP}	gross domestic product per capita

GEA	Global Environmental Action
GECHS	Global Environmental Change and Human Security
GEF	Global Environment Facility
GEFIA	Global Environment Facility Interim Approval
GEF-IN	Global Environment Facility International Notes
GEF-IW	Global Environment Facility International Waters
GEFOP	Global Environment Facility Operations Committee
GEFPID	Project Information Document (GEFWB)
GEFRC	Global Environment Facility Regional Coordinator
GEFSEC	Global Environment Facility Secretariat
GEFTF	Global Environment Facility Trust Fund
GEG	Global Environmental Governance
GEM	Global Environmental Mechanism
GEMI	Global Environmental Management Initiative
GEMS	Global Environment Monitoring System (UNEP)
GEO (1)	Global Environment Outlook report (UNEP)
GEO (2)	Global Environmental Organization
GEOHAB	Global Ecology and Oceanography of Harmful Algal Blooms (UNESCO)
GEOS	Global Environmental and Oceans Sciences
GEOSS	Global Earth Observing System of Systems
GESAMP	Group of Experts on the Scientific Aspects of Marine Pollution
GESI	Global Environmental Sanitation Initiative
GEST	Global Evaluation of Sediment Transport
GET	Global Environment Trust Fund
GETF	Global Environment Technology Foundation
GEWEX	Global Energy and Water Cycle Experiment
GFAR	Global Forum on Agricultural Research
GFE	Global Fund for the Environment
GFMC	Global Fire Monitoring Center
GFO	Global Forum on Oceans, Coasts and Islands
GFRA	Global Forest Resources Assessment
GFSE	Global Forum on Sustainable Energy
Gg	gigagram
GHG	greenhouse gas
GHP	GEWEX Hydrometeorology Panel
GIBIP	Green Industry Biotechnology Platform
GIDP	Gender in Development Programme (UNDP)
GIFAR	Global Forum on Agricultural Research
GIPME	Global Investigation on Pollution in the Marine Environment
GIS	geographic information system
GISD	Geographic Information for Sustainable Development
GISP	Global Invasive Species Programme
GIWA	Global International Waters Assessment (GEF)
GLASOD	Human Induced Soil Degradation
GLIDE	global identifier number (UN)

GLIMS	global land ice measurements from space
GLOBE	Global Legislators Organization for a Balanced Environment
GM (1)	genetically modified
GM (2)	global mechanism
GMA	global assessment on the marine environment
GMEF	Global Ministerial Environment Forum
GMES	Global Monitoring for Environment and Security
GMET	General Multilingual Environmental Thesaurus
GMFS	Global Monitoring for Food Security
GMO	genetically modified organism
GMSR	Greater Mekong (River) Sub-region
GNF	Global Nature Fund
GNI	gross national income
GNIP	Global Network for Isotopes in Precipitation
GNP	gross national product
GO	Global Environmental Objective (GEF)
GOE	Group of Experts
GOFC	global observation of forest cover
GONGO	government-organized NGO
GOOS	Global Ocean Observing System
GOS	Global Observing System (WMO)
GOs	governmental organizations
GOSIC	Global Observation Systems Information Center
'GOUTHE'	Global Observatory of Units for Teaching, Training and Ethics (UNESCO)
GP (1)	Government of Portugal
GP (2)	good practice
GP (3)	Greenpeace International
GPA	Global Programme of Action
GPCC	Global Precipitation and Climatology Centre
GPF	Global Policy Forum
GPG (1)	global public goods
GPG (2)	good practice guide
gpgNet	Global Public Goods Network
GPI	gender parity index
GPS	global positioning system
GRACE	gravity recovery and climate experiment
GRAIN	Genetic Resources Action International
GRAPHIC	Groundwater Resources Assessment under Pressures of Humanity and Climate Change
GRASP	Great Ape Survival Project
GRAVITY	global risk and vulnerability index trend per year
GRC	Governance-related European Forestry Commission Conditionalities
GRDC	Global Runoff Data Center
GRI	global reporting initiative
GRID	Global Resource Information Database (UN)

GRINGO	government-run NGO
GRIWAC	Gansu Research Institute on Water Conservation (China)
GRO	grassroots organization
GROMS	Global Register of Migratory Species
GroWI	Global Review of Wetland Resources and Priorities for Wetland Inventory
GRSO	grassroots support organization
GRULAC	Latin American and Caribbean Group
GRWHC	Global Rainwater Harvesting Collective (India, The Netherlands)
GS (1)	gold standard
GS (2)	General Secretariat
GSCO	Global Social Change Organization
GSFC	Goddard Space Flight Center
GSP	Generalized System of Preferences
GSPC	Global Strategy for Plant Conservation (CBD)
GSTP	Global System of Trade Preferences (UNCTAD)
GTI	Global Taxonomy Initiative
GTN-H	Global Terrestrial Network on Hydrology
GTOS	Global Terrestrial Observing System
GTRZ	German Association for Technical Cooperation
GTSC	GTOS Steering Committee
GTZ	German Technical Cooperation Agency
GURTs	genetic use restriction technologies
GVP	gross village product
G-WADI	Global Network – Water and Development Information for Arid Lands
GW	global warming
GWA	Gender and Water Alliance
GwES	groundwater in emergency situations
GWI (1)	Global Water Initiative
GWI (2)	global water intelligence
GWI (3)	Ground Water Institute
GWP (1)	Global Warming Potential (UNFCCC)
GWP (2)	Global Water Partnership
GWP-CA	Central American Programme of the GWP
GWP-CACENA	Central Asia and the Caucasus Programme of the GWP
GWP-CEE	Central and Eastern Europe Programme of the GWP
GWP-China	China Programme of the GWP
GWP-EA	Eastern Africa Programme of the GWP
GWP-MED	Mediterranean Programme of the GWP
GWP-PAC	Australia and the Pacific Programme of the GWP
GWP-SA	Southern Africa Programme of the GWP
GWP-SAM	South American Programme of the GWP
GWP-SAS	South Asia Programme of the GWP
GWP-SEA	Southeast Asia Programme of the GWP
GWP-TACs	Global Water Partnership – Technical Advisory Committees 2000

GWP-WA	Western Africa Programme of the GWP
GWPO	Global Water Partnership Organization
GWS (1)	George Wright Society
GWS (2)	Global Water Systems
GWSATC	Global Water Science, Assessment and Training Center
GWSP	Global Water System Project
GYF	Global Youth Forum (UNEP)

H

H2020	IAHS Working Group on Hydrology
HABITAT	United Nations Centre for Human Settlement
HAS	Hungarian Academy of Sciences
HCFC	halogenated CFCs
HCFCs	hydrochlorofluorocarbons
HD	Human Development Network
HDI	Human Development Index (UNDP)
HDP	Human Dimensions of Global Environmental Change Programme
HDR	Human Development Report (UNDP)
HELCOM	Baltic Marine Environment Protection Commission (Helsinki Commission)
HELP	Hydrology for the Environment, Life and Policy (UNESCO-IHP)
HEM	harmonization of environmental measurement unit
HFCs	hydrofluorocarbons
HG	Head of Government
HGWP	high global warming potential
HI/HYVs	high-input and high yield hybrid crop varieties
HIA	Health Impact Assessment
HIPC	Heavily Indebted Poor Countries
HIV/AIDS	human immunodeficiency virus (UN)
HLCOMO	high-level committee of ministers and officials (UNEP)
HLM	High Level Meeting
HNP	health, nutrition and population
HNS (1)	International Convention on Liability and Compensation for Damage in Connection with the Carriage of Hazardous and Noxious Substances (IMO)
HNS (2)	hazard and noxious substances (IMO)
HOMS	Hydrological Operational Multipurpose System
HPI	human poverty index
HQ	headquarters
HRC	Human Rights Commission
HRD	human resources development
HRH	His/Her Royal Highness
HRI	Hydraulic Research Institute (Egypt)
HS	Head of State

HSI	health status index
HSRC	Human Sciences Research Council
HST	Hubble Space Telescope
HTPI	handling, transport, packaging and identification
HTS	harmonized tariff schedule
HURPEC	Human Rights and Peace Campaign
HWI	human wellbeing index
HWP	harvested wood products (UNFCCC)
HWRP	Hydrology Water Resources Programme

I

I-CMAP	First Mesoamerican Congress on Protected Areas
IA (1)	implementing agency (GEF)
IA (2)	implementing arrangements (IEA)
IA (3)	institutional analysis (WB)
IA (4)	Irrigation Association (USA)
IAB	Industry Advisory Board (IEA)
IABIN	Inter-American Biodiversity Information Network
IAC	Informal Advisory Committee
IACD	Inter-American Agency for Cooperation and Development (OAS)
IACNDR	Inter-American Committee for Natural Disaster Reduction
IACSD	Interagency Committee on Sustainable Development (UN)
IADB (1)	Inter-American Development Bank (IDB)
IADB (2)	Inter-American Defense Board
IADRIP	Inter-American Declaration on the Rights of Indigenous Peoples
IADWM	Inter-American Dialogue on Water Management
IAEA	International Atomic Energy Agency (UN)
IAEC	Inter-American Economic Council
IAEE	International Association for Energy Economics
IAF (1)	Inter-American Foundation
IAF (2)	Inter-American Fund
IAF (3)	International Arrangement on Forests
IAH (1)	International Association of Hydrologists
IAH (2)	International Association of Hydrogeologists
IAHR	International Association of Hydraulic Engineering and Research
IAHS	International Association of Hydrological Sciences
IAI	Inter-American Institute for Global Change Research
IAIA	International Association for Impact Assessment
IAM	integrated area management
IANAS	Inter-American Network of Academies of Science
IAP	Inter-Academy Panel on International Issues (TWAS)

IAP-WASAD	International Action Programme on Water and Sustainable Agricultural Development (FAO)
IARC	International Agriculture Research Center
IAS (1)	Academy of Sciences (Indonesia, Iran, Iraq)
IAS (2)	Islamic Academy of Science (Jordan)
IASI	Inter-Americas Sea Initiative
IASP	Inter-American Strategic Plan for Policy and Vulnerability Reduction
IAST	Institute of Applied Science and Technology (Guyana)
IASWS	International Association for Sediment and Water Science
IATF	Interagency Task Force on Sustainable Development (OAS)
IATFDR	Inter-Agency Task Force on Disaster Reduction (UNISDR)
IATTC	Inter-American Tropical Tuna Commission
IBA	International Bird Area
IBAMA	Institute of Environment and Renewable Resources (Brazil)
IBC	International Bioethics Committee
IBE	International Bureau of Education (Geneva, Switzerland) (UNESCO)
IBNET	Water and Sanitation International Benchmarking Network
IBP	International Biological Programme
IBPGR	International Board for Plant Genetic Resources (CGIAR)
IBRD	International Bank for Reconstruction and Development (WB)
IBSP	International Basic Science Programme
IBTA	institution-building/technical assistance
IC (1)	Implementation Committee (GEF/STAP)
IC (2)	initial communication
IC (3)	Inter-Sessional Committee
ICAD	Integrated Conservation and Development Project (GEF)
ICALPE	International Centre for Alpine Environments
ICAO	International Civil Aviation Organization
ICARDA	International Center for Agricultural Research in the Dry Areas
ICARM	Integrated Coastal and River Basin Management
ICASE	International Council of Associations for Science Education
ICBA	International Center for Biosaline Agriculture
ICC (1)	International Chamber of Commerce
ICC (2)	International Criminal Court
ICC (3)	Inuit Circumpolar Conference
ICCAT	International Convention on the Conservation of the Atlantic Tuna

ICCBD	Intergovernmental Committee on the Convention on Biological Diversity
ICCD (1)	Intergovernmental Committee on the Convention to Combat Desertification
ICCD (2)	Intergovernmental Climate Change Directorate
ICCE	IAHS International Commission on Continental Erosion
ICCEB	International Center for Genetic Engineering and Biotechnology (UNIDO)
ICCP	Intergovernmental Committee on the Cartagena Protocol on Biosafety (CBD)
ICCPR	International Covenant on Civil and Political Rights
ICCROM	International Centre for the Study of the Preservation and Restoration of Cultural Property
ICDA	International Coalition of Development Action
ICDDR	International Centre for Diarrhea Diseases Research (Bangladesh)
ICDI	Independent Commission on International Development Issues (The Brandt Commission)
ICDP	Integrated Conservation Development Project (GEF)
ICES	International Council for the Exploration of the Sea
ICESA	International Commission for Earth Sciences in Africa (Botswana)
ICESCR	International Covenant on Economic, Social and Cultural Rights
ICFD	International Conference on Financing for Development
ICFPA	International Council of Forest and Paper Associations
ICFTU	International Confederation of Free Trade Unions
ICG	International Crises Group
ICH	International Heritage Convention
ICHARM	International Centre for Water Hazard and Risk Management (Japan)
ICID	International Commission on Irrigation and Drainage
ICIMOD	International Centre for Integrated Mountain Development
ICJ	International Court of Justice (UN)
ICLARM	International Centre for Living Aquatic Resources Management
ICLEI	International Council for Local Environmental Initiatives
ICLR	Institute for Catastrophic Loss Reduction
ICM (1)	Integrated Coastal Management
ICM (2)	International Conflict Management
ICM (3)	Information and Communication Management
ICO	*Instituto de Crédito Oficial* (Spain)
ICOH	International Commission on Occupational Health
ICOLD	International Commission on Large Dams
ICOMOS	International Council of Monuments and Sites
ICP	Informal Consultative Process on Oceans and the Law of the Sea

ICPD	International Conference on Population and Development
ICPDR	International Commission for the Protection of the Danube River
ICPs	International Cooperative Programmes
ICRAF	International Centre for Research in Agroforestry
ICRAN	International Coral Reef Action Network
ICRC (1)	Interim Chemical Review Committee
ICRC (2)	International Committee of the Red Cross, Red Crescent and Red Crystal Societies
ICRG	International Consulting Resources Group
ICRI	International Coral Reef Initiative
ICRISAT	International Crops Research Institute for the Semi-Arid Tropics
ICS (1)	International School for Science (UNIDO)
ICS (2)	International Coordinating Secretariat
ICSID	International Centre for Settlement of Investment Disputes (WB)
ICSU	International Council of Science Unions
ICT (1)	information and communications technology
ICT (2)	internet communication technology
ICT (3)	international communication technology
ICTP	International Centre for Theoretical Physics (Trieste, Italy) (UNESCO)
ICUC	International Centre for Underutilized Crops
ICUS	International Center for Urban Safety Engineering (Japan)
ICWC	Interstate Commission for Water Coordination (Central Asian States)
ICWE	International Conference on Water and the Environment (Dublin)
ICZM	International Coastal Zone Management
ID	Institutional Development
IDA (1)	International Development Association (WB)
IDA (2)	International Decade(s) for Action
IDA (3)	International Desalination Association
IDAC	International Disaster Advisory Committee
IDB (1)	Inter-American Development Bank
IDB (2)	Inter-American Defense Board
IDB (3)	Islamic Development Bank
IDDRI	Institute of International Relations and Sustainable Development (France)
IDE	International Development Enterprises
IDEA	International Institute for Democracy and Electoral Assistance
IDF	Institutional Development Facility
IDGEC	Institutional Dimensions of Global Environmental Change

IDGs	International Development Goals
IDNDR	International Decade for Natural Disaster Reduction
IDP (1)	Integrated Development Plan
IDP (2)	internal discussion paper (WB)
IDP (3)	internally displaced person (UN)
IDR	in-depth review (UNFCCC)
IDRC	International Development Research Centre (Canada)
IDS	Institute of Development Studies
IDT	International Development Target
IDU	internal document unit (WB)
IEA (1)	International Energy Agency
IEA (2)	International Environmental Agreement
IEEP	Institute for European Environment Policy
IEG	International Environmental Governance
IEGS	Institute for Global Environmental Strategies
IEHS	Institute for Environment and Human Security (UNU)
IEN	Indigenous Environment Network (US)
IEO	Industry and Environment Office (UNEP)
IEP	intergenerational equity principle
IEPS	Initial Executive Project Summary (GEF)
IESALC	International Institute for Higher Education in Latin America and the Caribbean (UNESCO/Venezuela)
IET	International Emissions Trading (UNFCCC)
IETA	International Emissions Trading Association
IETC	International Environmental Technology Centre
IFAD	International Fund for Agricultural Development
IFAP	International Federation of Agricultural Producers
IFAS	International Fund for the Aral Sea
IFAW	International Fund for Animal Welfare
IFC	International Finance Corporation (WB)
IFCS	International Forum on Chemical Safety
IFEJ	International Federation of Environmental Journalists
IFF (1)	Intergovernmental Forum on Forests
IFF (2)	International Finance Facility
IFI (1)	International Financing Institution
IFI (2)	International Flood Initiative (UNESCO, WMO, UNU, UNISDR, IAHS)
IFIP	International Funders for Indigenous Peoples
IFM	integrated flood management
IFNet	International Flood Network and Flood Alert System
IFPRI	International Food Policy Research Institute
IFRC	International Federation of Red Cross, Red Crescent and Red Crystal Societies
IFREMER	French Research Institute for the Exploitation of the Sea
IG	inter-governmental
IGAD	International Authority on Development
IGBC	Intergovernmental Bioethics Committee
IGBP	International Geosphere-Biosphere Programme
IGC (1)	International Green Cross

IGC (2)	intergovernmental consultation
IGCP	International Geoscience Programme
IGES	Institute for Global Environmental Strategies (Japan Environment Agency)
IGFA	International Group of Funding Agencies for Global Change
IGLU	International Union of Local Authorities
IGM	Open-ended Intergovernmental Group of Ministers or their Representatives
IGO	Inter-Governmental Organization
IGOS (1)	Integrated Global Observing Strategy
IGOS (2)	Integrated Global Water Cycle Observations
IGR	intergovernmental review
IGRAC	International Groundwater Resources Assessment Centre, Utrecht, The Netherlands (UNESCO, WHO)
IGU	International Geographical Union
IGWAC	International Ground Water Assessment Committee (UNESCO)
IGY	International Geophysical Year
IHA	International Hydropower Association
IHD	International Hydrological Decade (1965–1974)
IHDP	International Human Dimensions Programme on Global Change
IHE-Delft	International Institute for Infrastructural, Hydraulic and Environmental Engineering (1957–2002, replaced by UNESCO-IHE in 2003, The Netherlands)
IHO	International Hydrographic Organization
IHP	International Hydrological Programme (UNESCO)
IHP-V	fifth phase of IHP (1996–2001)
IHP-VI	sixth phase of IHP (2002–2007)
IHP-VII	seventh phase of IHP (2008–2013)
IHS	International Institute for Housing and Urban Development (The Netherlands)
IIASA (1)	International Institute for Applied Systems Analysis
IIASA (2)	Institute of Islamic and Arabic Sciences in America
IICA	Inter-American Institute for Cooperation on Agriculture
IICBA	International Institute for Capacity-Building in Africa (UNESCO/Ethiopia)
IICD	International Institute for Communication and Development
IICG	International Initiative on Corruption in Governance
IIDEA	International Institute for Democracy and Electoral Assistance
IIE	Institute for International Economics
IIED	International Institute for Environment and Development
IIEP	International Institute for Educational Planning (UNESCO/Argentina)
IIFB	International Indigenous Forum on Biodiversity
IIMI	International Irrigation Management Institute

IIMS	Integrated Information Management System
IIP	International Implementation Priorities
IIRR	International Institute for Rural Reconstruction
IISD	International Institute for Sustainable Development (Canada)
IIT	Indian Institute of Technology
IITA	International Institute of Tropical Agriculture
IITE	Institute for Information Technologies in Education (UNESCO/Russian Federation)
IJC	International Joint Commission
i-learning (1)	innovative learning
i-learning (2)	internet learning
ILA	International Law Association
ILAC	Latin American and Caribbean Initiative for Sustainable Societies
ILC	International Law Commission
ILEC	International Lake Environment Committee (Japan)
ILO (1)	International Labor Organization (UN)
ILO (2)	International Landslide Organization
ILRAD	International Laboratory for Research on Animal Disease
ILRI	International Livestock Research Institute
ILSI	International Life Sciences Institute
ILTER	International Long-Term Ecological Research
IMCAM	Integrated Marine and Coastal Area Management
IMCO	Intergovernmental Maritime Consultative Organization
IME	*Institut Méditerranéen de l'Eau* (France)
IMF	International Monetary Fund
IMO	International Maritime Organization
IMP	Information Management Plan
IMS	information management specialist
IMT	irrigation management transfer
IMTA	*Instituto Mexicano de Tecnologia del Agua*
INBAR	International Network for Bamboo and Rattan
INBO	International Network of Basin Organizations
INC	International Negotiation Committee
INCB	International Narcotics Control Board
INC/FCCC	Intergovernmental Negotiation Committee for a Framework Convention on Climate Change
INCD	International Negotiation Committee on Desertification
INDOEX	Indian Ocean Experiment
INEAM	Institute for Advanced Studies for the Americas (OAS)
INENCO	Centre for International Environmental Cooperation
Inf	information (documents identification)
INFN	National Institute for Nuclear Physics (Italy)
INFOCAP	Information Exchange Network on Capacity Building for the Sound Management of Chemicals
INFOTERRA	International Environmental Information System
INGO (1)	individual-based NGO

INGO (2)	international NGO
INPE	National Institute for Space Research (Brazil)
INPIM	International Network on Participatory Irrigation Management
INRA	National Institute for Agricultural Research (France)
INSA	Indian National Science Academy
INSERM	French National Institute for Health and Medical Research
INSTRAW	International Research and Training Institute for the Advancement of Women (UN)
INSULA	International Scientific Council for Sustainable Development
INTAL	Institute for the Integration of Latin America and the Caribbean
INTECOL	International Association of Ecology
INV00	Inventory Submission for the Year 2000
INWEB	International Network of Water Environment Centres for the Balkans
INWEH	International Network on Water, Environment and Health (UNU)
INWENT	Capacity Building International (Germany)
INWEPF	International Network for Water and Ecosystem in Paddy Fields
INWRDAM	Inter-Islamic Network on Water Resources Development and Management (Iran)
IO (1)	international organization
IO (2)	input-output
IOC (1)	Intergovernmental Oceanographic Commission (UNESCO)
IOC (2)	Indian Ocean Commission
IOCARIBE	Intergovernmental Oceanographic Commission – Caribbean (UNESCO)
IOCC	Inter-Organization Coordinating Committee
IOCU	International Organization of Consumers Unions
IODE	International Data and Information Exchange
IOI	International Oceans Institute
IOS	Internal Oversight Service (UN)
IOSEA	Indian Ocean-South East Asia
IP (1)	implementation progress (GEF)
IP (2)	intellectual property
IPAD	Portuguese Institute for Development Assistance
IPC (1)	integrated pest control
IPC (2)	integrated pollution control
IPCC	Intergovernmental Panel on Climate Change (UNEP/WHO)
IPDP	Indigenous Peoples Development Plan (WB)
IPE	independent panel of experts
IPED	International Panel of Experts on Desertification

IPF (1)	Intergovernmental Panel on Forests
IPF (2)	Indicative Planning Figure (UNDP)
IPGR	International Plant Genetic Resources Institute
IPGRI	International Plant Genetic Resources Institute
IPIECA	International Petroleum Industry Environmental Conservation Association
IPM (1)	integrated pest management
IPM (2)	International Preparatory Meeting
IPO (1)	Indigenous Peoples Organization
IPO (2)	Initial Public Offering
IPPC (1)	International Plant Protection Convention
IPPC (2)	integrated pollution prevention and control
IPPF	International Planned Parenthood Federation
IPR	intellectual property rights
IPS	Institute for Policy Studies
IPTRID	International Programme for Technology and Research in Irrigation and Drainage
IPU	Inter-Parliamentary Union
IQC	indefinite quantity contract (USAID)
IR	International River Foundation (Australia)
IRBM	Integrated River Basin Management
IRC	International Research Centre for Water Supply and Sanitation (The Netherlands)
IRCSA	International Rainwater Catchment Systems Association
IRD	Scientific Research Institute for Cooperative Development (France)
IREA	International Renewable Energy Alliance
IRFD	International Research Foundation for Development
IRHA	International Rainwater Harvesting Alliance
IRI (1)	International Resource Institute
IRI (2)	International Research Institute for Climate Prediction
IRI (3)	International Research Institute for Climate and Society
IRIS	Institute for Research and Innovation in Sustainability (Canada)
IRN	International Rivers Network
IRPTC	International Register of Potentially Toxic Chemicals
IRR	internal rate of return
IRRI	International Rice Research Institute
IRTCES	International Research and Training Centre on Erosion and Sedimentation (UNESCO/China)
IRTCUD	International Research and Training Center on Urban Drainage (UNESCO/Malaysia)
IRWR	internal renewable water resource
ISA	International Seabed Authority
ISARM	International Shared Aquifer Resource Management
ISBN	International Standard Book Numbers
IsDB	Islamic Development Bank
ISDF	International Sustainable Development Foundation
ISDN	Integrated Services Digital Network

ISDR (1)	International Strategy for Disaster Reduction (UN)
ISDR (2)	Institute for Sustainable Development and Research (India)
ISESCO	Islamic Educational, Scientific and Cultural Organization
ISET	Institute for Social and Environmental Transition
ISEW	Index of Sustainable Economic Welfare
ISGWAS	International Symposium on Groundwater Sustainability
ISI	International Sediment Initiative (UNESCO)
ISIC	International Standard Industrial Classification
ISM	Integrated Island Management
ISNAR	International Service for National Agricultural Research
ISO	International Organization for Standardization
ISOC	Inter-Sessional Meeting on the Operations of the Convention
ISP (1)	Inter-American Strategy for the Promotion of Public Participation in Decision-making for Sustainable Development
ISP (2)	integral sustainable production units
ISRIC	International Soil and Reference Information Center
ISS	Institute of Social Studies (The Netherlands)
ISSC	International Social Science Council
ISSN	International Standard Series Numbers
ISW	International Secretariat for Water (Canada)
IT (1)	information technology
IT (2)	industrial transformation
ITAIPU	*Central Hidroélectrica Itaipu Binacional* (Brazil, Paraguay)
ITC (1)	International Institute for Geo-Information Science and Earth Observation (The Netherlands)
ITC (2)	International Trade Centre
ITCSD	International Centre for Trade and Sustainable Development
ITDG	Intermediate Technology Development Group
ITE	Institute for Terrestrial Ecology
ITESM	*Instituto Tecnológico de Estudios Superiores de Monterrey* (México)
ITFF	Interagency Task Force on Forests
ITLOS	International Tribunal for the Law of the Sea
ITNs	insecticide-treated nets
ITO	International Telecommunication Union
ITOPF	International Tanker Owners Pollution Federation
ITPGR(FA)	International Treaty on Plant Genetic Resources for Food and Agriculture (formerly the International Undertaking)
ITQs	individual iransferable quotas
ITR	independent technical review (GEF)
ITTA	International Tropical Timber Agreement
ITTC	International Tropical Timber Council
ITTO	International Tropical Timber Organization
ITU	International Telecommunications Union
IU	international undertaking (CGRFA)

IUBS	International Union of Biological Sciences
IUCN	World Conservation Union (formerly the International Union for the Conservation of Nature and Natural Resources)
IUFRO	International Union of Forestry Research Organizations
IUGG	International Union of Geodesy and Geophysics
IUPGR	International Undertaking on Plant Genetic Resources
IUTAM	International Union of Theoretical and Applied Mechanics
IUU	illegal, unregulated, unreported fishing
IU-WG	International Undertaking Working Group
IVA	industrial value added
IVM	Institute for Environmental Studies
IW	International Waters Focal Area of the GEF
IW-LEARN	International Water Learning Exchange and Resource Network (UNDP)
IWA	International Water Association
IWALC	International Water Associations Liaison Committee
IWC (1)	International Whaling Commission
IWC (2)	International Water Centre (Australia)
IWCF	International Water Cooperation Facility (UNESCO, WWC)
IWGENV	Inter-secretariat Working Group on Environment Studies
IWGMP	Intergovernmental Working Group on Marine Pollution
IWHA	International Water History Association
IWI	indigenous water initiative
IWM	Institute of Water Modeling (Bangladesh)
IWMI	International Water Management Institute (Sri Lanka)
IWP	International Waters Protection
IWR	Institute for Water Resources (USACE)
IWRA	International Water Resources Association
IWRB	International Waterfowl Research Bureau
IWRM	Integrated Water Resource Management
IWRN	Inter-American Water Resources Network (OAS)
IWSD	Institute of Water and Sanitation Development
IWT	inland water transport
IYDD	International Year of Deserts and Desertification
IYF	International Year of Freshwater (2003)
IYFW	International Year of Freshwater (2003)
IYM	International Year of Mountains

J

JAC	Joint Advisory Committee
JAROS	Japan Resources Observation System Organization
JAWA	Japan Water Resource Association
JBIC	Japan Bank for International Cooperation

JCEDAR	Joint Committee on Environment and Development in the Arab Region
JCF	Japan Carbon Finance
JCOMM	Joint WMO/IOC Technical Commission for Oceanography and Marine Meteorology
JDEC	Japan Dam Engineering Center
JGRF	Japan GHG Reduction Fund
JI	joint implementation (UNFCCC)
JICA	Japan International Cooperation Agency
JIID	Japanese Institute of Irrigation and Drainage
JIN	Joint Implementation Network
JIQ	Joint Implementation Quarterly
JIU	joint inspection unit
JIWET	Japan Institute of Wastewater Engineering Technology
JMP	Joint Monitoring Programme (for water supply and sanitation; UNICEF, WHO)
JMPR	Joint Meeting on Pesticide Residues (FAO/WHO)
JPAC	Joint Public Advisory Committee (CEC)
JPO	junior professional officer
JPOI	Johannesburg Plan of Implementation
JRA	Japan River Association
JRC (1)	Joint Research Council
JRC (2)	Joint River Commission
JSTC	Joint Scientific and Technical Committee (GCOS)
JUSSCANNZ	Japan, US, Switzerland, Canada, Australia, Norway and New Zealand (the non-EU industrialized countries)
JUWFI	Joint UNESCO/WMO Flood Initiative
JWA	Japan Water Agency
JWF	Japan Water Forum
JWG	Joint Working Group on Compliance (UNFCCC)
JWRA	Japan Water Resources Association
JWRC	Japan Water Reclamation Committee

K

KARI	Kenya Agricultural Research Institute
KFAS	Kuwait Foundation for the Advancement of Science
KFW	*Kreditanstalt für Wiederaufbau* (Germany)
KI	knowledge index
KIT	Royal Tropical Institute (The Netherlands)
KM	knowledge management
KMOE	Korean Ministry of Environment
KMS	Knowledge Management System
KNAW	Royal Netherlands Academy of Arts and Sciences
KNMI	Royal Netherlands Meteorological Institute
KOICA	Korea International Cooperation Agency
KOWACO	Korean Water Resources Corporation (see Kwater)

KP	Kyoto Protocol
KWAHO	Kenya Water for Health Organization
Kwater	Korean Water Resources Corporation

L

L	limited distribution (document identification)
LA (1)	Local Administration (Italy)
LA (2)	Latin America
LA21s	Local Agendas 21
LA-RED	Network for Social Studies on Disaster Prevention in Latin America
LAC	Latin America and the Caribbean
LACFC	Latin American and Caribbean Forestry Commission
LAIA	Latin American Integration Association
LAN	local area network
LANBO	Latin American Network of Basin Organizations
LAS (1)	League of Arab States
LAS (2)	Lithuanian Academy of Sciences
LAWETnet	Latin American Water Education and Training Network
LBA (1)	land-based activities
LBA (2)	Large Scale Biosphere-Atmosphere Experiment in Amazonia
LBI	legally binding instrument
LBS	land-based sources protocol
LC (1)	Latin America and the Caribbean (document identification)
LC (2)	life cycle
LCA	life-cycle assessments
LCCP	life-cycle climate performance
LCIA	life-cycle impact assessments
LCSES	Latin American and Caribbean Environmentally and Socially Sustainable Development Unit (WB)
LDC	least developed country
LEAD	leadership for environment and development
LEG	legal department (GEF-WB)
LEGEN	Environment Negotiations Unit of the Legal Department (WB)
LFCC	low forest cover countries (UNFF)
LFG	landfill gas
LG	liaison group
LIL	learning and innovation loan
LINKS	Local and Indigenous Knowledge Systems
LISA	low-impact sustainable agriculture
LLDC	land-locked developed countries
LME (1)	large marine ecosystems
LME (2)	learning management environments (WB)

LMMC	like-minded megadiverse countries
LMO	living modified organism (CBD)
LOA	letter of agreement (GEF)
LogFrame	logical framework
LOI	letter of inquiry
LOICZ	land-ocean interaction in the coastal zone
LOS	Law of the Sea Convention
LP (1)	loan proposal (IDB)
LP (2)	*Laissez-Passer*, UN travel document
LPI	Living Planet Index
LR	liability and redress
LRRD	linking relief, rehabilitation and development
LRS	large river system
LRT	long-range transportation
LRTAP	Convention on Long-Range Transboundary Air Pollution (EU)
LTAs	Long-term Agreements (IEA)
LTER	long-term ecological research
LUCC	land-use and land-cover change (IGBP/HDP)
LUCF	land use change and forestry (UNFCCC)
LULUCF	land use, land use change and forestry (UNFCCC)
LUP	land use planning

M

M&E	monitoring and evaluation
MA	Millennium Ecosystem Assessment (UN)
MAB	Man and the Biosphere Programme (UNESCO)
MAC (1)	maximum allowable concentration
MAC (2)	marginal abatement costs
MAC (3)	Marine Aquarium Council
MAD	marginal avoided damage costs
MAE	*Ministére des Affaires Étrangéres* (France)
MAI	Multilateral Agreement on Investment
MAP (1)	Mediterranean Action Plan
MAP (2)	Millennium African Programme
MAR (1)	monitoring, assessment and reporting
MAR (2)	managed aquifer recharge
MAR (3)	mean annual runoff
MARPOL	International Convention for the Prevention of Pollution from Ships
MAS	Mexican Academy of Sciences
MAT	mutually agreed terms
MB (1)	methyl bromide
MB (2)	marginal benefit
MBD	maritime boundary delimitation
MBI	market-based instrument

MC	*Mediocrecito Centrale* (Italy)
MCA	Millennium Challenge Account (US)
MCC	Millennium Challenge Corporation (US)
MCED	Ministerial Conference on Environment and Development
MCPFE	Ministerial Conference on the Protection of Forests in Europe
MCS	monitoring, control and surveillance
MCSD	Mediterranean Commission for Sustainable Development (EU)
MDB	Multilateral Development Bank
MDF	Mediterranean Development Forum
MDGs	Millennium Development Goals
MDG +5	Millennium +5 Summit; World Summit 2005
MDI	Multilateral Development Institution
MDIs	material-dose inhalers
MDIAR	monitoring-data-information-assessment-reporting (EU)
ME-Japan	Ministry of Environment
MEA	Multilateral Environmental Agreement
MEDA	Mediterranean Economic Development Assistance
MEDD	*Ministère de l'Ecologie et du Développement Durable* (France)
MEDECOS	Mediterranean Ecosystems
MEDIES	Mediterranean Education Initiative for Environment and Sustainability
MEDPOL	Programme for the Assessment and Control of Pollution in the Mediterranean Region
MEDTAC	Mediterranean Technical Committee (GWP)
MEP (1)	Member European Parliament
MEP (2)	Mediterranean Environmental Plan
MEP (3)	Memorandum of Economic Policies
MEPC	Marine Environment Protection Committee
MER (1)	market exchange rates
MER (2)	monitoring, evaluation, reporting (WB)
MERCOSUR	Southern Common Market (Argentina, Brazil, Chile, Paraguay, Uruguay, Venezuela)
MERRAC	Marine Environment Emergency Preparedness Response – Regional Activity Centre
MES (1)	markets for environmental services
MES (2)	Ministry of Environment and Science
MESCT	Ministry of Higher Education, Science and Technology
MESRS	Ministry of Higher Education and Scientific Research (D.R. Congo)
METI	Ministry of Economy, Trade and Industry of Japan
MEW	measure of economic welfare
MF (1)	multilateral fund
MF (2)	Ministry of Finance (Belgium)
MFA	Ministry of Foreign Affairs
MFI	micro finance institutions

MFMP	Multilateral Fund for the Montreal Protocol
MFN	most favored nation (Status)
Mg	megagram
MHLC	Multilateral High-Level Conference
MICIT	Ministry of Science and Technology (Latin America)
MICS	Multiple Indicator Cluster Surveys
MIF	multinational investment fund (IDB)
MIGA	Multilateral Investment Guarantee Agency (WB)
MIND	Munasinghe Institute for Development (Sri Lanka)
MinLNV	Ministry of Agriculture, Nature and Food Quality (The Netherlands)
MINREST	Ministry of Scientific and Technological Research (Cameroon)
MIS (1)	management information system
MIS (2)	methods, inventory and science programme (UNFCCC)
MLF	multilateral fund
MLIT	Ministry of Land, Infrastructure and Transport (Japan)
MMA	Ministry of Environment (Brazil)
MMSD	mining, minerals and sustainable development
MMTCDE	million metric tons of carbon dioxide equivalents
MNC	multinational corporation
MNP	Netherlands Environment Assessment Agency
MOC	memorandum of cooperation
MoD	Ministry of Defense
MODIS	moderate resolution imaging spectroradiometer
MOE (1)	Ministry of Environment
MOE (2)	Ministry of Energy
MOEA	Ministry of External Affairs
MOER	Ministry of External Relations
MOEST	Ministry of Education, Science and Technology
MOET	Ministry of Environment and Territory (Italy)
MÖF	Swedish Association for Environmental Journalists
MOFA	Ministry of Foreign Affairs
MOI	Memorandum of Intent
MOJ	Ministry of Justice
MOP (1)	Meeting of the Parties (for a Protocol)
MOP (2)	Memorandum and Recommendation of the President (WB)
MOPH	Ministry of Public Health
MOPW	Ministry of Public Works
MOST (1)	Management of Social Transformations
MOST (2)	Ministry of Science and Technology
MOSTEC	Ministry of Science, Technology, Education and Culture
MOU	Memorandum of Understanding
MOWE	Ministry of Water and Electricity
MOWR	Ministry of Water Resources
MP (1)	Montreal Protocol
MP (2)	Member of Parliament
MPA	marine protected area

MPANET	Marine Parks and Protected Areas Management Network
MPD	maximum permissible doses
MRA	mutual recognition agreement
MRC	Mekong River Commission
MRET	mandatory renewable energy targets (Australia)
MRI	Mitsubishi Research Group
MS (1)	multilateral system (CGRFA)
MS (2)	multistakeholder
MSC	Marine Stewardship Council
MSD	multi-stakeholder dialogue
MSF	Doctors Without Borders (*Médecins Sans Frontières*)
MSP	medium sized project
MSRT	Ministry of Science, Research and Technology (Iran)
MSSD	Mediterranean Strategy for Sustainable Development
MSTCDE	million short tons of carbon dioxide equivalents
MSY	maximum sustainable yield
MTA	material transfer agreement
MTCR	Missile Technology Control Regime
MTNs	multilateral trade negotiations
MTP	medium term plan
MtPA	mountain protected area
MTPW	medium-term programme of work
MTPWWM	Ministry of Transport, Public Works and Water Management (The Netherlands)
MTS	multilateral trading system
MUN	Model United Nations
MUSE	multilateral system for exchange
MV-EU	Majority vote – European Union
MVP	minimum viable population
MWC	International Convention on the Protection of the Rights of all Migrant Workers and Members of their Families
MWR	Ministry of Water Resources
MWRI	Ministry of Water Resources and Irrigation
MXCID	International Commission on Irrigation and Drainage (Mexican National Committee)
MyCapNet	Malaysia Capacity Building Network
MYPOW	multi-year programme of work

N

N_2O	nitrous oxide
NA	North America
NAAEC	North American Agreement on Environmental Cooperation (NAFTA)
NAAS	National Academy of Agricultural Sciences (India)
NABIN	North American Biodiversity Information System
NAC	New Agenda Coalition

NACEC	North American Commission for Environmental Cooperation
NADBANK	North American Development Bank
NAFEC	North American Fund for Environmental Cooperation (CEC)
NAFO	North Atlantic Fisheries Organization
NAFTA	North American Free Trade Agreement (Canada, US, Mexico)
NAFTA-CEC	North American Free Trade Agreement Commission on Environmental Cooperation
NAM	Non-Aligned Movement
NAMEA	national accounting matrix including environmental accounts (The Netherlands)
NAO	National Administrative Office
NAP (1)	National Action Programme
NAP (2)	National Allocation Plan
NAPA	National Adaptation Programme of Action (UNFCCC)
NAPE	National Associations of Professional Environmentalists (Africa)
NAPRI	North American Pollutant Release Inventory
NARBO	Network of Asian River Basin Organization
NARS	National Agricultural Research System
NAS	National Academy of Sciences (US, India, Nigeria)
NASA	National Aeronautics and Space Administration (US)
NASAC	Network of African Science Academies
NASCO	North Atlantic Salmon Conservation Organization
NASDA	National Space Development Agency (Japan)
NASPD	National Association of State Park Directors
NAST	National Academy of Science and Technology (the Philippines)
NATO	North Atlantic Treaty Organization
NAWMP	North American Waterfowl Management Plan
NBCBN-RE	Nile Basin Capacity Building Network for River Engineering
NBI	Nile Basin Initiative (Egypt, Ethiopia, Eritrea, Kenya, D.R. Congo, Tanzania, Rwanda, Burundi, Uganda, Sudan)
NBSAP	National Biodiversity Strategies and Action Plans
NC	National Committee (WB)
NC1	First National Communication
NCAR	National Center for Atmospheric Research (US)
NCB	National Coordinating Body
NCC (1)	National Coordinating Committee
NCC (2)	net contributor country
NCEA	National Center for Environmental Assessment
NCESD	National Council for Environment and Sustainable Development
NCSE	National Council for Science and Environment (US)
NCSP (1)	National Communications Support Programme (GEF)

NCSP (2)	National Country Studies Programme (UNFCCC)
NCST	National Council for Science and Technology (English-speaking Caribbean/Africa)
NDF	Nordic Development Fund
NDMC	National Drought Mitigation Center (US)
NDP	net domestic product
NEA	Nuclear Energy Agency (OECD)
NEAFF	Northeast Asian Forest Forum
NEAP	National Environmental Action Plan
NEC	National Environment Committee
NEDA	Netherlands Development Assistance, Ministry of Foreign Affairs
NEPA	National Environmental Policy Act (US)
NEPAD	New Partnership for Africa's Development
NERC	Natural Environment Research Council (UK)
NETWA	Global Network of Water Anthropology for Water Action
NEX	National Execution (GEF)
NFF	National Forest Foundation (US)
NFI	National Forest Initiative
NFP (1)	National Forest Programme
NFP (2)	National Focal Point
NFP (3)	Netherlands Fellowship Programme
NFPF	National Forest Programme Facility
NGA	nongovernmental actor
NGIP	NonGovernment Investment Program (IBRD)
NGLS	NonGovernmental Liaison Services (UN)
NGO	nongovernmental organization
NGOSC	NGO Steering Committee
NGS	National Greenhouse Strategy (Australia)
NGWA	National Ground Water Association (US)
NH$_3$	ammonia
NHI	National Heritage Institute
NHP	National Historic Park
NHRI	Nanjing Hydraulic Research Institute (China)
NIB	Nordic Investment Bank
NIE	National Institute for the Environment
NIEO	new international economic order
NIH (1)	National Institute of Health
NIH (2)	National Institute for the Humanities
NileIWRnet	IWRM Capacity Building Network for the Nile Basin
NIMBY	not in my backyard
NIPH	National Institute for Public Health
NIR	national inventory reporting
NIS	newly independent states
NLBI	Non-legally Binding Instrument
NMFS	National Marine Fisheries Service (NOAA-US)
NMHS	National Meteorological and Hydrological Service (WMO)
NMSS	National Marine Sanctuary System (NOAA-US)

NMVOC	non-methane volatile organic compounds
NNGO	national NGO
NNP	net national product
NNWS	non-nuclear-weapon state
NOAA	National Oceanic and Atmospheric Administration (US)
NORAD	Norwegian Agency for Development Cooperation
NoWNET	Northern Water Network
NOWPAP	North-West Pacific Action Plan
NO_x	nitrogen oxide
NPO	non-profit organization
NPP	net primary production
NPR	National Park Reserve
NPSP	non-point source pollution
NPT (1)	Treaty on the Non-Proliferation of Nuclear Weapons
NPT (2)	Netherlands Programme for Institutional Strengthening of Post-secondary Education and Training Capacity
NPV	net present value
NRC (1)	National Research Centre (Egypt)
NRC (2)	National Research Council (US)
NRCAN	National Resources Canada
NRCC	National Research Council of Canada
NRDC	Natural Resources Defense Council
NRG4SD	Network of Regional Governments for Sustainable Development
NRSE	new and renewable sources of energy
NRTEE	National Round Table on the Environment and the Economy (Canada)
NS	natural step
NSC	National Selection Committee
NSDC	National Sustainable Development Councils
NSDWDC	Network on Safe Drinking Water in Developing Countries (TWNSO/UNDP/WMO/UNESCO)
NSF	National Science Foundation (US)
NSFC	National Natural Science Foundation of China
NSSD	National Strategies for Sustainable Development
NSTC	National Science and Technology Council (English-speaking Caribbean)
NTFP	non-timber forest products
NUFFIC	Netherlands Organization for International Cooperation in Higher Education
NVE	Norwegian Water Resources and Energy Directorate
NWA	national wildlife area
NWCF	Nepal Water Conservation Foundation
NWFP	non-wood forest products
NWO-WOTRO	Netherlands Organization for Scientific Research-Foundation for the Advancement of Tropical Research
NWP (1)	Nepal Water Partnership
NWP (2)	Netherlands Water Partnership
NWRC	National Water Research Center

NWRI	National Water Research Institute (Canada, Nigeria)
NWS (1)	nuclear-weapon state
NWS (2)	National Weather Service
NZAID	New Zealand Agency for International Development
NZODA	New Zealand Official Development Assistance

O

O_3	ozone
O&M	operations and maintenance
OA	official assistance/aid
OAS	Organization of American States
OAS/USDE	OAS Unit for Sustainable Development and Environment
OAU	Organization of African Unity
OBA	output based aid
OCA/PAC	Oceans and Coastal Areas Programme Activity Center (UNEP)
OCC	operational and capital costs
OCHA	Office for the Coordination of Humanitarian Affairs (USDOS)
OCM	Ocean and Coastal Management
OD	operational directive (WB)
ODA (1)	official development assistance
ODA (2)	Overseas Development Administration (UK)
ODAE	ODA equity
ODAG	ODA grant
ODAL	ODA loan
ODF	Official Development Finance (ODA + OA + other ODF)
ODI	Overseas Development Institute (UK)
ODP	ozone depleting potential (also ozone destroying potential)
ODPt	ozone depleting potential in tons
ODS (1)	ozone depleting substance
ODS (2)	official document system (UN)
OECD	Organisation for Economic Co-operation and Development
OECD-DAC	OECD Development Assistance Committee
OECS	Organization of Eastern Caribbean States
OED	Operations Evaluation Department (IBRD)
OeKB	*Oesterreichische Kontrollbank* AG (Austria)
OEWG	open-ended working group
OFAC	Office of Foreign Assets Control (US)
OFDA	Office of Foreign Disaster Assistance (US)
OHP	Operational Hydrology Programme (WMO)
OIC (1)	Organization of Islamic Countries
OIC (2)	Organization of the Islamic Conference

OIEAU	*Office International de l'Eau* (France)
OILPOL	International Convention for the Prevention of Pollution of the Sea by Oil
OLADE	Latin American Energy Development Organization
OM	operations manual
OMVS	Organization for the Development of the Senegal River
ONGO	operational NGO
OOFL	other official flows of non-concessional lending by multilateral banks (OECD)
OP (1)	operational policy
OP (2)	optional protocol
OPCW	Organization for the Prohibition of Chemical Weapons
Op. Obj.	operational objective
OP/BP	operation plan/business plan (GEF-WB)
OPEC	Organization of Petroleum Exporting Countries
OPG	operational policy guidelines
OPIC	Overseas Private Investment Corporation (US)
OPPRC	Oil Pollution Preparedness, Response and Co-operation Convention
OPRF	Ocean Policy Research Foundation (Japan)
OPS (1)	Overall Performance Study (GEF)
OPS (2)	Office of Project Services (UNDP)
OPS (3)	Pan-American Health Organization (WHO)
ORSTOM	Office of Overseas Scientific and Technical Research (France)
ORV	off-road vehicles
OSCE	Organization for Security and Cooperation in Europe
OSPAR	Convention for the Protection of the Marine Environment of the North-East Atlantic
OSS	Sahara and Sahel Observatory
OTCA	Amazonian Cooperation Treaty Organization
OTF	ozone trust fund
OTS	Organization for Tropical Studies
OV	On-line Volunteering
Ox	Oxfam

P

P	Preamble
P5	Permanent Five (Members of the UN Security Council)
P&Ms	policies and measures
PA	Participants Assembly (GEF)
PAC (1)	Inter-Bureau Project Appraisal Committee
PAC (2)	Project Advisory Committee
PACADIRH	Central American Water Resources Action Plan
PACD	Plan of Action to Combat Desertification
PACSICOM	Pan-African Conference on Sustainable Integrated Coastal Management

PACTIV	political leadership, accountability, capacity, transparency, implementation, voice
PAD	project appraisal document (WB)
PADF	Pan American Development Foundation
PADU	protected area data unit (WCMC)
PAG	Project Approval Group (UNEP)
PAGE	Pilot Analysis of Global Ecosystems (MA)
PAHO	Pan American Health Organization (WHO)
PALOP	official Portuguese-speaking African countries
PAM (or P&Ms)	policies and measures
PAME	Programme for the Protection of the Arctic Marine Environment
PAP	Priority Actions Programme
PAP-RAC	Regional Activity Centre for Priority Actions Programme (UNEP)
PARC	Performance Assessment Resource Centre
PAS	protected area strategy
PAVE	Pan African Vision for the Environment
PAWG	Protected Areas Working Group
PBI	programme budget implications
PBRs	plant breeders rights
PC (1)	Plant Committee (CITES)
PC (2)	Permanent Council (OAS)
PC-CP	From Potential (water) Conflicts to Cooperation Potential (UNESCO)
PC&I	principles, criteria and indicators
PCA	Permanent Court of Arbitration (UN)
PCBs	polychlorinated biphenyls
PCBAP	Plan for the Conservation of the Upper Paraguay River Basin
PCF (1)	Prototype Carbon Fund (WB)
PCF (2)	Portuguese Carbon Fund
PCM	project cycle management
PCV	Peace Corps Volunteer (US)
PD/GG	participatory development/good governance (OECD)
PDD	Project Design Document (UNFCCC)
PDF (1)	Project Preparation and Development Facility (GEF)
PDF (2)	Project Development Funds (GEF)
PDO	project development objective
PDT	project delivery team
PEAP	Poverty Eradication Action Plan
PEBLDS	Pan-European Biological and Landscape Diversity Strategy
PEDAS	potentially environmentally detrimental activities in space
PEEM	Panel of Experts on Environmental Management for Vector Control (WHO)
PEMSA	Partnerships in Environmental Management for the Seas of East Asia
PEP	Poverty-Environment Partnership (UNDP-UNEP)

PERRL	Pilot Emission Removals, Reductions and Learnings Initiatives
PERSGA	Regional Organization for the Conservation of the Environment of the Red Sea and Gulf of Aden
PES	payment for environmental services
PET	polyethylene terephthalate
PETE	polyethylene terephthalate
PETS	Public Expenditure Tracking Survey (WB)
PFA	proposal for action
PFCs	perfluorocarbons
PFII	United Nations Permanent Forum on Indigenous Issues
PG	planning group
PFP	Policy Framework Papers
PGRFA	Plant Genetic Resources for Food and Agriculture (CGRFA)
PHARE	EU's Assistance Programme in CE
PhExp	physical exposure for drought
PHVA	population and habitat viability assessment
PIANC	international navigation association
PIC	prior informed consent
PIC-INC	Intergovernmental Negotiating Committee for the Preparation of the Conference of Parties of the Rotterdam Convention for the Application of the Prior Informed Consent Procedure for Certain Hazardous Chemicals and Pesticides in International Trade
PID	project information document (WB)
PIDP	Pacific Island Development Program
PIDS	Inter-American Program for Sustainable Development (OAS)
PIF	Pacific Island Forum
PIMBY	please in my backyard
PINGO	public interest NGO
PIPR	Project Implementation Performance Report (GEF)
PIR	Project Implementation Review (GEF)
PJTC	Permanent Joint Technical Commission for Nile Waters (Egypt)
PM (1)	Prime Minister
PM (2)	particulate matter
PM (3)	permanent member
PMA	Plan for the Modernization of Agriculture (DFID)
PMS	Project Monitoring System (IDB)
PNA	Parties to the Nauru Agreement
PNG	Papua New Guinea
PO (1)	Private Organization
PO (2)	Peoples' Organization
PON	Program on Negotiations
POPs	Persistent Organic Pollutants (Stockholm Convention)
POR	period of record

PoWER	Partnership for Water Education and Research (UNESCO-IHE)
PP (1)	project purpose
PP (2)	project preparation (IDB)
PP (3)	precautionary principle (EU)
PPA (1)	Project Preparation Advance (GEF)
PPA (2)	Project Preparation Assistance (GEF)
PPA (3)	Programme on Protected Areas (IUCN)
PPA (4)	participatory poverty assessment
PPD	proposed project document (IDB)
PPDOP	participatory process for the definition of options and priorities
PPM	production and processing methods
ppmv	parts per million by volume
PPP (1)	public–private partnership
PPP (2)	purchasing power parity (WB)
PPP (3)	polluter pays principle
PPPUE	public private partnership for the urban environment
PPR	Project Performance Review (GEF)
PPRC	Practical Solutions for Environmental and Economic Vitality (US)
PRA (1)	participatory rural appraisal
PRA (2)	participatory rapid appraisal
PRC	People's Republic of China
PREC	Project Review and Evaluation Committee
PREM	Poverty Reduction and Economic Management Network (WB)
PRI	principles for responsible investment
PRIF (1)	pre-investment financing
PRIF (2)	pre-investment facility
PRINCE	Program for Measuring Incremental Costs for the Environment (GEF)
PROBASE	Procedures for Accounting and Baselines for Projects under Joint Implementation and the Clean Development Mechanism
ProDoc	project document
PROFOR	Programme on Forests (UNDP/WB)
PRS	poverty reduction strategy (WB)
PRSP	poverty reduction strategy paper (WB)
PRTR	pollutant release and transfer register
PSIA	poverty and social impact analysis (WB)
PSM	public sector management
PSP (1)	point-source pollution
PSP (2)	private sector participation
PTC	Program of Technical Cooperation (IDB)
PUB	prediction in ungauged basins
PV	photovoltaic
PVO	private voluntary organization
PVP	plant variety protection

PWA	Portfolio of Water Actions (UNESCO)
PWP (1)	Pakistan Water Partnership
PWP (2)	Philippines Water Partnership
PWRI	Public Works Research Institute (Japan)
PWWA	Philippines Water Works Association

Q

QA/QC	quality assurance/quality control
QALY	quality adjusted life year
QAPP	quality assurance project plan
QELRC	quantified emission limitation and reduction commitment
QMS	qualified majority voting system
QMV-EU	qualified 'double' majority voting – European Union
QSP	quick start programme
QUELROs	quantified emission limitation and reduction objectives
QuNGO	quasi-governmental NGO

R

R&D	research and development
R2P	responsibility to protect
RAC	Regional Activity Center
RAFI	Rural Advancement Fund International
RAI	Regional Activity Institute
RAIS	Regional Agricultural Information System
RAM	research and monitoring
RAMSAR	Convention on Wetlands of International Importance Especially as Waterfowl Habitat
RAN	Rainforest Action Network
RANDP	resource-adjusted net domestic product
RAP (1)	remedial action plan
RAP (2)	regional action plan
RAP (3)	resettlement action plan
RAP (4)	rapid assessment project
RAP (5)	rapid assessment procedures
RAS (1)	Regulatory Action Strategy
RAS (2)	Royal Academy of Sciences
RBC	River Basin Commission
RBD	River Basin District
RBI	River Basin Initiative
RBM	results based management
RBO	River Basin Organization
RCs	resource centers
RCMRD	Regional Centre for Mapping of Resources for Development
RCSA	Rainwater Catchment Systems Association (Brazil)

RCTWS	Regional Center for Training and Water Studies in Arid and Semi-Arid Zones (Egypt)
RCU	Regional Coordinating Unit
RCUWM	Regional Centre on Urban Water Management (UNESCO/Iran)
RDB	Regional Development Bank
RDP (1)	reconstruction development plan
RDP (2)	regional development plan
REACH	Registration Evaluation, and Authorization of Chemicals (EU)
Rec	recommendation (document identification)
REC	Regional Environmental Centre for Central and Eastern Europe
RECOFTC	Regional Community Forestry Training Centre for Asia and the Pacific
REDICA	*Red Centroamericana de Instituciones de Ingenieria*
REEEP	Renewable Energy and Energy Efficiency Partnership
REEF	Renewable Energy and Energy Efficiency Fund (GEF)
REIA	Renewable Energy in the Americas Initiative (OAS)
REN21	Renewable Energy Policy Network for the 21st Century
REReP	Regional Environmental Reconstruction Programme (GEF)
Res	resolution (document identification)
Res. Rep.	UNDP Resident Representative/Coordinator
Rev	revision (document identification)
RFA	recommendations for action
RFC	Regional Forestry Commission (FAO)
RFP	request for proposal
RH	reproductive health
RI	Rotary International
RIIA	Royal Institute of International Affairs (UK)
RIM	Regional Implementation Meetings
RING (1)	Alliance of Policy Research Organizations
RING (2)	Regional and International Networking Group
RINGO	research and independent NGOs
RIO+10	The World Summit on Sustainable Development (Johannesburg 2002)
RIOs	Regional Indigenous Organizations
RIPANAP	Ibero-American Network of National Park Institutions and other Protected Areas
RIRH	*Red Inter-Americana para Recursos Hidricos* (OAS)
RIS	Ramsar Information System
RIVM	Netherlands National Institute for Public Health and Environment
RIZA	Netherlands Institute for Inland Water Management and Waste Water Treatment (EWA)
RLB	Latin American Plant Sciences Network
RM	risk management
RMUs	removal units (UNFCCC)

RO	renewable obligation
ROAP	Regional Office for Asia and the Pacific (UNEP)
ROC	Renewable Obligation Certificate
ROE	Regional Office for Europe (UNEP)
ROLAC	Regional Office for Latin America and the Caribbean (UNEP)
RONA	Regional Office for North America (UNEP)
RONAST	Royal Nepal Academy of Science and Technology
ROPME	Regional Organization for the Protection of the Marine Environment
RPA	research priority area
RPC	Regional Programming Committee
RPT95	Report Submitted in 1995
RR	rules and regulations (IMF)
RRA	rapid rural appraisal
RRC-AP	Regional Resource Centre for Asia and Pacific
RSO	Research and Systematic Observation (UNFCCC)
RSPCA	Royal Society for the Prevention of Cruelty to Animals
RSS	Royal Scientific Society (Jordan)
RT	Rain Trust (US, Holland, Brazil)
RTAC	Regional Technical Advisory Committee (GWP)
RU (1)	Removal Unit (LULUCF)
RU (2)	Regional Unit of IBRD (AFR, Africa; EAP, East Asia and Pacific; ECA, Europe and Central Asia; LCR, Latin America and the Caribbean; MNA, Middle East and North Africa; SAR, South Asia)
RVP	Regional Vice President (WB)
RWP	Regional Water Partnership (GWP)
RWS	*Rijkswaterstraat* (Water Management Agency, The Netherlands)

S

SAARC	South Asian Association for Regional Cooperation
SAC	Scientific Advisory Committee (UNEP)
SACE	*Sezione Speciale per l'Assicurazione del Credito all'Esportazione* (Italy)
SACEP	South Asian Cooperative Environment Programme
SACN	South American Community of Nations
SADC	Southern African Development Community
SADCC	Southern African Development Coordination Conference
SAEFL	Swiss Agency for Environment, Forests and Landscape (BUWAL)
SAF (1)	Society of American Foresters
SAF (2)	South Asia Foundation
SAFTA	South American Free Trade Area
SAICM	Strategic Approach on International Chemicals Management

SAIL	Cooperation on International Post-Graduate Institutes (The Netherlands)
SAL	structural adjustment loan
SAMTAC	South American Technical Advisory Committee (GWP)
SANDEC	Swiss Department of Water and Sanitation in Developing Countries
SANIGMI	Central Asia Hydro-Meteorological Research Institute (Uzbekistan)
SAOPID	Secretariat for Water, Public Works and Infrastructure for Development (Mexico)
SAP (1)	Strategic Action Plan (GEF)
SAP (2)	Scientific Assessment Panel
SAPTA	South Asian Preferential Trade Agreement
SAR (1)	Second Assessment Report (IPCC)
SAR (2)	Staff Appraisal Report (WB)
SAR-TA	Staff Appraisal Report-Technical Annex (WB)
SARD	Sustainable Agriculture and Rural Development
SARDC	South African Research and Documentation Center
SAREC	Department of Research Cooperation (Sweden)
SARPN	South African Regional Poverty Network
SAS	South Asian Seas Programme
SASTAC	South Asian Seas Technical Advisory Committee (GWP)
SATAC	Southern Africa Technical Advisory Committee (GWP)
SB	subsidiary body
SBA	sustainable business advisory
SBC	Secretariat of the Basel Convention
SBD	Secretariat for Biological Diversity (UNEP)
SBI	Subsidiary Body for Implementation (UNFCCC)
SBSTA	Subsidiary Body for Scientific and Technological Advice (UNFCCC)
SBSTTA	Subsidiary Body on Scientific, Technical and Technological Advice (CBD)
SC (1)	Standing Committee
SC (2)	Steering Committee (GWP)
SC (3)	sale of children
SCAR	Scientific Committee on Antarctic Research
SCBD	Secretariat of the Convention on Biological Diversity
SCCF	Special Climate Change Fund (UNFCCC)
SCI	Site of Community Importance (EU)
SCM	Sectoral Crediting Mechanisms
SCOPE	Scientific Committee on Problems of the Environment (ICSU)
SCOR	Scientific Committee on Oceanic Research (ICSU)
SCP (1)	socio-cultural profile
SCP (2)	sustainable consumption-production
SD	sustainable development
SDC (1)	Swiss Agency for Development and Cooperation
SDC (2)	solar development capital (GEF)
SDG	Sustainable Development Governance

SDIN	Sustainable Development Issues Network
SDR	special drawing rights
SDV	Social Development Department (WB)
SEA (1)	strategic environmental assessment
SEA (2)	Sustainable Enterprise Academy (Canada)
SeaCapNet	South East Asia Capacity Building Network
SEAGA	socio-economic and gender analysis
SEATAC	South East Asia Technical Advisory Committee (GWP)
SEAWUN	South East Asia Water Utilities Network
SECO	*Secrétariat d'État á l'Économie* (Switzerland)
SeCyT	Secretariat of Science and Technology (Argentina)
SEDAC	Socioeconomic Data and Applications Center (CIESIN)
SEED	Sustainable Energy and Environment Division (UNDP)
SEEDS	Sustainable Environment and Ecological Development Society
SEFI	Sustainable Energy Finance Initiative
SEGA	socio-economic and gender analysis
SEI	Stockholm Environment Institute
SEM	*Société des Eaux de Marseille* (France)
SEMARNAT	*Secretaria de Medio Ambiente y Recursos Naturales*
SENACYT	National Secretariat of Science and Technology (Ecuador)
SEP	*Secretaria de Educación Pública*
SEQ	Standing Group on Emergency Questions (IEA)
SER (1)	Series (OAS documents)
SER (2)	Society for Ecological Restoration International
SESEC	Swiss Environmental Solutions for Emerging Countries
SETAC	Society of Environmental Toxicology and Chemistry
SETPC	Sino-Europe Technology Promotion Center
SEWA	Self-Employed Women's Association (India)
SF	Sumitra Foundation (India)
SFI	Sustainable Forestry Initiative
SFM	sustainable forest management (UNFF)
SFWMD	South Florida Water Management District
SG	Secretary General
SGP	small grants programme
SHD	sustainable human development
SHF	*Société Hydrotechnique de France*
SHO	self-help organization
SHP	small hydropower
SHPO	self-help support organization
SI	international system of units
SIC	Scientific Information Center
SICA	Central American Integration System
SICAP	Central American System of Protected Areas
SICICWC	Scientific Information Center Interstate Water Coordination Commission of Central Area
SID	Society for International Development
SIDA (Sida)	Swedish International Development Agency

SIDB	Small Industries Development Bank
SIDS	Small Island Developing States
SIL (1)	International Association of Theoretical and Applied Limnology
SIL (2)	*Societas Internationalis Limuologiae (France)*
SIMDAS	Sustainable Integrated Management and Development of Arid and Semi-arid regions of Southern Africa
SINAP	National System of Protected Areas (Mexico)
SINDAS	Sustainable Integrated Management and Development of Arid and Semi-Arid Regions of Southern Africa (UNESCO)
SINGER	System-Wide Information Network on Genetic Resources
SIRG	Summit Implementation Review Group (OAS)
SISSA	International School for Advanced Studies (Italy)
SIWI	Stockholm International Water Institute
SLR	side-looking radar
SLT	Standing Group on Long-Term Cooperation (IEA)
SMART	specific, measurable, agreed, realistic, time bound
SME	small and medium-sized enterprises
SME/SMI	small and medium-scale enterprise/industry
SMME	small, micro and medium-sized enterprises
SMO	social movement organization
SMPR	Secretariat Managed Project Review (GEF)
SMR	Sustainability Management and Reporting
SMS	safe minimum standards
SNA	System of National Accounts
SNV	Swedish Environment Protection Agency
SNW	Sustainable Northwest (US)
SO	strategic objective
SO$_2$	sulfur dioxide
SOA (1)	Summit of the Americas
SOA (2)	State Oceanic Administration (China)
SOD	Summary, Overview and Development Report (ICDA)
SODIS	solar water disinfection system
SOER	State of the Environment Report (EU)
SOFO	State of the World's Forests Report
SOG	Sustainable Ocean Governance
SOGE	Seminar of Governmental Experts
SOM	Standing Group on Oil Market (IEA)
SOPAC	South Pacific Applied Geoscience Commission
SPA (1)	specially protected areas (EU, CAP)
SPA (2)	Strategic Partnership for UNCCD Implementation in Central Asian Countries
SPA-SANIRI	Scientific Production Association Central Asian Irrigation Research Institute
SPAW	Protocol on Specially Protected Areas and Wildlife of the Cartagena Convention
SPC (1)	South Pacific Commission
SPC (2)	Secretariat for the Pacific Community

SPF	South Pacific Forum
SPFS	Special Programme for Food Security
SPM	Summary for Policy Makers (IPPC/Reviews)
SPMs	sanitary and phytosanitary measures
SPOT	*Système Probatoire d'Observation de la Terre*
SPREP (1)	Secretariat of the Pacific Regional Environment Programme
SPREP (2)	South Pacific Regional Environmental Programme (UNEP)
SPS	Sanitary and Phytosanitary Agreement (WTO)
SRAP	Sub-Regional Action Plan
SRC	Scientific Research Council (Jamaica, Iraq)
SRCCS	Special Report on Carbon Dioxide Capture and Storage
SRES	Special Report on Emissions Scenarios
SRFC	Sub-Regional Fisheries Commission
SRH	Secretariat for Water Resources (Brazil)
SRI	socially responsible investment
SRLFC	Special Report on Land Use, Land Use Change and Forestry and Carbon Sinks (IPCC)
SS	special session
SSC	Species Survival Commission (IUCN)
SSNC	Swedish Society for Nature Conservation
SSP	Social Policy Programme (IUCN)
SSWP	small scale water provider (ADB)
ST	Scheduled Tribe
STAF	short term assistance facility (CDB)
STAP	Scientific and Technical Advisory Panel (GEF)
START (1)	Global Change Systems for Analysis, Research and Training (IHDP, IGBP, WCRP) (Secretariat in the US)
START (2)	Strategic Arms Reduction Treaty
STATE	US State Department
STC	short-term consultant (WB)
STI	sexually transmitted infection
STREAMS	Streams of Knowledge Coalition of Water and Sanitation Resource Centres
STRP	Scientific and Technical Review Panel (Ramsar)
SUI	Sustainable Use Team (IUCN)
SWAP	sector wide approach to planning
SWCC	Second World Climate Conference
SWF	State of the World Forum
SWG	sub working group
SWH	Swedish Water House
SWITCH	Urban Water Management in the City of the Future
SWOT	strengths, weaknesses, opportunities and threats
SWR	Sub-Committee on Water Resources (ACC)
SWRRC	Sustainable Water Resources Research Center (Korea)
SWS (1)	safe water systems
SWS (2)	Stockholm Water Symposium
SYKE	Environment Institute of Finland

T

TA	technical assistance
TAC (1)	total allowable catch
TAC (2)	Technical Advisory Committee
TACIS	Technical Assistance for the Commonwealth of Independent States (EU)
TAG	Technical Advisory Group
TAR	Third Assessment Report (IPPC)
TBD	tropical biodiversity (CHM)
TBT	technical barrier to trade
TCAs	transboundary conservation areas
TCBO	training, capacity building and outreach
tCe	tons of carbon equivalent
TCP	Technical Cooperation Programme (FAO)
TDA (1)	transboundary diagnostic analysis (GEF)
TDA (2)	US Trade and Development Agency
TE	total expenditures
TEAP	Technology and Economic Assessment Panel
TEC	Technical Committee (GWP)
TED	turtle excluder device
TEK	traditional ecological knowledge
TEMS	Terrestrial Ecosystem Monitoring Sites (EU Database)
TERI (1)	Terrestrial Ecosystem Resource Inventory (CI)
TERI (2)	The Energy and Resources Institute
TERI (3)	Tata Energy and Resources Institute
TERM	Transport and Environment Reporting Mechanism
TERRIS	Terrestrial Environment Information System (EU)
TEST	transfer of environmentally sound technology
TFAP	Tropical Forestry Action Plan
TFCA	Tropical Forest Conservation Act (USA)
TFCP	Tropical Forest Canopy Programme
TFDD	Transboundary Freshwater Dispute Database (US)
TFDT	Task Force on Destruction Technologies
TFF	Tropical Forestry Foundation
TFI	Task Force for National Greenhouse Inventories
TFRK	traditional forest-related knowledge (CBD)
TGCIA	Task Group on Scenarios for Climate and Impact Assessment (IPCC)
TGF	testing ground facility
TI	Transparency International
TICLEAR	Technology Information Clearing House
TIIWE	Taiwan (of China) International Institute for Water Education
TKBD	traditional knowledge and biological diversity
TM	task manager
TMB	Trust Management Board
TNC (1)	The Nature Conservancy
TNC (2)	transnational corporation

TNO	Netherlands Organization for Applied Scientific Research
TOC	Technological Options Committee
TOE	tons of oil equivalent
TOPS	The Ocean Policy Strategy
TOR	terms of reference
ToT	training of trainers
TPR	Tripartite Review (GEF)
TRAFFIC	Trade Record Analysis of Flora and Fauna in Commerce
TREES	Tropical Ecosystem Environment Observations by Satellite (EEC)
TRI	toxic release inventory
TRIMs	trade-related investment measures
TRIPS	Agreement on Trade-related Aspects of Intellectual Property Rights (IU)
TRN	Taiga Rescue Network
TRP	Technical Review Panel (GEF)
TRR	traditional resource rights
TS (1)	technical summary
TS (2)	Technical Secretariat
TSF	Tropical Synergy Foundation
TSP	total suspended particulates
TSS	total suspended solids
TSU	Technical Support Unit (IPCC)
TT	technology transfer
TTF	Thematic Trust Fund
TUAC	Trade Union Advisory Committed (OTC)
TWAS	Third World Academy of Sciences (Italy)
TWG	Technical Working Group
TWNSO	Third World Network of Scientific Organizations (Italy)
TWOWS	Third World Organization for Women in Science (Italy)
TWUWS	Transportation, Water and Urban Development Department (UNDP-WB)
TWWF	Third World Water Forum

U

$U5_{MORT}$	under five years old mortality rate
UATI	International Union of Technical Associations and Organizations
UAWS	Union of African Water Suppliers
UCLG	United Cities and Local Governments
UDHR	Universal Declaration of Human Rights
UESNET	Urban Environmental Sanitation Network (GWP)
UIE	UNESCO Institute for Education (UNESCO/Germany)
UIS	UNESCO Institute for statistics (UNESCO/Canada)
UN	United Nations
UN-Habitat	United Nations Programme for Human Settlements
UN-NGO-IRENE	United Nations NGO Informal Regional Network

UNACABQ	UN Advisory Committee on Administrative and Budgetary Questions
UNACC	Administrative Committee on Coordinating of the United Nations
UNACC/SCWR	United Nations Administrative Committee on Coordination Subcommittee on Water Resources
UNAIDS	United Nations Fund for HIV/AIDS
UNCAC	United Nations Convention against Corruption
UNCAF	United Nations Economic Commission for Asia and the Far East
UNCBD	United Nations Secretariat of the Convention on Biological Diversity
UNCCD	United Nations Convention to Combat Desertification
UNCCPCJ	United Nations Commission on Crime Prevention and Criminal Justice
UNCEB	United Nations Chief Executives Board
UNCED	United Nations Conference on Environment and Development
UNCEF	United Nations Capital Development Fund
UNCFB	United Nations System Chief Executive Board for Coordination
UNCHE	United Nations Conference on Human Environment
UNCHR	United Nations Commission on Human Rights
UNCHS	United Nations Centre for Human Settlements
UNCLOS	United Nations Convention on the Law of the Sea
UNCND	United Nations Commission on Narcotic Drugs
UNCPD	United Nations Commission on Population and Development
UNCRC	United Nations Convention on the Rights of the Child
UNCRD	United Nations Centre for Regional Development
UNCSD (1)	United Nations Commission on Sustainable Development
UNCSD (2)	United Nations Commission for Social Development
UNCSTD	United Nations Commission on Science and Technology for Development
UNCSW	United Nations Commission on the Status of Women
UNCTAD	United Nations Conference on Trade and Development
UNCUEA	United Nations Centre for Urgent Environmental Assistance
UNDAC	United Nations Disaster Assessment and Coordination Team
UNDAF	United Nations Development Assistance Framework
UNDCP	United Nations Drug Control Program
UNDESA	United Nations Department of Economic and Social Affairs
UNDESD	United Nations Decade – Education for Sustainable Development
UNDHR	United Nations Declaration on Human Rights
UNDOALOS	United Nations Division on Ocean Affairs and Law of the Sea

UNDP	United Nations Development Programme
UNDP-IW-LEARN	International Waters Learning Exchange and Resource Network
UNDPI	United Nations Department of Public Information
UNDPRF	United Nations Development Programme Revolving Fund
UNDP/SU/TCDC	UNDP Special Unit for Technical Cooperation among Developing Countries
UNDRO	United Nations Office of Disaster Relief
UNECA	United Nations Economic Commission for Africa
UNECE	United Nations Economic Commission for Europe
UNECLAC	United Nations Economic Commission for Latin America and the Caribbean
UNECWA	United Nations Economic Commission for Western Asia
UNEMG	United Nations Environmental Management Group
UNEO	United Nations Environment Organization
UNEP	United Nations Environment Programme
UNEP-CAR/RCU	Caribbean Regional Coordinating Unit of the Cartagena Convention (UNEP)
UNEP-CEP	United Nations Environment Programme Caribbean Environment Programme
UNEP-DELC	United Nations Division of Environmental Law and Conventions
UNEP-DTIE	United Nations Environment Programme Division of Technology, Industry, and Economics
UNEP-EAS/RCU	United Nations Environment Programme East Asia Seas Regional Coordinating Unit
UNEP-ENRIN	United Nations Environment Programme Environment and Natural Resource Information Group
UNEP-GC	United Nations Environment Programme Governing Council
UNEP-GPA	United Nations Environment Programme Global Programme of Action on the Protection of the Marine Environment from Land-based Activities
UNEP-GRID	United Nations Environment Programme Global Resources Information Database
UNEP-HEM	United Nations Environment Programme Harmonization of Environmental Measurement
UNEP-IETC	United Nations Environment Programme International Environment Technology Centre
UNEP-MEDU	United Nations Environment Programme Coordinating Unit of the Mediterranean Action Plan
UNEP-OS	United Nations Environment Programme Ozone Secretariat
UNEP-RCUs	United Nations Environment Programme Regional Coordinating Units of the Regional Seas Programme
UNEP-ROA	United Nations Environment Programme Regional Office for Africa
UNEP-ROAP	United Nations Environment Programme Regional Office for Asia and the Pacific

UNEP-ROE	United Nations Environment Programme Regional Office for Europe
UNEP-ROLAC	United Nations Environment Programme Regional Office for Latin America and the Caribbean
UNEP-RONA	United Nations Environment Programme Regional Office for North America
UNEP-ROWA	United Nations Environment Programme Regional Office for West Asia
UNEP-SPAW	Specially Protected Areas and Wildlife Protocol of the Cartagena Convention
UNEP-WCMC	UNEP World Conservation Monitoring Center
UNESCAP	United Nations Economic and Social Commission for Asia and the Pacific
UNESCO	United Nations Educational, Scientific, and Cultural Organization
UNESCO-CATHALAC	Center for Water in the Humid Tropics for Latin America and the Caribbean (Panama)
UNESCO-CAZALAC	Centre for Arid and Semi-Arid Regional of Latin America and the Caribbean (Chile)
UNESCO-CIH/HIC	International Hydroinformatics Centre for Integrated Water Resources Management (Brazil – proposed)
UNESCO-CINARA	Regional Centre on Urban Water management for Latin America and the Caribbean (Colombia)
UNESCO-HELP (1)	Centre for Water Law, Policy and Science (Scotland)
UNESCO-HELP (2)	International Centre of Water for Food Security (Australia – proposed)
UNESCO-HTC	Regional Humid Tropics Hydrology and Water Resources Centre for Southeast Asia (Malaysia)
UNESCO-ICE-PAS	European Regional Centre for Ecohydrology (Poland)
UNESCO-ICHARM	International Centre for Water Hazard and Risk Management (Japan)
UNESCO-ICQHHS	International Center on Qanats and Historic Hydraulic Structures (Iran)
UNESCO-IHC	International Heritage Convention
UNESCO-IHE	Institute for Water Education (The Netherlands)
UNESCO-IHE-PoWER	Partnership for Water Education and Research (The Netherlands)
UNESCO-IHE-PWE	Partnership for Water Education (The Netherlands)
UNESCO-IHP	International Hydrological Programme
UNESCO-IRTCES	International Research and Training Centre for Erosion and Sedimentation (China)
UNESCO-IRTCUD	International Research and Training Center on Urban Drainage (Serbia)
UNESCO-RCTWS	Regional Center for Training and Water Studies of Arid and Semi-Arid Zones (Egypt)
UNESCO-RCUWM	Regional Center on Urban Water Management (Iran)
UNESCO-SWEM	Centre on Sustainable Water Engineering and Management (Thailand – proposed)
UNESCO-WWAP	World Water Assessment Programme (Italy)

UNEVOC	International Centre for Technical and Vocational Education and Training (UNESCO/Germany)
UNF	United Nations Foundation
UNFAO	United Nations Food and Agricultural Organization
UNFCCC	United Nations Framework Convention on Climate Change
UNFF	United Nations Forum on Forests
UNFIP	United Nations Fund for International Partnerships
UNFPA	United Nations Fund for Population Activities
UNG@ID	United Nations Global Alliance for Information and Communication Technologies for Development
UNG/WG	United Nations Geographical Information Working Group
UNGA	United Nations General Assembly
UNGARP	United Nations Global Atmospheric Research Programme
UNGASS	United Nations General Assembly Special Session
UNGIWG	United Nations Geographic Information Working Group
UNHCR (1)	United Nations High Commissioner for Refugees
UNHCR (2)	United Nations Commission on Human Rights
UNHLCP	United Nations High Level Committee on Programmes
UNHRC	United Nations Human Rights Council
UNIA	United Nations Implementing Agreement
UNICEF	United Nations Children's Fund
UNICJ	United Nations International Court of Justice
UNICPOLOS	United Nations Informal Consultative Process on Oceans and the Law of the Sea
UNIDCP	United Nations International Drug Control Programme
UNIDO	United Nations Industrial Development Organization
UNIDROIT	International Institute for the Unification of Private Law
UNIFEM	United Nations Development Fund for Women
UNISDR	United Nations International Strategy for Disaster Reduction
UNISDR-PPEW	UNISDR Platform for the Promotion of Early Warning
UNITAR	United Nations Institute for Training and Research
UNJPO	United Nations Junior Professional Officer
UNMDGs	United Nations Millennium Development Goals
UNMOVIC	United Nations Monitoring, Verification and Inspection Commission
UNMP	United Nations Millennium Development Project
UNNGLS	United Nations NonGovernmental Liaison Service
UNOCHA	United Nations Office for Coordination of Humanitarian Affairs
UNON	United Nations Office at Nairobi
UNOOSA	United Nations Office for Outer Space Affairs
UNOPS	United Nations Office for Project Services
UNPFFI	United Nations Permanent Forum on Indigenous Issues
UNPRI	United Nations Principles for Responsible Investment
UNRC	United Nations Resident Coordinator

UNRR	United Nations Resident Representative
UNRWA	United Nations Relief and Works Agency
UNSC (1)	United Nations Security Council
UNSC (2)	United Nations Statistical Commission
UNSD	United Nations Statistics Division
UNSIA	United Nations Special Initiative for Africa
UNSO	United Nations Sudano-Saheilian Office
UNSTAT	United Nations Statistical Division
UNT	United Nations Treaty Collection
UNU	United Nations University (Japan)
UNU-BIOLAC	UNU Programme for Biotechnology in Latin America and the Caribbean (Venezuela)
UNU-CRIS	UNU Programme for Comparative Regional Integration Studies (Belgium)
UNU-EHS	UNU Institute for Environment and Human Security (Germany)
UNU-FNP	UNU Food and Nutrition Programme for Human and Social Development (US)
UNU-FTP	UNU Fisheries Training Programme (Iceland)
UNU-GTP	UNU Geothermal Training Programme (Iceland)
UNU-IAS	UNU Institute for Advanced Studies (Japan)
UNU-IIST	UNU International Institute for Software Technology (Macao)
UNU-ILI	UNU International Leadership Institute (Jordan)
UNU-INRA	UNU Institute for Natural Resources in Africa (Ghana)
UNU-INWEH	UNU International Network on Water, Environment, and Health (Canada)
UNU-MERIT	UNU Maastricht Economic and Social Research and Training Center on Innovation Technology (The Netherlands)
UNU-WIDER	UNU World Institute for Development Economics Research (Finland)
UNV	United Nations Volunteer
UNW	United Nations Wire
UN-WADOC	United Nations Water Decade Office on Capacity Development
UNWater	United Nations Committee on Fresh Water
UNWIPO	United Nations World Intellectual Property Organization
UNWTO	United Nations World Tourism Organization
UNWWAP	United Nations World Water Action Programme
UPOV	International Union for the Protection of New Varieties of Plants
UPS	uninterrupted power supply
UPTW	University Partnership for Transboundary Water (UNESCO)
UPU	Universal Postal Union
URC	UNEP RISOE Center
URF	universal reporting format
URWH	Urban Rain Water Harvesting

US	United States of America
USA	United States of America
USACE	United States Army Corps of Engineers
USAID	United States Agency for International Development
USAID/OFDA	USAID Office of Foreign Disaster Assistance
USBOR	United States Bureau of Reclamation
USCCSP	United States Climate Change Science Program
USDA	United States Department of Agriculture
USDE	Unit of Sustainable Development and Environment (OAS)
USDOI	United States Department of Interior
USDOS	United States Department of State (Foreign Secretary)
USEPA	United States Environmental Protection Agency
USFS	United States Forest Service
USFWS	United States Fish and Wildlife Service
USGS	United States Geological Survey
USNGWA	United States National Ground Water Association
USNPS	United States National Park Service/System
USPC	United States Peace Corps
UTF	Unilateral Trust Fund (FAO)
UV	ultraviolet
UW	United Water (USA)
UWI	University of the West Indies
UWICED	UWI Center for Environment and Development

V

V&A	vulnerability and adaptation assessment
VA	voluntary agreement (IEA)
VASTRA	Swedish Water Management Research Programme
VAT	value added tax
VC (1)	video conference
VC (2)	Vienna Convention
VCLT	Vienna Convention on the Law of Treaties between States and International Organizations or between International Organizations (1986)
VEA	voluntary environmental agreement
Vienna/Montreal	Vienna Convention for the protection of the Ozone Layer and its Montreal Protocol on Substances that Deplete the Ozone Layer
VietCapNet	Vietnam Capacity Building Network
VIP (1)	very important person
VIP (2)	ventilated pit latrine
VISTA	Volunteers in Service to America (US)
VITA	Volunteers in Technical Assistance
VMS	vessel monitoring system
VOCA	Volunteers International Cooperatives Association
VP	Vice President

VPP	victim pays principle
VRA	Volta River Authority
VTPI	Victoria Transport Policy Institute (Canada)

W

W-E-T	Water-Education-Training (UNESCO)
WAC	Water Management for African Cities (UN-Habitat)
WACLAC	World Association of Cities and Local Authorities Coordination
WAEMU	West African Economic and Monetary Union
WANA	West Asia and North Africa
WANet	West African Network in Integrated Water Resource Management
WAP (1)	Water Awareness Program
WAP (2)	Water Action Plan
WARAP	West African Regional Action Plan for Integrated Water Resources Management
WARDA	West Africa Rice Development Association
WARFSA	Water Research Foundation for Southern Africa
WASA	Water and Sewage Authority
WASER	World Association for Sedimentation and Erosion Research
WATAC	West Africa Technical Advisory Committee (GWP)
WAT_{RUR}	percentage of population having access to improved water supply in rural areas
WAT_{TOT}	percentage of population having access to improved water supply
WAT_{URB}	percentage of population having access to improved water supply in urban areas
WaterNet	South and East African Network in Integrated Water Resource Management
WAYS	World Academy of Young Scientists
WB	World Bank
WB-BIP	World Bank – Bank Internship Program
WB-JPA	World Bank – Junior Professional Associates Program
WB-YPP	World Bank – Young Professional Program
WBCSD	World Business Council for Sustainable Development
WBER	World Bank Economic Review
WBG	World Bank Group
WBGU	German Advisory Council on Global Change
WBI	World Bank Institute
WC	WIDECAST – Wider Caribbean Sea Turtle Conservation Network
WCA	Water Conservation in Agriculture (GWP)
WCAR	World Conference against Racism
WCASP	World Climate Application and Service Programme
WCC	World Conservation Congress

WCD	World Commission on Dams
WCDP	World Climate Data Programme
WCDR	World Conference on Disaster Reduction
WCED	World Commission on Environment and Development (The Brundtland Commission)
WCF	Water Cooperation Facility (UNESCO, WWC)
WCFSD	World Commission on Forests and Sustainable Development
WCIP	World Climate Impact Study Programme (UNEP)
WCMC	World Conservation Monitoring Centre
WCO	World Customs Organization
WCP	World Climate Programme
WCPA	World Commission on Protected Areas (IUCN)
WCRP	World Climate Research Programme
WCS (1)	World Conservation Strategy
WCS (2)	Wildlife Conservation Society
WCSIW	Wider Caribbean Initiative for Ship-Generated Waste
WDC	World Data Centre (ICSU)
WDCS	Whale and Dolphin Conservation Society
WDI	World Development Indicators
WDPA	World Data Base on Protected Areas
WDR	World Development Report
WE	Western Europe
WEA	World Energy Assessment
WEC (1)	World Energy Council
WEC (2)	World Environment Center
WEC (3)	World Environment Capacity
WEC (4)	Water Resources Environment Technology Center (Japan)
WECB	water, education and capacity building
WEDO	Women's Environment and Development Organization
WEF (1)	World Economic Forum
WEF (2)	Water Environment Federation (US)
WEHAB	Water, Energy, Health, Agriculture and Biodiversity Objectives (WSSD)
WEI	World Environment Institute
WEO (1)	World Environmental Organization
WEO (2)	World Energy Outlook
WEOG	Western Europe and Others Group
WERRD	Water and Environmental Resources in Regional Development
WES	Water, Environment and Sanitation Programme
WET	Water Education for Teachers (US)
Wetsus	Center for Sustainable Water Technology (The Netherlands)
WFC	World Food Council
WFD	Water Framework Directive (EU)
WFE	water, food and environment
WFED	World Foundation for Environment and Development

WFEO	World Federation of Engineering Organizations
WFP (1)	World Food Programme
WFP/WFp (2)	water footprint
WFS	World Food Summit of 1996
WFUNA	World Federation of United Nations Associations
WG	Working Group
WGEM	Ad Hoc Working Group on Environmental Monitoring of the UNECE
WGI	Working Group on Planning (CITES)
WGMS	World Glacier Monitoring Service
WHA	World Health Assembly
WHC (1)	World Heritage Convention (UNESCO)
WHC (2)	World Heritage Committee (UNESCO)
WHO	World Health Organization
WHYCOS	World Hydrological Observing System
WHYMAP	World-Wide Hydrological Mapping and Assessment Programme
WICE	World Industry Council for the Environment
WID	Women in Development
WIDECAST	Wider Caribbean Sea Turtle Conservation Network
WIN	Water Integrity Network
WIPO	World Intellectual Property Organization
WIS	Water Information Summit (IWRN)
WMA	Water Monitoring Alliance
WMO	World Meteorological Organization
WOC	Water Operating Center
WOCAR	World Conference against Racism
WPC	World Parks Congress
WPI	Water Poverty Index
WQMP	Water Quality Management Programme (GWP)
WRA	Water Resource Assessment
WRC (1)	Water Resources Commission (AfDB)
WRC (2)	World Research Commission
WRI (1)	World Resources Institute (US)
WRI (2)	Water Resources Institute (Ghana)
WRI (3)	Water Research Institute (Iran)
WS	water supply (WB)
WSC	Water Sector Committee (ADB)
WSCU	Water Sector Coordination Unit
WSDF	World Sustainable Development Forum
WSDP	Water Sector Development Programme
WSF (1)	World Solidarity Fund (UN)
WSF (2)	World Social Forum
WSI (1)	World Sindhi Institute (US)
WSI (2)	water stress index
WSIS	World Summit on the Information Society
WSP (1)	water safety plans
WSP (2)	Water and Sanitation Programme (GWP)

WSS	Water Supply and Sanitation (WWC; AIDIS)
WSSCC	Water Supply and Sanitation Collaborative Council
WSSD	World Summit on Sustainable Development
WSTA	Water Science and Technology Association (Bahrain)
WTA (1)	World Trade Agreement
WTA (2)	willingness to accept compensation
WTO (1)	World Trade Organization
WTO (2)	World Tourist Organization
WTP	willingness to pay
WTTERC	World Tourism and Travel Environment Research Center
WUA	Water Users Association
WUC	Water Users Cooperative
WUF	Water Users Federation
WUP	Water Utilities Partnerships in Africa (GWP)
WW2BW	from white water to blue water
WWA-WAU	World Water Council-Water Action Unit
WWAP	World Water Assessment Programme (UNESCO)
WWC	World Water Council
WWDR	World Water Development Report
WWF (1)	World Wide Fund for Nature (World Wildlife Fund, World Wide Fund International)
WWF (2)	World Water Forum (WWC)
WWI	World Water Institute
WWP	Women for Water Partnership
WWV	World Water Vision
WWW	World Weather Watch (WMO)

Y

YCELP	Yale (University) Center for Environmental Law and Policy
YFEU	Youth Forum of the EU
YLYL	years of life lost
YP	Yellow Pages
YRCC	Yellow River Conservancy Commission (China)
YWAT	Young Water Action Team

Z

ZAMCOM	Zambezi Watercourse Convention
ZEF	Centre for Development Research (Germany)
ZIL	Swiss Centre for International Agriculture
ZNWP	Zimbabwe National Water Partnership
ZOPP	objectives-oriented project planning
ZWA	Zero Waste Alliance

Bibliography

Abbott, K. W. and Snidal, D. (2000) 'Hard and soft law in international governance,' *International Organization*, vol 54, no 3, pp421–456

Abbott, M. B. (1991) *Hydroinformatics: Information Technology and the Aquatic Environment*, Aldershot, Avebury Technical

Albert, A. (ed) (1995) *Chaos and Society*, Amsterdam, IOS Press

Alexander, D. E. and Fairbridge, R. W. (eds) (1999) *Encyclopedia of Environmental Science*, Dordrecht, Kluwer Academic Publishers

Antweiler, W. (2006) 'European Currency Unit (ECU): A brief history of the ECU, the predecessor of the Euro,' Vancouver, Sauder School of Business, The University of British Columbia, accessed 2 December 2006 at http://fx.sauder.ubc.ca/ECU.html

Arthur, W. B. (1993) 'Why do things become more complex?' *Scientific American*, May, p144

Asian Development Bank (1986) *Environmental Guidelines for the Development of Ports and Harbours*, Manila, ADB

Axelrod, R. (1997) *The Complexity of Cooperation*, Princeton, Princeton University Press

Beattie, A. (2005) 'Welcome to the Group of 78,' *The Financial Times*, 16 April

Benedick, R. E. (1993) 'Perspectives of a negotiation practitioner,' in

Sjostedt, G. (ed) *International Environmental Negotiation*, London, Sage Publications, pp219–243

Bharati, V. (2001) *Yoga Sutras of Patanjali with the Exposition of Vyasa: A Translation and Commentary*, Delhi, Motilal Banarsidas Publishers

Biermann, F., Brohm, R. and Dingwerth, K. (eds) (2002) *Proceedings of the 2001 Berlin Conference on the Human Dimensions of Global Environmental Change: Global Environmental Change and the Nation State*, PIK Report No 80, Potsdam, Potsdam Institute for Climate Impact Research

Bigg, T. (2003) 'The World Summit on Sustainable Development: Was it worthwhile?' in Bigg, T. (ed) *Survival for a Small Planet*, London, Earthscan

Birnie, P. and Boyle, A. E. (1992) *International Law and the Environment*, Oxford, Clarendon Press

Boot, M. (2002) 'The big enchilada: American hegemony will be expensive,' *The International Herald Tribune*, 15 October

Botkin, D. B. (1990) *Discordant Harmony: A New Ecology for the Twenty-first Century*, Oxford, Oxford University Press

Brown, B. J., Hanson, M. E., Liverman, D. M. and Merideth, R. W., Jr. (1987) 'Global sustainability: Toward definition,' *Environmental Management*, vol 11, no 6, pp713–719.

Brunwassar, M. (2006) 'For Europe, a lesson in ABCs (of Cyrillic),' *The International Herald Tribune*, 9 August

Caldwell, L. (1980) *International Environmental Policy and Law*, Durham: Duke University Press

Caldwell, L. (1990) *Between Two Worlds: Science, the Environmental Movement, and Policy Choice*, Cambridge, Cambridge University Press

Cambel, A. B. (1993) *Applied Chaos Theory: A Paradigm for Complexity*, San Diego, Academic Press, Inc.

Carnegie Council (2004) 'Human rights dialogue: Environmental rights,' *Human Rights Dialogue*, series 2, no 11, Spring

Centre for Global Development and the Carnegie Endowment for International Peace. (2003) 'Ranking the rich,' *Foreign Policy*, May/June, pp56–66

Chayes, A. and Chayes, A. H. (1991) 'Adjustment and compliance processes in international regulatory regimes,' in Tuchman Mathews, J. (ed) *Preserving the Global Environment: The Challenge of Shared Leadership*, New York and London, W. W. Norton and Company, pp280–308

Chirac, J. (2006) 'Message from the President of the French Republic to the Closing Session of the 4th World Water Forum', at www.elysee.fr/elysee/elysee.fr/anglais/speeches_and_documents/2006/message_from_the_president_of_the_french_republic_to_the_closing_session_of_the_4th_world_water_forum.44782.html, accessed 30 November 2006

Cohen, R. (2004) 'As world leaders meet, UN is at a crossroads,' *The International Herald Tribune*, 22 September

Columbia University (nd) CIESIN Data Base, at http://sedac.ciesin.columbia.edu

COMEST (2005) *The Precautionary Principle*, Paris, UNESCO

Commission on Global Governance (1995) 'The concept of global governance,' in CGG (ed) *Our Global Neighborhood: The Report of the Commission on Global Governance*, Oxford, Oxford University Press

Commission on Global Governance (1999) 'The millennium year and the reform process', at www.cgg.ch

Cooper, A. F., English, J. and Thakur, R. (2002) *Enhancing Global Government: Towards a New Diplomacy*, Tokyo, UNU Press

Corell, E. and Betsell, M. M. (2001) 'A comparative look at NGO influence in intergovernmental environmental negotiations: Desertification and climate change,' *Global Environmental Politics*, vol 1, no 4, pp86–107

Daly, H. E. (1996) *Beyond Growth: The Economics of Sustainable Development*, Boston, Beacon Press

Deardorff, A. V. (2006) *Terms of Trade: Glossary of International Economics*, London, World Scientific Publishers.

Diamond, J. (2005) *Collapse: How Societies Choose to Fail or Succeed*, New York, Viking Press

Dodds, F. and Strauss, M. (2004) *How to Lobby at Intergovernmental Meetings*, London, Earthscan

Domoto, A. (2001) 'International environmental governance: Its impact on social and human development,' *Inter-linkages*, World Summit for Sustainable Development. United Nations University Centre, 3–4 September

Dresner, S. (2004) *Principles of sustainability*, London, Earthscan

Drezner, D. W. (2002) 'Bargaining, enforcement, and multilateral sanctions: When is cooperation counterproductive?' *International Organization*, vol 54, no 1, 73–102

Dupont, C. (1993) 'The Rhine: A study of inland water negotiations,' in Sjost-edt, G. (ed) *International Environmental Negotiation*, London, Sage Publications, pp135–148

Esty, D. C. and Ivanova, M. H. (eds) (2002) *Global Environmental Governance: Options and Opportunities*, New Haven, Yale Center for Environmental Law and Policy

European Commission (2000) *Communication from the Commission on the Precautionary Principle*, EU COM(2000)1, at http://europa.eu.int/comm/environmental/docum/20001_en.htm

Fauth, J. E. (1997) 'Working toward operational definitions in ecology: Putting the system back into ecosystem,' *Bulletin of the Ecological Society of America*, vol 78, no 4, p295

Flavin, C. et al. (eds) (2002) *State of the World 2002 – Progress Towards a Sustainable Society*, London, Worldwatch Institute and W.W. Norton and Company

French, H. (2001) *Vanishing Borders*, London, Worldwatch Institute and W.W. Norton and Company

French, H. (2002) 'Reshaping global governance,' in Flavin, C. et al. (eds) *State of the World 2002 – Progress Towards a Sustainable Society*, London, Worldwatch Institute and W.W. Norton and Company, pp174–198

Fridtjof Nansen Institute (2001) *Yearbook of International Cooperation on Environment and Development*, London, Earthscan

Gallopin, G. C. (1981a) 'Human systems: Needs, requirements, environments and quality of life,' in Lasker, G. E. (ed) *Applied Systems and Cybernetics. Vol. 1. The Quality of Life: Systems Approaches*, Oxford, Pergamon Press

Gallopin, G. C. (1981b) 'The abstract concept of environment,' *International Journal of General Systems*, vol 7, pp139–149

Global Water Partnership. (2003) 'Effective water governance: Learning from the dialogues, Stockholm,' at www.gwpforum.org/gwp/library/effective%20water%20governance.pdf, accessed on 30 November 2006

Goulet, D. (1986) 'Three rationalities in development decision-making,' *World Development*, vol 14, no 2, pp301–317

Gupta, J. (2002) *"On behalf of My Delegation..." A Survival Guide for Developing Country Climate Negotiators*. Climate Change Knowledge Network/Center for Sustainable Development in the Americas,' at http://www.unitar.org/cctrain/Survival%20Negotiators%(nAIP)www/index.htm

Haas, P. (1992) 'Introduction,' *Epistemic Communities and International Policy*

Coordination, International Organization, vol 46, no 1, pp1–35

Hanson, V. D. (2004) 'The U.N.? Who Cares...' *The Wall Street Journal – Europe*, 23 September

Hardin, G. (1968) 'The tragedy of the commons,' *Science*, vol 162, pp1243–1248

Hawley, A. H. (1986) *Human Ecology: A Theoretical Essay*, Chicago, The University of Chicago Press

Hempel, L. (1996) *Environmental Governance: the Global Challenge*, Washington DC, Island Press

Henley, J. (2005) 'Parlez-vous bureaucratique?' *The Guardian*, 18 February

Hewson, M. and Sinclair, T. J. (eds) (1999) *Approaches to Global Governance Theory*, Albany, State University of New York Press

Hollings, C. S. (1973) 'Resilience and stability of ecological systems,' *Annual Review of Ecology and Systematics*, vol 4, pp1–24

Hunter, D., Salzman, J. and Zaelke, D. (1998) *International Environmental Law and Policy*, New York, Foundation Press

IISD (2001) 'Summary Report from the UNEP Expert Consultations on International Environmental Governance,' 2nd Round Table, 29 May 2001, *IISD Linkages*, vol 53, no 1

Ingerson, A. E. (2002) 'A critical user's guide to "ecosystem" and related concepts in ecology,' Institute for Cultural Landscape Studies, the Arnold Arboretum of Harvard University, at www.icls.harvard.edu/ecology/ecology.html, accessed 2003

International Herald Tribune (2004) 'Editorial: The cloud of Iraqi sanctions over the United Nations,' *International Herald Tribune*, 15 October

IPCC (2001) 'Climate Change 2001: Impacts, adaption and vulnerability,' *IPCC Third Assessment Report*. WHO/UNEP, at www.ipcc.ch accessed 16 July, 2003

IUCN, UNEP and WWF (1980) *World Conservation Strategy: Living Resource Conservation for Sustainable Development*, Gland, IUCN

Jakobson, M. (2002) 'Preemption: Shades of Roosevelt and Stalin,' *The International Herald Tribune*, 17 October

Kagan, R. (2002) 'Power and weakness,' *Policy Review on Line*, at www.policyreview.org/JUN02/kagan.html, accessed 15 August, 2002

Kay, J. J. (1991) 'A non-equilibrium thermodynamic framework for discussing ecosystem integrity,' *Environmental Management*, vol 15, no 4, pp483–495

Keating, M. (1993) *The Earth Summit's Agenda for Change: A Plain Language Version of Agenda 21 and the Other Rio Agreements*, Geneva, Centre for Our Common Future

Kellert, S. (1995) 'When is the economy not like the weather? The problem of extending chaos theory to the social sciences,' in Albert, A. (ed) *Chaos and Society*, Amsterdam, IOS Press

Kremenyuk, V. and Lang, W. (1993) 'The political, diplomatic, and legal background,' in Sjostedt, G. (ed) *International Environmental Negotiation*, London, Sage Publications, pp3–16

Lackey, R. T. (2001) 'Values, policy, and ecosystem health,' *BioScience*, vol 51, no 6, pp437–443

Lawrence, P., Meigh, J. and Sullivan, C. (2002) 'The water poverty index,' Keele Economics Research Papers 2002/19, Department of Economics, Keele University, Keele

Lean, G. (2002) 'U.N. creates watchdog group in lieu of future summits,' *London Independent*, 8 September

Lipschutz, R. D. (1999) 'From local knowledge and practice to global environmental governance,' in Hewson, M. and Sinclair, T. J. (eds) *Approaches to Global Governance Theory*, Albany, NY State University of New York Press, pp259–283

Lipschutz, R. D. (2003) *Global Environmental Politics from the Ground Up*, at http://ic.ucsc.edu/~rlipsch/pol174/syllabus.html, accessed on 15 July, 2003

Loescher, G. (2004) 'Make aid a demilitarized zone,' *The International Herald Tribune*, 21–22 August

Lorenz, E. N. (1993) *The Essence of Chaos*, Seattle, University of Washington Press

Lugo, A. E. (1978) 'Stress and ecosystems,' in Thorp, J. H. and Gibbons, J. W. (eds) *Energy and Environmental Stress in Aquatic Systems*, DOE Symposium Series (1978)

Maerz, J. C. (1994) 'Ecosystem management: A summary of the Ecosystem Management Roundtable of 19 July 1993,' *Bulletin of the Ecological Society of America*, vol 75, no 2, pp93–95

Manners, I. R. and Mikesell, M. W. (eds) (1974) *Perspectives on Environment*, Washington DC, Association of American Geographers

Marín, V. (1997) 'General system theory and the ecosystem concept,' *Bulletin of the Ecological Society of America*, vol 78, no 1, pp102–103

Markandya, A., Perelet, R., Mason, P. and Taylor, T. (2001) *Dictionary of Environmental Economics*, London, Earthscan

McConnell, F. (1996) *The Biodiversity Convention: A Negotiating History*, London, Klawer Law International

McDonough, W. and Braungart, M. (2002) *Cradle to Cradle: Remaking the Way we Make Things*. North Point Press

Millennium Project (2005) Investing in Development: A Practical Plan to Achieve the Millennium Development Goals, at www.unmillenni-umproject.org/reports/fullreport.htm, accessed at 25 June, 2006

McDonough, W. and Braungart, M. (2003) *The Hanover Principles*, at www.mbdc.com

Miller, K. R. (1980) 'Cooperación y asistencia internacional en la dirección de parques nationales', *Planificación de Parques Nacionales para el Ecodesarrollo en Latinoamerica*, Madrid, Fundación para la Ecologia y la Protección del Medio Ambiente

Mitchell, R. B. (2002a) 'International environment,' in Risse, T., Simmons, B. and Carlsnaes, W. (eds) *Handbook of International Relations*, London, Sage Publications

Mitchell, R. B. (2002b) 'Of course international institutions matter: But when and how?' in Biermann, F., Brohm, R. and Dingwerth, K. (eds) *Proceedings of the 2001 Berlin Conference on the Human Dimensions of Global Environmental Change: Global Environmental Change and the Nation State*, PIK Report No. 80, Potsdam, Potsdam Institute for Climate Impact Research, pp16–25

Mitchell, R. B. (2003) 'International environmental agreements defined', at www.uoregon.edu/~rmitchel/IEA/overview/definitions/htm, accessed on 15 October

Najan, A. (1995) 'An environmental negotiation strategy for the South,' *International Environmental Affairs*, vol 7, no 3, pp249–287

Nonaka, I. and Takeuchi, H. (1995) *The Knowledge-Creating Company; How Japanese Companies Create the Dynamics of Innovation*, New York, Oxford University Press

OAS (1987) *Minimum Conflict: Guidelines for Planning the Use of American Humid Tropic Environments*, Washington DC, General Secretariat, Organization of American States

OAS (1998) 'First meeting of experts for the establishment of the Inter-American Biodiversity Information Network-IABIN,' 6–7 October 1997, Washington, DC, General Secretariat, Organization of American States

OAS (2001) *Inter-American Strategy for the promotion of Public Participation in Decision-Making for Sustainable Development*, Washington, DC, General Secretariat, Organization of American States

OECD (2006) 'OECD risk awareness tool for multicultural enterprises in weak governance zones,' at www.oecd.org/dataoecd/26/21/36885821.pdf, accessed on 26 June, 2006

O'Riordan, T. and Cameron, J. (1994) *Interpreting the Precautionary Principle*, London, Earthscan

O'Riordan, T., Cameron, J. and Jordan, A. (eds) *Reinterpreting the Precautionary Principle*, London, Cameron May

Pannell, D. J. and Schilizzi, S. (1997) 'Sustainable agriculture: A question of ecology, equity, economic efficiency or expedience?' *Sustainability and Economics in Agriculture*, SEA Working Paper 97/1, GRDC Project, University of Western Australia

Pavard, B. and Dugale, J. (2003) 'An introduction to complexity in social science,' at www.irit.fr/cosi/training/Complexity-tutorial/htm, accessed 15 July

Pezzey, J. (1992) *Sustainable Development Concepts: An Economic Analysis*, World Bank Environment Paper No. 2, Washington, DC, The World Bank

Pfaff, W. 2004. 'The debate on humanitarian intervention,' *The International Herald Tribune*, 31 August

Pomeroy, R. (2002) 'Earth summiteers cast doubt on future world meets,' *Reuters News Publication Service*, 4 September

Ramsundersingh, A. (2003) *Introducing Creative Learning at UNESCO-IHE*, Proceedings of the Conference on Water Education and Capacity Building (WECB), Third World Water Forum, Kyoto

Risse, T., Simmons, B. and Carlsnaes, W. (eds) (2002) *Handbook of International Relations*, London, Sage Publications

Rubin, J. Z. (1993) 'Third party roles: Mediation in international environmental disputes,' in Sjostedt, G. (ed) *International Environmental Negotiation*, London, Sage Publications, pp275–290

Saarinen, T. F. (1974) 'Environmental perception,' in Manners, I. R. and

Mikesell, M. W. (eds) *Perspectives on Environment*, Washington DC, Association of American Geographers, pp252–289

Sachs, I. (1976) 'Ecodevelopment', *Ceres*, Rome, UNFAO

Saunier, R. E. (1999) *Perceptions of Sustainability: A Framework for the 21st Century*, Trends for a Common Future 6, Washington, DC, CIDI/Organization of American States

Schnabel, A. and Thakur, R. (2000) 'Kosovo and the challenge of humanitarian intervention', UNU, Peace and Governance Programme, at www.unu.edu/p&g/kosovo_full.htm, accessed 25 November 2006

Sebenius, J, K. (1993) 'The Law of the Sea Conference: Lessons for negotiations to control global warming,' in Sjostedt, G. (ed) *International Environmental Negotiation*, London, Sage Publications, pp189–215

SER (2003) 'Global rationale for ecological restoration' IUCN-CEM 2nd Ecosystem Restoration Working Group Meeting, 2–5 March 2003, Taman Negara, Malaysia

Sharma, A., Mahapatra, R. and Polycarp, C. (2002) 'Dialogue of the deaf,' *Down to Earth*, Delhi, Centre for Science and Environment, pp25–33, at www.downtoearth.org.in/cover.asp?foldername=20020930&filename=ana/&sec_id=9&sid=1, accessed 20 January 2003

Sjostedt, G. (ed) (1993) *International Environmental Negotiation*, London, Sage Publications

Speth, J. G. and Haas, P. M. (2006) *Global Environmental Governance*, Washington, DC, Island Press

Suskind, R. (2006) *The ONE Percent Doctrine: Deep Inside America's Pursuit of its Enemies Since 9/11*, New York, Simon & Schuster

Taverne, D. (2005) *The March of Unreason: Science, Democracy and the New Fundamentalism*, London, Oxford University Press

The Aspen Institute (1996) 'Preventive intervention: Report of conference key findings, ideas and recommendations,' in The Aspen Institute (eds) *Managing Conflict in the Post-Cold War World: The Role of Intervention*, Report of the 2–6 August 1995 Aspen Institute Conference, Aspen, at www.colorado.edu/conflict/peace/example/aspe7032.htm, accessed on 1 December 2006

The Economist (2006) 'A Question of Definition?' *The Economist*, 14 September
The Frozen Ark (nd) *The Frozen Ark: Saving the DNA of Endangered* Species, at www.frozenark.org/index.html, accessed 3 December 2006

Third Millennium Foundation (2002) *Briefing on Japan's 'Vote-buying' Strategy in the International Whaling Commission*, Paciano, Third Millennium Foundation

Thorp, J. H. and Gibbons, J. W. (eds) (1978) *Energy and Environmental Stress in Aquatic Systems*, DOE Symposium Series

Trzyna, T., Margold, E. and Osborn, J. K. (1996) *World Directory of Environmental Organizations*, Sacramento, California Institute of Public Affairs, at www/cipahq/prg/landmarks.htm

Tuchman Mathews, J. (ed) (1991) *Preserving the Global Environment: The Challenge of Shared Leadership*, New York and London, W. W. Norton and Company

United Nations (nd) United Nations Treaty Data Base, at http://untreaty.un.org

UNCHS (2002) *Cities in a Globalizing World: Global Report on Human Settlements 2001*, London, Earthscan

UNDESA/DSD (2003) 'Partnerships for Sustainable Development' at www.un.org/esa/sustdev/partnerships/htm.com, accessed 13 November, 2003

UNDP (1996) *Environmental Projects Compendium for 1985–1995*, Han Noi, United Nations Development Programme

UNECE (2002) *Introducing the Aårhus Convention*, at www.buwal.ch/inter/e/ea_zugan.htm, accessed 15 August, 2001

UNEP (2002) *Global Environment Outlook 3*, London, Earthscan

UNEP (1997) *Compendium of Legislative Authority 1992–1997*, Oxford, United Nations Environment Programme/Express Litho Service

United Nations Food and Agriculture Organization (1997) *Food Production: The Critical Role of Water*, Rome, Technical background document 7, World Food Summit, 13–17 November, 1996

UNGA (1982) *World Charter for Nature*, UNGA RES 37/7

United Nations Millennium Development Goals (2000) at www.un/org/millenniumgoals/

Van Woerden, R. S. N., Meinder, J. and Rietjijk, T. (2006) 'World water exchange: Introducing a water exchange with the accompanying financial derivatives,' unpublished paper, Amsterdam

Varady, R. G. and Iles-Shih, M. (2005) 'Global water initiatives: What do the experts think' Paper presented at the Workshop on Impacts of Mega-Conferences on Global Water Development and Management, Bangkok, Thailand

Vatikiotis, M. (2005) 'A troubled world seen from a Swedish idyll,' *The International Herald Tribune*, 10 August

Waldrop, M. M. (1993) *Complexity: The Emerging Science at the Edge of Order and Chaos*, New York, Touchstone

Wali, M. (1995) 'eco Vocabulary: A glossary of our times,' *Bulletin of the Ecological Society of America*, vol 76, pp106–111

WBCSD (nd) *Eco-efficiency Learning Module*, World Business Council for Sustainable Development, Five Winds International, at www.wbcsd.ch/DocRoot/5XIVdoQGPMFEwDdM1xhh.eco-efficiency-module.pdf, accessed 30 November 2006

Weeks, D. (1992) *Eight Essential Steps to Conflict Resolution*, New York, G.P. Putnam's Sons

Wenger, E. (1998) *Communities of Practice; Learning, Meaning and Identity*, Cambridge, Cambridge University Press

WCED (World Commission on Environment and Development) (1987) *Our Common Future*, Oxford, Oxford University Press

World Resources Institute (2003) 'WRI expresses disappointment over many WSSD outcomes', at http://newsroom.wri.org, accessed 6 October, 2003

WRI, IUCN, UNEP (1992) *Global Biodiversity Strategy*, Washington, DC, World Resources Institute

Wyant, J, G., Meganck, R, A. and Ham, S. H. (1995) 'The need for an environmental restoration decision framework,' *Ecological Engineering*, vol 5, pp417–420

Young, O. R. (ed) (1997a) *Global Environmental Accord: Strategies for Sustainability and Institutional Innovations*, Cambridge, MIT Press

Young, O. R. (1997b) 'Global governance: Drawing insights from the environmental experience,' in Young, O. R. (ed) *Global Environmental Accord: Strategies for Sustainability and Institutional Innovations*, Cambridge, MIT Press

Zartman, W. I. (1993) 'Lessons for analysis and practice,' in Sjostedt, G. (ed) *International Environmental Negotiation*, London, Sage Publications, pp262–274

Appendix 1:
Selected Intergovernmental Environmental Agreements

Early agreements

1 The Universal Declaration of Human Rights (1944)
2 Charter of the United Nations (1945)
3 The Convention on the Rights of the Child (1959)
4 UNESCO Convention Concerning the Protection of the World Cultural and Natural Heritage (1972)
5 Convention on the Elimination of all Forms of Discrimination Against Women (1979)

UNCED (1992) preparations

6 A/Res/42/186 (1987)
7 A/Res/42/187 (1987)
8 A/Res/44/228-85 (1989)

UNCED related documents

9 The Rio Declaration on Environment and Development (1992)
10 *Agenda 21*: Global Programme of Action on Sustainable Development (1992)
11 Statement of Principles for the Sustainable Management of Forests (1992)
12 Declaration of Barbados and the Programme of Action for the Sustainable Development of Small Island Developing States (1994)

13 Programme of Action adopted at the Special Session of the General Assembly to Review the Implementation of *Agenda 21* (Earth Summit+5) (1997)
14 United Nations Millennium Declaration and Goals (2000)

Social issues

15 Programme of Action of the International Conference on Population and Development (1994)
16 The Report of the World Summit for Social Development (1995)
17 The Habitat Agenda and the Istanbul Declaration on Human Settlements (1996)
18 WHO-policy Health for All in the 21st Century (1999)

Economic issues

19 Final Act of the Uruguay Round and Related Agreements (1994)
20 The Marrakech Ministerial Decision on Trade and Environment (1994)
21 WTO Doha Ministerial Declaration (2001)

Natural resources

22 Convention on Wetlands of International Importance Especially as Waterfowl Habitat (1975)
23 Convention on International Trade in Endangered Species of Wild Fauna and Flora (1975)
24 Convention on the Conservation of Migratory Species of Wild Animals and further agreements under this convention (1979)
25 Vienna Convention for the Protection of the Ozone Layer (1985)
26 The Montreal Protocol (1987)
27 World Declaration on Nutrition/Plan of Action for Nutrition (1992)
28 Convention on Biological Diversity (1993)
29 UN Framework Convention on Climate Change (1994)
30 Rome Declaration on World Food Security and the World Food Summit Plan of Action (1996)
31 Report of the World Food Summit (1996)
32 United Nations Convention to Combat Desertification in Countries Experiencing Serious Drought and/or Desertification, Particularly in Africa (1996)

Hazardous wastes

33 Basel Convention on the Control of Transboundary Movements of Hazardous Wastes and their Disposal (1982)
34 Convention on Early Notification of a Nuclear Accident (1986)

Oceans

Appendix 2: Principles and Values of Global Environmental Governance

Most GEG meetings, conferences and summits such as UNCED or WSSD produce a final product, normally divided into a Declaration of Principles and a Plan of Action (POA). The Declaration of Principles, which is generally signed by the Ministers or Heads of State, is a broad document that provides the context for understanding the detailed initiatives or substantive mandates elaborated in the plan of action. These collected principles now help 'guide' GEG and, although many of them appear in declarations and are, therefore, soft law, others, because they are essential parts of universally ratified accords that have entered into force, have taken on the stature of international law. We list a few of the more important here.

Although not Principles or Values in a strict sense, the Millennium Development Goals (MDGs) are included in this appendix because for the first time in history all 189 UN Member States (number of Member States in 2000) agreed to a concerted effort to address the fundamental issues affecting sustainable development. To build strong partnerships at all levels, the MDGs place responsibilities on both rich and poor nations. Rich nations are specifically called on to relieve debt, increase aid and give poor countries fair access to their markets and their technology. Developing countries have the responsibility to undertake policy reforms and strengthen governance. The Goals, which will guide both technical assistance and investment in developing countries for the next decade, offer the world a means to accelerate the pace of development and to actually measure the results.

United Nations Universal Declaration of Human Rights (1948)

Article 1

All human beings are born free and equal in dignity and rights.They are endowed with reason and conscience and should act towards one another in a spirit of brotherhood.

Article 2

Everyone is entitled to all the rights and freedoms set forth in this Declaration, without distinction of any kind, such as race, colour, sex, language, religion, political or other opinion, national or social origin, property, birth or other status. Furthermore, no distinction shall be made on the basis of the political, jurisdictional or international status of the country or territory to which a person belongs, whether it be independent, trust, non-self-governing or under any other limitation of sovereignty.

Article 3

Everyone has the right to life, liberty and security of person.

Article 4

No one shall be held in slavery or servitude; slavery and the slave trade shall be prohibited in all their forms.

Article 5

No one shall be subjected to torture or to cruel, inhuman or degrading treatment or punishment.

Article 6

Everyone has the right to recognition everywhere as a person before the law.

Article 7

All are equal before the law and are entitled without any discrimination to equal protection of the law. All are entitled to equal protection against any discrimination in violation of this Declaration and against any incitement to such discrimination.

Article 8

Everyone has the right to an effective remedy by the competent national tribunals for acts violating the fundamental rights granted him by the constitution or by law.

Article 9

No one shall be subjected to arbitrary arrest, detention or exile.

Article 10

Everyone is entitled in full equality to a fair and public hearing by an independent and impartial tribunal, in the determination of his rights and obligations and of any criminal charge against him.

Article 11

(1) Everyone charged with a penal offence has the right to be presumed innocent until proved guilty according to law in a public trial at which he has had all the guarantees necessary for his defense.

(2) No one shall be held guilty of any penal offence on account of any act or omission which did not constitute a penal offence, under national or international law, at the time when it was committed. Nor shall a heavier penalty be imposed than the one that was applicable at the time the penal offence was committed.

Article 12

No one shall be subjected to arbitrary interference with his privacy, family, home or correspondence, nor to attacks upon his honour and reputation. Everyone has the right to the protection of the law against such interference or attacks.

Article 13

(1) Everyone has the right to freedom of movement and residence within the borders of each state.

(2) Everyone has the right to leave any country, including his own, and to return to his country.

Article 14

(1) Everyone has the right to seek and to enjoy in other countries asylum from persecution.

(2) This right may not be invoked in the case of prosecutions genuinely

arising from non-political crimes or from acts contrary to the purposes and principles of the United Nations.

Article 15

(1) Everyone has the right to a nationality.

(2) No one shall be arbitrarily deprived of his nationality nor denied the right to change his nationality.

Article 16

(1) Men and women of full age, without any limitation due to race, nationality or religion, have the right to marry and to found a family. They are entitled to equal rights as to marriage, during marriage and at its dissolution.

(2) Marriage shall be entered into only with the free and full consent of the intending spouses.

(3) The family is the natural and fundamental group unit of society and is entitled to protection by society and the State.

Article 17

(1) Everyone has the right to own property alone as well as in association with others.

(2) No one shall be arbitrarily deprived of his property.

Article 18

Everyone has the right to freedom of thought, conscience and religion; this right includes freedom to change his religion or belief, and freedom, either alone or in community with others and in public or private, to manifest his religion or belief in teaching, practice, worship and observance.

Article 19

Everyone has the right to freedom of opinion and expression; this right includes freedom to hold opinions without interference and to seek, receive and impart information and ideas through any media and regardless of frontiers.

Article 20

(1) Everyone has the right to freedom of peaceful assembly and association.

(2) No one may be compelled to belong to an association.

Article 21

(1) Everyone has the right to take part in the government of his country, directly or through freely chosen representatives.
(2) Everyone has the right of equal access to public service in his country.
(3) The will of the people shall be the basis of the authority of government; this will shall be expressed in periodic and genuine elections which shall be by universal and equal suffrage and shall be held by secret vote or by equivalent free voting procedures.

Article 22

Everyone, as a member of society, has the right to social security and is entitled to realization, through national effort and international co-operation and in accordance with the organization and resources of each State, of the economic, social and cultural rights indispensable for his dignity and the free development of his personality.

Article 23

(1) Everyone has the right to work, to free choice of employment, to just and favourable conditions of work and to protection against unemployment.
(2) Everyone, without any discrimination, has the right to equal pay for equal work.
(3) Everyone who works has the right to just and favourable remuneration ensuring for himself and his family an existence worthy of human dignity, and supplemented, if necessary, by other means of social protection.
(4) Everyone has the right to form and to join trade unions for the protection of his interests.

Article 24

Everyone has the right to rest and leisure, including reasonable limitation of working hours and periodic holidays with pay.

Article 25

(1) Everyone has the right to a standard of living adequate for the health and well-being of himself and of his family, including food, clothing, housing and medical care and necessary social services, and the right to security in the event of unemployment, sickness, disability, widowhood, old age or other lack of livelihood in circumstances beyond his control.
(2) Motherhood and childhood are entitled to special care and assistance. All children, whether born in or out of wedlock, shall enjoy the same social protection.

Article 26

(1) Everyone has the right to education. Education shall be free, at least in the elementary and fundamental stages. Elementary education shall be compulsory. Technical and professional education shall be made generally available and higher education shall be equally accessible to all on the basis of merit.

(2) Education shall be directed to the full development of the human personality and to the strengthening of respect for human rights and fundamental freedoms. It shall promote understanding, tolerance and friendship among all nations, racial or religious groups, and shall further the activities of the United Nations for the maintenance of peace.

(3) Parents have a prior right to choose the kind of education that shall be given to their children.

Article 27

(1) Everyone has the right freely to participate in the cultural life of the community, to enjoy the arts and to share in scientific advancement and its benefits.

(2) Everyone has the right to the protection of the moral and material interests resulting from any scientific, literary or artistic production of which he is the author.

Article 28

Everyone is entitled to a social and international order in which the rights and freedoms set forth in this Declaration can be fully realized.

Article 29

(1) Everyone has duties to the community in which alone the free and full development of his personality is possible.

(2) In the exercise of his rights and freedoms, everyone shall be subject only to such limitations as are determined by law solely for the purpose of securing due recognition and respect for the rights and freedoms of others and of meeting the just requirements of morality, public order and the general welfare in a democratic society.

(3) These rights and freedoms may in no case be exercised contrary to the purposes and principles of the United Nations.

Article 30

Nothing in this Declaration may be interpreted as implying for any State, group or person any right to engage in any activity or to perform any act aimed at the destruction of any of the rights and freedoms set forth herein.

Declaration of Rio de Janerio on Environment and Development, June 1992

Principle 1

Human beings are at the centre of concerns for sustainable development. They are entitled to a healthy and productive life in harmony with nature.

Principle 2

States have, in accordance with the Charter of the United Nations and the principles of international law, the sovereign right to exploit their own resources pursuant to their own environmental and developmental policies, and the responsibility to ensure that activities within their jurisdiction or control do not cause damage to the environment of other States or of areas beyond the limits of national jurisdiction.

Principle 3

The right to development must be fulfilled so as to equitably meet developmental and environmental needs of present and future generations.

Principle 4

In order to achieve sustainable development, environmental protection shall constitute an integral part of the development process and cannot be considered in isolation from it.

Principle 5

All States and all people shall cooperate in the essential task of eradicating poverty as an indispensable requirement for sustainable development, in order to decrease the disparities in standards of living and better meet the needs of the majority of the people of the world.

Principle 6

The special situation and needs of developing countries, particularly the least developed and those most environmentally vulnerable, shall be given special priority. International actions in the field of environment and development should also address the interests and needs of all countries.

Principle 7

States shall cooperate in a spirit of global partnership to conserve, protect and restore the health and integrity of the Earth's ecosystem. In view of the different contributions to global environmental degradation, States have common but differentiated responsibilities. The developed countries acknowledge the responsibility that they bear in the international pursuit to sustainable development in view of the pressures their societies place on the global environment and of the technologies and financial resources they command.

Principle 8

To achieve sustainable development and a higher quality of life for all people, States should reduce and eliminate unsustainable patterns of production and consumption and promote appropriate demographic policies.

Principle 9

States should cooperate to strengthen endogenous capacity-building for sustainable development by improving scientific understanding through exchanges of scientific and technological knowledge, and by enhancing the development, adaptation, diffusion and transfer of technologies, including new and innovative technologies.

Principle 10

Environmental issues are best handled with participation of all concerned citizens, at the relevant level. At the national level, each individual shall have appropriate access to information concerning the environment that is held by public authorities, including information on hazardous materials and activities in their communities, and the opportunity to participate in decision-making processes. States shall facilitate and encourage public awareness and participation by making information widely available. Effective access to judicial and administrative proceedings, including redress and remedy, shall be provided.

Principle 11

States shall enact effective environmental legislation. Environmental standards, management objectives and priorities should reflect the environmental and development context to which they apply. Standards applied by some countries may be inappropriate and of unwarranted economic and social cost to other countries, in particular developing countries.

Principle 12

States should cooperate to promote a supportive and open international economic system that would lead to economic growth and sustainable development in all countries, to better address the problems of environmental degradation. Trade policy measures for environmental purposes should not constitute a means of arbitrary or unjustifiable discrimination or a disguised restriction on international trade. Unilateral actions to deal with environmental challenges outside the jurisdiction of the importing country should be avoided. Environmental measures addressing transboundary or global environmental problems should, as far as possible, be based on an international consensus.

Principle 13

States shall develop national law regarding liability and compensation for the victims of pollution and other environmental damage. States shall also cooperate in an expeditious and more determined manner to develop further international law regarding liability and compensation for adverse effects of environmental damage caused by activities within their jurisdiction or control to areas beyond their jurisdiction.

Principle 14

States should effectively cooperate to discourage or prevent the relocation and transfer to other States of any activities and substances that cause severe environmental degradation or are found to be harmful to human health.

Principle 15

In order to protect the environment, the precautionary approach shall be widely applied by States according to their capabilities. Where there are threats of serious or irreversible damage, lack of full scientific certainty shall not be used as a reason for postponing cost-effective measures to prevent environmental degradation.

Principle 16

National authorities should endeavour to promote the internalization of environmental costs and the use of economic instruments, taking into account the approach that the polluter should, in principle, bear the cost of pollution, with due regard to the public interest and without distorting international trade and investment.

Principle 17

Environmental impact assessment, as a national instrument, shall be undertaken for proposed activities that are likely to have a significant adverse impact on the environment and are subject to a decision of a competent national authority.

Principle 18

States shall immediately notify other States of any natural disasters or other emergencies that are likely to produce sudden harmful effects on the environment of those States. Every effort shall be made by the international community to help States so afflicted.

Principle 19

States shall provide prior and timely notification and relevant information to potentially affected States on activities that may have a significant adverse transboundary environmental effect and shall consult with those States at an early stage and in good faith.

Principle 20

Women have a vital role in environmental management and development. Their full participation is therefore essential to achieve sustainable development.

Principle 21

The creativity, ideals and courage of the youth of the world should be mobilized to forge a global partnership in order to achieve sustainable development and ensure a better future for all.

Principle 22

Indigenous people and their communities and other local communities have a vital role in environmental management and development because of their knowledge and traditional practices. States should recognize and duly support their identity, culture and interests and enable their effective participation in the achievement of sustainable development.

Principle 23

The environment and natural resources of people under oppression, domination and occupation shall be protected.

Principle 24

Warfare is inherently destructive of sustainable development. States shall therefore respect international law providing protection for the environment in times of armed conflict and cooperate in its further development, as necessary.

Principle 25

Peace, development and environmental protection are interdependent and indivisible.

Principle 26

States shall resolve all their environmental disputes peacefully and by appropriate means in accordance with the Charter of the United Nations.

Principle 27

States and people shall cooperate in good faith and in a spirit of partnership in the fulfilment of the principles embodied in this Declaration and in the further development of international law in the field of sustainable development.

Specialized Summit of the Americas on Sustainable Development, December 1996

1 We, the elected Heads of State and Government of the Americas, gathered in Santa Cruz de la Sierra as decided at the Summit of the Americas held in Miami in 1994, reaffirm our determination to move forward toward sustainable development and to implement the decisions and commitments set forth in the Rio Declaration and Agenda 21, which were adopted at the United Nations Conference on Environment and Development, held in Rio de Janeiro in 1992.

We also reaffirm the commitments undertaken in the Declaration of Principles and the Plan of Action of the Summit of the Americas. We undertake to promote the agreements reached at the Global Conference on the Sustainable Development of Small Island Developing States, held in Barbados in 1994, and recognize the importance of the principles enunciated at recent United Nations conferences concerning sustainable development.

We support the efforts launched at the hemispheric, regional, and subregional levels, such as the Central American Alliance for Sustainable Development, the North American Agreement on Environmental Cooperation, the Treaty for Amazonian Cooperation, and the Permanent South Pacific Commission.

2   We reaffirm that human beings are entitled to a healthy and productive life in harmony with nature and, as such, are the focus of sustainable development concerns. Development strategies need to include sustainability as an essential requirement for the balanced, interdependent, and integral attainment of economic, social, and environmental goals.

3   One essential feature of the Americas is their natural and cultural diversity. Our countries share a unique and rich political tradition grounded in democratic values and significant potential for economic growth and technological development in a context of open, market-based economies. These characteristics are of fundamental importance for the promotion of economic development and social welfare and for the preservation of a healthy environment.

We will adopt policies and strategies that will encourage changes in production and consumption patterns in order to attain sustainable development and a better quality of life, as well as to preserve our natural environment and contribute to the alleviation of poverty.

We reaffirm our commitment to the fundamental principle of the Charter of the Organization of American States, restated at the Summit of the Americas, that representative democracy is essential for peace, justice, and development. Sustainable development requires that we strengthen and promote our democratic institutions and values.

4   Recognizing that globalization, efforts toward integration, and the complexity of environmental issues pose challenges and offer opportunities to the countries in the Hemisphere, we pledge to work together.

5   We recognize that the needs and responsibilities facing the countries of the Hemisphere today are diverse. Sustainable development does not assume that all the countries are at the same level of development, have the same capabilities, or can necessarily use the same model to attain it. In view of the different contributions to global environmental degradation, states have common but differentiated responsibilities in the global quest for sustainable development. We should make efforts to ensure that the benefits of sustainable development reach all countries in the Hemisphere, in particular those that are less developed, and all segments of our populations.

We will give special attention to the small island states, whose environmental vulnerability, especially with regard to natural disasters, is greater owing to their geographic situation, their size, and the scale of their economies, among other factors.

6   The alleviation of poverty is an integral part of sustainable development. The benefits of prosperity will only be attained through policies that address the interrelationship between human beings and nature. In developing policies and programs for sustainable development, special attention should be given to the needs of indigenous people, minority

communities, women, youth, and children and to facilitating their full participation in the development process. The living conditions of persons with disabilities and the elderly also merit special attention.

7 We will establish or strengthen our programs, policies, and institutional frameworks in support of sustainable development objectives. National efforts should be complemented by ongoing international cooperation in furtherance of the commitments made at the Rio conference related to financial resources, and the transfer of technology on fair and favorable terms, including preferential terms, as mutually agreed.

8 We will support and encourage, as a basic requisite for sustainable development, broad participation by civil society in the decision-making process, including policies and programs and their design, implementation, and evaluation. To this end, we will promote the enhancement of institutional mechanisms for public participation.

9 This Summit Conference on Sustainable Development is the cornerstone of a partnership for cooperation among the states of the Americas in their common pursuit of a higher quality of life for their peoples, founded on integrated and complementary economic, social, and environmental objectives.

Taking the current experience of our countries and region as a point of departure, we hereby frame a plan of action that will commit the states to timely action and ensure the availability of the resources needed for that purpose.

10 In keeping with the principles stated above, we emphasize the following points regarding application of the Plan of Action for the Sustainable Development of the Americas:

a *Equitable economic growth*

Implement effective and ongoing measures to ensure that the international economic and financial system supports the growth of local economies and their sustainable development with a view to establishing greater social justice for all of our peoples. Reinforce the mutually supportive relationship between trade and the environment by acting to conserve the environment, while safeguarding an open, equitable, and nondiscriminatory multilateral trade system, taking into account the efforts currently being deployed in this field by the Committee on Trade and Environment of the World Trade Organization. We recognize the great need of our countries to improve access to markets while maintaining effective and appropriate environmental policies. In this regard, we will avoid hidden trade restrictions, in accordance with the General Agreement on Tariffs and Trade/World Trade Organization (GATT/WTO) and other international obligations. Full participation by the private sector – especially small, medium-sized, and micro-enterprises, as well as cooperatives and other forms of productive organization – in a sustainable development strategy essential to take advantage of its resources and dynamism. This strategy should balance comprehensive policies to address environmental and development problems.

b   *Social dimensions*

There is an urgent need to intensify efforts to reduce the poverty and the marginalization which broadly affect our societies, and especially women and children. We will promote, through the relevant measures and programs, including those established in the Plan of Action, adequate levels of nutrition, a greater degree of food security, equitable and effective access to basic health care and drinking water and to employment and housing, and we will seek to ensure pollution control and a clean environment for all people, taking into account, in particular, the most vulnerable groups. We will also develop strategies that value human dignity while respecting and fostering the cultural diversity of our societies, gender equity, and educational programs promoting peace, democracy, and respect for nature, with special attention to children and young people. In this context, the principles and priorities established in the Pan American Charter: Health and Environment in Sustainable Human Development will be put into practice as appropriate.

c   *A healthy environment*

Planning and decision-making for sustainable development require understanding and integrating environmental considerations, as well as social and economic factors. We will assess the environmental impact of our policies, strategies, programs, and projects nationally and in the framework of international agreements to ensure that adverse environmental effects are identified, prevented, minimized, or mitigated, as appropriate.

d   *Public participation*

We will promote increased opportunities for the expression of ideas and the exchange of information and traditional knowledge on sustainable development between groups, organizations, businesses, and individuals, including indigenous people, as well as for their effective participation in the formulation, adoption, and execution of decisions that affect their lives.

e   *The development and transfer of technology*

The development, adoption, adaptation, and application of environmentally sound, effective technology play an important role in ensuring sustainable development.

To this end, efforts to promote the transfer of, and access to, appropriate technology should continue in the Hemisphere. We recognize the important role played by market-based mechanisms and will promote opportunities for technology transfer through training and cooperative work programs and through improved access to sources of information. In addition, we will strengthen national scientific and technological capacities, complemented by international cooperation.

f *Financing*

Implementation of the initiatives set forth in the Plan of Action requires the mobilization of financial resources in keeping with the commitments made at the Rio Summit. These should be complemented with innovative financing mechanisms. In this context, we highlight the importance of international organizations and financial institutions in strongly supporting the efforts of the Hemisphere.

g *Strengthening of the legal framework*

Relations between countries of the Hemisphere, within the framework of this partnership for sustainable development, will be grounded in the rules and principles of international law. We will consider the progress in international environmental law and promote the reform and modernization of national laws, as appropriate, to reflect sustainable development concepts. We will also develop national mechanisms for effective enforcement of applicable international and national laws and provisions. We will seek to secure ratification of, or accession to, international instruments on sustainable development and will fulfill all commitments made therein.

Thus we sign the Declaration of Santa Cruz and adopt the Plan of Action for the Sustainable Development of the Americas on this seventh day of December in the year one thousand nine hundred and ninety-six, in Spanish, French, English, and Portuguese.

Millennium Values and Development Goals (2000)

Values

Freedom
> Men and women have the right to live their lives and raise their children in dignity, free from hunger and from the fear of violence, oppression or injustice. Democratic and participatory governance based on the will of the people best assures these rights.

Equality
> No individual and no nation must be denied the opportunity to benefit from development. The equal rights and opportunities of women and men must be assured.

Solidarity

Global challenges must be managed in a way that distributes the costs and burdens fairly in accordance with basic principles of equity and social justice. Those who suffer or who benefit least deserve help from those who benefit most.

Tolerance

Human beings must respect one other, in all their diversity of belief, culture and language. Differences within and between societies should be neither feared nor repressed, but cherished as a precious asset of humanity. A culture of peace and dialogue among all civilizations should be actively promoted.

Respect for nature

Prudence must be shown in the management of all living nature species and natural resources, in accordance with the precepts of sustainable development. Only in this way can the immeasurable riches provided to us by nature be preserved and passed on to our descendants. The current unsustainable patterns of production and consumption must be changed in the interest of our future welfare and that of our descendants.

Shared

Responsibility for managing worldwide economic and responsible social development, as well as threats to international peace and security, must be shared among the nations of the world and should be exercised multilaterally. As the most universal and most representative organization in the world, the United Nations must play the central role.

Millennium Development Goals (MDGs)

By the year 2015, the then 191 UN Member States pledged to:

Goal I
Eradicate extreme poverty and hunger

- Reduce by half the proportion of people living on less than one US dollar per day.
- Reduce by half the proportion of people who suffer from hunger.

Goal 2
Achieve universal primary education

- Ensure that all boys and girls complete a full course of primary schooling.

Goal 3
Promote gender equality and empower women

- Eliminate gender disparity in primary and secondary education preferably by 2005, and at all levels by 2015.

Goal 4
Reduce child mortality

- Reduce by two-thirds the mortality rate among children under five.

Goal 5
Improve maternal health

- Reduce by three-quarters the maternal morality ratio.

Goal 6
Combat HIV/AIDS, malaria and other diseases

- Halt and begin to reverse the spread of HIV/AIDS.
- Halt and begin to reverse the incidence of malaria and other major diseases.

Goal 7
Ensure environmental sustainability

- Integrate the principles of sustainable development into country policies and programs; reverse loss of environmental resources.
- Reduce by half the proportion of people without sustainable access to safe drinking water.
- Achieve significant improvement in lives of at least 100 million slum dwellers, by 2020.

Goal 8
Develop a global partnership for development

- Develop further an open trading and financial system that is rule-based, predictable and non-discriminatory. Includes a commitment to good governance, development and poverty reduction – nationally and internationally.
- Address the least developed countries' special needs. This includes tariff- and quota-free access for their exports; enhanced debt relief for heavily indebted poor countries; cancellation of official bilateral debt; and more generous official development assistance for countries committed to poverty reduction.
- Address the special needs of landlocked and Small Island Developing States.
- Deal comprehensively with developing countries' debt problems through national and international measures to make debt sustainable in the long-term.
- In cooperation with the developing countries, develop decent and productive work for youth.
- In cooperation with pharmaceutical companies, provide access to affordable essential drugs in developing countries.

- In cooperation with the private sector, make available the benefits of new technologies – especially information and communications technologies.

Johannesburg Declaration on Sustainable Development, September 2002

From our origins to the future

1   We, the representatives of the peoples of the world, assembled at the World Summit on Sustainable Development in Johannesburg, South Africa, from 2 to 4 September 2002, reaffirm our commitment to sustainable development.

2   We commit ourselves to building a humane, equitable and caring global society, cognizant of the need for human dignity for all.

3   At the beginning of this Summit, the children of the world spoke to us in a simple yet clear voice that the future belongs to them, and accordingly challenged all of us to ensure that through our actions they will inherit a world free of the indignity and indecency occasioned by poverty, environmental degradation and patterns of unsustainable development.

4   As part of our response to these children, who represent our collective future, all of us, coming from every corner of the world, informed by different life experiences, are united and moved by a deeply felt sense that we urgently need to create a new and brighter world of hope.

5   Accordingly, we assume a collective responsibility to advance and strengthen the interdependent and mutually reinforcing pillars of sustainable development – economic development, social development and environmental protection – at the local, national, regional and global levels.

6   From this continent, the cradle of humanity, we declare, through the Plan of Implementation of the World Summit on Sustainable Development and the present Declaration, our responsibility to one another, to the greater community of life and to our children.

7   Recognizing that humankind is at a crossroads, we have united in a common resolve to make a determined effort to respond positively to the need to produce a practical and visible plan to bring about poverty eradication and human development.

From Stockholm to Rio de Janeiro to Johannesburg

8   Thirty years ago, in Stockholm, we agreed on the urgent need to respond to the problem of environmental deterioration. Ten years ago, at the United Nations Conference on Environment and Development, held in Rio de Janeiro, we agreed that the protection of

the environment and social and economic development are fundamental to sustainable development, based on the Rio Principles. To achieve such development, we adopted the global programme entitled Agenda 21 and the Rio Declaration on Environment and Development, to which we reaffirm our commitment. The Rio Conference was a significant milestone that set a new agenda for sustainable development.

9 Between Rio and Johannesburg, the world's nations have met in several major conferences under the auspices of the United Nations, including the International Conference on Financing for Development, as well as the Doha Ministerial Conference. These conferences defined for the world a comprehensive vision for the future of humanity.

10 At the Johannesburg Summit, we have achieved much in bringing together a rich tapestry of peoples and views in a constructive search for a common path towards a world that respects and implements the vision of sustainable development. The Johannesburg Summit has also confirmed that significant progress has been made towards achieving a global consensus and partnership among all the people of our planet.

The challenges we face

11 We recognize that poverty eradication, changing consumption and production patterns and protecting and managing the natural resource base for economic and social development are overarching objectives of and essential requirements for sustainable development.

12 The deep fault line that divides human society between the rich and the poor and the ever-increasing gap between the developed and developing worlds pose a major threat to global prosperity, security and stability.

13 The global environment continues to suffer. Loss of biodiversity continues, fish stocks continue to be depleted, desertification claims more and more fertile land, the adverse effects of climate change are already evident, natural disasters are more frequent and more devastating, and developing countries more vulnerable, and air, water and marine pollution continue to rob millions of a decent life.

14 Globalization has added a new dimension to these challenges. The rapid integration of markets, mobility of capital and significant increases in investment flows around the world have opened new challenges and opportunities for the pursuit of sustainable development. But the benefits and costs of globalization are unevenly distributed, with developing countries facing special difficulties in meeting this challenge.

15 We risk the entrenchment of these global disparities and unless we act in a manner that fundamentally changes their lives the poor of the world may lose confidence in their representatives and the democratic systems to which we remain committed, seeing their representatives as nothing more than sounding brass or tinkling cymbals.

Our commitment to sustainable development

16 We are determined to ensure that our rich diversity, which is our collective strength, will be used for constructive partnership for change

and for the achievement of the common goal of sustainable development.

17 Recognizing the importance of building human solidarity, we urge the promotion of dialogue and cooperation among the world's civilizations and peoples, irrespective of race, disabilities, religion, language, culture or tradition.

18 We welcome the focus of the Johannesburg Summit on the indivisibility of human dignity and are resolved, through decisions on targets, timetables and partnerships, to speedily increase access to such basic requirements as clean water, sanitation, adequate shelter, energy, health care, food security and the protection of biodiversity. At the same time, we will work together to help one another gain access to financial resources, benefit from the opening of markets, ensure capacity-building, use modern technology to bring about development and make sure that there is technology transfer, human resource development, education and training to banish underdevelopment forever.

19 We reaffirm our pledge to place particular focus on, and give priority attention to, the fight against the worldwide conditions that pose severe threats to the sustainable development of our people, which include: chronic hunger; malnutrition; foreign occupation; armed conflict; illicit drug problems; organized crime; corruption; natural disasters; illicit arms trafficking; trafficking in persons; terrorism; intolerance and incitement to racial, ethnic, religious and other hatreds; xenophobia; and endemic, communicable and chronic diseases, in particular HIV/AIDS, malaria and tuberculosis.

20 We are committed to ensuring that women's empowerment, emancipation and gender equality are integrated in all the activities encompassed within Agenda 21, the Millennium development goals and the Plan of Implementation of the Summit.

21 We recognize the reality that global society has the means and is endowed with the resources to address the challenges of poverty eradication and sustainable development confronting all humanity. Together, we will take extra steps to ensure that these available resources are used to the benefit of humanity.

22 In this regard, to contribute to the achievement of our development goals and targets, we urge developed countries that have not done so to make concrete efforts to reach the internationally agreed levels of official development assistance.

23 We welcome and support the emergence of stronger regional groupings and alliances, such as the New Partnership for Africa's Development, to promote regional cooperation, improved international cooperation and sustainable development.

24 We shall continue to pay special attention to the developmental needs of small island developing States and the least developed countries.

25 We reaffirm the vital role of the indigenous peoples in sustainable development.

26 We recognize that sustainable development requires a long-term perspective and broad-based participation in policy formulation, decision-making and implementation at all levels. As social partners,

we will continue to work for stable partnerships with all major groups, respecting the independent, important roles of each of them.

27 We agree that in pursuit of its legitimate activities the private sector, including both large and small companies, has a duty to contribute to the evolution of equitable and sustainable communities and societies.

28 We also agree to provide assistance to increase income-generating employment opportunities, taking into account the Declaration on Fundamental Principles and Rights at Work of the International Labour Organization.

29 We agree that there is a need for private sector corporations to enforce corporate accountability, which should take place within a transparent and stable regulatory environment.

30 We undertake to strengthen and improve governance at all levels for the effective implementation of Agenda 21, the Millennium development goals and the Plan of Implementation of the Summit.

Multilateralism is the future

31 To achieve our goals of sustainable development, we need more effective, democratic and accountable international and multilateral institutions.

32 We reaffirm our commitment to the principles and purposes of the Charter of the United Nations and international law, as well as to the strengthening of multilateralism. We support the leadership role of the United Nations as the most universal and representative organization in the world, which is best placed to promote sustainable development.

33 We further commit ourselves to monitor progress at regular intervals towards the achievement of our sustainable development goals and objectives.

Making it happen!

34 We are in agreement that this must be an inclusive process, involving all the major groups and Governments that participated in the historic Johannesburg Summit.

35 We commit ourselves to act together, united by a common determination to save our planet, promote human development and achieve universal prosperity and peace.

36 We commit ourselves to the Plan of Implementation of the World Summit on Sustainable Development and to expediting the achievement of the time-bound, socio-economic and environmental targets contained therein.

37 From the African continent, the cradle of humankind, we solemnly pledge to the peoples of the world and the generations that will surely inherit this Earth that we are determined to ensure that our collective hope for sustainable development is realized.

Appendix 3:
Major Civil Society Alternative Agreements

(The NGO Alternative Treaties are from the Global Forum at Rio de Janeiro 1–15 June, 1992. Texts of these documents may be found at www.igc.org/habitat/treaties/index.html).

Declarations and General Principles

1   People's Earth Declaration
2   Rio de Janeiro Declaration
3   The Earth Charter
4   Ethical Commitments to Global Ecological Posture and Behavior

Education, Communication and Cooperation

5   Treaty on Environmental Education for Sustainable Societies and Global Responsibility
6   Communication, Information, Media and Networking Treaty
7   Treaty for Non-Governmental Organization Cooperation and Sharing of Resources
8   Treaty on a Technology Bank Solidarity System for Technological Exchange
9   Rio Framework Treaty on NGO Global Decision Making
10 Code of Conduct for NGOs

Alternative economic issues

Consumption, poverty, food and subsistence

Climate, energy and waste

Land and natural resources

Marine and ocean issues

Biodiversity and biotechnology

36 Marine Biodiversity Treaty
37 Draft Protocol on Scientific Research Components for the Conservation of Biodiversity
38 Citizen's Commitments on Biotechnology

Cross-sectoral issues

39 A Global Women's Treaty for NGOs Seeking a Just and Healthy Planet
40 Treaty on Population, Environment and Development
41 Youth Treaty
42 Treaty in Defense and Protection of Children and Adolescents
43 International Treaty between Non-Governmental Organizations and Indigenous Peoples
44 Treaty Against Racism
45 Treaty on Militarism, the Environment and Development
46 Treaty on Urbanization

Appendix 4:
Documenting Governance

Although the purpose of any GEG meeting is to produce a set of decisions to guide activities designed to meet the stated objectives of that meeting, it sometimes appears that a meeting's purpose is little more than to produce a set of documents of ever-increasing number. To keep track of all these documents, from three to five lines of document symbols or codes – a combination of letters and numbers – are placed in the upper right corner of the first page that indicate just what the document is: the responsible body and/or subsidiary body, the meeting, identification number, where it is in the process, when it was written or approved, and in what languages. There are similarities among the many agencies and agreements but there are also differences – for example, the UN uses symbols that are composed of upper case letters while other agencies may use lower case and the symbols used by the Organization of American States are in Spanish even though the document may be in English, French or Portuguese. How to decipher just what all the abbreviations mean is one of the first hurdles a beginner has to face – both to keep track of what is going on in a meeting and to find the document you are looking for in the future. We will present a few of the more common abbreviations here. Others can be found in the Acronyms and Abbreviations chapter of this book. The United Nations explains its documentation symbols at www.un.org/depts./dh/resguides/symbol.htm.

Generally, units of the code are divided by a diagonal line [/] (and sometimes by a period [.] or hyphen [-]). The first set of letters identify the parent organ or body and the second set identifies the subsidiary body responsible for the document. The next set identifies the meeting or activity and the number immediately following identifies the session of the meeting where the document is being, or was, presented and whether it is the original, an addendum, amendment or correction. Other symbols indicate the nature of the document's distribution (restricted, general, internal, limited, etc.) and additional information such as whether it is for information only, whether it is a statement by a named member party or observer, a verbatim or summary record, a resolution, a working paper or a petition. Information may also be found elsewhere on the cover sheet that indicates the full name of the sponsoring institutions, location and date of the meeting, and the title of the paper. The following is an example of what would appear in the upper right corner of the first page (the main line of which is often repeated on each page of the entire document):

Dist
GENERAL
UNEP/CBD/COP/3/Inf.20
20 September 1996
ORIGINAL: ENGLISH

This notation says that the document was originally written in English for general distribution on 20 September, 1996 and is the twentieth informational paper in a series prepared for the third meeting of the Conference of the Parties to the Convention on Biological Diversity being sponsored by the United Nations Environment Programme. This is an easy example. When they get a lot more difficult, and they do, don't panic. You can go through the following table and maybe work it out. Or you can just ask your neighbor what they mean. Of course, your neighbor won't know either, but it is always more comforting when you realize that you are not alone.

Document identifications

Abbreviation	Full Name/Description	Organization(s)
A	Assembly, General Assembly	GEF, UN
A1, A2 ...	Annex 1, 2 ...	UN
Add.	Addendum, the second part of a document previously submitted	UN
AC	Ad hoc committee	UN
AG	General Assembly (*Asamblea General*)	OAS
Amend.	Alteration, by decision of a competent authority, of a portion of an adopted text	UN
C	Council	GEF
C	Standing/permanent/main committee	UN
CN	(1) Conference Notes, (2) Committee Notes, (3) Commission	UN

Conf.	Conference paper	
CONF.	Conference paper	UN
COPdoc	Conference of the Parties (meeting) document	UN
Corr.	Corrigendum, corrections to a document	
CP	Pre-conference documents (provisional and	
	regular documents and agenda)	UN
CP	Permanent Council (*Consejo Permanente*)	OAS
CRP	Conference Room Papers (working	
	documents for use during negotiations)	
Dist.	Distribution of the document	
DP	United Nations Development Programme	UN
E	Economic and Social Council	UN
E	Extraordinary session	OAS
E	(1) English, (2) Edited, (3) Executive	UN
ED	Executive Directive	UNEP
G	General Distribution	UN
GC	Governing Council	UN
GET/PMA	Special Working Group on Environmental	
	Protection	OAS
GT	Working Group (*Grupo de Trabajo*) of	
	the Permanent Council	OAS
IDP	Internal discussion paper	WB
IDR	In-depth reviews (of national communications)	WB
Inf.	Information document	
INF	Information series	UN
INF. docs	Information documents (background)	
JD	Board of Directors (*Junta Directiva*)	OAS
L	Limited distribution	
L. docs	Limited documents (draft reports and texts)	
LC	Latin America and the Caribbean	

Misc. Docs	Miscellaneous documents	
	(views of parties/observers; participant lists)	
NC	National communication	UN
Non-paper	Unofficial document (informal, in-session	
	documents to assist negotiations)	UN
OEA	OAS	OAS
OP	Operational procedure	WB
P	Preamble	UN
PC	Preparatory committee	UN
PET	Petitions	UN
PRST	Statements by the President of the Security Council	UN
PV	Verbatim records of meetings	UN
R	Restricted distribution; restricted access	UN
Rec.	Recommendation (Rec.1, Rec.2, etc)	
RES (or Res)	Resolution	
Rev.	Revision (revised document)	
S	Security Council	UN
SA	Synthesis of the minutes	OAS
SC	Subcommittee	UN
Ser.	Series	
Ser. A	Multilateral agreements, conventions and	
	treaties open for signature in the OAS	OAS
Ser. B	Agreements to which the OAS is party	OAS
Ser. G	Permanent Council	OAS
Ser. L	Inter-American Specialized Organizations	OAS
Ser. M	Bilateral and regional conventions deposited	
	at the OAS	OAS
Ser. P	General Assembly	OAS
SR	Summary records of meetings	UN
SS	Special session	

ST	Secretariat	UN
Sub.	Subcommission	UN
Summary	Summarized version	
TD	United Nations Conference on Trade and	
	Development	UN
TP	Technical papers	
UNEP	United Nations Environment Programme	UN
WG	Working group	
WP	Working papers	UN

Appendix 5: Random Definitions

The following are definitions given by graduate students and professionals working in the 'environmental' offices of government and some NGOs when asked to give their definitions to the terms 'environment,' 'ecology,' 'ecosystem' and 'sustainable development.' The questions were asked at the beginning of short courses in spatial planning, environmental governance and natural resource management. (Source: Personal files of Richard E. Saunier)

Environment

- National parks, wilderness, and wildlife.
- A combination of many different elements occurring both naturally and artificially.
- Surroundings, relating to land, water and air systems.
- The physical and chemical domains in which living and nonliving things exist.
- The bios surrounding a particular area.
- All things, be it natural or man made, that surround a person(s) or are within a defined space.
- Plants, animals, water, soils, air, ... everything involved in our surrounding area. All inter-reliant. Therefore in any one thing affect others.
- Group of ecosystems.
- The flora, fauna, geological, hydrological and atmospheric components functioning together.
- The external factors that affect the going concern of any system.

- The group of natural elements such as climatology, soil, water, plants and animals.
- Ensemble of place where people, animals and all living things interact with each other.
- Many aspects occur in small or large area like pollution, etc.
- The surroundings that living things live in. This includes inorganic and organic matter.
- Any surrounding habitable or non-habitable by living things.
- The amount of factors such as climate, vegetation, soils, etc. that are around.
- In a broad sense, the concept of environment refers to the surroundings that have some influence on the life of the subjects in it.
- The media that contains many different parts working together or depending on each other in a specific area.
- Man's (or any living thing) surroundings.
- … the area or space in which human beings interact.
- One's environment is that which surrounds him (her).
- A combination of natural inputs including animals (both human and wildlife), water, air, land, etc. Without environment there is no life.
- The care of the surroundings. Protecting the country resources.
- Every aspect of surroundings that in some way affects all forms of life – human, plant, animal, etc.
- The natural and artificial surroundings.
- The environment is everything.
- The assemblage of many ecosystems which produce the five renewable natural resources.
- Space.
- Atmosphere. Everything to do with nature – land, sun, air, sea. Man and his surroundings.
- Collection of natural conditions that condition human activities.
- Space that surrounds us.
- Main characteristics that are present in a given place.
- Group of elements that form the natural surroundings that are interdependent in terms of their development. Ecosystem.
- The physical-social-economic surroundings including the interrelationships that are established between them, in which life is developed and which influences a being's life in general.
- Natural environment includes water, air, land, etc. animals and people also. (2) Broader definition to include homes, education, and other human development indicators.
- All of nature that surrounds and affects the entire universe.
- What I want or need, when I want or need it, where I want or need it.
- The interdependent whole made up of divers entities.
- The reason to be alive.
- Where we live, work and play.

- The space in which we live and that sustains us.
- All physical and social aspects influencing and sustaining life.

Ecology

- The science that study the different associations of organisms and their relationship with the environment.
- Science which goal is to study the environment.
- It means there are many aspects of ecology in the sea, river, lakes, etc.
- A combination of ecosystems and how they interact with one another both in the ecosystems and between the ecosystems.
- The study of living things and their relationship with the environment.
- The science that study the environment.
- The discipline which is related to the weather, in other words to the way of live of living beings in a given environment.
- The science of dealing with living things.
- The study of environment and all its inhabitants.
- The study of the interrelationship of living things with their environment.
- The scientific discipline [or] study of Earth's different systems and environments.
- The study of the Earth's natural resources and their interactions.
- The study of the interactions between the biotic and abiotic constituents of an environment.
- The study of the environment surrounding and the way it works.
- The study of the environment.
- The study of ecosystems (plants, animals within the ecosystem).
- Science of particulars (flora/fauna).
- Science of understanding the interactions of plants, animals, environment.
- The science that take care of matters regardless of natural resources.

Ecosystem

- A classification for an area including plants, animals, trees and environment. They are areas that have specific characteristics in terms of ecological significance.
- The natural environment of the earth and the interaction with animals and other living things.
- The biotic and abiotic constituents of an environment.

- The components that make up a natural environmental system.
- The natural environment within a particular area.
- A natural system and all related plant/animal species within the system. Also the environment of the system (i.e. weather/climate, geography).
- Balanced concentration of particulars.
- The plants, animals, water, land, etc. that comprise a definable ecological system. For example, the everglades ecosystem comprises water flowing from N to S, alligators, gar, anhingas, coral/limestone based soils, subtropical climate, etc.
- The group of natural factors that are components in an occurrence, that can be measured.

Sustainable development

- The concept of having development be more geared toward environmental, public, social issues to foster better 'smart growth' in the future, trying to keep or make better what is being built in the future.
- Utilization of the Earth's resources in a manner that allows for controlled depletion. Using these resources in a way which allows the environment to recover as quickly as possible, thereby allowing for further development.
- May be better entitled, 'sustainable existence,' because to 'develop' something in human terms is inherently to exploit and drain the natural resources provided.
- The idea to perpetuate the existing ecosystem and environment at its ideal, optimal level for our existence to survive.
- Development that is self-reliant and is able to continue without outside intervention.
- A level of development which does not deteriorate other things (i.e. sustain current habitat, sustain current runoff quantities) levels of development beyond this negatively impact surrounding area.
- Balanced environments.
- Development that preserves biological diversity (doesn't cause extinctions/preserves unique ecosystems and preserves enough 'green space' for current and future generations.
- Continued improvement of any system.
- Improving the quality of life.
- Improving the human condition.